Religious Freedom in Au

– a new *Terra Nullius*?

Edited by

Iain T. Benson, Michael Quinlan and

A. Keith Thompson

SHEPHERD
STREET PRESS

Published in 2019 by Connor Court Publishing Pty Ltd under the imprint
Shepherd Street Press.

SHEPHERD
STREET PRESS

Shepherd Street Press is an imprint of Connor Court Publishing and The School of Law, The
University of Notre Dame Australia, Broadway.

Shepherd Street Press Editorial Executive:
Michael Quinlan
A. Keith Thompson
Iain T. Benson
Greg Blatch

Connor Court Publishing Pty Ltd
PO Box 7257
Redland Bay QLD 4165
sales@connorcourt.com
www.connorcourtpublishing.com.au
Phone 0497-900-685

Printed in Australia

ISBN: 9781925826623

Front Cover Image: By Melchisédech Thévenot - Thevenot's Relations de divers voyages curieux,
Paris, J., Public Domain, https://commons.wikimedia.org/w/index.php?curid=353379

Table of Contents

INTRODUCTION

RELIGIOUS LIBERTY IN THE CONTEXT OF HISTORY AND CULTURE: WHY RELIGION OUGHT NOT TO BECOME A CONTEMPORARY *TERRA NULLIUS*[1]

IAIN T. BENSON

In his justly celebrated Gifford Lectures from three quarters of a century ago,[2] historian Christopher Dawson's sustained analysis of the relationship between religion and culture reminds us that law, like culture itself, has its roots in the sacred. From the Greeks we get the idea of cosmos, in which natural reason engages the world around us and perceives it to be ordered and to have purposes we can understand. The Romans adopt this understanding of an ordered universe and, in Cicero's famous aphorism, law is understood to be 'right reason in accordance with nature.'[3] The Judeo-Christian moral tradition further develops the understanding of law as revelation that accords, in some significant measure, with what reason has already disclosed about reality.

Thus, as a result of over two millennia of thought and development of

---

[1]   In international law, *terra nullius* is a term that denotes a territory that is owned by nobody. Once a territory was adjudged to be *terra nullius* occupation could occur without taking into account other questions of sovereignty as long as possession and administration followed. See, Stephen Hall, *Principles of International Law* (LexisNexis Butterworths, 5th ed, 2016) 383-385. The adjudging by British administration of Australia as a *terra nullius* meant that any local indigenous right or claims under settled principles of International Law could be, as they were, ignored.

[2]   Christopher Dawson, *Religion and Culture* (Sheed and Ward, 1947).

[3]   Cicero, *De Re Publica* in M D A Freeman (ed), *Lloyd's Introduction to Jurisprudence* (Sweet & Maxell, 2001) 140.

culture, in what we still call, though with less and less confidence, "Western Civilization", religion and law developed side-by-side and the result of the inter-relationship formed the cultures that developed.

The relationship between law, culture and religion has varied in theory and in practice. How we understand history in part determines how we consider the questions of culture, religion and law and there are signs now that the terms of the relationship are being reconsidered but without adequate attention to the history of their philosophy and theology. This has serious consequences for our ability to protect the moral traditions that are the root of law. Many argue that the terms of the arrangement should no longer give public place to the religion that Dawson and many others understood as foundational to law and culture itself.[4]

From all points of the political and philosophical spectrum there are voices that call for increasing secularism defined, as George Jacob Holyoake intended, as the restructuring of the public order on a "material basis" with religion both privatized and marginalized. As has been written about elsewhere, Holyoake was able to convince not just himself, but others as well, that his theory of "secularism" (for it was he who coined the term in 1851) was "neutral" when closer examination showed it was anything but.[5] Yet today many, including those who would call themselves religious, speak of an "open secularism" in the manner of an incompetent biologist who might speak of "healthy botulism."

Still others believe that the public sphere can be "neutral" only if stripped

---

[4]   See also, Harold Berman, *Faith and Order: The Reconciliation of Law and Religion* (Eerdmans, 1993).

[5]   Iain T Benson, 'Considering Secularism' in Douglas Farrow (ed), *Recognizing Religion in a Secular Age* (McGill-Queens, 2004) 83-98.

of express involvement by religions;[6] others, including many of the authors in this volume, contest this sort of political or legal position as anything but neutral and point out that the stripping of religious beliefs and involvements is, in fact, an interference with the beliefs of religious citizens while giving a pride of place to the beliefs of non-religious citizens.

Many, including religious believers who should know better, speak of the non-religious as "unbelievers" when they are anything but. It is not a question of whether humans believe, but, rather, what they believe in. Many of our key beliefs are non-empirical - justice for instance cannot be weighed on a scale. As it is with the false idea of the "neutral state" so it is with metaphysical beliefs – they are not optional. Metaphysical beliefs such as what we hold to be the nature of human being, the nature of what is good and the nature of what is true and beautiful are of fundamental importance to a culture and the society that emerges from it. Metaphysical beliefs frame our understanding not only of the holy but of what is just and what is right and wrong and therefore what should be legal or illegal. Metaphysical beliefs do not belong only to those who ground them in religious convictions about the nature of the cosmos.

---

6   See, eg, John Rawls, *The Law of Peoples* (Harvard University Press, 1999) 152-154, where he said comprehensive doctrines including religious ideas, could only enter public debate if they are 'proper political reasons' and manifest 'commitment to constitutional democracy'. In her celebrated commentary upon Rawls, Martha C Nussbaum, *Frontiers of Justice* (Belknap, 2006) comments upon the grounds of Rawls' conception of pluralism and perpetuates the shibboleth that politics and "metaphysics" can be separated. She states, that with respect to religion, Rawls has 'robust protections for religious freedom, freedom of association and so forth' (296) and gives a list of principles that she says represent: 'a free-standing partial moral conception' that is:

'...introduced for political purposes only, and without any grounding in metaphysical ideas of the sort that divide along lines of culture and religion, such as the idea of the immortal soul, or the idea of god or gods. It provides the basis for an overlapping consensus" (297).

This is all very convenient but hardly comprehends how complete the metaphysical claims are that have been outlined in this Introduction so far. Somehow eliding the cosmos of ordered purpose and meaning, not something most contemporary "liberals" even begin to take on, and eliding the "soul" that as we have seen the Greeks and Romans, believed to be essential to being and culture itself, there simply is no neat demarcation into "metaphysics" (optional) and "politics" (obligatory) of the sort wished for by Rawls and supported by Nussbaum. With this sort of truncation it is no wonder that contemporary theories of liberalism are increasingly described as no longer commanding a consensus and are said to be in "crisis." See, Benson, below n 6. Politics better understood must necessarily be metaphysical however much that jars with the presuppositions of those moderns who find metaphysics too connected to traditions of an ordered (therefore intelligible) cosmos.

Metaphysics are present in convictions even if the persons holding them do not understand them to be metaphysical. To paraphrase Aldous Huxley, you can have good metaphysics or bad metaphysics but one thing you cannot have is no metaphysics.[7] To judge by our systems of schooling, ours is a time when the general consensus is that metaphysics is an optional course we can do without. It is the case, however, that we will still operate with metaphysics implicit if not explicitly expressed and inarticulate if not articulated. We are, in fact, in a condition of metaphobia – a practical fear of the very metaphysics we need so desperately. When our societies no longer understand the linkage between metaphysics, beliefs and all aspects of culture it is difficult to explain why religious citizens and projects should be considered able to have a presence in the public sphere, a sphere Charles Taylor reminds us is, after all, a 'social imaginary'.[8] Instead of understanding the foundational metaphysics, the technical side of education (*techné*, the Greek word for art or skill from which we get our English words: technique, technology and technician) has dominated discussion and teaching. The ends of education (its *telos*, the Greek word for purpose) has been subordinated for almost two centuries according to the writings of those learned in this area.[9] When techniques stand in for purposes what is lost is the proper ability to evaluate techniques in relation to their purposes. Thus, it becomes impossible to evaluate technology in moral terms because we have, without realizing it, allowed or even encouraged a gap between techniques and the purposes necessary to evaluate whether they are right or wrong, good or bad. To understand law, for example, one needs to teach and learn the moral basis of specific areas of law not just the techniques (case-law, statutes etc.) that form the practical framework for the moral conceptions. All too often, however, it is the "case- law" method deprived of its context that stands in for a more complete legal education. The same kind of reductionism is prevalent in many disciplines today. A starting point for considerations of politics and culture, for example, might not be the position of rival parties, which is pointless without first knowing what politics is about, but rather, be a reflection on Aristotle's observation that 'the student of politics must first study the soul....and virtues above all things.'[10] We are

---

7   Aldous Huxley, *Ends and Means* (Chatto and Windus, 1937) 252.

8   Charles Taylor, *A Secular Age* (Belknap, 2007) 176 ff.

9   George Grant, *Philosophy in the Mass Age* (Copp Clark, 1959, 1966). The analysis of *techné* and *telos* throughout this Introduction, and its connection to *cosmos*, is taken from this important short work of Grant's.

10   Aristotle, *Nicomachean Ethics*, Chapter 13, 1102a5-1103a10.

trying to have the fruits without the roots.

A full-scale drift of schooling (that is, schooling that is directionless) is evident in area after area of contemporary culture. Consider the following: politicians who seem unaware of the proper role of politics (beyond mere party politics); journalists who are more concerned with staging events (manipulating opinions) than covering truthfully and deeply the issues of the day; business leaders who seem unaware that business has a moral role in culture that goes considerably beyond merely the so-called "bottom-line" of profit making; a legal fraternity who are largely unaware that each subject they study or studied in law school has a moral and principled core more essential than the merely technical dimensions of the study; medical doctors who view human patients as material entities merely, devoid of soul, spirit and psyche. In each of these examples, and there are obviously many more, we see the split, the exclusion that happens when *techné* dominates *telos* and the impoverishment of culture that results.

The moral dimension in all disciplines is essential. In relation to business, for example, this moral basis is the creation of just employment and the production of "goods" that are fit for purpose; the very words "good" and "fitness for purpose" should alert us to the metaphysical and physical importance of what business does for culture. In those situations where the mere *techniques* of business and the ubiquitous term "values", a term from the market place, stand in for a more connected and objective set of moral ideas connected to business practices. Business is like an out of control machine merely for profit and has lost its cultural purpose. Morals without techniques may not deliver the goods, and techniques allowed to proliferate without a connection to properly considered purposes will not realise the common good and are likely to be dangerous: consider recent statements by leaders in the world of technology that human-kind is behaving irresponsibly in relation to artificial intelligence.

It is important to note, as well, the centrality here of what I have termed elsewhere a "cuckoo's egg" in our moral lexicon.[11] How curious that the term "values" which fails to bridge from the person using it to others in any way perceived as obligatory (after all, we know "you have *your* values and I have mine"), is exactly as the Canadian philosopher George Grant once memorably

---

[11]   Iain T Benson, 'Values Language: A Useful Moral Framework or a Cuckoo's Egg' in D. Daintree (ed), *Subverting Modernity: The Liberal Arts and Human Educational Fulfilment* (Connor Court, 2018) 1-43.

put it: 'an obscuring language for morality used when the idea of purpose has been destroyed.'[12] Purpose has been destroyed when we use "values" and are assuming we are employing a shared moral term. Values, as they have come to be expressed are ambiguous, subjective and are merely preferences which are not obligatory on others. Values do not require anything of us. Genuine moral language, such as "virtues", require that we conform ourselves to what was understood to be good and obligatory and shared. The long synthesis from the Greeks and Romans that framed our conceptions of virtues, one of the cardinal virtues of which was justice itself, cannot be thought or spoken in the language of "values."[13] As Grant said, "values" is an obscuring and confusing language better left merely for matters of personal opinion.

Virtues such as justice entail, as "values" do not, the long traditions that framed our cultures. Religion is informed by mercy and compassion that, along with the other cardinal virtues of wisdom, moderation and courage, all perfected by the theological virtues of faith, hope and love, formed the understanding of the moral structure of Western Education until quite recently. Now not one person in a hundred can list what the cardinal virtues are or explain why it once was that we understood that "Grace perfected nature." This is the sorry background to this volume of papers which, in their own ways, seek to shine light on aspects of what religious liberty is and why it matters to Australia today.

The importance of religion to Australia is now being widely discussed but sometimes against strange preconceptions. Tens of thousands of people presented recently to a Government Commission (the Ruddock Commission) and the Commission stated in its Report that religious liberty needs protections.[14] Yet, the early responses from State and Commonwealth governments suggest

---

[12]   David Cayley, *George Grant in Conversation* (Anansi, 1995) 120-122.

[13]   The four cardinal virtues were: justice, wisdom, moderation and courage. The three theological virtues are faith, hope and charity. See, generally, Romano Guardini, The Virtues (Henry Regnery, 1963). See, also, D S Hutchinson, *The Virtues of Aristotle* (Routledge and Kegan Paul, 1986), who notes: 'This sense of "good", then, is objective, and, if you like, scientific, for it is part of Aristotle's philosophy of nature, which recognizes goals, functions, and purposes and therefore good and bad as part of the reality of things' (68). For a more popular account and useful discussion of virtues in relation to vices as classically and theologically understood, see Peter Kreeft, *Back to Virtue* (Ignatius Press, 1992).

[14]   Religious Freedom Review Expert Panel, *Religious Freedom Review: Report of the Expert Panel* (18 May 2018) Department of the Prime Minister and Cabinet, 109.

that protections would be *removed* not created or augmented![15] Rather than acknowledging the importance of religion, the process seems to have gone in the opposite direction. The only explanation is that secularism, with its exclusionary strategies, is now more important to policy makers than the protection of religious liberty and the fair treatment of all citizens. Two directions are in play. First, secularism as an ideology opposed to religion is being defined in ways which oppose its original meaning. Second, religions and religious education in the form of a properly based historical religious education are becoming rarer and less clear about their own moral narratives. Many citizens, the religious included, believe they inhabit a "secular" society by which they mean one not based upon any sacred commitments. Yet this is contrary to what the term "secular" meant for centuries when it stood for the times or the age, *saeculorum,* that period of time between when Jesus departed and when he would return. In the Catholic tradition to this day the "secular clergy" are those "in the world" as opposed to "regular clergy" who operate under a regulation or a rule "in the cloister." This shift in language, as with the term "secularism" being recast as "open" or anti-religion with a pleasant face, goes largely unnoticed even by religious people who should know better. Alongside the slippage of moral language to "values" these directions work only in one way: the increasing exclusion from common life of the traditions that give solid grounding to the moral language of the West at the same time as unchallenged secularism strengthens its grip on our understanding of what we mean by "secular" and "public."

In many settings leaders speak vaguely about "Australian values" just as surely as, in other countries, they speak of the "values" of those other places - yet nobody has a clue what these "values" entail and if anything substantive is mentioned at all, it is usually bits and pieces from a more coherent tradition that we fail to understand because of the inadequate attention given to the history of the relationship between religion law and culture. For example, "human dignity" which cannot be derived from current assumptions, is still widely affirmed as essential to human rights. Yet it was the Western tradition's insight about how we are made for life in an ordered and meaningful cosmos (later we understand this as our creation "in the image and likeness of God") that grounded why all people had dignity. Law recognised this dignity it did not create it. This is important because what law gives it can take away. Such

---

[15] David Crowe, 'Winding back gay discrimination in schools is a pragmatic response from Morrison', *Sydney Morning Herald* (Online) 12 October 2018.

notions as "human dignity" could emerge only from an ordered cosmos rationally comprehensible where human nature was, in fact, universal and nature taught us something real about reality.[16] This structure and lineage has also been largely destroyed.

Such is our fate and times. This volume hopes to shine light on what is becoming darker and more obscure with each passing year; that is, the relationships that underlie moral structures. The editors hope that you will find something here of interest and worth passing on. The chapters that follow try and reverse trends that place religious liberty in peril and push culture further off its shared moral understandings - beliefs that, after all, framed our very conceptions of justice, fairness and moral goodness. Just as the British Crown and administrators of the day defined Australia as a *terra nullius*, so contemporary secularists believe they occupy a land in which religion is irrelevant.

Our cultures, made up in significant measure by legal and political traditions morally informed by millennia of religious and philosophical insights, can continue to exist only because they understand what makes these traditions coherent and reasonable and alive. These traditions may be judged as just or unjust only if we have meaningful moral frameworks against which to evaluate them.

BIBLIOGRAPHY

Aristotle, *Nicomachean Ethics*, in Jonathan Barnes (ed), *The Complete Works of Aristotle:* The Revised Oxford Translation (Princeton University Press, 1984)

Benson, Iain T. 'Civic Virtues and the Politics of Full Drift Ahead' (Centre for Independent Studies, 2017)

Benson, Iain T., 'Considering Secularism' in Douglas Farrow (ed), *Recognizing Religion in a Secular Age* (McGill-Queens, 2004) 83

Benson, Iain T., 'Values Language: A Useful Moral Framework or a Cuckoo's Egg' in D. Daintree (ed), *Subverting Modernity: The Liberal Arts and Human Educational Fulfilment* (Connor Court, 2018) 1

Berman, Harold, *Faith and Order: The Reconciliation of Law and Religion* (Eerdmans, 1993)

---

[16]   Recent attempts in Australia to ground citizenship on "Australian values" has been analysed elsewhere. See, Iain T Benson, *Civic Virtues and the Politics of Full Drift Ahead* (May 2017) Centre for Independent Studies.

Cayley, David, *George Grant in Conversation* (Anansi, 1995)

Cicero, 'De Re Publica' in M.D.A. Freeman (ed), *Lloyd's Introduction to Jurisprudence* (Sweet & Maxell, 2001) 140

Crowe, David, 'Winding back gay discrimination in schools is a pragmatic response from Morrison' Sydney Morning Herald (12 October 2018) <https://www.smh.com.au/politics/federal/winding-back-gay-discrimination-in-schools-is-a-pragmatic-response-from-morrison-20181012-p509ct.html>

Dawson, Christopher, *Religion and Culture* (Sheed and Ward, 1947)

Grant, George, *Philosophy in the Mass Age* (Copp Clark, 1966)

Guardini, Romano, *The Virtues* (Henry Regnery, 1963)

Hall, Stephen, *Principles of International Law* (LexisNexis Butterworths, 5th ed, 2016)

Hutchinson, D.S., *The Virtues of Aristotle* (Routledge and Kegan Paul, 1986)

Huxley, Aldous, *Ends and Means* (Chatto and Windus, 1937)

Kreeft, Peter, *Back to Virtue* (Ignatius Press, 1992)

Nussbaum, Martha C., *Frontiers of Justice* (Belknap, 2006)

Rawls, John, 'The Idea of Public Reason Revisited' in John Rawls (ed), *The Law of Peoples* (Harvard University Press, 1999) 152

Taylor, Charles, *A Secular Age* (Belknap, 2007)

Ruddock, Philip, Report of the Expert Panel Religious Freedom Review (18 May 2018) <https://www.ag.gov.au/RightsAndProtections/HumanRights/Documents/religious-freedom-review-expert-panel-report-2018.pdf>

The Contributors

About our contributors in the order in which they first appear in the book

Iain T. Benson is a Professor at the Sydney School of Law of The University of Notre Dame Australia and is an Extraordinary Professor of Law at the University of the Free State in Bloemfontein, South Africa. Born in Scotland and raised in Canada, Iain has practised and taught comparative constitutional law and philosophy all over the world but particularly in Canada, South Africa, France and Australia.

Peter Kurti is a Senior Research Fellow in the Culture, Prosperity and Civil Society program at the Centre for Independent Studies. He is also an Adjunct Associate Professor at the Sydney School of Law of The University of Notre Dame Australia, an Adjunct Research Fellow at the Australian Centre for Christianity and Culture at Charles Sturt University, and an ordained minister in the Anglican Church of Australia.

Robert Forsyth is a Senior Fellow at the Centre for Independent Studies. He was previously the Anglican of South Sydney and before that, Rector of St Barnabas, Broadway and chaplain to the University of Sydney.

Michael Quinlan is a Professor and Dean at the Sydney School of Law of The University of Notre Dame Australia. Before that Michael specialised in insolvency and insurance litigation for 23 years at Allens including 14 years as a partner. He also serves as the Junior Vice President of the St Thomas More Society and as a Director of Freedom for Faith.

Lorraine Finlay is a Lecturer in the School of Law at Murdoch University in Western Australia and a PhD candidate at the University of Queensland. She has previously worked as a State Prosecutor in Western Australia and as an Associate to Justice J.D. Heydon at the High Court of Australia.

Joshua Forrester is a PhD candidate at Murdoch University in Western Australia. Before commencing that research, he practised as a commercial litigation lawyer. He is also a co-author of *No Offence Intended: Why 18C is Wrong.*

Augusto Zimmermann is Professor of Law at Sheridan College in Western Australia and an Adjunct Professor at the Sydney School of Law at The University of Notre Dame Australia. He has published widely in Legal History, Constitutional Law and in Law and Religion space. He is also a former member of West Australia's Law Reform Commission.

Alex Deagon is a Senior Lecturer in the Faculty of Law at the Queensland University of Technology. He specialises in legal philosophy, law and theology, freedom of religion, and constitutional protections for freedom of speech and religion. He teaches Theories of Law, Constitutional Law, and Evidence

Brian Adams is the Director of the Centre for Interfaith and Cultural Dialogue at Griffith University in Queensland. Involved in peace building around the world for more than 15 years particularly in the Pacific and Africa, Brian's most well-known initiative is the G20 Interfaith Summit which began in the Gold Coast, Queensland in 2015 and has since convened in Istanbul, Turkey, Beijing, China, Potsdam Germany, Buenos Aries, Argentina and Osaka, Japan. He is also the Chair of the Board of Trustees for ACWAY, A Common Word Among the Youth, an international youth interfaith NGO.

Brendan Long is an economist and religious writer who has worked for central agencies of the Commonwealth government, held national leadership roles in the not-for profit sector, and was a political adviser to 4 Cabinet ministers. He is a Senior Research fellow at Charles Sturt University and is a strategic policy adviser to the Australian Catholic Bishops Conference. He writes on Adam Smith thought, economics and theology.

A. Keith Thompson is a Professor and Associate Dean at the Sydney School of Law of The University of Notre Dame Australia. He previously worked as International Legal Counsel for The Church of Jesus Christ of Latter-day Saints through the Pacific and African continent and as a partner in a commercial law firm in Auckland, New Zealand.

Rick Sarre is a Professor and Dean of Law and Criminal Justice at the University of South Australia and previously served as Chair of the Academic Board and as a member of the University Council. He has also taught law in the United States, in Hong Kong and in Sweden.

The editors also wish to make a special acknowledgement of the assistance they have received from Pascal Moussa. Pascal graduated first in the 2018 class of the Sydney School of Law at The University of Notre Dame Australia. Part of her brief was to conform the various citation styles of the several authors with the requirements of the publisher at the same time enabling a volume that would be readable and consistent. We do not know how she found the time to assist us, but we wish she never had to leave! The authors also thank the various student research assistants who helped prepare their papers for publication in this volume.

This book has been prepared to comply with the Peer Review Policy of the Shepherd Street Press which provides for double blind peer review by at least two expert reviewers.

The Contents of this Book

This volume of essays emerged from, but is not limited to, various presentations and formal papers delivered at a Conference, "Varieties of Diversity and the Law" held at The University of Notre Dame Australia, Sydney in February 2018. Some of the presentations were less formal than others but we wished to capture their contents here so have included those in Part 1 as "editorial commentaries." Following the Conference a more general invitation was given for additional papers and several of those are also included in this volume in Parts 2 and 3.

The Second group are the more general papers about religious liberty in Australia, dealing, in various ways, with the legal and philosophical framework for religious rights and liberty, arguing that the existing frameworks (Commonwealth, State and Territory) are an insufficient patchwork that fail in one way or another to satisfy Australia's responsibility to domesticate norms agreed to (and in force as of 1980) in the *International Covenant on Civil and Political Rights*.[1] Papers take differing views on the advisability of a Commonwealth Act for Conscience and Religion Discrimination Protection but all agree that strengthening measures are overdue in Australia.

The Third group deals with topics in relation to the freedom of religion and religious liberty across a wide variety of areas including religious diversity in political discourse; the religious roots of the separation of church and state in Australia; interfaith dialogue and the financial impact of religiosity; the removal of confessional privilege in Australia; conscientious objection in the first World War; legal implications of "equal voice liberalism" and a review of recent scholarship by two American scholars, Sullivan and Hurd.

Where the law is stated in the papers that follow efforts have been made to ensure it is current but, generally, the date of the Conference can be taken as the date to which the law was current throughout. What follows are more detailed abstracts for each paper in all three parts.

---

[1] *International Covenant on Civil and Political Rights*, opened for signature 19 December 1966, 999 UNTS 171 (entered into force 23 March 1976).

Part 1

Editorial Commentary on Religious Liberty in Australia
1: RELIGIOUS LIBERTY: A FORGOTTEN FREEDOM?

PETER KURTI

This editorial piece reflects on balancing freedom of religion against other fundamental rights and freedoms. The author highlights that religious freedom is profoundly at risk in Australia given the constant attempts made to limit the scope and protection of the freedom. The author ultimately suggests that all rights and freedoms recognised in an open, secular, and multicultural society such as Australia ought to be capable of coexisting and being recognised together.

2: FREEDOM OF RELIGION: THE NEW CONTEXT AND A REAL THREAT

ROBERT FORSYTH

This editorial piece examines religious freedom in the context of the *Marriage Amendment (Definition and Religious Freedoms) Bill 2017* (Cth). The author observes that the "no" campaign should have presented their claims in an alternative manner to enable proper understanding of their position. Instead, the rhetoric and approach adopted by the "no" meant that many were not comprehending the stance of classic Christians, indeed Christianity was often discounted as unconvincing and even immoral. The author also explores a second issue, which he coins as 'the existential threat to [religious] faith communities' that is caused by repeated criticisms about the "discriminatory" policies of religious organisations.

Part 2

General Framework Governing Religious Liberty in Australia
3: AN UNHOLY PATCHWORK QUILT: THE INADEQUACY OF PROTECTIONS OF FREEDOM OF RELIGION IN AUSTRALIA

MICHAEL QUINLAN

This chapter considers whether freedom of religion should be protected more comprehensively in contemporary Australia, particularly given the sweeping social changes that have occurred in recent times. The chapter also considers whether the recommendations of the Ruddock Review are adequate to address the modern challenges facing freedom of religion in Australia. The principal conclusion of the author is that religious freedom should not remain protected via a patchwork of different laws across the nation. Rather the freedom ought to be securely guarded in a more uniform and less piecemeal manner.

4: THE CONSTITUTIONAL LIMITATIONS & IMPLICATIONS OF A RELIGIOUS FREEDOM ACT

LORRAINE FINLAY

This chapter further explores the question of whether Australia ought to introduce a national *Religious Freedom Act* (RFA). It focuses specifically on the constitutional issues associated with the enactment of a RFA, such as determining the appropriate constitutional head of power to support the Commonwealth law and also the constitutional limitations involved with the federal government exercising its law-making capacity. Further, the chapter considers the potential implications of a Commonwealth RFA, particularly the legislation's propensity to intersect with other fundamental rights and freedoms that are usually enshrined in state anti-discrimination laws. The chapter recognises or affirms the Commonwealth government's capacity to enact a RFA, but questions whether it is advisable that the Commonwealth exercise such power.

5: DOES AUSTRALIA NEED A RELIGIOUS FREEDOM ACT?

LORRAINE FINLAY, JOSHUA FORRESTER AND AUGUSTO ZIMMERMANN

This chapter examines whether religious freedom is sufficiently protected in Australia or whether it should be legislatively safeguarded in a national *Religious Freedom Act*. The chapter concludes that the existing status of freedom of religion in Australia is insufficiently protected; recent developments such as the same-sex marriage campaign and the follow on legislation (i.e. *Marriage Amendment (Definition and Religious Freedoms) Act 2017* (Cth) exemplify the failure to protect religious freedom in Australia. The authors, however, are sceptical that a dedicated *Religious Freedom Act* is the antidote. Rather, they propose an alternative solution that works with or within the existing legal mechanisms. The idea is that anti-discrimination laws ought to be reformed to address the collisions that regularly occur between fundamental rights and freedoms.

Part 3

Specific Topics in Religious Liberty:

6: A CHRISTIAN FRAMEWORK FOR RELIGIOUS DIVERSITY IN POLITICAL DISCOURSE

ALEX DEAGON

Many scholars and politicians argue that excluding religious perspectives from political decision-making is the only way to guarantee genuine neutrality, freedom and equality. This addresses the common view that religion should not directly influence public policy and law because it can be sectarian and divisive. However, this chapter argues that secular liberalism is not neutral between faith perspectives (religious and non-religious) as it is, itself, a kind of faith. More significantly, it is an approach which relies on violence. Christian theology provides an alternative framework which relies on peace rather than violence, and this is the 'law of love'. This chapter makes the case for Christianity as the most desirable framework for religious diversity in political discourse, arguing in particular that the neutrality, freedom and equality sought by liberalism cannot be sustained by liberalism, and are actually better fulfilled in Christianity.

7: THE RELIGIOUS ROOTS OF "SEPARATION OF CHURCH AND STATE": CONSTITUTIONAL IMPLICATIONS FOR MODERN AUSTRALIA

AUGUSTO ZIMMERMANN

This chapter explores the common misconception that the anti-establishment clauses in the *United States and Australian Constitutions* were created to ensure a rigid separation between church and state. The author argues that both the context behind the drafting of the clauses, and the religious roots of the concept of separation of church and state, cumulatively negate the proposition that the *Australian or American Constitutions* were intended to establish a strict partitioning of church and state as opposed to their co-operation.

8: WHERE WOULD THE CONSTITUTIONAL SPACE BE LOCATED? FORB (Freedom of Religion and Belief) EFFORTS IN PARTNERSHIP WITH INTERFAITH DIALOGUE

BRIAN ADAMS

This chapter outlines an educational model of social institutional relationships that is key to influencing or strengthening social norms in society. The proposed tripartite model of Definers, Defenders and Developers is intended to assist us to achieve Freedom of Religion and Belief ends in otherwise impossible contexts.

9. THE ECONOMIC IMPACT OF RELIGIOUS VOLUNTEERING AND DONATION

A. KEITH THOMPSON

This chapter introduces the idea of research into the economic impact of religion in society. It introduces SEIROS, an interfaith think tank which has commissioned peer reviewed research into 'the economic impact of religion in society'. The detail of the analysis involved is spelled out in more detail in the following chapter.

10: MEASURING THE ECONOMIC IMPACT OF RELIGIOSITY IN AUSTRALIA

BRENDAN LONG

This chapter explores a missing or overlooked topic in public discourse, namely the question of how religion enhances the economic life of the nation. The chapter presents sophisticated economic and statistical research in order to determine whether the religiosity of Australians has any bearing upon their giving behaviour, in the sense of volunteering (i.e. giving of time) and donations (i.e. giving of money). The proposition of the author is that, if religious Australians are more prone to giving time and money, then we can, firstly, measure the economic impact of religious life in Australia and, secondly, consider whether we ought to adopt a public policy that supports or encourages such contributions.

11: RELIGIOUS FREEDOM UNDER THE *AUSTRALIAN CONSTITUTION* AND RECOMMENDATIONS THAT RELIGIOUS CONFESSION PRIVILEGE BE ABOLISHED

A. KEITH THOMPSON

This chapter discusses the Royal Commission into Institutional Responses to Child Sexual Abuse, in particular, the 'abolish religious confession privilege' recommendation made by the statutory body and the criticisms this recommendation has provoked. The chapter reviews the history and nature of the constitutional religious freedom provision (s 116), with a particular focus on the belief-manifestation dichotomy that is associated with the constitutional clause. The chapter concludes by offering an alternative approach to that adopted by the Commission, namely a "reconciliation and healing" strategy as opposed to a "compensatory and fault-based" framework.

12: SECTION 116 OF THE *AUSTRALIAN CONSTITUTION* IN THE CONTEXT OF FIRST WORLD WAR CONSCIENTIOUS OBJECTION

RICK SARRE

This chapter reviews the issue of conscientious objection on the basis of religious belief, specifically in the context of mandatory military service. Pursuant to this objective, the author retraces the intersection of law and religion in Anglo-Australian legal history before turning to analyse the contemporary law, namely s 116 of the *Constitution*. The author concludes that the guarantee in s 116 is over-stated, however, there remains a qualified right to conscientiously object on the basis of religious belief in Australian law.

13: EQUAL VOICE LIBERALISM AND FREE PUBLIC RELIGION: SOME LEGAL IMPLICATIONS

ALEX DEAGON

This chapter proposes some potential legal implications for free public religion in the context of 'equal voice liberalism'. Equal voice liberalism and its antecedent connections to priority for democracy are first outlined in conjunction with an analysis of free public religion. The chapter subsequently argues that equal voice liberalism is a framework conducive to facilitating free public religion while preserving equality. In this context the chapter attempts to give more analytical and evaluative precision to the commonplace ideas of freedom and equality in terms of proportionate, reasonable accommodation of difference. Finally, the chapter argues in support of religious associations requiring the space to form independently and develop unique perspectives which such groups can contribute to public discourse, which in turn enhances the importance of freedom and equality.

14: GETTING RELIGION AND BELIEF WRONG BY DEFINITION: A RESPONSE TO SULLIVAN AND HURD

IAIN T. BENSON

This chapter reviews two influential contemporary theorists writing from America and rejects their approaches. First the chapter reviews and rejects the definitional 'vagueness' argument against religious freedom of Winnifred Fallers Sullivan; next it reviews and rejects the 'good religion/bad religion' paradigm and associated arguments of Elizabeth Shakman Hurd and their express or implied recourse to 'equality' as a supposed ground for liberty. The first argument is, that religion is not as evasive of legal definition and utility as has been made out. Secondly, that all other terms argued as superior, such as 'equality' are even more difficult to define; they depend, in fact, on a context and a realization that religion is an equality right itself – being universally listed as such within Constitutions and Bills of Rights in both domestic and international settings. Finally, the "sceptical about religion" and "highly statist approach" taken by Hurd, which purports to express concern about categorizing religions as 'good' or 'bad', harmful or unharmful is rejected as relativistic and unworkable when viewed alongside that author's concerns about religion itself. Both theories are, it is argued, a sort of 're-warmed' secularism – concerns about religion in general are dressed up as a concern about International Relations which fail to respect religions themselves in their associational and lived dimensions. In conclusion the chapter argues that these approaches amount to a lack of respect for religious believers and their communities from scholars who, as these two under review, overly 'problematize' religion in ways common to secularist, anti-religious, globalist and sceptical sensibilities.

Part 1

Editorial Commentary on
Religious Liberty in Australia

1

RELIGIOUS LIBERTY: A FORGOTTEN FREEDOM?[1]

PETER KURTI

Balancing the right to religious liberty against other rights and freedoms enjoyed by Australians is likely to be one of the biggest political challenges facing the Turnbull government in 2018.

Religious freedom has been front-page news primarily because of debates in the Commonwealth Parliament about religious amendments to Senator Dean Smith's same-sex marriage bill that subsequently passed into law in December 2017.

The concern then was whether or not the new marriage law gave adequate protections to people who decline to be involved with same-sex marriage ceremonies on the grounds of their religious beliefs.

The amended *Marriage Act* addressed many of these worries.[2] But broader concerns about religious freedoms remain — such as parental rights to educate children, and the status of faith-based charities.

And how much protection will a Muslim or a Christian have if they express a view about same-sex marriage or voluntary euthanasia … or the curriculum of a religious school?

The heat of the topic makes it easy to believe reports the Religious Freedom Inquiry chaired by Philip Ruddock has received more than 3000 submissions.

Religious freedom is a fundamental human right because it allows people

---

[1]   This paper draws on material previously published in Peter Kurti, *The Tyranny of Tolerance: Threats to Religious Liberty in Australia* (Connor Court, 2017).

[2]   *Marriage Amendment (Definition and Religious Freedoms) Act 2017* (Cth)

to make the most important decisions about how they live their lives, raise their children, and participate in their communities.

Opponents of religious freedom protections tell us that believers already have all the freedom they could possibly want.

'There are strong grounds for a campaign to counter the expansion of religious freedoms and to reduce the ones that already exist,' says commentator, Richard Ackland.[3]

But that sort of hyperbole hardly does justice to the cultural, religious, and ethnic diversity of Australia's thriving multicultural society - a diversity reflected in successive returns for the Census conducted by the Australian Bureau of Statistics.[4]

This diversity is acknowledged by the right of religious groups and communities in Australia to order their affairs according to their beliefs and traditions – recognised in every state, to varying degrees, by anti-discrimination legislation.

Where legislation grants protections for religious freedom, it does so not simply to justify what would otherwise be unlawful discrimination: rather, it does so to protect religious liberty, and to ensure that right is balanced against other rights.

But today even these protections are under threat from what Augusto Zimmermann has described as 'a radical anti-Western ideological project'.[5]

The threat comes from the contemporary corrective tendency to minimise cultural differences as a way of managing diversity. This tendency, powered by the legislative fuel of anti-discrimination laws, promotes minority identity to the status of an end in itself.

Although passed with the intention of inhibiting intolerance, anti-discrimination laws have effectively pursued equality by removing from the public sphere all that distinguishes one group of citizens from another.

---

[3]   Richard Ackland, 'Why extend the church's 'freedom' when it's abused what it already has?', *The Guardian* (Online) 14 December 2017.

[4]   In the 2016 Census, Australians were asked to identify their religion in response to the question, "What is your religion?" with the option of "No Religion" placed at the top of the list of available answers. Whereas the 2011 Census showed that 22 per cent of Australians identified as having no religion, by 2016 the figure had risen to 30 per cent, indicating that more than two thirds of Australians continue to retain some degree of religious allegiance and affiliation. See, Australian Bureau of Statistics, *2016 Census data reveals "no religion" is rising fast* (27 June 2017).

[5]   Augusto Zimmermann, 'The Intolerance of Religious Tolerance Laws' (2013) 57(7/8) *Quadrant* 52, 56.

Whether these distinguishing factors are religious forms of address or the performance of public roles and rituals, their removal serves only to undermine the very diversity and tolerance the legislation effects to promote, thereby inhibiting the freedom of all citizens.

The resulting outlook for religious liberty is not likely to be encouraging. Of course, limits to religious freedom can be imposed by the state — but only when public safety, national security, or social cohesion is threatened. Otherwise, citizens should enjoy complete religious liberty.

Increasingly, however, expressing a religious point of view or expounding a matter of doctrine is liable to be condemned as an act of "hate speech".

Religion has almost come to be seen as a new form of racism making the defence of religious freedom a matter of urgency.

Religious freedom must always be about more than internally held beliefs: it must be about the external practice and manifestation of belief. The freedom to believe must always be accompanied by the freedom to speak and by the freedom to associate or dissociate.

As we know, most definitions of religious freedom begin with, or at least take into account, that set out in the *United Nations Universal Declaration of Human Rights 1948* ('*Universal Declaration*').[6]

The *Universal Declaration* is supplemented by the *International Covenant on Civil and Political Rights 1966* ('ICCPR') which sets out a specific freedom from coercion.[7] The ICCPR also permits the state to set limitations to external expressions of religious freedom.[8]

Both treaties have been ratified by Australia. Ratification entails a legal

---

[6]   *Universal Declaration of Human Rights*, GA Res 217A (III), UN GAOR, 3rd sess, 183rd plen mtg, UN Doc A/810 (10 December 1948). Article 18(1) of the *Universal Declaration of Human Rights 1948* states:
Everyone has the right to freedom of thought, conscience and religion; this right includes freedom to change his religion or belief, and freedom, either alone or in community with others and in public or private, to manifest his religion or belief in teaching, practice, worship and observance.

[7]   *International Covenant on Civil and Political Rights*, opened for signature 19 December 1966, 999 UNTS 171 (entered into force 23 March 1976)

[8]   These provisions are set out in art 18(2) of the ICCPR: 'No one shall be subject to coercion which would impair his freedom to have or to adopt a religion or belief of his choice.' Whilst, art 18(3) states: 'Freedom to manifest one's religion or beliefs may be subject only to such limitations as are prescribed by law and are necessary to protect public safety, order, health, or morals or the fundamental rights and freedoms of others.' Article 18(3) was adopted from art 9(2) of the *Convention for the Protection of Human Rights and Fundamental Freedoms*, opened for signature 4 November 1950, 213 UNTS 221 (entered into force 3 September 1953).

obligation to act consistently with the treaty but it does not automatically make the treaty provisions part of Australian law unless they are specifically included in legislation by the Commonwealth Parliament.

Now, one possible recommendation from the Ruddock Inquiry is for a federal *Religious Freedom Act* — an idea first proposed 20 years ago by the forerunner of the Australian Human Rights Commission.

Such an Act would put into law the kind of obligations Australia has already assumed by ratifying these international covenants. In other words, a federal *Religious Freedom Act* would allow the government to turn Australia's moral obligations into legal ones.

Of course, such a proposal is not quite that straightforward. For example, proponents of states' rights would likely resist any interference with the legislative independence of states and territories.

But advocates of a federal religious freedom law might argue, in turn, that no new rights are being created — such as the right to be ruled by sharia law or the right to religious polygamous marriages.

A *Religious Freedom Act* would not enforce religious law, such as sharia. It would simply protect existing freedoms and ensure Australian law is always consistent with freedoms protected by international law.

'Religious freedom means nothing,' says Jeremy Waldron, a legal philosopher, 'if it does not mean that those who offend others are to be recognised as fellow citizens and secured in that status, if need be, by laws that prohibit the mobilization of social forces to exclude them.'[9]

No fair-minded and free-thinking citizen should advocate hatred of, or discrimination against, another person on the basis of ethnicity, gender, or belief. The problem, however, is that where such advocacy does occur, it is met not by counter-argument and social ostracism but by immediate recourse to law.

A consequence of this tendency is that a hardened form of secularism is now developing in Australia in such a way as to deny what Waldron calls 'the compossibility of rights.'[10]

And it is in this context that the Ruddock Inquiry has set about its work. The debate about religious freedom last year threatened to derail passage of same-sex marriage legislation.

---

[9]   Jeremy Waldron, *The Harm in Hate Speech* (Harvard University Press, 2012) 130.
[10]   Ibid 135

Legislating for human rights can, sometimes, lead to unintended consequences, and the Prime Minister was keen for religious freedom to be given careful consideration. That is why he sought to ensure discussions about the two topics were kept separate.

Initial submissions to the Ruddock Inquiry were due by 31 January 2018, and the Inquiry is expected to hand down its report at the end of March 2018.

Ruddock, himself, recognizes that any recommendations his Inquiry makes about religious freedom will have to take into account the existence of other, important freedoms. It is a matter of proportionality; and, as Ruddock has said, '[p]roportionality demands an element of compromise.'[11]

It remains to be seen whether the Ruddock Inquiry can strike the appropriate balance of compromise in its recommendations.

But it seems that the Inquiry is clear that the rights and freedoms recognized in an open, secular, and multicultural society must be capable of coexisting and being recognised together.

As I said at the outset, religion's opponents insist that believers already have all the freedom they could possibly want and shouldn't be given licence to indulge in further acts of "hate speech" or discrimination.

Driven by the advocates of identity politics, this drive against religion threatens to make it harder for Australian society to be truly tolerant of diversity.

The Ruddock Inquiry must now step up to the plate to help strike the right balance of freedoms.

Bibliography

Ackland Richard, 'Why extend the church's 'freedom' when it's abused what it already has?', *The Guardian* (Online) 14 December 2017 <https://www.theguardian.com/australia-news/2017/dec/14/dont-extend-churches-freedom-when-theyve-abused-those-they-already-have>

Australian Bureau of Statistics, *2016 Census data reveals "no religion" is rising fast* (27 June 2017) <http://www.abs.gov.au/AUSSTATS/abs@.nsf/mediareleasesbyReleaseDate/7E65A144540551D7CA258148000E2B85>

Convention for the Protection of Human Rights and Fundamental Freedoms, opened for signature 4 November 1950, 213 UNTS 221 (entered into force 3

---

11   Michelle Grattan, 'Protecting religious freedom is a matter of balance, says head of Turnbull's inquiry', *The Conversation* (Online) 22 November 2017.

September 1953).

Grattan Michelle, 'Protecting religious freedom is a matter of balance, says head of Turnbull's inquiry', *The Conversation* (Online) 22 November 2017 <http://theconversation.com/protecting-religious-freedoms-is-a-matter-of-balance-says-head-of-turnbulls-inquiry-87933>

International Covenant on Civil and Political Rights, opened for signature 19 December 1966, 999 UNTS 171 (entered into force 23 March 1976)

Kurti Peter, *The Tyranny of Tolerance: Threats to Religious Liberty in Australia* (Connor Court, 2017).

Marriage Amendment (Definition and Religious Freedoms) Act 2017 (Cth)

Universal Declaration of Human Rights, GA Res 217A (III), UN GAOR, 3rd sess, 183rd plen mtg, UN Doc A/810 (10 December 1948)

Waldron Jeremy, *The Harm in Hate Speech* (Harvard University Press, 2012)

Zimmermann Augusto, 'The Intolerance of Religious Tolerance Laws' (2013) 57(7/8) *Quadrant*

2

FREEDOM OF RELIGION: THE NEW CONTEXT AND A REAL THREAT

ROBERT FORSYTH

Let me begin by stressing that my views are not necessarily those of the Centre for Independent Studies. Certainly the Centre for Independent Studies is very concerned about the preservation of religious freedom, even though it is a secular organisation. Here, however, I talk more as a Christian minister.

I wish briefly to cover two topics. The first is the new context of the issue of religious freedom at the end of 2017 and the second is the real potential threat that needs to be guarded against.

Leaving aside for a moment the religious freedom implications of the passing of the *Marriage Amendment (Definition and Religious Freedoms) Bill 2017* (Cth), the process and events around it have revealed that there are profound differences in fundamental beliefs in Australia between the orthodox Christian churches and a great deal of the wider society.

Much of the disagreement about same-sex marriage reflected deeper disagreements about other questions; what is marriage itself, what is the moral status of same-sex relationships, and even how such questions are decided in the first place. The differences go all the way down. As ancient historian Kyle Harper recently wrote:

> In our secular age, just as in the early years of Christianity, differences in sexual morality are really about the clash between different pictures of the universe and the place of the individual within it.[1]

---

[1] Kyle Harper, 'The First Sexual Revolution' (2018) *First Things*.

This was unacknowledged in the debate and yet is one reason why neither side seemed to be actually talking to the other. The churches' campaign for the 'no' case never really said why same-sex marriage should not be legal because, whether they realised it or not, the real Christian case for 'no' is incomprehensible to those who share so little of the Christian understanding of reality. Harper captures this well.

> An avowed secularist is as likely as a Christian activist to proclaim the universal dignity of all individuals and insist upon the individual's freedom. And yet, however moralized the domain of sex might be, the vast, vacant universe seems to have left only authenticity and consent as the shared, public principles of sexual morality. These axioms derive from a picture of the universe different from the one imagined by [Saint] Paul, who always envisioned the individual—including the sexual self— within the larger story of the gospel and its picture of a created cosmos in the throes of restoration.[2]

That is why the 'no' case was all about unwelcome consequences to same-sex marriage, not the issue itself. In hindsight, I believe that this was a significant mistake. It would have been much better to try to explain the real issues in depth, even though they will not be grasped and certainly not believed. But what happened was that the 'no' case appeared to many to be engaging in disingenuous scare mongering. The opportunity to engender respect for sincere, if not shared, convictions was lost. That, in turn, has made the conditions for the churches in the peace that has followed the same-sex marriage war much more difficult.

Since then, not unexpectedly, what the change in the law means is deeply contested also. In the second reading, then Attorney General George Brandis, described the passing of the bill as saying 'to those vulnerable young people [who are homosexual or lesbian] – There is nothing wrong with you. You are not unusual. You are not abnormal. You are just you.'[3] The Prime Minister in his second reading speech on the bill said that in amending the *Marriage Act 1961* (Cth) the clear message to every gay person was '…we love you. We respect you. Your relationship is recognised by the Commonwealth as legitimate and honourable as anybody else's. You

---

2   Ibid
3   Debbie Schipp, 'Senate votes against Liberal Senator Dean Smith's private same-sex marriage bill amendments', *News.Com.Au* (Online) 29 November 2017.

belong.'[4] Peter van Onselen writing in *The Australian* on 27 November 2017 likened those who voted 'no' with 'people who wanted blacks to continue to ride at the back of the bus, or racial segregation of toilets, or bans on interracial marriage. When the laws changed they realised they were on the wrong side of history.'[5]

If the logic of such rhetoric were to be taken seriously, it would mean that, no matter how much they deny it, those who did not vote 'yes,' and in particular those who continue to hold to a view of marriage that is not the one endorsed by the passing of the Act, are in effect saying the opposite to gay people, that is, "you are abnormal," "you are not loved or respected," and that such people are the moral equivalent to segregationists in America's deep south in the 1960s. In other words, it is not just that such leaders remain unconvinced as to the stance of classic Christians, they are uncomprehending, and worse, regard them as immoral.

By chance all this was followed immediately by the final report of the Royal Commission into Institutional Responses to Child Sexual Abuse, which reported that:[6] 'Of those survivors who told us about the types of institution where they were abused, 58.6 per cent said they were sexually abused in an institution managed by a religious organisation.'

If that wasn't bad enough, the press reports of this terrible conclusion gave the impression that it was closer to 100%.

In 2017, Christian pastor and blogger Stephen McAlpine correctly linked these two events in the perception of religious institutions today.

> For let's face it, the wider culture does not look at the two events separately, no matter how much we say "Yes, but." ... The wider culture has signalled that it has made the precipitous move to celebrate sexuality in a manner that the church does not, and will, if pressed, simply state that the church has not been practising sexuality in the way that the church has publicly celebrated. ... For whether or not this is true of all churches, indeed of the majority, is not the point. In this post-Christian

---

4   Commonwealth, *Parliamentary Debates*, House of Representatives, 4 December 2017, 12342, (Malcom Turnbull, Prime Minister)

5   Peter Van Onselen, 'Malcom Turnbull is showing leadership – against conservatives on SSM', *The Australian* (Online) 29 November 2017.

6   Commonwealth, Royal Commission into Institutional Responses to Child Sexual Abuse, *Final Report - Preface and Executive Summary*, 11.

culture as far as the world is concerned, we're all in this together.[7]

While we are still close to these events it is not easy to know how long lasting such attitudes are. Public debates have short attention spans. Indeed, things seem to be cooler in the New Year. But the long-term reality of incomprehension and disgust is lasting. We can be sure that the six in ten Australians, who according to the *Ipsos* survey released in October 2017, believe that religion does more harm than good are not going away soon.[8]

And that is not good for religious freedom questions. I am thankful for the setting up of the Expert Panel to examine whether Australian law adequately protects the human right to freedom of religion. However I do hope that further discussion on religious freedom is not taken, by either side, as round two of the marriage equality debate. That would be most regrettable. And a disaster for religious freedom.

There have been some rumblings. David Gillespie in *Courier Mail* on 22 November 2017 in an article entitled 'Forget bakers, why can private schools be bigots?' wrote:[9]

> If you want a job in, or your child educated in, a very large chunk of the Australian education system your protections against discrimination are non-existent. Your tax dollars are funding institutions which can legally discriminate against you. And yet the debate of the day is whether a baker can refuse to supply a cake to a same-sex couple.
>
> The nation's attention is now firmly focused on the rights of same-sex couples, so let's use that opportunity to remove the ridiculous protections afforded to the taxpayer funded businesses we call private schools. That is where 'religious freedom' can really bite, not at the local cake-shop or florist.

To which Stephen McAlpine commented:[10]

> Nailed it, didn't he? Religious freedom is really biting. We need to render it toothless. Why do we need to render it toothless? Because we don't wish mediating institutions to teach an alternate sexual ethic to what the

---

[7]   Stephen McAlpine, 'Church: Plan for a "Plan B" Future' on *Stephen McAlpine Blog* (18 December 2017).

[8]   Ipsos, *Ipsos global study shows half think that religion does more harm than good* (12 October 2017).

[9]   David Gillespie, 'Forget bakers, why can private schools be bigots?', *The Courier Mail* (Online) 22 November 2017.

[10] Stephen McAlpine, 'Forget the Bakers and Florists, It's About Schools' on *Stephen McAlpine Blog* (23 November 2017).

Secular State wishes to teach. We need compliance.

He thinks, and I agree, this really is not a church-state divide. The danger is not that the church will have undue influence in society but the other way round. He writes:

> The political institutions we live within are not simply seeking to shape our thinking, but to capture our hearts with a vision of the good life which they inculcate. So in that sense they are rival cults; competing centres of worship to the church.[11]

The challenge is to the integrity and ultimate existence of minority dissenting religious institutions and communities. Which leads to my second topic, a real possible threat, a real possible threat that needs to be guarded against. The real issue is not bakers, florists and wedding photographers. It is the existential threat to faith communities of all kinds. Let me give you an example from the university sector.

I was Anglican Chaplain to the University of Sydney from 1983 to 2000. Universities are funny places. But in my time the only problem we had on the religious freedom front was when the Sydney University Evangelical Union, or EU, a non-denominational Christian student group I will return to in a moment, ran a series of provocatively titled talks. A staff member of the Sydney University Union called us in to complain about our advertising. Someone had been "accosted by a poster" she said. An inconclusive discussion followed and that was it.

More recently, something much more serious occurred. That same Sydney University Union changed its rules so that any student club to be affiliated with the Union would be required to be open to any student member of the Union at the University. Sounds reasonable? No doubt some tidying up to the rules to insure inclusiveness.

But the effect of that policy was to present an existential threat to one significant student society: the EU. The EU had been founded in 1930 and has been one of the biggest and most active student societies in that time. It is rumoured it was the EU who first created something like an O Week to recruit new members. Today it has about 600 members and runs three public lectures a week, countless small groups and bible studies and training events. But it is not a society of any students. As its own self

---

[11]   Stephen McAlpine, 'The Church is Always Political. Always' on *Stephen McAlpine Blog* (4 January 2017).

designation puts it, 'The EU are a group of around 600 Christian students who join together to present Jesus Christ to the University, to encourage each other to stand firm in Christ, and to help each other prepare for a lifetime of Christian service.'[12] And that means to join the EU you must declare your faith in the Lord Jesus Christ as your Saviour, your Lord and your God, identify yourself with the EU community and commit yourself to its Objects.[13] Those elected to leadership have to go further and assent to a more full statement of basic Christian doctrine. In passing let me say that I believe that the EU and similar bodies in other universities are some of the most strategic Christian institutions in Australia.

The Sydney University Union change in policy meant that the EU had to remove these requirements for membership and leadership if it was to be a registered club. Anyone, whatever they believed, had to be able to join and even elected to the leadership group of the EU. If the appropriate change was not made to the constitution then the EU would cease to be a registered club and lose access to rooms and lecture theatres to meet in as well as supportive funding from the Sydney University Union. But if the EU did make the change, then it faced the threat of losing its Christian character and *raison-d'etre*. There was much discussion of what to do. Long negotiations with the Student Union followed. Surprisingly the EU was one of the only student societies to raise an objection. After all, things had gone well for 86 years without this requirement. And this posed an existential risk; the threat of being deregistered; or forced to change and try and survive by a strong culture, not constitution.

At one point the EU agreed to show good faith by putting the required changes to its constitution to a vote of a meeting of members. There was no doubt what they stood for. The proposed changes to remove the faith requirements were lost 71 to 1. Finally, after a stand-off, external legal advice was ought which changed the Union's tune. A special Religious Club category was created and the EU was able to keep its integrity.[14]

The whole exercise was unnecessary and costly. My fear is that such

12   Sydney University Evangelical Union, *What is the EU?* (2018).
13   Sydney University Evangelical Union, *Constitution* (2018), cl 3.
14   See, Eryk Bagshaw, 'University of Sydney evangelical students vote to keep Jesus', *Sydney Morning Herald* (Online) 26 March 2016; Andrew Judd, 'University of Sydney's Evangelical Union shouldn't have to give up its faith in fight against discrimination', *Sydney Morning Herald* (Online) 23 March 2016.

things will increasingly occur in the real world, threatening religious organisations, employment policies and funding or tax breaks because of their so called "discriminatory" membership or employment requirements.

The submission to the Expert Panel conducting the Review into Religious Freedom by Freedom for Faith, a Christian legal think tank with a particular interest in religious freedom, well expresses this issue in acknowledging that the freedom to select is an existential issue for faith communities of all kinds.[15]

> The most important issue for Christians, and, we understand, for most other faith groups, is not the freedom to discriminate, but the freedom to select on the basis of religious belief and practice, and freedom to take adverse action against an employee if necessary, where issues of personal conduct are incompatible with the values of the employing organisation.[16]

Unless this freedom is protected in a way that is compatible with other anti-discrimination law, the existence and flowering of religious bodies in this country is at risk.

Bibliography

Bagshaw Eryk, 'University of Sydney evangelical students vote to keep Jesus', *Sydney Morning Herald* (Online) 26 March 2016 <www.smh.com. au/education/university-of-sydney-evangelical-students-vote-to-keep-jesus-20160325-gnr38u.html>_

Commonwealth, *Parliamentary Debates*, House of Representatives, 4 December 2017, 12342, (Malcom Turnbull, Prime Minister)

Commonwealth, Royal Commission into Institutional Responses to Child Sexual Abuse, *Final Report - Preface and Executive Summary*

Freedom for Faith, Submission No 2520 to the *Expert Panel conducting the Religious Freedom Review*, 29 January 2018

Gillespie David, 'Forget bakers, why can private schools be bigots?', *The Courier Mail* (Online) 22 November 2017 <https://www.couriermail. com.au/rendezview/forget-bakers-why-can-private-schools-be-bigots/news-story/eb5d430febabb5dbda0036f7b861a130>

---

15   Freedom for Faith, Submission No 2520 to the *Expert Panel conducting the Religious Freedom Review*, 29 January 2018, 63.

16   Ibid 59

Harper Kyle, 'The First Sexual Revolution' (2018) *First Things*

Ipsos, *Ipsos global study shows half think that religion does more harm than good* (12 October 2017) <https://www.ipsos.com/en-au/ipsos-global-study-shows-half-think-religion-does-more-harm-good>

Judd Andrew, 'University of Sydney's Evangelical Union shouldn't have to give up its faith in fight against discrimination', *Sydney Morning Herald* (Online) 23 March 2016 <https://www.smh.com.au/opinion/university-of-sydneys-evangelical-union-shouldnt-have-to-give-up-its-faith-in-fight-against-discrimation-20160322-gnnxvp.html>

McAlpine Stephen, 'Church: Plan for a "Plan B" Future' on *Stephen McAlpine Blog* (18 December 2017) <https://stephenmcalpine.com/church-plan-for-a-plan-b-future/>

McAlpine Stephen, 'Forget the Bakers and Florists, It's About Schools' on *Stephen McAlpine Blog* (23 November 2017) <https://stephenmcalpine.com/forget-the-bakers-and-florists-its-about-schools/>

McAlpine Stephen, 'The Church is Always Political. Always' on *Stephen McAlpine Blog* (4 January 2017) <https://stephenmcalpine.com/the-church-is-always-political-always/>

Onselen Van Peter, 'Malcom Turnbull is showing leadership – against conservatives on SSM', *The Australian* (Online) 29 November 2017

Schipp Debbie, 'Senate votes against Liberal Senator Dean Smith's private same-sex marriage bill amendments', *News.Com.Au* (Online) 29 November 2017 <https://www.news.com.au/national/politics/you-are-not-unusual-you-are-not-abnormal-you-are-just-you/news-story/c1665d5b21255bdf6471fa6054f5dc34>

Sydney University Evangelical Union, *Constitution* (2018) <https://www.sueu.org.au/constitution>

Sydney University Evangelical Union, *What is the EU?* (2018) www.sueu.org.au/what-is-the-eu

Part 2

General Framework Governing Religious Liberty in Australia

AN UNHOLY PATCHWORK QUILT: THE INADEQUACY OF PROTECTIONS OF FREEDOM OF RELIGION IN AUSTRALIA

MICHAEL QUINLAN

Make every effort to live in peace with everyone and to be holy.[1]

Australia is at a crossroads in its approach to religious freedom. Although Australia has entered into a number of international obligations to protect religious freedom, the approach to date has tended to be a minimalist one. Rather than introducing a national law to prevent religious discrimination or to protect religious freedom, a less structured approach of particular protections in specific Commonwealth and State and Territory legislation has been preferred. At the time of writing, the recommendations of a review of religious freedom in Australia colloquially known as "the Ruddock Review" have been made public. In December 2018 the Coalition government announced its response and as part of that response the Commonwealth Attorney-General referred questions concerning the legal freedoms of religious schools and religious bodies to the Australian Law Reform Commission. A Federal election took place on Saturday 18 May, 2019 and the results there, particularly in the Senate will have a significant impact on the ability of the government to legislate in relation to religious freedom and religious discrimination. At the present time, the extent to

---

[1]   Hebrews 12:14 (Bible New International Version).

which Australia's Commonwealth, State and Territory governments may adopt a more considered and holistic approach to religious discrimination and religious freedom consequent on the recommendations of the Ruddock Review is not yet known. This chapter argues that a number of changes to Australian society suggest that there is a need for broader Commonwealth protection of freedom of religion and belief than may have been the case in the past. The chapter also makes some preliminary observations about the adequacy of the recommendations of the Ruddock Review as a means of addressing those challenges.

The chapter begins with a very brief analysis of the historical background, falling religious affiliation and increasing ignorance of religion taking place before considering some of the social and legal responses to date in connection with religious freedom. The chapter then examines some of the legislative challenges to religious freedom which have and are taking place. The chapter then turns to the recommendations of the Ruddock Review, considers the adequacy of those changes and makes some preliminary observations on them.

The Historical background

Australia is and it always has been a pluralist, multi-faith and multi-ethnic society.[2] Whilst most Australians have self-identified with a Christian denomination in each national census, there has been significant growth in followers of non-Christian faiths primarily as the result of immigration. Followers of non-Christian religions grew from 4.9 per cent in 2001 to 7.8 per cent of the Australian population in 2016.[3] Whilst other faith traditions are growing the percentage of Christians in Australia is falling. This category fell from 88.2 per cent in 1966 to 52.1 per cent in 2016.[4] There is an overall trend away from religious belief towards "no religion" which is the fastest growing category. It grew from 0.8 per cent in 1966 to

---

[2] Australian Bureau of Statistics, *Report 2071.0 - Reflecting a Nation: Stories from the 2011 Census, 2012–2013* (21 June 2012); Roy Williams, *Post God Nation? How religion fell off the radar in Australia – and what might be done to get it back on* (ABC Books, 2015) 113-114. This has been recognised by a number of Australian Courts. See, eg, *Canterbury Municipal Council v Moslem Alawy Society* (1985) I NSWLR 525, 543; *Christian Youth Camps Ltd v Cobaw Community Health Service Ltd* [2014] VSCA 75, [560] (Redlich JA).

[3] Ibid.

[4] Australian Bureau of Statistics, *2016 Census: religion* (27 June 2017).

30.1 per cent in 2016.[5] As Sheridan has observed:

> … [i]t is no exaggeration to say that Christianity is in nearly existential crisis in the West. Australia is about to become, a majority atheist nation. This is something unprecedented in all the long Aboriginal and European and modern multicultural history of our land. [6]

Learning to live together with tolerance

Australian history shows the benefits of accommodating differing cultures and religious beliefs. This has usually been done without much intrusion by law. It has instead involved acts of tolerance, understanding, accommodation and good sense by everyday Australians. Such acts enable people to work and live with their traditions and their religious faith. Examples of such behaviours include that:

- the National Rugby League team, Canterbury-Bankstown, agreed to an employment contract with star player Will Hopoate which enabled him to not play rugby league on Sundays to accommodate his faith. He has now decided that he will play on Sundays, which is his choice to make;[7]

- the Australian Cricket Board and Big Bash League teams agreed that Usman Khawaja, and Fawad Ahmed, who are both cricketers of Islamic faith, need not wear advertisements for alcohol on their jerseys;[8] and

- perhaps most importantly, the freedom of conscience that politicians, when dealing with issues such as abortion and euthanasia are granted in Australia's two largest political parties: the Australian Labor Party and the Liberal Party – theoretically, at

---

5   Ibid.

6   Greg Sheridan, *God is Good For You* (Allen & Unwin, 2018) 2.

7   NRL Network, *Hopoate to play on Sunday* (15 May 2017) Official website of the Canterbury-Bankstown Bulldogs.

8   Maik Dunnbier, *One scene that says it all about alcohol and sports* (12 November 2015) Drink Tank.

least – on all issues.[9]

However Australia was not like this from the beginning and this kind of tolerant good sense is not uniformly so today. The new settlers brought religious intolerance and sectarianism with them. A public and official demonstration of this was the oath of office taken by governors, from Arthur Phillip on. In taking office the early colonial governors swore their allegiance not just to the Crown but to 'the Protestant succession' and each repudiated 'Romish beliefs in the transubstantiation of the Eucharist'.[10] Protestant/Catholic sectarianism plagued Australia's history well into the 1970s.[11] Intolerance was even more manifest in the disregard of the customs, traditions and beliefs of Australia's Aboriginal and Torres Strait Islander peoples. From their arrival, the British treated Australia as "terra nullius" or uninhabited. This reflected a particular view of the importance of Western understandings of property and cultivation of land as indicia of ownership and civilization.[12] Aboriginal peoples were subject to British law and recognition of their own customary law was rejected.[13] Conflicts between colonists on the frontier and the original inhabitants of the country had much to do with the colonists' ignorance of traditional customs and laws. As explorer Edward Eyre observed in 1845:

> As we ourselves have laws, customs or prejudices, to which we attach considerable importance, and the infringement of which we consider either criminal or offensive, so have the natives theirs, equally perhaps, clear to them, but which, from our ignorance or heedlessness, we may be continually violating, and can we wonder that they sometimes exact the penalty of infraction? Do we not do the same.[14]

The principle of "terra nullius" was not short lived. It obtained until its

---

9   The Australian Labor Party decided in 1984 that 'the matter of abortion can be freely debated at any state or federal forum of the Australian Labor Party, but any decision reached is not binding on any member of the Party.'
See, Australian Labor Party, *ALP National Constitution* (26 July 2015), [52]; Deirdre McKeown and Rob Lundie, 'Free Votes in Australian and some Overseas Parliaments' (Current Issues Brief No 1, Parliamentary Library, Parliament of Australia, 2002-2003) ('The Liberal Party does not have a pledge which binds members to a party line.'); Gerard Henderson, *How Menzies would have dealt with conscience votes is guesswork* (22 August 2015) The Sydney Institute ('Liberal Party MPs were given a conscience vote on all pieces of legislation.').

10   Williams, above n 2, 28.

11   Roy Williams, *In God They Trust*, (Bible Society, 2013) 20.

12   Patrick Parkinson, *Tradition and Change in Australian Law* (Law Book Co, 5th ed, 2013) 129 [5.20].

13   Ibid 132-133 [5.40].

14   Quoted in Parkinson, above n 12, 133 [5.49].

rejection by the High Court in *Mabo v Queensland* (No 2) (1992) 175 CLR 1.[15] The consequences of the failure to recognise the reality of the customary laws and religious traditions of Australia's indigenous peoples is no doubt reflected in their proportionally high rates of incarceration, poor education and ill-health. Today whilst there are examples of tolerant behaviours as mentioned above, acts of vilification, discrimination, harassment, intimidation, verbal and physical abuse, property damage and vandalism and hate crimes on the grounds of religious belief take place in Australia.[16] The sort of ignorance of the motivations of the Aboriginal peoples that Eyre identified among European Australians can now be seen in ignorance and misunderstanding of religion and religious motivations for behaviour in Australia. As Christian Brugger has observed, '[I]n Australia, there is an astonishing level of religious ignorance and oblivion. Religion is simply not in the daily categories of thinking.'[17] Looking at the largest religious category

---

[15]   Ibid 133 [5.50].

[16]   Adam Possamai et al, 'Muslim Students' Religious and Cultural Experiences in the Micro-publics of University Campuses in NSW, Australia' (2016) 47 *Australian Geographer* 319- 321; Derya Iner et al, *Islamophobia in Australia 2014-2016* (June 2017) Charles Sturt University Research Output 39, 42. The report adopts Salmad Sayyis's definition of 'Islamophobia' which is 'a form of racism that includes various forms of violence, violations, discrimination and subordination that occur across multiple sites in response to the problematisation of Muslim identity.' It defines 'Incident' to mean '[a]n event or occurrence of an Islamophobic nature that is either physical or online event or occurrence characterised as Islamophobia/Islamophobic including physical attacks, assault, damage to property, offensive graffiti, non-verbal harassment, intimidation and online threats.'; Joint Standing Committee on Foreign Affairs, Defence and Trade, Parliament of Australia, *Conviction with Compassion: A Report on Freedom of Religion and Belief* (2000) [5.6], [5.7], [5.10]- [5.12],[5.19]-[5.21], [5.23]-[5.24]; Justine Kearney and Mohamed Taha, 'Sydney Muslims experience discrimination at three times the rate of other Australians: study', *ABC News* (Online) 30 November 2015; International Centre for Muslim and non-Muslim Understanding, 'Islamophobia, social distance and fear of terrorism in Australia: A Preliminary report' (Report, University of South Australia, 2015); Abdullah Saeed, *Islam in Australia* (Allen & Unwin, 2003) 6-7, 209-212; Deepti Goel, 'Perceptions of Immigrants in Australia after 9/11' (2010) 86 *The Economic Record* 275, 596-597, 600-601, 605-608; Kristine Frederickson, BYU's Chris Collinsworth had angels on his left and right sides' (16 January 2011) *Deseret News*; Julie Nathan, '2014 Report on Antisemitism in Australia' (Report, Executive Council of Australian Jewry, 9 November 2014) 6-8, 15-42; Gary D Bouma and Michael Mason, 'Babyboomers downunder: the case of Australia' in W Roof, J Carroll and D Roozen (eds), *The Post-War Generation and Establishment Religion: Cross-cultural Perspectives* (Westview Bolder Co, 1995) 27-28, 44-45, 65-69, 72, 81; Margaret Thornton and Trish Luker, 'The Spectral Ground: Religious Belief Discrimination' (2009) 9 *Macquarie Law Journal* 75-84;

[17]   Christian Brugger, quoted in Eddie O'Neill, 'Lifting Up the Faith Down Under', *National Catholic Register* (Online) 29 July 2017.

Christianity, for example, 8 per cent of Australians know no Christians[18] and nearly 18 per cent know nothing about the Church in Australia.[19] Ignorance can lead to suspicion and misunderstanding with the result that more than a quarter of Australians (26 per cent) have a negative view of Christianity.[20] Six percent of Australians have strong reservations about Christianity and 7 per cent are passionately opposed to it.[21] Many associate Christians with negative stereotypes such as being judgmental, opinionated, hypocritical, intolerant, insensitive, rude, greedy, with outdated beliefs that they seek to impose on others.[22] Some consider that even discussing the traditional Christian – particularly the Catholic – position on, for example, sexual morality, confession, abortion, euthanasia or marriage - is hateful, bigoted and offensive and merely an excuse for protecting child abusers, covering up child sexual assault, sexism, homophobia, transphobia and discrimination akin to racism, apartheid and slavery.[23]

---

[18] McCrindle Research, *Faith and Belief in Australia Report: A national study on religion, spirituality and worldview trends* (May 2017) 10.

[19] Ibid 10.

[20] Ibid 9.

[21] Ibid 31.

[22] Ibid 30, 35.

[23] For example the *Sydney Morning Herald* and *Sun Herald* feature weekly columns from the militant atheist Peter Fitzsimons who regularly includes anti-Christian and anti-Catholic diatribes in his columns. See, eg, Peter Fitzsimmons, 'Folau's thoughtless comments are an anathema to the greatest of rugby's values' (Online) *The Sydney Morning Herald* (April 7–8 2018) 51. Media personality Andrew Denton has called on religious people to withdraw from the debate about euthanasia referring to Catholic businessmen and politicians who oppose legalising euthanasia as a 'subterranean Catholic force' (Michael Edwards, 'Andrew Denton lashes out at 'subterranean Catholic force' blocking voluntary euthanasia laws' (Online) *ABC News* (10 August 2016); Staff writers, 'Andrew Denton trying to exclude Catholic voices from euthanasia debate' (17 August 2016) *The Catholic Weekly*. It is also common in the popular media to seek to undermine rational arguments if they are presented by persons of faith. For example, in an episode of the ABC television program, '*Q and A*', dealing with euthanasia which featured Nikki Gemmell (journalist), Penny Wong (Australian Labor Party Federal parliamentarian), Mitch Fifield (Federal Minister for Communications), Billy Bragg (singer/songwriter) and Margaret Somerville (The University of Notre Dame Australia, bio-ethicist Professor), the moderator Tony Jones asked only the panellist from a Catholic university, Professor Margaret Somerville, if she was 'a religious person': ABC, 'Assad, Assisted Suicide and Satire', *Q and A*, 10 April 2017 (Tony Jones). A final example of this is the boycotting of Coopers' lager because of their involvement in a video featuring a very civil respectful debate on marriage between same-sex attracted advocate for the redefinition of marriage Liberal MP Tim Wilson and Liberal MP Andrew Hastie who was a supporter of maintaining the then definition of marriage: Rachel Olding, 'Pubs boycott Coopers beer following Bible Society marriage equality marketing campaign', *Sydney Morning Herald*, 14 March 2017.

Legislative accommodations for culture, tradition and religious freedom

In 1901 the colonies of Australia federated. They did so 'primarily due to the issues of commerce and defence.'[24] As a consequence the *Australian Constitution* is 'a pragmatic rather than an inspiring document.'[25] It gave the Commonwealth powers in 'what may be broadly described as public economic or financial subjects.'[26] Whilst it protects or confers very few rights on individuals, it does include religious freedom in s 116. This section prevents the Commonwealth from establishing a State religion or imposing any religious test for the holding of any Commonwealth office. It also prevents the Commonwealth from prohibiting the free exercise of religion.[27] The few cases to date on this section have not found a Commonwealth law to have breached the free exercise of religion.[28] The limited jurisprudence to date would suggest that the High Court focusses on the intention of the legislation in applying the test and that unless the law was passed by the Commonwealth with the specific intention to interfere with religion it is unlikely to be found to fall foul of the section. Section 116 has no application to the legislatures of the Australian States. The *Australian Constitution* gives the Commonwealth powers only in specifically identified areas. It gave the Commonwealth no general power in relation to religion or religious freedom. It did, however, give the Commonwealth power 'to make laws, for the peace, order, and good government of the Commonwealth with respect to external affairs.'[29] Relevantly this provision

---

[24]   Sarah Joseph and Melissa Castan, *Federal Constitutional Law: A Contemporary View* (Lawbook Co, 3rd ed, 2010) [1.80]

[25]   Ibid [1.150]

[26]   *Russell v Russell* [1976] 134 CLR 495, 546 ('*Russell v Russell*').

[27]   Section 116 of the *Australian Constitution* provides that: 'The Commonwealth shall not make any law for establishing any religion, or for imposing any religious observance, or for prohibiting the free exercise of any religion, and no religious test shall be required as a qualification for any office or public trust under the Commonwealth.'

[28]   *Krygger v Williams* (1912) 15 CLR 366; *Adelaide Company of Jehovah's Witnesses v Commonwealth* (1943) 67 CLR 116; *Attorney-General (Vic); Ex Rel Black v Commonwealth* (1981) 146 CLR 559; *Church of the New Faith v Commissioner of Pay-Roll Tax (Vic)* (1983) 154 CLR 120; *Williams v Commonwealth* (2012) 288 ALR 410. See discussion in Denise Meyerson, 'The Protection of Religious Rights Under Australian Law' (2009) 3 *BYU Law Review* 529, 538-540; Paul Babie and Neville Rochow, 'Feels Like Déjà vu: An Australian Bill of Rights and Religious Freedom' (2010) 3 *BYU Law Review* 821, 829-832.

[29]   *Australian Constitution*, s 51(xxix).

has been interpreted by the High Court as providing the Commonwealth with legislative power to give effect to Australia's international obligations. This extends to obligations which arise under a treaty or agreement.[30] Australia is party to a number of international agreements which recognise the right to freedom of religion. For example, Article 18 of the 1948, *Universal Declaration of Human Rights* provides that:[31]

> Everyone has the right to freedom of thought, conscience and religion; this right includes freedom to change his religion or belief, and freedom, either alone or in community with others and in public or private, to manifest his religion or belief in teaching, practice, worship and observance.

Article 18(1) of the *International Covenant on Civil and Political Rights* ('ICCPR'), which Australia has been a party to since 1980, provides that:[32]

> Everyone shall have the right to freedom of thought, conscience and religion. This right shall include freedom to have or to adopt a religion or belief of his choice, and freedom, either individually or in community with others and in public or private to manifest his religion or beliefs in worship, observance, practice and teaching.

The United Nations Human Rights Committee, established under Article 29 of the *ICCPR*, has recognised that:

> The freedom to manifest religion or belief may be exercised "either individually or in community with others and in public or private". The freedom to manifest religion or belief in worship, observance, practice and teaching encompasses a broad range of acts.[33]

Under Article 2 of the *ICCPR*, Australia undertook to respect and ensure that everyone within Australia and subject to Australian jurisdiction, recognises the rights in the *ICCPR*. Article 9 of the *European Convention on Human Rights* ('ECHR'),[34] is in substantially the same terms as Article 18(1) of the *ICCPR*. The European Court of Human Rights has observed that the maintenance of pluralism is dependent on maintaining freedom of

---

[30] *Commonwealth v Tasmania* (1983) 158 CLR 1

[31] *Universal Declaration of Human Rights*, GA Res 217A (III), UN GAOR, 3rd sess, 183rd plen mtg, UN Doc A/810 (10 December 1948).

[32] *International Covenant on Civil and Political Rights*, opened for signature 19 December 1966, 999 UNTS 171 (entered into force 23 March 1976)

[33] Human Rights Committee, *CCPR General Comment No 22: Article 18 (Freedom of Thought, Conscience or Religion)*, 48th sess, UN Doc CCPR/C/21/Rev.1/Add.4 (30 July 1993).

[34] *Convention for the Protection of Human Rights and Fundamental Freedoms*, opened for signature 4 November 1950, 213 UNTS 221 (entered into force 3 September 1953)

religion.[35] In *Sindicatul "Pastorul Cel Bun" v Romania* (2014) 58 ECHR 10 the Grand Chamber of the European Court of Human Rights stated that:

> The autonomous existence of religious communities is indispensable for pluralism in a democratic society and is an issue at the very heart of the protection which Article 9 affords. It directly concerns not only the organisation of these communities as such but also the effective enjoyment of the right to freedom of religion by all their active members. Were the organisational life of the community not protected by Article 9, all other aspects of the individual's freedom of religion would become vulnerable.[36]

While Australia has committed to these international instruments, there is presently no general Commonwealth religious anti-discrimination or religious freedom legislation. By contrast, the Commonwealth has enacted laws prohibiting discrimination in a range of areas such as age, race, disability, sex and sexual identity primarily relying on the external affairs power and its obligations under international instruments. Such legislative protections as are afforded to religion are contained in a patchwork of exemptions in some Commonwealth laws and a range of approaches in State and Territory laws. Legislative accommodations have sometimes been given when conflicts with religion or belief or with the laws, traditions and customs of Australia's Aboriginal and Torres Strait Islander peoples have arisen. An example is Part 4.4 of the *Succession Act 2006* (NSW) ('*Succession Act*'), which was applied in Re *Estate Jerrard, Deceased*.[37] This case considered the application of a distribution order following the death of Mr Jerrard. Mr Jerrard was a young aboriginal man of the Nucoorilma Clan of the Gomeroi People from Tingha. He died intestate. The estate of a person who dies intestate in NSW is usually shared evenly by their mother and father if they are alive pursuant to s 128 of the *Succession Act*. Recognising 'the fact that, in an indigenous community, the concept of "family" relationships may differ radically from the general concept of "family" relationships upon which [the usual distribution arrangements provided by the *Succession Act* are based]', where an indigenous person dies intestate a Part 4.4 application can be made. This provides for a

---

[35] *Case of Eweida And Ors v The United Kingdom* [2013] Eur Court HR 30, [79] ('*Eweida*').

[36] *Sindicatul "Pastorul Cel Bun" v Romania* [2014] 58 ECHR 10 [136], quoted in *Iliafi v Church of Jesus Christ Of Latter Day Saints Australia* (2014) 311 ALR 354, [77] ('*Iliafi*').

[37] [2018] NSWSC 781 (8 June, 2018) ('*Jerrard*')

different scheme of distribution of the estate in accordance with the laws, customs, traditions and practices of the community or group to which the intestate belonged under s 133(2) of the *Succession Act*. In *Jerrard*, the deceased's mother brought such an application seeking the whole of the estate. Under the customary law of the relevant clan a deceased person's estate should go to 'the person who has borne responsibility for, cared for and provided for the deceased person throughout his life.'[38] Mr Jerrard's mother was this person as she brought Mr Jerrard up and he had a close personal relationship with her. By contrast Mr Jerrard had limited social contact with his father. The Court accepted the evidence of the relevant customary law and ruled that the estate should go wholly to Mr Jerrard's mother but awarded a modest allowance to his father applying principles of justice and equity.[39] This case demonstrates the sort of accommodation that Australian law – in this case a State law – can provide in favour of citizens with different 'laws, customs, traditions and practices.'

When the law has sought to accommodate freedom of religion and conscience it has generally done so by specific exemptions in legislation dealing with other matters. Some examples of this approach are:

- the exemption under electoral laws for people whose beliefs prevent them from voting on particular days or at all;[40]

- exemptions for religious bodies from discrimination laws to enable them to operate schools and ordain clergy in compliance with their own doctrines;[41]

---

[38]   Ibid.

[39]   Ibid [137].

[40]   Although voting is compulsory in Australia, if an elector has a religious belief that it is his or her religious duty to abstain from voting, this will constitute a reasonable excuse under s 245(14) of the *Commonwealth Electoral Act* (1918) and s 45(13A) of the *Referendum (Machinery Provisions) Act* (1984): See, Australian Electoral Commission, *Electoral Backgrounder: Compulsory Voting*, [41]

[41]   Exemptions are provided to religious bodies from a range of discrimination provisions to enable them to operate schools and to comply with their own doctrines in managing their own operations. See, eg, *Sex Discrimination Act 1984* (Cth), ss 5, 5A, 14, 21(3), 23(3)(b), 37(1)(a), 37(1)(d), 37(2) and 38; *Age Discrimination Act 2004* (Cth), s35; *Anti-Discrimination Act, 1977* (NSW), ss 8, 38S(2)(c), 49ZT(2)(c), 49ZXB(2)(c), 49ZYB, 49Y and 56; *Equal Opportunity Act 2010* (Vic), ss 83(1)-(2). For a summary of the exemptions from various discrimination provisions which are afforded to religious (and other) schools in Australia, see Greg Walsh, *Religious Schools And Discrimination Law* (Central Press, 2015) 1-11.

- exemptions for conscientious objectors in the *Defence Act,1903* (Cth);[42] and

- the protection of the contents of religious confessions from disclosure in court by statute in Commonwealth law and by the laws of most states and territories.[43] As discussed below this protection has now been removed or is under review in a number of jurisdiction.

As Mark Fowler has observed there are deficiencies in treating protections for religion as exemptions:

> [T]he language of "exemptions" contains some beguiling and at times untested philosophical presumptions. What are termed religious "exemptions" are not true *exemptions* at all, but are legitimate *expressions* of religious freedom rights. We do not say, for instance, that the right of the press to free speech is an "exemption" from majoritarian imposed control. It is a legitimate stand-alone right. Similarly, we do not say the citizen's freedom to associate around common interests is an "exemption" granted by the state from compelled forms of association. Why is it that religious freedom is singled out for such laden terminology?[44]

Exemptions of this kind are not always given even where the potential for conflict with religiously impelled or motivated activities are recognised in advance. For example, an increasing number of States and Territories

---

42   Department of the Parliamentary Library, 'Conscientious Objection to Military Service in Australia' (Research Note No 31, Parliamentary Library, Parliament of Australia, 2003)

43   The Commonwealth and NSW protect religious confession privilege by s 127 of the NSW and Commonwealth *Evidence Acts*. It provides:
(1) A person who is or was a member of the clergy of any church or religious denomination is entitled to refuse to divulge that a religious confession was made, or the contents of a religious confession made, to the person when a member of the clergy.
(2) Subsection (1) does not apply if the communication involved in the religious confession was made for a criminal purpose.
(3) This section applies even if an Act provides:
(a) that the rules of evidence do not apply or that a person or body is not bound by the rules of evidence, or
(b) that a person is not excused from answering any question or producing any document or other thing on the ground of privilege or any other ground.
(4) In this section:
"religious confession" means a confession made by a person to a member of the clergy in the member's professional capacity according to the ritual of the church or religious denomination concerned.
Victoria and other "Evidence Act" States (that is, all jurisdictions except Western Australia, South Australia and Queensland) have also protected religious confession privilege specifically by this statutory privilege since 1995.

44   Mark Fowler, 'Why are we talking about "exemptions" rather than the right to free religious expression?', *ABC Religion & Ethics* (Online) 18 October 2018.

in Australia have passed laws mandating the referral of patients seeking an abortion by health professionals with a conscientious objection to the practice. Another example is the increasing number of States and Territories which have criminalised a wide range of activities within designated exclusion zones near facilities where terminations of pregnancies take place. These examples are considered below.

Referral or direction legislation

Whilst these provisions impact on all health professionals who have a conscientious objection to abortion, they have a particular impact on observant Catholics given the teachings of that Church that direct abortion is gravely immoral.[45] This is due to the belief that human life is to be respected and protected from conception.[46] Given that specific impact this discussion concentrates on the impact of such provisions on Catholic health professions to whom they apply. A Catholic who formally cooperates by facilitating an abortion (such as by providing a patient with a referral to a medical practitioner known to have the skills to perform an abortion and to be willing so to do) would automatically excommunicate him or herself from the Church by doing so.[47] The Catholic Church teaches that a civil law permitting abortion is 'an intrinsically unjust law,'[48] that it is never legitimate to obey such a law,[49] and that there is 'a grave and clear obligation to oppose [such a law] by conscientious objection.'[50] For Catholic health professionals who seek to live in accordance with the official teachings of their Church, being obliged to refer a patient for an abortion is akin to a country extraditing a criminal to face the death penalty. The United Nations Human Rights Commission ('UNHRC') and the European Court of Human Rights have both held that extradition in such circumstances would be a contravention of human rights.[51] In *Judge*

---

45   *Catechism of the Catholic Church*, (St Pauls Publications, 2nd ed, 2000) ('*CCC*') [2271]

46   Ibid [2258], [2270].

47   Ibid [2272]; Ernest Caparros, Michel Thériault, and Jean Thorn, *Code of Canon Law Annotated* (Wilson & Lafleur, 1993) 1398, 1329.2 ('*Code of Canon Law*'). See also, Pope John Paul II, *Evangelium Vitae: On the Value and Inviolability of Human Life* (25 March 1995) The Holy See; [62]. This precludes the reception of the sacraments (including communion, reconciliation, confirmation, marriage, anointing of the sick and Holy Orders).

48   Pope John Paul II, above n 47, [20], [57], [73].

49   Ibid [73].

50   Ibid.

51   See discussion in Stephen Hall, *Principles of International Law* (LexisNexis Butterworths, 5th ed, 2016) 621-623 [11.46]-[11.47].

v Canada [52] the UNHRC found that by deporting a criminal to the US to face the death penalty, 'Canada established the crucial link in the causal chain that would make possible the execution.'[53] For a Catholic health professional providing a referral is such a crucial link in the causation of a subsequent abortion. As a result, freedom of conscience and religion in their professional lives when it comes to abortion is very important. It is not respected by an increasing number of States and Territories. An example of the operation of such a provision is the 2013 investigation and disciplining of a Victorian Catholic pro-life doctor, Dr Mark Hobart, for failing to comply with a Victorian law. This law requires doctors with a conscientious objection to abortion to provide a referral to a doctor known not to share their objection. Dr Hobart failed to refer a patient seeking a sex-selection abortion. Similar laws apply in the Northern Territory[54] and Queensland[55] and a Department of Health policy is in a similar form in New South Wales.[56] These laws exist even though information about abortion and abortion procedures are widely available and no referral or direction is required to access the procedure.[57] Like laws which seek to compel the breach of the seal of confession by Catholic priests, which are discussed below, these laws oblige faithful Catholics to either break the law or automatically excommunicate themselves from their Church by complying with the law. Excommunication is a serious matter for a faithful Catholic as it precludes participation in the sacraments of the Church.[58]

---

[52]   Human Rights Committee, *Views: Communication No 829/1998*, 78th sess, UN Doc CCPR/C/78/D/829/1998 (20 October 2003) [11.46] ('*Judge v Canada*'), quoted in Hall, above n 51, 621.

[53]   Ibid.

[54]   *Termination of Pregnancy Law Reform Act 2017* (NT).

[55]   *Termination of Pregnancy Act 2018* (Qld).

[56]   NSW Ministry of Health, *Policy Directive: NSW Health Policy Directives And Other Policy Documents* (May 17, 2016) ('*the NSW Policy*'). The NSW Policy does not apply to all medical practitioners in NSW. Compliance with the NSW Policy is mandatory for Area Health Services/Chief Executive Governed Statutory Health Corporations, Board Governed Statutory Health Corporations, Affiliated Health Organizations — Non-Declared, Affiliated Health Organizations — Declared, and Divisions of General Practice and Public Hospitals NSW Department of Health.

[57]   See discussion in Michael Quinlan, 'When the State Requires Doctors to Act Against their Conscience: The Religious Freedom Implications of the Referral and the Direction Obligations of Health Practitioners in Victoria and New South Wales' (2016) 4 *BYU Law Review* 1237, 1245, 1248.

[58]   *CCC*, [1463].

Exclusion zone legislation

An increasing number of States and Territories have introduced exclusion zones around facilities where terminations of pregnancies are carried out. In Tasmania,[59] the ACT,[60] New South Wales,[61] the Northern Territory,[62] Victoria[63] and Queensland[64] communication including by prayer (unless it is silent and not likely to be identified by others),[65] counselling and protest (no matter how quiet, respectful or caring) is a criminal offence if it occurs within designated areas around abortion clinics. People may be driven to communicate about abortion in these areas for a range of reasons. These laws have a particular impact on those Australians who are driven to protest about abortion for religious motives. To date only Christians have been prosecuted for breaching these laws and the impact on Christians is the particular focus here. Three elderly Christians (Mr and Mrs Stallard and Mr Graeme Preston) were successfully prosecuted in Tasmania for protesting too close to an abortion clinic in 2016.[66] Motivated by their faith they conducted a peaceful and quiet protest outside an abortion clinic within the exclusion zone in Hobart in 2016.[67] The Magistrate made these observations on motive:

> [Mr Preston] has been a Christian since he was 14 and he believes that human life has been created in the image of God uniquely and that human life is of absolute importance as referred to in the Scriptures. That God knows us even when we are growing in our mother's womb and in particular he believes in the incarnation of Jesus as God coming into the world born in his mother's womb and that that validates human life at every stage. Mr Preston explained that the Bible teaches people to care for one another and in particular to help those who are most vulnerable or defenceless. He considers that a child in the womb would be probably the most vulnerable category of human beings and that they are completely defenceless. He believes that it is right and necessary that people come to the aid of those who are vulnerable and defenceless

---

59 *Reproductive Health (Access to Terminations) Act 2013* (Tas), s9.

60 *Health Act 1993* (ACT).

61 *Public Health Amendment (Safe Access to Reproductive Health Clinics) Act 2018* (NSW).

62 *Termination of Pregnancy Law Reform Act 2017* (NT).

63 *Public Health and Wellbeing Amendment (Safe Access Zones) Act 2015* (Vic).

64 *Termination of Pregnancy Act 2018* (Qld).

65 *Bluett v Popplewell* [2018] ACTMC 2 (9 March 2018).

66 *Police v Preston and Stallard* [2016] TASMC (27 July 2016). An unsuccessful appeal from this decision grounded on the implied freedom of political communication (rather than on religious freedom) was heard by the High Court of Australia in October 2018.

67 *Police v Preston and Stallard* [2016] TASMC (27 July 2016).

which includes unborn children.[68]

> Essentially as I understood Mrs Stallard's evidence she regards herself as a practicing Christian, and as part of her Christian beliefs she believes that every life is sacred, that an unborn life does not have a voice, and that as part of her Christian beliefs she needs to stand up for people without a voice which led her to protest with Mr Preston.[69]

Uniquely of all Australian Constitutions the *Tasmanian Constitution*, provides protections for freedom of conscience[70] and religion. In this case the restrictive approach taken by the High Court to date in applying s 116 of the *Australian Constitution* was applied to the application of the provisions of the *Tasmanian Constitution*. Although the protestors presented no physical obstacle to entrance to the facility, badgered, harangued and attacked no one and posed no threat of violence or intimidation, the religious motivations of the accused did not prevent their conviction.[71] A similar result was reached in relation to a lone peaceful protester in Victoria where religious freedom was not an available argument.[72] In the ACT, three Christians were successful in overturning a fine issued for praying silently and individually outside an office block where terminations of pregnancy were performed.[73] The Court did not find that prayer could not amount to a prohibited "protest" but that the actions of the three Christians did not involve any protest because they were simply walking in public areas around an office block and doing nothing to communicate or act in any way to stand out.[74] Exclusion zone legislation criminalises religiously motivated non-violent and non-threatening behaviour. It does so with very limited evidence that such actions cause harm to anyone.[75]

---

[68]   Ibid [58].

[69]   Ibid [65].

[70]   Section 46(1) of the *Constitution Act 1934* (Tas) provides that: 'Freedom of conscience and the free profession and practice of religion are, subject to public order and morality, guaranteed to every citizen.'

[71]   *Police v Preston and Stallard* [2016] TASMC (27 July 2016) [58]-[59], [64]-[65].

[72]   *Edwards v Clubb* [2017] MCV (6 October 2017); *Edwards v Clubb* [2017] MCV (23 December 2017).

[73]   *Bluett v Popplewell* [2018] ACTMC 2 (9 March 2018).

[74]   Ibid [84]-[85].

[75]   Joseph Turner, Debbie Garratt and Simon McCaffrey, *The High Court, Abortion Clinic Speech Restrictions and the Assessment of Harm* (1 October 2018) The Western Australian Legal Theory Association.

The sacrament and the seal of confession

The Royal Commission into Institutional Responses to Child Sexual Abuse ('*the Commission*') concluded that many institutions in Australia – including institutions associated with religious traditions – had repeatedly failed to adequately protect children in their care or to take adequate steps to minimize the risk of such behaviours being repeated. The Final Report of the Commission made many recommendations. Most of these recommendation have received approval and support from the religious traditions concerned including the Catholic Church.[76] The recommendations included a recommendation that 'State and territory governments amend laws concerning mandatory reporting to child protection authorities to achieve national consistency in reporter groups' and that those obligations should extend to 'people in religious ministry'.[77] The Commission further recommended that such laws 'should not exempt persons in religious ministry from being required to report knowledge or suspicions formed, in whole or in part, on the basis of information disclosed in or in connection with a religious confession.'[78] The Catholic Church has not accepted or endorsed that recommendation. Nevertheless South Australia and the ACT have already passed legislation consistent with these recommendations and Tasmania, Western Australia and Victoria have all expressed an intention of doing so.[79] It is noteworthy however that the Commission did not make recommendations to override legal professional privilege by recommending that the reporting obligations ought to be extended to lawyers whose clients may confess child sexual assaults committed by them or for the abrogation of the right to silence enjoyed by persons accused of crimes including child sexual assault in Australia.

The Commission thereby recognised that there are some privileges that society considers to have such value that they ought not be abrogated even where doing so might produce probative evidence. It is also noteworthy that the Commission did not identify any instance anywhere in the world

---

[76] John Sandeman, 'Catholics accept most of the Royal Commission recommendations,' *Eternity News* (Online) 31 August 2018.

[77] Commonwealth, Royal Commission into Institutional Responses to Child Sex Abuse, *Final Report - Recommendations* (2017) 17 [7.3].

[78] Ibid, [7.4].

[79] Catherine Sheehan, 'Priests face life in jail,' *The Catholic Weekly* 7 October 2018, 1,4.

of any person being convicted of a child sexual assault on the basis of any information reported by a priest following disclosure within the sacrament of confession.[80] Whilst religious confessions are not limited to the Catholic faith tradition, legislation of this kind has two significant implications for the religious freedom of lay Catholics and their priests and this discussion focusses on those implications. The analysis starts with a consideration of the significance of the sacrament and "seal" of confession for Catholics and the nature of what occurs – or is understood by Catholics to occur - in that sacrament.

What is this sacrament and what is the seal of confession?

In the Catholic faith tradition, confession is a sacrament.[81] Whilst many Christian Churches (and other religious traditions) recognise the need for repentance from sin and the need to seek the forgiveness of God, in the Catholic tradition, it is essential for serious sins to be confessed to God verbally via a priest. In hearing a confession a priest is 'fulfilling the ministry of the Good Shepherd,'[82] and acting *in personi Christi*.[83] As such, in the sacrament of confession the penitent is effectively speaking to God through the priest. If absolution is granted the priest is not personally forgiving sin – God is forgiving sin.[84] Catholics are strongly recommended to regularly attend confession[85] and they are 'bound by an obligation faithfully to confess serious sins at least once a year.'[86] Catholics aware of having committed a serious sin may not receive communion without first

---

[80]   For example, in Ireland despite the passage of the *Criminal Justice (Withholding of Information on Offences against Children and Vulnerable Persons) Act 2012* (Ire) which made it an offence for a person not to report any information relating to a sexual offence committed against a child and the *Children First Act 2015* (Ire) which created a statutory duty on mandated persons including Catholic priests to report suspicions, knowledge or a risk of a child being abused to Tusla (the Child and Family Agency).

[81]   *CCC* [1425]-[1429]. It is also known as penance or most commonly today as the sacrament of reconciliation

[82]   Ibid [1465].

[83]   Ibid. The scriptural foundation for this view includes Proverbs 28:13 which provides that '[n]o man who conceals his sins will prosper, whoever confesses and renounces them will find mercy.' (New Jerusalem Bible)

[84]   Ibid.

[85]   Ibid [1459].

[86]   Ibid [1457] [references given in CCC omitted]

making a good confession.[87]

In the Catholic tradition, particular emphasis is given to the words of Saint John's Gospel which record Christ's appearance to the disciples, his breathing on them and saying: '... receive the Holy Spirit. If you forgive anyone's sins, they are forgiven; if you retain anyone's sins they are retained.'[88] According to this tradition when a good confession is made to the disciples – whose role is now performed by the priests of the Church - and the penance imposed served, a penitent can receive God's forgiveness.[89] In contrast, in many other religious traditions it is believed that the forgiveness of God can be sought and obtained by a direct communication by the penitent to God – that is by way of silent thought. In reaching its recommendations on religious confession the Commission referred in detail to changes in the approach to confession in some parts of the Anglican communion. In doing so it failed to identify the significant differences in the prevalence, emphasis, sacramental and mandatory nature of confession and in the structure of the two religious traditions. In the Catholic Church areas such as doctrine and Canon law are universal and outside the scope of a local or domestic part of the church to vary.[90]

In the sacrament of confession, the priest does not purport to and does not, act in any way on behalf of the State or forgive the crimes of a criminal vis a vis the State. Criminals are no less liable to imprisonment or any other form of State punishment for crimes which they have committed whether they have confessed them to a priest or not. The position is no different to that of a criminal from another faith tradition who had made an honest confession directly to God, within the theology of that faith tradition, who may believe he or she has been forgiven by his or her God but remain liable for criminal prosecution by the State for that crime. Catholics are not confused about the difference between the laws of the

---

87   Ibid [1457].

88   John 20:22-23 (New Jerusalem Bible)

89   CCC [1441].

90   The universal operation of the Canon Law is important when considering, for example, if Canon Law ought require all bound by it to report any and all breaches of the criminal or civil law which they suspect may have occurred to the State authorities. There are many countries which punish same-sex sexual activity and ten countries in which such activities are punishable by death: Max Bearak and Darla Cameron, 'Here are the 10 countries where homosexuality may be punished by death', *Washington Post* (Online) 16 June 2016.

Church and the laws of the State. In contrast, should State intrusion into confidential communications occurring within the sacrament of confession involve confusion in the role of the State and the Church. The verbal communications that occur in a Catholic confession occur only because of the particular religious teaching of that faith. Confession is not optional for faithful Catholics. Laws which seek to override the seal of confession are a significant intrusion in the sacramental life of lay Catholics who are obliged to confess their sins because of their religious beliefs. Requiring disclosure of the content of a confession involves the State seeking to intrude into and benefit from a religious tradition. It is akin to overriding an accused's right to silence because it requires the disclosure of a person's innermost thoughts, which would absent the tradition of the sacrament of confession be their prayerful silent communication with their God. How a person communicates with their God and what is said in those communications is a matter which is intensely private and ought to be recognised by the State as such.

The maintenance of a penitent's privacy by the seal of confession is so fundamental to Catholics that the Code of Canon law provides that:

> The sacramental seal is inviolable. Accordingly, it is absolutely wrong for a confessor in any way to betray the penitent, for any reason whatsoever, by word or in any fashion.[91]

> The confessor is wholly forbidden to use knowledge acquired in confession to the detriment of the penitent even when all danger of disclosure is excluded.[92]

A priest who breaches the seal in doing so excommunicates himself from the Church. As a consequence he may no longer receive the sacraments or exercise any priestly role. Such laws may discourage men from seeking ordination as priests to the detriment of the laity. They are also a serious intrusion into the religious freedom of priests. Should a confession of relevant crimes be made, the priest must then choose between breaching the law and committing a criminal offence or effectively surrendering his vocation by complying with the law. This then raises the question of whether there may be a State interest sufficient to justify such an intrusion. Answering this question requires a consideration of the benefits and detriments to the State of confession.

---

[91]   Caparros, Thériault, and Thorn, above n 47, [982].

[92]   Ibid [984]. See also, *CCC* [1467].

Does the State Benefit from Confession?

Leaving aside the benefit to the State of respecting religious freedom and complying with its international obligations so to do, the fact that a Catholic confession must be verbal provides an opportunity for priests to hear of actions of penitents which might not otherwise be disclosed to anyone. Priests hearing confession are not required or expected to be silent sponges. On the contrary. Where a penitent has committed sins which have injured another confession is not enough, satisfaction is required. As the Catechism states:

> Many sins wrong our neighbour. One must do what is possible in order
> to repair the harm (e.g. return stolen goods, restore the restoration of
> someone slandered, pay compensation for injuries).[93]

Were a child sex abuser to disclose his or her crimes to a priest in confession in a manner which enabled the priest to become aware of the actual nature of the activities to which the penitent was confessing, the priest would have the opportunity of encouraging that penitent to make satisfaction by confessing his or her crimes to the police. Some priests take the view that they could refuse absolution to a penitent who refused to go to the police and confess their crimes to them and that they could set that step as penance which forms a condition of forgiveness in the sacrament.[94]

Some priests may argue that this accords with the Catechism's description of penance:

> The *penance* the confessor imposes must take into account the penitent's
> personal situation and must seek his spiritual good. It must correspond
> as far as possible with the gravity and nature of the sins committed.[95]

and with Canon Law which provides that:

> The confessor is to impose salutary and appropriate penances, in
> proportion to the kind and number of sins confessed, taking into
> account, however, the condition of the penitent. The penitent is bound
> personally to fulfil these penances.[96]

Whether or not reporting to the police should or should not properly be set as a condition of absolution or as a penitential step, confession at the very least, may provide an opportunity for a priest to encourage the perpetrator

---

[93]   *CCC* [1459].

[94]   Commonwealth, Royal Commission into Institutional Responses to Child Sex Abuse, *Criminal Justice Report: Parts III-VI* (2017) 206 ('*Criminal Justice Report*')

[95]   *CCC* [1460].

[96]   Caparros, Thériault, and Thorn, above n 47, [981].

to report to the police. Without confession – for example, in a faith tradition in which sins are forgiven by silent admonition – such an opportunity may never present. The Catholic sacrament of confession provides a potential opportunity to encourage an abuser to come forward.

What would be gained by abrogating the seal?

For anything to be gained by abrogating the seal child molesters would need to confess to child sexual assault and provide their identity and probative evidence in doing so knowing that the erstwhile seal of confession has been abrogated by the State and priests would need to comply with the law rather than their faith. Each of those propositions seems most unlikely.

Child sexual abusers and confession

Confessions can be made to any priest. They are often held in a confessional in which the penitent cannot be seen by the priest and the identity of the penitent is not revealed. A confession is not an inquisition. Sins are often confessed by broad category. Confession does not require disclosure of the penitent's identity or the giving of any specific details such as names, places, dates and so on. This lack of detail in the celebration of the sacrament has only been exacerbated in the contemporary Catholic Church in Australia by the popularity and preponderance of the sacrament being celebrated in the form of the Second Rite. This form involves a public liturgy. Whilst private confession forms part of the Second Rite, the time is truncated and penitents are often requested to confess in categories of sin – selfishness, lying etc – rather than in specifics. To the limited extent to which priests who engaged in child sexual assault might confess their sins there are therefore good reasons for concluding that whatever was said in the sacrament would be of no probative value. First, confession usually occurs anonymously in which the priest does not know who is confessing to him. Secondly, there is no requirement for a penitent to disclose their name let alone their occupation or contact details in confession. Thirdly, confession is not a forensic or police investigation of sins involving an interrogation of dates, times, locations and so on. Fourthly, research conducted by Marie Keenan in Ireland which involved her interviewing priests convicted of child sexual assault supports this view. Keenan found that child abusing priests who alleged they confessed, did not confess the true nature of their acts or disclose that their sins had involved a minor.[97] Child molesters have a great capacity for self-deception and engage in all kinds of minimisation and rationalisation to excuse their aberrant behaviour. This makes it unlikely that they would seek to confess, what to others obviously are and what the Catechism and Canon Law clearly recognise, are grievous sins.[98] The Royal Commission 'heard evidence from clergy who told [the Commission] that they had never heard a confession in which a penitent confessed they had sexually abused a child or in which a child told them they had been sexually abused.'[99] The Commission also heard from infamous child sexual offender Gerard Risdale that he never confessed these sins. Assertions from perpetrators – persons who, as noted above, engage in all kinds of minimisation and rationalisation - that they confessed their sins are inherently unreliable, but even if accepted, support the view that what might have been confessed would have had no probative value. For example, the Royal Commission relied on the evidence of Father Brennan that a woman told him that her serial abusing father had told her that he had regularly confessed his sins and this made the abuser feel vindicated and the abuse continued.[100] It is impossible to draw any conclusions from this because we do not have the evidence of the woman to whom the father spoke, we do not have the evidence of the father himself, we do not know what was said by him assuming that he did make confession, we do not know whether anything he might have said may have been of any probative value and we do not know whether the offending father was seeking to justify his own offending by falsely stating that he made confession of his sins. On analysis there is no foundation for a conclusion that perpetrators of child abuse disclose that sexual abuse of children in confession. There is also no foundation for the view that, if child sexual abusers did make any such disclosures, what they disclosed might be of any probative value in any subsequent legal proceedings or in any investigation of the possibility of a crime having taken place.

Whilst not all Catholics regularly seek out the sacrament of confession in the contemporary Catholic Church[101] and some may not even do so once a year as the Church mandates they ought,[102] it remains a fundamental aspect

---

97 Marie Keenan, *Child Sexual Abuse and the Catholic Church: Gender, Power and Organizational Culture* (Oxford University Press, 2012), 162-164.

98 Ibid

99 Royal Commission into Institutional Responses to Child Sexual Abuse, *Criminal Justice Report*, above n 94, 204.

100 Ibid, 202-203.

101 Ibid.

102 *CCC* [1457].

and sacrament of the Church. It is not the role of the State to determine whether or not confession is a requirement of the forgiveness of sins, nor whether God does or does not exist, nor whether life after death exists, nor whether a failure to confess one's sins may lead to eternal damnation. In a pluralist, multi-faith and multi-cultural society persons should be able to fully participate in their religious faith as international law recognises. For the State to intrude on a Church sacrament so as to undermine both the penitent's continued certainty in the confidentiality of the confession of his or her sins and to place priests in the invidious position of maintaining the seal of confession or complying with laws requiring the disclosure of such intimately confidential communications and in doing so automatically excommunicating themselves from their Church, would be a major intrusion by the State into Church and faith. This would be even more so were such an intrusion to be retrospective in nature. As Archbishop Julian Porteous has observed:

> [I]n seeking to break the seal on confession the government, would be essentially making priests agents of the state, fundamentally [this] would breach the principle of separation of power between state and the church. This would be a worrying and dangerous precedent.[103]

Should the State act in this way in relation to one crime the logical foundation for it to do so in relation to other crimes would have been laid leaving the faithful unsure as to whether their confidences will be protected in the future and as to whether they may be putting their priests at risk of future prosecution by confessing to them. Mandating the disclosure of religious confessions made within the Catholic sacrament would be to unfairly treat Catholic priests and the Catholic faithful and that it would do so for no adequately established reason.

The law at the moment and the Recommendations of the Ruddock Review

Religious affiliation may be declining in Australia but religious belief and experience have been a feature of all human societies[104] and it is likely that

---

[103]   Julian Porteious, 'Children will be no safer by forcing priets to break the seal of confession', *Weekend Australian* 20-21 October 2018.

[104]   Mario Beauregard and Denyse O'Leary, *The Spiritual Brain* (Harper Collins, 2008) 7; John Finnis, *Natural Law and Natural Rights* (Oxford University Press, 2nd ed, 2011) 90; Candace S Alcorta and Richard Sosis, 'Ritual, Emotion and Sacred Symbols' (2005) 16 *Human Nature* 4, 323, 346.

a substantial proportion of the population will always be religious.[105] The increasing variation in the percentages of followers of particular religious traditions in Australia is also likely to continue. The need for adequate protection of religious freedom grows rather than diminishes as the number of believers falls as a proportion of the population and less people understand or think positively of religion. As this chapter has shown by considering the examples of conscientious objection of health professions, the introduction of exclusion zones and actions and calls for the abolition of religious confession privilege, laws are being passed and amended in Australia today which fail to protect religious freedom and this is done without any necessity or compelling State interest so to do.

On 12 October, 2018 the twenty recommendations of the Ruddock Review were reported by the press and on 13 December 2018 the full report and the recommendations ('*the Ruddock Recommendations*') took place. This chapter does not endeavour to provide any full critique of the recommendations but makes some initial comments on the Ruddock Recommendations. The release of the Ruddock Recommendations Review followed a leak of two recommendations of the Review on 9 October 2018. This occurred in the midst of the hotly contested Wentworth by-election consequent on the replacement and resignation of former Prime Minister, the Hon. Malcolm Turnbull. The leaked recommendations were published under the banner, 'Religious freedom review enshrines right of schools to turn away gay children and teachers.'[106] In fact the Ruddock Review had recommended amendments to existing exclusions in the *Sex Discrimination Act 1984* (Cth). Both major parties quickly rejected the recommendations of the unreleased Ruddock Review and indicated an intention to withdraw the exemptions for religious schools at least as far as they applied to students.[107] This sort of political response does not augur well for religious freedom in Australia. About 30 per cent of Australian schools

---

[105] Most people have been religious believers throughout history: Dimitrios Kapagiannis et al, 'Cognitive and Neural Foundations of Religious Belief' (2009) 106(12) *Proceedings of the National Academy of Sciences of the United States of America* 4876. Religious belief and experience come naturally to us: Justin L Barrett, *Born Believers* (Free Press, 2012) 16; M R Trimble, *The Soul in The Brain* (John Hopkins University Press, 2009) 9-10, 17-23, 178.

[106] Jewel Topsfield, 'Religious freedom review enshrines right of schools to turn away gay children and teachers', *Sydney Morning Herald* (Online) 9 October 2018.

[107] David Crowe, 'Winding back gay discrimination in schools is a pragmatic response from Morrison', *Sydney Morning Herald* (Online) 12 October 2018.

have a religious affiliation[108] with more than 390 of such schools in the Sydney metropolitan area alone.[109] They represent many faiths including Christianity, Islam and Judaism and many different forms of those traditions. Current exemptions to the *Sex Discrimination Act, 1984* (Cth) are in broad terms but they need to be in order to cater for the variety that exists within the religious traditions operating schools. As John Anderson has observed:

> In a liberal democracy, if a clash of interests can be resolved without limiting anybody's freedom then it should be the preferred way. In the case of religious schools in a highly developed country like Australia, most people have the option of more than just one school to work or study in. Furthermore as the Ruddock review recommends, schools can develop strategies for making their doctrinal and moral expectations clear from the beginning in a sensitive way, seeking to avoid any unnecessary hurt.[110]

Rather than a quick political response, any change to the law which will reduce the religious freedoms of religious schools requires careful consideration because what is appropriate for one school may not be so in another. It appears that following the results of the Wentworth by-election further consideration is being given to the changes which might be made in this area and as noted above this issue has now been referred to the Australian Law Reform Commission.[111] Hopefully a more considered response will be the result.

The Ruddock Review continues the practice of treating religion, not as a human right deserving of protection in its own right, but as an exemption from other rights legislation. Fowler's criticism of this approach has been set out above. Patrick Parkinson has made this observation:

> In political workplaces such as party offices, political allegiance matters; for environmental advocacy groups, views about climate change matter. In ethnic associations, ethnicity matters. And yes, in religious workplaces, religion matters.
>
> Christian leaders have for years argued strenuously that they do not want religious freedom to rest upon exemptions. They would much rather have a positive right for faith-based organisations to select staff, or

---

[108] Emma Rowe, 'Religion in Australian schools: an historical and contemporary debate', *School News* (Online) 26 August 2017.

[109] John Trevill Scott and Ann Cherly Armstrong, 'Faith-based Schools and the Public Good: Purposes and Perspectives' (Paper presented at the AARE Annual Conference, Melbourne 2010) 1.

[110] John Anderson, 'We can't let the aggressive secularists drive out religion', *The Weekend Australian*, 27-28 October 2018, 16.

[111] Joe Kelly, 'Major parties at odds over gay students law', *The Australian*, 26 October 2018, 4.

prefer staff, that adhere to the beliefs and values of the faith and, to the extent necessary, to insist upon codes of conduct consistent with those values. Christians do not want the right to "discriminate." They want the freedom to select.[112]

The Ruddock Recommendations are not for the grant of more exemptions or for a national *Religious Freedom Act* to better protect religious freedom more consistently and coherently across the nation but many are for the review, removal or amendment of existing religious exemptions.[113] Even the recommendation to finally make discrimination on the grounds of a person's 'religious belief or activity' or absence of such belief illegal across the country, through federal legislation, does not recommend the enactment of a Commonwealth *Religious Discrimination Act* but puts that only as an alternative to including such religious discrimination protections by way of amendment to the *Racial Discrimination Act 1975* (Cth).[114] This is unfortunate. The title and placement of legislation – even in identical language – are not unimportant for the message that they send. If proscribing discrimination against a person on the basis of a person's religion is at least as important as such a proscription on the basis of other protected characteristics a separate Act is required. It is to its credit that as part of its response to the Ruddock Review the Coalition government announced an intention to enact a Commonwealth *Religious Discrimination Act*. Whether this occurs is yet to be seen.

As noted earlier in this chapter, there is evidence of religious intolerance and discrimination in Australia but there is no systematic national record of such behaviours across all religious traditions. It was evident during the Ruddock Review that the Chair and the panel were interested in evidence of infringements of religious freedom and incidents of religious discrimination in their deliberation.

Recommendation 17 is for the commissioning of the collection and analysis of evidence of these actions. Evidence can be of assistance to decision makers and it is good that such information be collected and analysed. However, when dealing with fundamental human rights – such as freedom of religion and belief – their protection ought not depend upon the presence or absence of evidence of infringement. Laws send important messages about what a

---

112 Patrick Parkinson, 'Religious leaders seek right to believe not power to discriminate', *The Australian*, 26 October 2018, 26.

113 Religious Freedom Review Expert Panel, *Religious Freedom Review: Report of the Expert Panel* (18 May 2018) Department of the Prime Minister and Cabinet, See, Recommendations 1, 5, 6 and 78.

114 Ibid, Recommendation 15. See also Recommendation 16 specifically in relation to the current anti-discrimination laws of New South Wales and South Australia.

society considers important.

The Ruddock Recommendations if enacted would take away, amend, restrict or remove some existing religious freedom protections. It is not at all clear that they would provide a grounding for different results to apply in relation to the legislative challenges to religious freedom the subject of this chapter. In my view they would not send any clear signal that religious freedom is more important in Australia than Australia's current inadequate, incomplete and unravelling patchwork quilt of exemptions. Religious freedom is a fundamental human right. It is not appropriate that such a right be the subject of a patchwork of different laws in different parts of Australia. A refocusing of the legislative protections of religious freedom is necessary to ensure a national uniform response. This may best be achieved by a Commonwealth *Religious Freedom Act* with application across the nation.

Bibliography

ABC Q and A Assad, *Assisted Suicide and Satire: Transcript Extract* (10 April 2017) <https://dwdnsw.org.au/wp-content/uploads/2017/06/transcript-QandA-100417-section-on-voluntary-euthanasia.pdf.>

Adelaide Company of Jehovah's Witnesses v Commonwealth (1943) 67 CLR 116 Alcorta, Candace S and Richard Sosis, "Ritual, Emotion and Sacred Symbols" (Winter 2005) 16 *Human Nature* 4

Anderson, John, "We can't let the aggressive secularists drive out religion," *The Weekend Australian* 27-28 October, 2018, 16

Attorney-General (Vic); Ex Rel Black v Commonwealth (1981) 146 CLR 559

Australian Bureau of Statistics, 2016 *Census: religion* (27 June 2017) <http://www.abs.gov.au/AUSSTATS/abs@.nsf/mediareleasesbyReleaseDate/7E65A144540551D7CA258148000E2B85?OpenDocument>

Australian Bureau of Statistics, Report 2071.0 - Reflecting a Nation: Stories from the 2011 Census, 2012–2013 <http://www.abs.gov.au/ausstats/abs@.nsf/Lookup/2071.0main+features902012-2013 accessed 26 October 2015.>

Australian Constitution

Australian Electoral Commission, *Electoral Backgrounder: Compulsory voting* [41] < http://www.aec.gov.au/About_AEC/Publications/backgrounders/compulsory-voting.htm>

Australian Labor Party, National Constitution 2015 <https://cdn.australianlabor.

com.au/documents/ALP_National_Constitution.pdf.https://
d3n8a8pro7vhmx.cloudfront.net/australianlaborparty/pages/121/
attachments/original/1439953357/ALP_National_Platform____
Constitution.pdf?1439953357>

Babie, Paul and Neville Rochow, *Feels Like Déjà vu: An Australian Bill of Rights and Religious Freedom*, BYU.L.Rev.821 (2010), 829-832

Bearak, Max and Darla Cameron, "Here are the 10 countries where homosexuality may be punished by death" *Washington Post*, June 16, 2016 https://www.washingtonpost.com/news/worldviews/wp/2016/06/13/here-are-the-10-countries-where-homosexuality-may-be-punished-by-death-2

Bouma and Mason, 'Babyboomers downunder: the case of Australia' in W Roof, J Carroll and D Roozen (eds), *The Post-War Generation and Establishment Religion: Cross-cultural Perspectives* (Westview Bolder Co, 1995) 66-73

Barrett, Justin L., *Born Believers* (Free Press, 2012)

Beauregard, Mario and Denyse O'Leary, *The Spiritual Brain* (Harper Collins 2008) Bluett v Popplewell [2018] ACTMC 2

Bulldogs.com.au "Hopoate to play on Sunday" 15 May 2017 https://www.bulldogs.com.au/news/2017/05/15/hopoate-to-play-on-sunday/

Catechism of the Catholic Church Church of the New Faith v Commissioner of Pay-Roll Tax (Vic) (1983) 154 CLR 120

Code Of Canon Law Annotated (E. Caparros et al. eds, 1993)

Commonwealth v Tasmania (1983) 158 CLR 1

Constitution Act, 1934 (Tas)

Crowe, David, "Winding back gay discrimination in schools is a pragmatic response from Morrison" *Sydney Morning Herald* 12 October 2018 <https://www.smh.com.au/politics/federal/winding-back-gay-discrimination-in-schools-is-a-pragmatic-response-from-morrison-20181012-p509ct.html>

Department of the Parliamentary Library," Conscientious Objection to Military Service in Australia," Library Research Note No 31 11 April 2003   <https://parlinfo.aph.gov.au/parlInfo/download/library/prspub/2E296/upload_binary/2e2964.pdf;fileType=application%2Fpdf#search=%22library/prspub/2E296%22>

Dunnbier, Maik,"One scene that says it all about alcohol and sports," *drinktank* 12 November 2015 <http://drinktank.org.au/2015/11/one-scene-that-says-it-all-about-alcohol-and-sports/>

Edwards v Clubb [2017] MCV

Edwards, Michael, "Andrew Denton lashes out at 'subterranean Catholic force' blocking voluntary euthanasia laws" *ABC News* ,10 August 2016, <http://www.abc.net.au/news/2016-08-10/denton-blames-catholic-force-blocking-voluntary-euthanasia/7718152>

Eweida And Ors v The United Kingdom ECHR 48428/10,59842/10,51671/10 and 36516/10 15 January 2013

Finnis, John, *Natural Law and Natural Rights* (Oxford University Press, 2nd ed 2011

Fitzsimmons, Peter, "Folau's thoughtless comments are an anathema to the greatest of rugby's values," *The Sydney Morning Herald* (Sydney) April 7 – 8 2018, 51.

Fowler, Mark, "Why are we talking about "exemptions" rather than the right to free religious expression?" *ABC Religion & Ethics,* 18 October, 2018 <https://www.abc.net.au/religion/not-exemptions-but-right-to-free-religious-expression/10391540>

Frederickson, Kristine, LDS World: "BYU's Chris Collinsworth had angels on his left and right sides" (16 January 2011) <http://www.deseretnews.com/article/705386994/BYUs-Chris-Collinsworth-had-angels-on-his-left-and-right-sides.html >

Goel, Deepti, 'Perceptions of Immigrants in Australia after 9/11' (2010) 86 *The Economic Record* 275

Hall, Stephen, *Principles of International Law* (5th ed, LexisNexis Butterworths, 2016)]

Henderson, Gerard, "How Menzies would have dealt with conscience votes is guesswork, *Sydney Institute.* (Aug. 22, 2015) http://thesydneyinstitute.com.au/blog/2015/08/22/how-menzies-would-have-dealt-withconscience-votes-is-guesswork/

Iliafi v Church of Jesus Christ Of Latter Day Saints Australia (2014) 311 ALR 354

Iner, Derya, "Islamophobia in Australia 2014-2016" (Centre for Islamic Studies and Civilisation, Charles Sturt University, 2017) 42.

International Centre for Muslim and non-Muslim *Understanding, 'Islamophobia, social distance and fear of terrorism in Australia - A Preliminary report'* (International Centre for Muslim and non-Muslim Understanding, 2015)

John Paul II, Encyclical Letter, *Evangelium Vitae* (Mar. 25, 1995), <http://w2.vatican.va/content/john-paul-ii/en/encyclicals/documents/hf_jp-ii_enc_25031995_evangelium-vitae.html>

Joint Standing Committee on Foreign Affairs, Defence and Trade,

'Compassion: A Report on Freedom of Religion and Belief' (November 2000)

Joseph, Sarah and Melissa Castan, *Federal Constitutional Law: A Contemporary View* (Lawbook Co, 3rd ed, 2010)

Kapagiannis, Dimitrios et al, 'Cognitive and Neural Foundations of Religious Belief' (2009) 106(12) Proceedings of the National Academy of Sciences of the United States of America 4876

Kearney, Justine and Mohamed Taha, Sydney Muslims experience discrimination at three times the rate of other Australians: study (30 November 2015) *ABC News* <http://www.abc.net.au/news/2015-11-30/muslims-discrimination-three-times-more-than-other-australians/6985138>

Keenan, Marie, *Child Sexual Abuse and the Catholic Church: Gender, Power and Organizational Culture* (Oxford University Press, 2012)

Kelly, Joe, "Major parties at odds over gay students law," *The Australian* October 26, 2018. 4

Krygger v Williams (1912) 15 CLR 366

McCrindle Research Pty Ltd, "Faith And Belief in Australia" (McCrindle Research Pty Ltd, May 2017)

McKeown, Deirdre & Rob Lundie, Information & Reference. Services Free Votes In Australian And Some Overseas Parliaments 8 (2002)

Meyerson, Denise *The Protection of Religious Rights Under Australian Law*, 2009 BYU L.Rev.529 (2009), 538-540.

Nathan, Julie, '2014 Report on Antisemitism in Australia' (Report, Executive Council of Australian Jewry, 9 November 2014)

News.com.au, "Panellists clash in TV debate over Israel Folau." News.com.au (on line) May 12, 2019 <https://www.news.com.au/sport/rugby/panellists-clash-in-tv-debate-over-israel-folau/news-story/f026a04925832da2361f91b24a78436c>

Olding, Rachel, "Pubs boycott Coopers beer following Bible Society marriage equality marketing campaign" *Sydney Morning Herald* 14 March 2017.

O'Neill, Eddie. "Lifting Up the Faith Down Under," *National Catholic Register* 29 July, 2017 http://www.ncregister.com/daily-news/lifting-up-the-faith-down-under

Parkinson, Patrick, "Religious leaders seek right to believe not power to discriminate," *The Australian* 26 October, 2018 26

Parkinson, Patrick, *Tradition and Change in Australian Law* (5th ed, 2013, Law Book Co)

Police v Preston [2016] TASMC

Porteous, Julian, "Children will be no safer by forcing priests to break the seal of confession," *Weekend Australian* 20-21 October, 20-18

Possamai, Adam et al, 'Muslim Students' Religious and Cultural Experiences in the Micro-publics of University Campuses in NSW, Australia' (2016) 47 *Australian Geographer* 319- 321

Quinlan, Michael, "When the State Requires Doctors to Act Against their Conscience: The Religious Freedom Implications of the Referral and the Direction Obligations of Health Practitioners in Victoria and New South Wales," 2016 BYU L. Rev. 1237

Rowe, Emma, "Religion in Australian schools: an historical and contemporary debate," *School News* 26 August, 2017 <https://www.school-news. com.au/education/religion-in-australian-schools-an-historical-and-contemporary-debate/>

Royal Commission into Institutional Responses to Child Sexual Abuse "Final Report Recommendations"

Russell v Russell [1976] 134 CLR 495

Saeed, Abdullah, *Islam in Australia* (Allen & Unwin, 2003)

Sandeman, John," Catholics accept most of the Royal Commission recommendations," 31 August 2018, *Eternity* <>https://www. eternitynews.com.au/australia/catholics-accept-most-of-the-royal-commission-recommendations/

Trevill Scott,John and Ann Cherly Armstrong, "Faith-based Schools and the Public Good: purposes and perspectives Paper presented at the AARE Annual Conference Melbourne 2010 <https://www.aare.edu.au/ publications-database.php/6087/Faith-based-Schools-and-the-Public-Good:-Purposes-and-Perspectives>

Sheehan, Catherine, "Priests face life in jail," *The Catholic Weekly,* 7 October 2018, 1,4

Thornton, Margaret and Trish Luker, 'The Spectral Ground: Religious Belief Discrimination' (2009) 9 *Macquarie Law Journal* 75-84

Sheridan, Greg, *God is Good For You,* (Allen & Unwin, 2018)

Staff writers, "Andrew Denton trying to exclude Catholic voices from euthanasia debate" *The Catholic Weekly,* 17 August 2016 <https://www. catholicweekly.com.au/andrew-denton-trying-to-exclude-catholic-voices-from-euthanasia-debate/.>

Trimble, M R, *The Soul in The Brain* (John Hopkins University Press, 2009)

Jewel Topsfield, "Religious freedom review enshrines right of schools to turn away gay children and teachers" Sydney Morning Herald 9 October 2018 <https://www.smh.com.au/politics/federal/religious-freedom-

review-enshrines-right-of-schools-to-turn-away-gay-children-and-teachers-20181009-p508o7.html

Turner, Joseph, Debbie Garratt and Dr Simon McCaffrey, "The High Court, Abortion Clinic Speech Restrictions and the Assessment of Harm." The Western Australian Legal Theory Association, 2018 <https://walta.net.au/2018/10/01/the-high-court-abortion-clinic-speech-restrictions-and-the-assessment-of-harm/>

Williams v Commonwealth (2012) 288 ALR 410.

Williams Roy, *In God They Trust,* (Sydney: Bible Society, 2013)

Williams, Roy, *Post God Nation?* (ABC Books, 2015)

4

THE CONSTITUTIONAL LIMITATIONS & IMPLICATIONS OF A *RELIGIOUS FREEDOM ACT*

LORRAINE FINLAY[1]

The idea that the Commonwealth Parliament should introduce a *Religious Freedom Act* ('*RFA*') has gained currency in Australia in recent times, notably during the recent debate surrounding the introduction of same-sex marriage laws. This is a proposal that has been supported by those on both the left and right of politics,[2] and has featured in many of the submissions that were made to the Expert Panel on Religious Freedom.[3] Putting to one side the question of whether we *should* enact a *RFA* (which this author has serious

---

[1]   BA (UWA), LLB (UWA), LLM (NUS), LLM (NYU), Lecturer in Constitutional Law, Murdoch Law School; Senior Lecturer (Adjunct), University of Notre Dame Australia (Sydney).
[2]   See, for example, Rachel Baxendale, 'Anti-discrimination exemptions for religious organisations should be removed, Amnesty says', *The Australian* (Online) 30 July 2018, which quotes both Amnesty International and the Minister for Social Services, Dan Tehan MP, as supporting the introduction of a *RFA*.
[3]   See, for example, submissions made to the Expert Panel by Freedom for Faith (Submission Number 2520), Centre for Independent Studies (Submission Number 14929), Australian Christian Lobby (in conjunction with the Human Rights Law Alliance (Submission Number 14932), Australian Federation of Islamic Councils (Submission Number 2832), the Australian Catholic Bishops Conference (Submission Number 11901), the Wilberforce Foundation (Submissions Number 6435), Neville Rochow SC (Submission Number 2539) and Associate Professor Keith Thompson (Submission Number 14157). All submissions can be accessed at: Department of the Prime Minister and Cabinet, *Religious Freedom Review – Submissions*.

doubts about),[4] there is a need to also consider *how* such a law could be enacted within the existing Australian constitutional framework and whether there are any constitutional limitations or implications that would need to be addressed.

This paper will consider the key constitutional issues that may arise with respect to any future *RFA,* and the constitutional limitations that need to be considered when drafting such a law. Part I will consider the preliminary question of what head of power might provide constitutional support for a future *RFA,* concluding that the external affairs power would be the most likely head of power through the treaty implementation mechanism and noting that this is the constitutional power already relied upon by the Commonwealth to primarily support existing anti-discrimination laws. Part II goes on to consider the constitutional limitations that would be imposed on a future *RFA* that relied upon the external affairs power, noting that s 51(xxix) of the *Australian Constitution* does not provide for a general power over religious freedom but is instead limited by the terms of the international treaty that the Commonwealth Parliament is seeking to enact into domestic law. A further issue that will undoubtedly arise with the introduction of a *RFA* concerns the interaction between the new Commonwealth law and existing State anti-discrimination laws. The constitutional implications of this are considered in Part III, which looks at the effect of s 109 of the *Australian Constitution* and concludes that any future *RFA* will have a potentially significant impact on the federal balance by further entrenching the policy dominance of the Commonwealth over the States in the areas of anti-discrimination and human rights. The paper concludes that while the Commonwealth Parliament ultimately does have the legislative power to introduce a *RFA,* there are constitutional limitations and implications that do need to be considered, both in terms of the way that any *RFA* is drafted and its inter-relationship with existing anti-discrimination laws.

Part I: Finding a Constitutional Head of Power

Although in recent years it may appear to a casual observer that the Commonwealth Parliament can legislate on almost anything it pleases, this is

---

[4]   See Lorraine Finlay, Joshua Forrester & Augusto Zimmermann, 'Does Australia Need a *Religious Freedom Act?*' in Iain T. Benson, Michael Quinlan and Keith Thompson (ed), *Religious freedom in Australia – a new* terra nullius? (Connor Court Publishing, 2019).

not actually the case under the Australian constitutional arrangements. The *Australian Constitution* in fact establishes a federal system of government, as is evident from the preamble to the *Constitution* in which the people of the colonies agreed 'to unite in one indissoluble Federal Commonwealth'.[5] The idea was to create a two-tiered system of government in which power was distributed between Commonwealth and State governments, with each tier of government being constitutional equals and sovereign within their own spheres of power.

The Australian founding fathers did not intend for the Commonwealth Government to have unlimited legislative powers. Quite the contrary, they intended for the Commonwealth Government to be a government of strictly limited powers, and to this end gave the Commonwealth Parliament enumerated legislative powers under ss 51 and 52 of the *Constitution*. That this was the original intention can be clearly seen in the comments made by Sir Samuel Griffith during the 1891 convention debates:[6]

> [W]e must not lose sight of the essential condition that this is to be a federation of States and not a single government of Australia … And here let me insist upon the essential condition – the preliminary condition – that the separate states are to continue as autonomous bodies, surrendering only so much of their powers as is necessary to the establishment of a general government to do for them collectively what they cannot do individually for themselves, and which they cannot do as a collective body for themselves.

It is true that the federal balance in Australia has shifted a long way from the original intentions of the founding fathers. For example, Alfred Deakin suggested in 1897 that 'so far from our Federal Government over-awing the States, it is more probable that the States will over-awe the Federal Government'.[7] In fact, the exact opposite has occurred, with the expansion of Commonwealth legislative and financial power over the past one hundred years creating a real risk 'that the Parliament of each State is progressively reduced until it becomes no more than an impotent debating society'.[8] Indeed, State Governments in present-day Australia have been described – perhaps

---

5   *Commonwealth of Australia Constitution Act 1900* (Imp) 63 & 64 Vict, c 12, preamble s 3.

6   *Official Record of the Debates of the Australasian Federal Convention*, Sydney, 4 March 1891, 30-31 (Samuel Griffith).

7   *Official Record of the Debates of the Australasian Federal Convention*, Adelaide, 30 March 1897, 298-9 (Alfred Deakin).

8   *New South Wales & Ors v Commonwealth* (2006) 229 CLR 1, [779] (Callinan J).

unkindly but, unfortunately, probably accurately – as 'enfeebled, emasculated creatures'.[9]

Whilst there has clearly been an expansion of Commonwealth legislative power over the last hundred years in practice, the limitations imposed by the constitutional framework cannot be entirely ignored. Whenever the Commonwealth Government is asked to introduce a new law, the first question that should be asked is always whether it actually lies within their constitutional power to do so.

The External Affairs Power

Is there a constitutional head of power that could potentially support the introduction of a RFA by the Commonwealth Parliament? There is no specific head of power amongst those listed under s 51 granted to the Commonwealth legislature over the areas of human rights, anti-discrimination or religion. Instead, we must look beyond a direct subject-matter power to find some other constitutional basis for any future RFA.

The most obvious possible option in this case is the external affairs power found in s 51(xxix),[10] which has been interpreted as giving the Commonwealth Parliament the ability to make laws with respect to Australia's management of relations with other countries,[11] the regulation of matters physically external to Australia and,[12] most significantly for this analysis, the implementation of

---

[9]   James Allan & Nicholas Aroney, 'An Uncommon Court: How the High Court of Australia has Undermined Australian Federalism' (2008) 30 *Sydney Law Review* 245, 247.

[10] It is important to note that this is not the only possible constitutional option, although other options also appear to give rise to considerable limitations and practical difficulties. For example, one option may be to use the referral power under s 51(xxxvii), which essentially allows any State Parliament to refer matters to the Commonwealth Parliament. The key difficulties here are, firstly, that it would be extremely unlikely that any State Parliament would realistically agree to refer these issues to the Commonwealth Parliament and, secondly, that any law made under the referrals power only extends to those States by whose Parliaments the matter is referred. Any use of the referral power raises the very real (and undesirable) prospect of a 'patchwork' approach whereby any federal RFA would only apply in certain States, and not in others.

[11] *R v Sharkey* (1949) 79 CLR 121; *Kirmani v Captain Cook Cruises Pty Ltd (No. 1)* (1985) 159 CLR 351.

[12] *Polyukhovich v Commonwealth* (1991) 172 CLR 501; *XYZ v Commonwealth* (2006) 227 CLR 532.

international agreements.[13] Australia is a dualist system with respect to our understanding of the inter-relationship between international and domestic law meaning that, unlike a monist system,[14] international obligations are not automatically incorporated into Australian domestic law. This means that '[t]he content of treaties have been held to have no effect in domestic law until they are implemented by legislation'.[15] The Commonwealth Parliament must introduce domestic legislation if it wishes to give effect to an international treaty within the Australian legal framework. The external affairs power under s 51(xxix) of the *Constitution* has been interpreted as giving the Commonwealth Parliament the constitutional capacity to do just this.

With respect to the implementation of international agreements, the Commonwealth Parliament will have the constitutional power to introduce a *RFA* if it can be established that the treaty the *RFA* is seeking to incorporate into domestic law is a *bona fide* treaty that was entered into in good faith,[16] concerns a matter of international character,[17] and imposes reasonably specific legal obligations on Australia (the 'specificity requirement'),[18] and that the *RFA* itself sufficiently conforms to the terms of the treaty (the 'conformity requirement').[19]

Existing Anti-Discrimination Laws

Indeed, the external affairs power is the primary constitutional head of power that has been relied upon by the Commonwealth Parliament to support most anti-discrimination laws at a federal level. This is the case for each of the four

---

[13]   *Commonwealth v Tasmania* (1983) 158 CLR 1 *('Tasmanian Dam Case'); Victoria v Commonwealth* (1996) 187 CLR 416 *('Industrial Relations Act Case').*

[14]   Professor David Sloss gives the examples of sixteen monist states, namely Austria, Chile, China, Columbia, Egypt, France, Germany, Japan, Mexico, Netherlands, Poland, Russia, South Africa, Switzerland, Thailand and the United States in 'Domestic Application of Treaties' contained in Duncan B Hollis (ed), *The Oxford Guide to Treaties* (Oxford University Press, 2012).

[15]   Senate Standing Committees on Legal and Constitutional Affairs (References Committee), *Inquiry into Sexuality Discrimination* (December 1997), [3.9].

[16]   *R v Burgess; ex parte Henry* (1936) 55 CLR 608, 687 (Evatt & McTiernan JJ); *Koowarta v Bjelke-Petersen* (1982) 153 CLR 168, 200 (Gibbs CJ).

[17]   *R v Burgess; ex parte Henry* (1936) 55 CLR 608, 687 (Evatt & McTiernan JJ); *Tasmanian Dam Case* (1983) 158 CLR 1, 125 (Mason J).

[18]   *Industrial Relations Act Case* (1996) 187 CLR 416, 486 (Brennan CJ, Toohey, Gaudron, McHugh and Gummow JJ).

[19]   Ibid 487 (Brennan CJ, Toohey, Gaudron, McHugh and Gummow JJ); *Richardson v Forestry Commission* (1988) 164 CLR 261.

key Commonwealth anti-discrimination laws, namely the *Racial Discrimination Act 1975* (Cth) ('RDA'), *Sex Discrimination Act 1984* (Cth) ('SDA'), *Disability Discrimination Act 1992* (Cth) ('DDA') and *Age Discrimination Act 2004* (Cth) ('ADA').

For example, the *RDA* expressly refers to the *International Convention on the Elimination of all Forms of Racial Discrimination*[20] and the external affairs power in its Preamble, and sets out the *Convention* as a Schedule to the Act. In *Koowarta v Bjelke-Peterson*[21] the High Court of Australia upheld the constitutional validity of ss 9 and 12 of the *RDA* by reference to the external affairs power. In particular, the majority found that the *RDA* was introduced to give domestic effect to Australia's international obligations under the *International Convention on the Elimination of All Forms of Racial Discrimination*.[22]

This express reliance on the external affairs power is also evident in the *SDA, DDA* and *ADA*. For example, s 3(a) of the *SDA* specifically notes that one of its objects is 'to give effect to certain provisions of the *Convention on the Elimination of All Forms of Discrimination Against Women* and to provisions of other relevant international instruments'. Section 3 of the *ADA* sets out the objects of the Act 'bearing in mind the international commitment to eliminate age discrimination reflected in the Political Declaration adopted in Madrid, Spain on 12 April 2002 by the Second World Assembly on Ageing', while s 10(7) makes further reference to the external affairs power by providing that certain provisions within the Act have effect to the extent that the provisions give effect to specific obligations contained within a range of international instruments, or relate to matters external to Australia or matters of international concern. This can also be seen in s 12(8) of the *DDA*, which relies particularly on the *Convention on the Rights of Persons with Disabilities*[23] and the *Discrimination (Employment and Occupation) Convention 1958*.[24]

These federal anti-discrimination laws also make reference within their

---

[20]   *International Convention on the Elimination of All Forms of Racial Discrimination*, opened for signature 21 December 1965, 660 UNTS 195 (entered into force 4 January 1969). ('*Convention on Racial Discrimination*')

[21]   (1982) 153 CLR 168.

[22]   *Convention on Racial Discrimination*, above n 20.

[23]   *Convention on the Rights of Persons with Disabilities*, opened for signature 30 March 2007, 2515 UNTS 3 (entered into force 3 May 2008).

[24]   *Discrimination (Employment and Occupation) Convention*, opened for signature 25 June 1958, 362 UNTS 31 (entered into force 15 June 1960). Adopted by the General Conference of the International Labour Organization on 25 June 1958.

terms to a range of other constitutional heads of power that could also be used to support aspects of the law. For example, s 9 of the *SDA* aims to extend the scope of the law as widely as possible through the use of a range of alternative constitutional powers to make laws with respect to territories (s 122), foreign, trading or financial corporations (s 51(xx)), banking (s 51(xiii)), insurance (s 51(xiv)), interstate or international trade and commerce (s 51(i)) and 'postal, telegraphic, telephonic or other like services' (s 51(v)). This can also be seen in s 10 of the *ADA* and s. 12 of the *DDA*. The legislative structure reflects an attempt to provide constitutional support for broad-based anti-discrimination laws despite the constitutional powers granted to the Commonwealth Parliament not including a general power relating to human rights or anti-discrimination. While the primary power supporting these laws would seem to be the external affairs power, there are also other constitutional heads of power that provide some level of support to various aspects of the laws.

Application to a Future RFA

In relation to a future *RFA* the core international instrument that would likely be relied upon to activate the external affairs power would be the *International Covenant on Civil and Political Rights ('ICCPR')*, which Australia ratified on 13 August 1980.[25] Article 2 of the *ICCPR* sets out a general obligation on each State Party to respect individuals without distinction of any kind, with religion given as one of the examples of a distinction that should not be drawn. Article 18 sets out the specific obligations with respect to religious freedom, providing that:

1. Everyone shall have the right to freedom of thought, conscience and religion. This right shall include freedom to have or adopt a religion or belief of his choice, and freedom, either individually or in community with others and in public or private, to manifest his religion or belief in worship, observance, practice and teaching.

2. No only shall be subject to coercion which would impair his freedom to have or to adopt a religion or belief of his choice.

3. Freedom to manifest one's religion or beliefs may be subject only to such limitations as are prescribed by law and are necessary to protect public

---

25 *International Covenant on Civil and Political Rights*, opened for signature 19 December 1966, 999 UNTS 171 (entered into force 23 March 1976).

safety, order, health, or morals or the fundamental rights and freedoms of others.

4. The States Parties to the present Covenant undertake to have respect for the liberty of parents and, when applicable, legal guardians to ensure the religious and moral education of their children in conformity with their own convictions.

There are also other articles contained within the *ICCPR* that deal with aspects of religious freedom. For example, Article 20 prohibits 'any advocacy of national, racial or religious hatred that constitutes incitement to discrimination, hostility or violence', Article 26 provides for equality before the law and prohibits discrimination on grounds including, *inter alia*, religion, and Article 27 protects the right of religious minorities 'to profess and practise their own religion'.

Of course, the *ICCPR* is not the only international instrument that refers to the protection of religious freedoms. Other relevant instruments that deal with freedom of religion in a broad sense include the *Universal Declaration of Human Rights* (specifically Articles 2 and 18)[26] and *Declaration on the Elimination of All Forms of Intolerance and of Discrimination Based on Religion or Belief* (*'1981 Declaration'*).[27] However, it is important to note that neither of these are actually treaties. For example, the *1981 Declaration* was adopted without a vote by the United Nations General Assembly on 25 November 1981. While it has been described as 'the most important contemporary codification of the principles of freedom of religion and belief',[28] as a resolution of the UN General Assembly it is only a recommendation, lacks enforcement mechanisms, and is not strictly legally binding as a matter of international law.[29] This has been

---

[26] *Universal Declaration on Human Rights*, GA Res 217A (III), UN GAOR, 3rd sess, 183rd plen mtg, UN Doc A/810 (10 December 1948).

[27] United Nations General Assembly, *Declaration on the Elimination of All Forms of Intolerance and of Discrimination Based on Religion or Belief*, A/RES/36/55, 36th sess, (25 November 1981).

[28] University of Minnesota Human Rights Library, *Study Guide: Freedom of Religion or Belief* (February 2016).

[29] Stephen M Schwebel, 'The Effect of Resolutions of the UN General Assembly on Customary International Law' (1979) 73 *American Society of International Law* 301; Secretariat of the United Nations, 'Questions relating to the voting procedure and decision-making process of the General Assembly', published in the *United Nations Juridical Yearbook* (1986) 274. See further Articles 10 and 14 of the *Charter of the United Nations* that describes the power of the General Assembly as being to 'make recommendations' to Members or the Security Council and to 'recommend measures for the peaceful adjustment of any situation'.

recognised by Carolyn Evans who notes that the *1981 Declaration* is not legally binding, but does suggest that it nevertheless 'may have significant effect if understood as an authoritative source for clarifying State's obligations as described in treaties such as the *ICCPR*'.[30]

The external affairs power appears to extend to giving the Commonwealth Parliament the power to legislate for the carrying out of international obligations that are contained in 'recommendations' or 'declarations' in certain circumstances. For example, in *R v Burgess; Ex parte Henry*,[31] Evatt and McTiernan JJ observed:

> ... it is not to be assumed that the legislative power over "external affairs" is limited to the execution of treaties or conventions; and the Parliament may well be deemed competent to legislate for the carrying out of "recommendations" as well as the "draft international conventions" resolved upon by the International Labour Organisation or of other international recommendations or requests upon other subject matters of concern to Australia as a member of the family of nations.

Strictly speaking, a treaty obligation does not appear to be technically essential. What is required is that there is an international obligation in some form that the legislation is seeking to give effect to. The High Court has recognised that the relevant obligation may be found in a variety of international instruments, or even potentially in customary international law. For example, in the *Industrial Relations Act Case* the High Court considered whether domestic laws that included (amongst other things) provisions concerning the right to strike and engage in industrial action were supported by the external affairs power.[32] While the Court ultimately found that the domestic provisions in question were supported by Article 8 of the *International Covenant on Economic, Social and Cultural Rights*,[33] it also considered a number of ILO Conventions, ILO Recommendations (adopted by the General Conference of the ILO), the ILO Constitution, the *Declaration Concerning the Aims and Purposes of the International Labour Organisation*,[34] and customary international law. In that case,

---

30   Carolyn Evans, 'Time for a Treaty? The Legal Sufficiency of the Declaration on the Elimination of All Forms of Intolerance and Discrimination' (2007) *Brigham Young University Law Review* 617, 628.

31   *R v Burgess; Ex parte Henry* (1936) 55 CLR 608, 687 (Evatt and McTiernan JJ).

32   *Victoria v Commonwealth* (1996) 187 CLR 416.

33   *International Covenant on Economic, Social and Cultural Rights*, opened for signature 16 December 1966, 993 UNTS 3 (entered into force 3 January 1976).

34   The General Conference of the International Labour Organisation, *Declaration concerning the aims and purposes of the International Labour Organisation*, 26th sess, (10 May 1944).

those other international instruments did not actually give rise to an obligation on Australia to provide a right to strike, however their consideration by the Court does implicitly suggest that, in the right circumstances, an international instrument other than a treaty might create a sufficiently specific international obligation so as to give rise to the operation of the external affairs power.

Similarly, in *Pape v Commissioner of Taxation* Heydon J rejected a submission by the defendants that recommendations by international agencies (in that case recommendations by the International Monetary Fund, G-20 meetings and the Organisation for Economic Co-operation and Development) could, in that particular case, support a law purportedly enacted in reliance on the external affairs power.[35] Justice Heydon rejected this submission on the basis that 'mere recommendations do not create international obligations'.[36] This supports the conclusion that the Court will look to substance over form. That is, the key criteria is the existence of an international obligation rather than the requirement that the obligation takes the precise form of an international treaty.

Given this, it may theoretically be possible for the *1981 Declaration* to provide a basis for a future *RFA*. This will, however, depend on whether or not the *1981 Declaration* can be seen to create binding international obligations on Australia. It certainly does appear that the actual terms of the *1981 Declaration* are more than merely aspirational, and impose what appear on their face to be specific obligations. However, the key difficulty is that the *1981 Declaration* takes the form of a United Nations General Assembly resolution and is not therefore legally binding on Australia. At best, it may be seen as representing a codification of customary international law, but basing a constitutional claim on international obligations created by way of customary international law would be a difficult task. For this reason, reliance on the *1981 Declaration* (or any other relevant General Assembly resolution) would not provide as solid a constitutional footing for any future *RFA* as would be provided by reliance upon the *ICCPR*.

There are also specific clauses relating to religious freedom in a range of other human rights instruments, with examples including Article 14 of the *Convention on the Rights of the Child*[37] and Article 4 of the *Convention concerning*

---

35 *Pape v Commissioner of Taxation* [2009] HCA 23, 176 [479] ff (Heydon J).

36 Ibid 177 [479].

37 *Convention on the Rights of the Child*, opened for signature 20 November 1989, 1577 UNTS 3 (entered into force 2 September 1990).

the Status of Refugees.[38] Further, instruments such as the International Labour Organisation *Discrimination (Employment and Occupation) Convention 1958*[39] deal with discrimination (including discrimination on the basis of religion) within specific fields, in this specific case being discrimination in the field of employment and occupation. While these instruments will not give the Commonwealth Parliament the constitutional capacity to enact a broad-based *RFA* they may provide constitutional support for aspects of the *RFA* insofar as the domestic provisions seek to reflect the specific provisions of the individual international instrument.

If the Commonwealth Government was seeking to enact a comprehensive *RFA*, the most secure and broadest constitutional foundation would be found by reliance on the *ICCPR* as the relevant international treaty. There are, however, important limits to the treaty-making aspect of the external affairs power, which will be considered in Part II below.

Part II: Limits to the External Affairs Power

While there is no doubt that the external affairs power provides the Commonwealth Parliament with a broad constitutional power to make laws implementing international treaties, it does not provide the Parliament with a blank cheque. Ultimately, the power is limited by the terms of the international treaty itself, and any law must reflect the treaty obligations to a reasonable degree. Therefore, the design of a possible *RFA* will necessarily be informed by these constitutional limitations, namely that there is a *bona fide* treaty entered into good faith, that the treaty concerns a matter of international character, and that both the specificity and conformity requirements are satisfied.

Bona Fide Treaty

The first requirement is that the treaty being relied upon under the external affairs power must be a *bona fide* treaty. That is, a treaty that is entered into merely to allow the Commonwealth to obtain legislative power will not enliven the external affairs power.[40] There can be no doubt that the *ICCPR* clearly satisfies this requirement. It is one of the key international

---

[38]   *Convention Relating to the Status of Refugees*, opened for signature 28 July 1951, 189 UNTS 137 (entered into force 22 April 1954).

[39]   *Discrimination (Employment and Occupation) Convention* (ILO No. 111), 362 UNTS 31 (entered into force 15 June 1960).

[40]   *R v Burgess; Ex parte Henry* (1936) 55 CLR 608, 687 (Evatt & McTiernan JJ).

human rights treaties, being one part of what is commonly known as the *International Bill of Human Rights*. The *ICCPR* has been ratified by 172 State Parties (including Australia), and has a further six States who are signatories but have not ratified.[41] The *ICCPR* was drafted over a number of years by the UN Human Rights Commission and was adopted without vote by the United Nations General Assembly in Resolution 2200 (XXI) of 16 December 1966. The Treaty entered into force on 23 March 1976. The fact that the Treaty intends to impact upon State behaviour can also be seen in the establishment of an individual complaints mechanism through the *Optional Protocol to the ICCPR ('First Optional Protocol').*[42] The *First Optional Protocol* currently has 116 State Parties and 35 signatories, with Australia becoming a State Party on 25 September 1991. This allows individuals from State Parties to take a complaint to the United Nations Human Rights Commission where they allege that their rights under the *ICCPR* have been violated. The *ICCPR* has been referred to and interpreted by international and regional courts, tribunals and committees[43] and has been referred to by the High Court of Australia on many occasions.[44] If the *ICCPR* did not meet the test of being a *bona fide* treaty, then it is difficult to envisage any other international treaty that would.

Matter of International Character

Some earlier cases took the view that the external affairs power would only provide the Commonwealth Parliament with the power to legislate if the treaty being implemented concerned a subject matter '… of sufficient international significance to make it a legitimate subject for international cooperation and

---

[41] United Nations Humans Rights Office of the High Commissioner, *Status of Ratification Interactive Dashboard* (1996-2014).

[42] *Optional Protocol to the International Covenant on Civil and Political Rights*, opened for signature 16 December 1966, 999 UNTS 171 (entered into force 23 March 1976).

[43] See, eg, references to the *ICCPR* by the International Court of Justice, including *Ahmadou Sadio Diallo (Republic of Guinea v Democratic Republic of the Congo) (Merits Judgment)* [2010] ICJ 639; *Legal Consequences of the Construction of a Wall in the Occupied Palestinian Territory (Advisory Opinion)* [2004] ICJ Rep 136.

[44] See, for example, *Mabo v Queensland [No. 2]* (1992) 175 CLR 1, 42 (Mason CJ, Brennan and McHugh JJ); *Al-Kateb v Godwin* [2004] 219 CLR 562; *Momcilovic v The Queen* [2011] HCA 34; *Re Kavanagh's Application* (2003) 204 ALR 1, [11] (Kirby J). Although it should be noted that the precise role that the *ICCPR* should have in the interpretation of Australian law (or, indeed, whether it should have any role at all) has been the subject of considerable debate and disagreement.

agreement'.[45] However, the current approach adopted by later cases views the entry by Australia into an international treaty itself as satisfying this criteria.[46] Given this, any requirement of 'international character' would be satisfied by the very fact that Australia ratified the *ICCPR* in the first place.

Specificity Principle

The specificity requirement provides that the external affairs power will only be enlivened where the relevant treaty imposes sufficiently specific legal obligations upon Australia. That is, a treaty that is purely aspirational or excessively general in its terms will not provide the Commonwealth Parliament with the capacity to legislate. It is not necessary for the treaty to prescribe a single course of action in minute detail. But if all that is stated is a 'broad objective with little precise content and permitting widely divergent policies by parties' that will not be enough.[47] Rather, the specificity requirement simply provides that '[t]he law must prescribe a regime that the treaty itself has defined with sufficient specificity to direct the general course to be taken by the signatory states'.[48]

The specificity requirement would likely be satisfied by the *ICCPR*. Article 18 sets out the individual right to freedom of thought, conscience and religion and operates primarily as a restriction upon States by effectively providing that the freedom of an individual to have or adopt the religion or belief of their choice is absolute and that the freedom to manifest that religion or belief 'may be subject only to such limitations as are prescribed by law and are necessary to protect public safety, order, health, or morals or the fundamental rights and freedoms of others'.[49] The general course of action to be taken by signatory states with respect to the freedom of religion is, however, outlined in Article 2(2) which states:[50]

> Where not already provided for by existing legislative or other measures, each State Party to the present Covenant undertakes

---

[45]   *R v Burgess; Ex parte Henry* (1936) 55 CLR 608, 658 (Starke J), 669 (Dixon J). See also, *Koowarta v Bjelke-Petersen* (1982) 153 CLR 168, 216-217.

[46]   *Tasmanian Dam Case* (1983) 158 CLR 1.

[47]   *Industrial Relations Act Case* (1996) 187 CLR 416, 486 (Brennan CJ, Toohey, Gaudron, McHugh and Gummow JJ), quoting Leslie Zines, *The High Court and the Constitution* (Lexis Law Publishing, 3rd ed, 1992), 250.

[48]   Ibid, 486 (Brennan CJ, Toohey, Gaudron, McHugh and Gummow JJ).

[49]   *ICCPR*, art 18(3).

[50]   *ICCPR*, art 2(2).

to take the necessary steps, in accordance with its constitutional processes and with the provisions of the present Covenant, to adopt such legislative or other measures as may be necessary to give effect to the rights recognized in the present Covenant.

Additionally, there are further obligations outlined in Article 2(3) with State Parties agreeing to provide an effective remedy to those whose rights or freedoms are violated, to ensure that claims to remedies are decided 'by competent judicial, administrative or legislative authorities'[51] and to ensure that such remedies are enforced.

That is, the effect of Articles 2 and 18 of the *ICCPR* is to impose on State Parties a legal obligation to give effect to the individual right to freedom of thought, conscience and religion, which encompasses both the right to hold religious beliefs and the right to manifest those beliefs. There is also a further obligation to provide effective and enforceable legal remedies if these rights are violated. While State Parties would appear to have a considerable margin of discretion in terms of the precise approach that they might take when meeting their obligations under Articles 2 and 18, there does appear to be sufficient specificity within the *ICCPR* itself 'to direct the general course to be taken by the signatory states'.[52] A *RFA* that was designed to reflect Australia's obligations under the *ICCPR* would most likely satisfy the requirements of the specificity principle.

Conformity Requirement

Finally, it is important to note that 'mere entry into a treaty does not create a new, plenary head of power for the Commonwealth to enact legislation with respect to the subject matter of the treaty'.[53] The external affairs power only gives the Parliament the ability to enact domestic laws that are 'capable of being reasonably considered to be appropriate and adapted to give effect to the treaty'.[54] In effect, the domestic law must conform to the terms of the

---

[51] *ICCPR*, art 2(3).

[52] *Industrial Relations Act Case* (1996) 187 CLR 416, 486 (Brennan CJ, Toohey, Gaudron, McHugh and Gummow JJ).

[53] Senate Standing Committees on Legal and Constitutional Affairs (References Committee), *Inquiry into Sexuality Discrimination* (December 1997), [3.11] (quoting Kristen Walker, Submission No 116/116A, Vol 5, 949).

[54] *Industrial Relations Act Case* (1996) 187 CLR 416, 487 (Brennan CJ, Toohey, Gaudron, McHugh & Gummow JJ).

international treaty that it is seeking to implement. This does not require precise conformity. In fact, it does not even necessarily require full implementation, with it being well established that partial or limited legislative implementation of a treaty is not in itself an objection to its validity under the external affairs power,[55] unless potentially the deficiency in implementation '… is so substantial as to deny the law the character of a measure implementing the Convention or it is a deficiency which, when coupled with other provisions of the law, make it substantially inconsistent with the Convention'.[56] Specifically in relation to a possible RFA this means that '[i]t would therefore be within Commonwealth power to implement art 18 of the ICCPR, for example, without comprehensive legislation protecting all the rights protected in the ICCPR'.[57]

However, while the domestic law does not have to reproduce the exact language of the treaty word for word, it cannot depart from the terms of the treaty in a substantive way. As Keith Thompson has observed, '[w]hat the Commonwealth Parliament cannot legislate is a regime that bears the name of an international convention but has no relationship to its terms'.[58] The Commonwealth Parliament does not have a general power to legislate with respect to religious freedoms, and would instead be limited to reflecting in domestic law the international obligations that have been accepted by Australia through the ICCPR and other international instruments.

The Commonwealth Parliament would, therefore, need to ensure that the terms of any proposed RFA broadly conformed to the scope of the obligations contained within the ICCPR, or any other international instrument being relied upon. This would appear to give the Parliament considerable latitude if they wished to introduce a comprehensive RFA. This reflects the observation by the Human Rights Committee that the Article 18 right is 'far-reaching and profound.'[59] Article 18 protects 'theistic, non-theistic and

---

55 *Tasmanian Dam Case* (1983) 158 CLR 1, 268 (Deane J); *Industrial Relations Act Case* (1996) 187 CLR 416, 488-489 (Brennan CJ, Toohey, Gaudron, McHugh & Gummow JJ).

56 *Industrial Relations Act Case* (1996) 187 CLR 416, 489 (Brennan CJ, Toohey, Gaudron, McHugh & Gummow JJ).

57 Carolyn Evans, *Legal Protection of Religious Freedom in Australia* (The Federation Press, 2012), 43.

58 Keith Thompson, 'A Commonwealth Religious Discrimination Act for Australia?' (2017) 7(1) *Solidarity: The Journal of Catholic Social Thought and Secular Ethics*, 11.

59 United Nations Human Rights Committee, *General Comment No. 22: The right to freedom of thought, conscience and religion (Art. 18)*, 48th sess, UN Doc CCPR/C/21/Rev.1/Add.4 (22 September 1993), [1]. ('*General Comment No. 22*')

atheistic beliefs, as well as the right not to profess any religion or belief'.[60] It provides that the freedom to have or adopt a particular religion or belief is protected unconditionally and cannot be derogated from, even in a time of public emergency. The freedom to have or to adopt a particular religion or belief is also protected from coercion that would impair that freedom, which the UN Human Rights Committee have observed, includes:[61]

> ...the use of threat of physical force or penal sanctions to compel believers or non-believers to adhere to their religious beliefs and congregations, to recant their religion or belief or to convert. Policies or practices having the same intention or effect, such as for example those restricting access to education, medical care, employment or the rights guaranteed by article 25 and other provisions of the Covenant are similarly inconsistent with article 18(2).

The unconditional protection of the freedom to have or to adopt a particular religion or belief is distinguished from the freedom to manifest one's religion or beliefs, which may be subject to limitations '... as are prescribed by law and are necessary to protect public safety, order, health or morals or the fundamental rights and freedoms of others'.[62] The freedom to manifest religion or belief under Article 18 may be exercised 'either individually or in community with others and in public or private' and 'encompasses a broad range of acts'.[63] The broad scope of this freedom can be seen in the examples given by the UN Human Rights Committee when describing the freedom to manifest religion or belief:[64]

> The concept of worship extends to ritual and ceremonial acts giving direct expression to belief, as well as various practices integral to such acts, including the building of places of worship, the use of ritual formulae and objects, the display of symbols, and the observance of holidays and days of rest. The observance and practice of religion or belief may include not only ceremonial acts but also such customs as the observance of dietary regulations, the wearing of distinctive clothing or headcoverings, participation in rituals associated with certain stages of life, and the use of a particular language customarily spoken by a group. In addition, the practice and teaching of a religion or belief includes acts integral to the conduct by religious groups of their basic affairs, such

---

[60]   Ibid [2].

[61]   Ibid [5].

[62]   *ICCPR*, art 18(3).

[63]   United Nations Human Rights Committee, above n 59, *General Comment No. 22*, [4].

[64]   Ibid [4].

> as, *inter alia*, the freedom to choose their religious leaders, priests and teachers, the freedom to establish seminaries or religious schools and the freedom to prepare and distribute religious texts or publications.

The broad scope of the freedom of religion outlined under Article 18 of the *ICCPR* would provide the Commonwealth Parliament with the ability to legislate to protect religious freedoms in a comprehensive way. In general terms, the Parliament would be able to validly legislate

> … to protect the right to freedom of religion and belief; to prohibit discrimination on the ground of religion and belief; to prohibit the advocacy of religious hatred that constitutes incitement to discrimination, hostility, or violence; and to protect the right of minorities, in community with the other members of their group, to profess and practice their own religion.[65]

It would, for example, allow the Parliament to include in a *RFA* provisions that would address specific areas of concern that were highlighted in Australia during the same-sex marriage debate and subsequent consultations by the Expert Panel on Religious Freedom. This may include provisions to protect the right of all celebrants to refuse to solemnise same-sex marriages where their genuine religious beliefs did not allow them to do so, to protect the legal status and funding of faith-based charities that continued to express support for traditional marriage, to protect people speaking publicly in support of traditional marriage, and to ensure parental rights in relation to the education of their children.

Again, however, this is not a plenary power. It is limited by the terms of the international instruments that are being relied on. While the Parliament is given some latitude in selecting the precise means by which it implements its international obligations, it must be guided by the terms of the relevant treaty when drafting the domestic law. An interesting example can be seen by considering whether the Commonwealth Parliament could legislate to enact s 8(1) of the *Racial and Religious Tolerance Act 2001* (Vic) at the federal level. Section 8(1) provides that:

> A person must not, on the ground of the religious belief or activity or another person or class of persons, engage in conduct that incites hatred against, serious contempt for, or revulsion or severe ridicule of, that other person or class of persons.

---

[65]   Denise Meyerson, 'The Protection of Religious Rights Under Australian Law' [2009] *Brigham Young University Law Review Law Review* 529, 530.

The most directly relevant provision within the *ICCPR* would appear to be Article 20(2) which provides that '[a]ny advocacy of national, racial or religious hatred that constitutes incitement to discrimination, hostility or violence shall be prohibited by law'. While both provisions are aimed at prohibiting expressions of religious hatred they are not identical in either their terms or intended reach. Whereas Article 20(2) directly targets advocacy of religious hatred,[66] the Victorian legislation is broader by prohibiting conduct that itself may not necessarily amount to advocacy of hatred but that incites that response in others. In its draft General Comment No. 34 (which concerned the interpretation of the right to freedom of expression under Article 19 of the *ICCPR*) the UN Human Rights Committee observed that there are many forms of 'hate speech' that although 'discriminatory, derogatory and demeaning' do not meet 'the level of seriousness set out in article 20'.[67] The Committee noted that it was 'only with regard to the specific forms of expression indicated in article 20 that States parties are obliged to have legal prohibitions'.[68]

Having regard to the conformity test, it is clear that the Commonwealth Parliament could enact a national law directly prohibiting the advocacy of religious hatred 'that constitutes incitement to discrimination, hostility or violence'. However, if they attempted to extend this to reflect the broader terms of the Victorian provision they would be on a more doubtful constitutional footing.

In a similar way, the standard set by s 18C of the *RDA* falls well short of the level of seriousness outlined in Article 20 of the *ICCPR*. Section 18C makes it unlawful for a person to an act, otherwise than in private if 'the act is reasonably likely, in all the circumstances, to offend, insult, humiliate or intimidate another person or a group of people' and 'the act is done because of the race, colour or national or ethnic origin of the other person or of some or all of the people in the group'.[69] It should be noted here that the

---

[66] United Nations Human Rights Committee, *General Comment No 11: Article 20 Prohibition for War and Inciting National, Racial or Religious Hatred*, 19th sess (29 July 1983), [2].

[67] United Nations Human Rights Committee, *Draft General Comment No. 34: Article 19*, UN Doc CCPR/C/GC/34/CRP.5 (25 November 2010), [54].

[68] Ibid.

[69] *Racial Discrimination Act 1975* (Cth), s 18C.

constitutional validity of s 18C itself has been called into question.[70] Any attempt to replicate the s 18C wording and extend it to religion as a protected attribute would face significant constitutional hurdles, with conduct that 'offends, insults, humiliates or intimidates' falling well short of the mandated Article 20(2) standard of advocacy of religious hatred that constitutes incitement to discrimination, hostility or violence. It is highly doubtful that a s 18C-style provision would meet the conformity requirement and, as a result, it would not receive constitutional support through the external affairs power.

Part III: State Laws & Inconsistency

Another potentially important constitutional implication that would arise from the introduction of a *REA* concerns its interaction with existing State human rights and anti-discrimination laws. Both Victoria and the Australian Capital Territory have introduced statutory Bills of Rights that include protections for the freedom of thought, conscience, religion and belief.[71] All State and Territory jurisdictions within Australia also have anti-discrimination laws, although not all of these laws include protection for religious freedom and their precise scope varies considerably across jurisdictions. Most jurisdictions – with the exception of New South Wales and South Australia[72] – include religious belief or activity as a protected attribute, at least in some respects.[73] Religious bodies and educational institutions are also provided with a variety of exemptions in relation to selected anti-discrimination provisions, although these have been described by the Australian Human Rights Commission as being 'inconsistent across jurisdictions'.[74] The important point to note here is that there are existing laws within each State and Territory jurisdiction that – to some extent – deal with issues concerning religious freedom.

Section 109 of the *Constitution* provides that '[w]hen a law of a State is

---

[70]   See, for example, Joshua Forrester, Lorraine Finlay and Augusto Zimmermann, *No Offence Intended; Why 18C is Wrong* (Connor Court Publishing, 2016).

[71]   *Human Rights Act 2004* (ACT), s 14; *Charter of Human Rights and Responsibilities Act 2006* (Vic), s 14.

[72]   Although s 85T(1)(f) of the *Equal Opportunity Act 1984* (SA) does include a limited protection aimed at religious freedom by making it unlawful to discriminate against a person on the ground of religious appearance or dress.

[73]   See *Discrimination Act 1991* (ACT), s 7(1)(u); *Anti-Discrimination Act* (NT), s 19(1)(m); *Anti-Discrimination Act 1991* (Qld), s 7(i); *Anti-Discrimination Act 1998* (Tas), ss 16(o) & (p); *Equal Opportunity Act 2010* (Vic), s 6(n); *Equal Opportunity Act 1984* (WA), Part IV.

[74]   Australian Human Rights Commission, *Religious Freedom Review: Australian Human Rights Commission Submission to the Expert Panel*, (February 2018), [92].

inconsistent with a law of the Commonwealth, the latter shall prevail, and the former shall, to the extent of the inconsistency, be invalid.' The first preliminary point to note here is that whilst s 109 only concerns State laws there are similar inconsistency rules that operate in relation to Territory laws, with it being well established that the Commonwealth law will prevail to the extent of any inconsistency.[75]

The second preliminary point to note is that s 109 only comes into operation when there is a valid Commonwealth law. If the Commonwealth Parliament purported to introduce a *RFA* that went well beyond the terms of the *ICCPR* and, as a result, could not be supported by the external affairs power then no question of inconsistency under s 109 would arise in the first place. The Commonwealth law would be invalid, and the States laws would continue to operate unaffected.

Assuming, however, that the *RFA* is constitutionally valid, any State law would be rendered inoperative by virtue of s 109 to the extent that it was inconsistent with the *RFA*. This may be because the two laws could not be simultaneously obeyed,[76] or 'if one law purports to confer a legal right, privilege or entitlement that the other law purports to take away or diminish'.[77]

One potential example of this type of direct inconsistency lies in the different way that the *ICCPR* (and therefore potentially a future *RFA*) and the *Charter of Human Rights and Responsibilities Act 2006* (Vic) ('*Victorian Charter*') deal with limitations. Under the *ICCPR* the freedom to have or to adopt a religion or belief of your choice is protected unconditionally and may not be

---

[75]   In relation to the Australian Capital Territory the question of inconsistency is dealt with under s 28 of the *Australian Capital Territory (Self-Government) Act 1998* (Cth), with a recent example being found in *Commonwealth v Australian Capital Territory* [2013] HCA 55. In relation to the Northern Territory, see *Attorney-General (NT) v Minister for Aboriginal Affairs* (1989) 90 ALR 59, 75 (Lockhart J), 110 (Von Doussa J); *University of Wollongong v Metwally* (1984) 158 CLR 447, 464 (Mason J); *Northern Territory of Australia v GPAO & Ors* (1999) 196 CLR 553, 579 (Gleeson CJ and Gummow J), 636 (Kirby J).

[76]   Examples of cases that have discussed the question of s 109 inconsistency on the basis that the State law cannot be obeyed at the same time as the Commonwealth law include *Mabo v Commonwealth* (1988) 166 CLR 186 and *R v Brisbane Licensing Court; Ex parte Daniell* (1920) 28 CLR 23.

[77]   George Williams, Sean Brennan and Andrew Lynch, *Australian Constitutional Law and Theory: Commentary and Materials* (Federation Press, 6th ed, 2014), 298. An example of this type of inconsistency can be found in *Clyde Engineering Co Ltd v Cowburn* (1926) 27 CLR 466.

subject to any limitations whatsoever, even in times of public emergency.[78] This contrasts with the right to manifest one's religion or belief, which may be subject to limitations in accordance with the criteria outlined in Article 18(3) of the *ICCPR*. Under the *Victorian Charter*, *any* aspect of the freedom of religion – including not only the right to manifest one's religion or belief but also extending to the freedom to have or to adopt a religion or belief of your choice – may be limited under the terms of s 7(2). This provides that a *Charter* right 'may be subject under law only to such reasonable limits as can be demonstrably justified in a free and democratic society based on human dignity, equality and freedom …'.[79]

If this aspect of the *ICCPR* was fully reflected in a future *RFA* there could potentially be a direct inconsistency concerning the freedom to have or to adopt a religion or belief of your choice, with the *RFA* providing that this freedom cannot be limited and the *Victorian Charter* allowing for limitations. Any inconsistency may be merely theoretical, with Carolyn Evans realistically observing that 'it is highly unlikely that any direct infringement of the freedom to have a religion would be held to be a reasonable limitation under s 7 of the *Victorian Charter*'.[80] Nevertheless, it underlines the point about the importance of the drafters of any future *RFA* needing to consider the interaction between Commonwealth and State laws concerning the freedom of religion and the potential impact of s 109 of the *Australian Constitution*.

In addition to these examples of direct inconsistency, s 109 will also operate in cases of indirect inconsistency where the Commonwealth law 'covers the field' in relation to a particular subject and a State law attempts to enter that same field. This expansive interpretation of s 109 was first outlined by Justice Isaacs in *Clyde Engineering Co Ltd v Cowburn*[81] as follows:

> If … a competent legislature expressly or impliedly evinces its intention to cover the whole field, that is a conclusive test of inconsistency where another legislature assumes to enter to any extent upon the same field.

The 'covers the field' test will be highly relevant in terms of the interaction between any future *RFA* and existing State anti-discrimination law. Indeed,

---

[78]   United Nations Human Rights Committee, above n 59, *General Comment No. 22*, [1].

[79]   *Charter of Human Rights and Responsibilities Act 2006* (Vic), s 7(2).

[80]   Carolyn Evans, above n 57, 99. See also Peter Kurti, 'The Forgotten Freedom: Threats to Religious Liberty in Australia' (*The Centre for Independent Studies: CIS Policy Monograph 139*, 2014), 8; Thompson, above n 58, 18.

[81]   (1926) 37 CLR 466, [486] (Isaacs J).

the operation of s 109 with respect to anti-discrimination laws at the Commonwealth and State levels has been considered by the High Court in numerous cases, notably in a number of cases concerning the *RDA*.[82] For example, in *Viskauskas v Niland*[83] the High Court found that Part II of the *Anti-Discrimination Act 1977* (NSW) was inconsistent with the *RDA* on the basis that the Commonwealth law purported to 'cover the field' of racial discrimination law. As a result, the relevant sections of the New South Wales law were declared inoperative due to s 109. In response, the Commonwealth Parliament amended the *RDA* by inserting s 6A(1), which provided:

> This Act is not intended, and shall be deemed never to have been intended, to exclude or limit the operation of a law of a State or Territory that furthers the objects of the *Convention* and is capable of operating concurrently with this Act.

The effect of this amendment was considered almost immediately in *University of Wollongong v Metwally*.[84] A majority of the Court found that the Commonwealth Parliament could not retrospectively avoid the conclusion that they had intended to 'cover the field' by introducing a 'no inconsistency' amendment with retrospective effect, but held that such an amendment could operate prospectively to remove an indirect inconsistency under s 109. In this way, a 'no inconsistency' clause may be effective insofar as it indicates that the Commonwealth did not intend to cover the particular field, and in this way avoid a prospective indirect inconsistency arising under s 109. Such a clause cannot, however, prevent the operation of s 109 if there is a direct inconsistency between the two laws.[85]

---

[82] See, for example, *Viskauskas v Niland* (1983) 153 CLR 280; *University of Wollongong v Metwally* (1984) 158 CLR 447; *Mabo v Queensland (No. 1)* 91988) 166 CLR 186; *Western Australia v Commonwealth; Wororra Peoples & Biljabu v State of Western Australia* (1995) 183 CLR 373; *Western Australia v Ward* (2002) 213 CLR 1; *Jango v Northern Territory of Australia* (2006) 152 FCR 150; *James v Western Australia* (2010) 184 FCR 582. These cases are all discussed in George Williams & Daniel Reynolds, 'The Racial Discrimination Act and Inconsistency under the Australian Constitution' (2015) 36 *Adelaide Law Review* 241 as examples of cases in which the Court has been asked to consider the validity of a State or Territory Act based upon a possible inconsistency with the *RDA*.

[83] [1983] HCA 15.

[84] (1983) 158 CLR 447.

[85] See, for example, *R v Credit Tribunal; ex parte General Motors Acceptance Corporation Australia* (1977) 137 CLR 545, 563 (Mason J); *Palmdale-AGCI Ltd v Workers Compensation Commission (NSW)* (1977) 140 CLR 236, 243 (Mason J); *University of Wollongong v Metwally* (1984) 56 ALR 1, 5-6 (Gibbs CJ), 9 (Mason J), 20 (Brennan J), 26-27 (Dawson J).

This can now be seen in all of the key Commonwealth anti-discrimination laws. Similar 'no inconsistency' clauses can be found in s 12(3) of the *Age Discrimination Act 2004* (Cth), s 13(3) of the *Disability Discrimination Act 1992* (Cth) and s 10(3) of the *Sex Discrimination Act 1984* (Cth).

Given the way that religious freedom is currently dealt with in State anti-discrimination laws, it is likely that any future *RFA* will necessarily have significant implications for these State laws based upon the effect of s 109, even if a 'no inconsistency' clause is included as part of the Commonwealth law. This is due to the limited protection that many State anti-discrimination laws currently offer to religious freedom, and the way in which existing laws seem to prioritize other anti-discrimination rights ahead of religious freedom. To the extent that religious freedom is protected only as a series of narrow exemptions that apply in tightly defined circumstances under State anti-discrimination laws, any *RFA* that provides for a more broadly protected right to religious freedom may well result in direct inconsistencies arising. In such cases, the State anti-discrimination laws will be declared inoperative to the extent of such inconsistency.

However, the constitutional analysis is necessarily more complicated given that State anti-discrimination laws will potentially intersect not only with any future *RFA*, but also with other existing Commonwealth laws concerning anti-discrimination and other human rights. For example, it is possible that a future *RFA* may seek to shield service providers (such as the often-mentioned baker, florist or wedding photographer) who, because of their religious beliefs, refuse to provide goods and services that will be directly used in same-sex marriage ceremonies or celebrations. Such a refusal would be contrary to existing State anti-discrimination laws being, for example, a potential breach of s 35Y of the *Equal Opportunity Act 1984* (WA) which makes it unlawful to discriminate against a person because of their sexual orientation by refusing to provide them with goods or services, or refusing to make facilities available to them. A straightforward application of s 109 of the *Constitution* would result in the *RFA* prevailing and the service provider being protected. In this way, the *RFA* will have a potentially significant impact on State anti-discrimination laws.

However, this fails to take into account the *Sex Discrimination Act 1984* (Cth) which in s 22(1) contains a provision similar to the State anti-discrimination law and yet, by virtue of amendments introduced as part of the *Marriage*

Amendment (Definition and Religious Freedoms) Act 2017 (Cth), contains only narrow exemptions that apply to ministers of religion, religious marriage celebrants or Defence Force chaplains who refuse to solemnise a same-sex marriage in certain circumstances. If the State law is deemed to be directly inconsistent with the RFA, then this will likely mean that almost-identical anti-discrimination provisions at the Commonwealth level will also be directly inconsistent.

This does not raise a constitutional issue *per se*, with any inconsistency between Commonwealth laws being dealt with through the application of ordinary principles of statutory construction (and presumably as an issue that is anterior to any s 109 analysis as it requires the valid scope of the Commonwealth law to be determined).

But it does highlight a key issue when it comes to human rights law, namely that human rights can never be considered in isolation as all too often protecting the rights of one individual necessarily means restricting the rights of another. The key question is how conflicting rights can be appropriately reconciled and balanced. Any RFA will need to be carefully drafted to deal with these obvious issues of inconsistency and the over-arching question of how religious freedoms are to be balanced with existing Commonwealth anti-discrimination laws.

From a constitutional perspective, perhaps the key issue that is highlighted here is the almost complete transfer of legislative power in the areas of human rights and anti-discrimination from the States to the Commonwealth by virtue of the combined operation of ss 51(xxix) and 109 of the *Australian Constitution*. These were not policy areas that were originally thought to be included in the legislative powers granted to the Commonwealth Parliament by the drafters of the *Australian Constitution*, and yet the federal balance has shifted sufficiently to have allowed the Commonwealth to assume almost complete control over them at the expense of the States.

Part IV: Conclusion

As can be seen above, there are a number of constitutional issues that would need to be kept in mind when drafting any future RFA. Most significantly, the law would need to be supported by a valid head of power. The most likely option is the external affairs power under s 51(xxix) of the *Australian Constitution*, with the treaty implementation aspect of this power allowing the Commonwealth Parliament to legislate to introduce a *RFA* that broadly conforms to the terms of Article 18 of the *ICCPR*. Given the broad anti-discrimination laws that are already in place in all States and Territories across Australia the inter-relationship between these existing laws and any future *RFA*, and the potential impact of s 109 of the *Australian Constitution*, would also need to be considered. While the Commonwealth Parliament does clearly have the constitutional capacity to introduce a future *RFA*, this is not a free-ranging power but is instead subject to significant constitutional limitations and considerations that need to be taken into account at an early stage of drafting any such law.

Bibliography

Age Discrimination Act 2004 (Cth)

Ahmadou Sadio Diallo (Republic of Guinea v Democratic Republic of the Congo) (Merits Judgment) [2010] ICJ 639

Al-Kateb v Godwin [2004] 219 CLR 562

Allan James & Aroney Nicholas, 'An Uncommon Court: How the High Court of Australia has Undermined Australian Federalism' (2008) 30 *Sydney Law Review* 245

Anti-Discrimination Act 1977 (NSW)

Anti-Discrimination Act (NT)

Anti-Discrimination Act 1991 (Qld)

Anti-Discrimination Act 1998 (Tas)

Attorney-General (NT) v Minister for Aboriginal Affairs (1989) 90 ALR 59

Australian Capital Territory (Self-Government) Act 1998 (Cth)

Australian Catholic Bishops Conference, Submission No 11901 to the Religious Freedom Review Expert Panel, *Religious Freedom Review*, 14 February 2018

Australian Christian Lobby (in conjunction with the Human Rights Law Alliance), Submission No 14932 to the Religious Freedom Review Expert Panel, *Religious Freedom Review*, 15 February 2018

Australian Constitution

Australian Federation of Islamic Councils, Submission No 2832 to the Religious Freedom Review Expert Panel, *Religious Freedom Review*, 30

January 2018

Australian Human Rights Commission, *Religious Freedom Review: Australian Human Rights Commission Submission to the Expert Panel*, (February 2018)

Baxendale Rachel, 'Anti-discrimination exemptions for religious organisations should be removed, Amnesty says', *The Australian* (Online) 30 July 2018 <https://www.theaustralian.com.au/national-affairs/antidiscrimination-exemptions-for-religious-organisations-should-be-removed-amnesty-says/news-story/ea4a9e08f99d4af7e5739867ddecd5b9>

Centre for Independent Studies, Submission No 14929 to the Religious Freedom Review Expert Panel, *Religious Freedom Review*, 12 February 2018

Charter of Human Rights and Responsibilities Act 2006 (Vic)

Clyde Engineering Co Ltd v Cowburn (1926) 27 CLR 466

Commonwealth v Australian Capital Territory [2013] HCA 55

Commonwealth v Tasmania (1983) 158 CLR 1

Commonwealth of Australia Constitution Act 1900 (Imp) 63 & 64 Vict, c 12

Convention on the Rights of Persons with Disabilities, opened for signature 30 March 2007, 2515 UNTS 3 (entered into force 3 May 2008)

Convention on the Rights of the Child, opened for signature 20 November 1989, 1577 UNTS 3 (entered into force 2 September 1990)

Convention Relating to the Status of Refugees, opened for signature 28 July 1951, 189 UNTS 137 (entered into force 22 April 1954)

Craven Greg (ed), *Official Record of the Debates of the Australasian Federal Convention* (Legal Books, 1986)

Discrimination Act 1991 (ACT)

Disability Discrimination Act 1992 (Cth)

Discrimination (Employment and Occupation) Convention (ILO No. 111), 362 UNTS 31 (entered into force 15 June 1960)

Discrimination (Employment and Occupation) Convention, opened for signature 25 June 1958, 362 UNTS 31 (entered into force 15 June 1960)

Equal Opportunity Act 1984 (SA)

Equal Opportunity Act 2010 (Vic)

Equal Opportunity Act 1984 (WA)

Evans Carolyn, *Legal Protection of Religious Freedom in Australia* (The Federation Press, 2012)

Evans Carolyn, 'Time for a Treaty? The Legal Sufficiency of the Declaration on the Elimination of All Forms of Intolerance and Discrimination' (2007) *Brigham Young University Law Review* 617

Finlay Lorraine, Forrester Joshua & Zimmermann Augusto, 'Does Australia Need a *Religious Freedom Act?*' in Iain T. Benson, Michael Quinlan & Keith Thompson (eds), *Religious Liberty in Australia – A New Terra Nullius?* (Connor Court, 2019)

Forrester Joshua, Finlay Lorraine and Zimmermann Augusto, *No Offence Intended; Why 18C is Wrong* (Connor Court Publishing, 2016)

Freedom for Faith, Submission No 2520 to the Religious Freedom Review Expert Panel, *Religious Freedom Review*, 29 January 2018

Human Rights Act 2004 (ACT)

International Covenant on Civil and Political Rights, opened for signature 19 December 1966, 999 UNTS 171 (entered into force 23 March 1976)

International Covenant on Economic, Social and Cultural Rights, opened for signature 16 December 1966, 993 UNTS 3 (entered into force 3 January 1976)

International Convention on the Elimination of All Forms of Racial Discrimination, opened for signature 21 December 1965, 660 UNTS 195 (entered into force 4 January 1969)

James v Western Australia (2010) 184 FCR 582

Jango v Northern Territory of Australia (2006) 152 FCR 150

Kirmani v Captain Cook Cruises Pty Ltd (No. 1) (1985) 159 CLR 351

Koowarta v Bjelke-Petersen (1982) 153 CLR 168

Kurti Peter, 'The Forgotten Freedom: Threats to Religious Liberty in Australia' (The Centre for Independent Studies: *CIS Policy Monograph 139*, 2014)

Legal Consequences of the Construction of a Wall in the Occupied Palestinian Territory (Advisory Opinion) [2004] ICJ Rep 136

New South Wales & Ors v Commonwealth (2006) 229 CLR 1

Mabo v Queensland [No. 2] (1992) 175 CLR 1

Marriage Amendment (Definition and Religious Freedoms) Act 2017 (Cth)

Meyerson Denise, 'The Protection of Religious Rights Under Australian Law' [2009] *Brigham Young University Law Review Law Review* 529

Momcilovic v The Queen [2011] HCA 34

Northern Territory of Australia v GPAO & Ors (1999) 196 CLR 553

Optional Protocol to the International Covenant on Civil and Political Rights, opened for signature 16 December 1966, 999 UNTS 171 (entered into force 23 March 1976)

Palmdale-AGCI Ltd v Workers Compensation Commission (NSW) (1977) 140 CLR 236

Pape v Commissioner of Taxation [2009] HCA 23

Polyukhovich v Commonwealth (1991) 172 CLR 501

R v Brisbane Licensing Court; Ex parte Daniell (1920) 28 CLR 23

R v Burgess; ex parte Henry (1936) 55 CLR 608

R v Credit Tribunal; ex parte General Motors Acceptance Corporation Australia (1977) 137 CLR 545

R v Sharkey (1949) 79 CLR 121

Racial Discrimination Act 1975 (Cth)

Re Kavanagh's Application (2003) 204 ALR 1

Richardson v Forestry Commission (1988) 164 CLR 261

Rochow Neville, Submission No 2539 to the Religious Freedom Review Expert Panel, Religious *Freedom Review,* 29 January 2018

Schwebel Stephen M, 'The Effect of Resolutions of the U.N General Assembly on Customary International Law' (1979) 73 *American Society of International Law* 301

Secretariat of the United Nations, 'Questions relating to the voting procedure and decision-making process of the General Assembly', published in the *United Nations Juridical Yearbook* (1986) 274

Senate Standing Committees on Legal and Constitutional Affairs (References Committee), Inquiry into Sexuality Discrimination (December 1997)

Sex Discrimination Act 1984 (Cth)

Sloss David, 'Domestic Application of Treaties' in Duncan B Hollis (ed), *The Oxford Guide to Treaties* (Oxford University Press, 2012)

The General Conference of the International Labour Organisation, *Declaration concerning the aims and purposes of the International Labour Organisation,* 26th sess, (10 May 1944)

Thompson Keith, 'A Commonwealth Religious Discrimination Act for Australia?' (2017) 7(1) Solidarity: *The Journal of Catholic Social Thought and Secular Ethics*

Thompson Keith, Submission No 14157 to the Religious Freedom Review Expert Panel, *Religious Freedom Review*, 20 January 2018

United Nations General Assembly, Declaration on the Elimination of All Forms of Intolerance and of Discrimination Based on Religion or Belief, A/RES/36/55, 36th sess, (25 November 1981)

United Nations Human Rights Committee, Draft General Comment No. 34: Article 19, UN Doc CCPR/C/GC/34/CRP.5 (25 November 2010)

United Nations Human Rights Committee, General Comment No 11: Article 20 Prohibition for War and Inciting National, Racial or Religious Hatred, 19th sess (29 July 1983)

United Nations Human Rights Committee, General Comment No. 22: The right to freedom of thought, conscience and religion (Art. 18), 48th sess, UN Doc CCPR/C/21/Rev.1/Add.4 (22 September 1993)

United Nations Humans Rights Office of the High Commissioner, Status of Ratification Interactive Dashboard (1996-2014) <http://indicators.ohchr.org/>

Universal Declaration on Human Rights, GA Res 217A (III), UN GAOR, 3rd sess, 183rd plen mtg, UN Doc A/810 (10 December 1948)

University of Minnesota Human Rights Library, Study Guide: Freedom of Religion or Belief (February 2016). <http://hrlibrary.umn.edu/edumat/studyguides/religion.html>

University of Wollongong v Metwally (1984) 158 CLR 447

Victoria v Commonwealth (1996) 187 CLR 416

Viskauskas v Niland (1983) 153 CLR 280

Western Australia v Commonwealth; Wororra Peoples & Biljabu v State of Western Australia (1995) 183 CLR 373

Western Australia v Ward (2002) 213 CLR 1

Wilberforce Foundation, Submission No 6435 to the Religious Freedom Review Expert Panel, *Religious Freedom Review*, 12 February 2018

Williams George, Brennan Sean and Lynch Andrew, *Australian Constitutional Law and Theory: Commentary and Materials* (Federation Press, 6th ed, 2014)

Williams George & Reynolds Daniel, 'The Racial Discrimination Act and Inconsistency under the Australian Constitution' (2015) 36 *Adelaide Law Review* 241

XYZ v Commonwealth (2006) 227 CLR 532

Zines Leslie, *The High Court and the Constitution* (Lexis Law Publishing, 3rd ed, 1992)

5

DOES AUSTRALIA NEED A *RELIGIOUS FREEDOM ACT?*

LORRAINE FINLAY,[1] JOSHUA FORRESTER[2] AND AUGUSTO ZIMMERMANN[3]

The protection of religious freedom has been a topic of considerable discussion and debate in Australia in recent years, particularly in the context of the campaign to legalise same-sex marriage. The significance of this issue can be seen by the numerous inquiries, reports and initiatives that have been undertaken in recent years focusing on the question of religious freedom and its protection in Australia. These have included the appointment by the Prime Minister of an Expert Panel on Religious Freedom,[4] a partially completed Inquiry into the Status of the Human Right to Freedom of Religion or Belief by the Parliamentary Joint Standing Committee on Foreign Affairs, Defence and Trade,[5] the Freedoms Inquiry conducted by the Australian Law Reform Commission,[6] and the launch in 2015 of a Religious Freedom Roundtable by

---

[1] BA (UWA), LLB (UWA), LLM (NUS), LLM (NYU), Lecturer in Constitutional Law, Murdoch Law School; Senior Lecturer (Adjunct), University of Notre Dame Australia (Sydney). This paper is based on the submission made by the three co-authors to the Expert Panel on Religious Freedom (9 February 2018).

[2] BA (Hons) (Murd), LLM (Hons) (UWA), PhD Candidate (Murdoch).

[3] LLB (Hons), LLM *cum laude*, PhD (Mon); Professor, Sheridan College; Professor of Law (Adjunct), University of Notre Dame Australia (Sydney); President, Western Australian Legal Theory Association (WALTA).

[4] See, Department of the Prime Minister and Cabinet, *Religious Freedom Review*

[5] See, Parliament of Australia, *Inquiry into the Status of the Human Right to Freedom of Religion or Belief*.

[6] See, Australian Law Reform Commission, *Traditional Rights and Freedoms - Encroachments by Commonwealth Laws ('ALRC Report 129')* (2 March 2016)

the Australian Human Rights Commission.[7]

A theme that has strongly emerged is that religious freedom is not sufficiently protected in Australia, and that this should be remedied through the introduction of a national *Religious Freedom Act* ('RFA'). While we would strongly agree with the first proposition, we have some serious doubts about the second. This paper will consider whether Australia does need to introduce a RFA and the implications that follow from this. Part I will begin by examining the existing status of freedom of religion in Australia, and concluding that religious freedom is not currently sufficiently protected. This will be illustrated in Part II by considering the particular example of the same-sex marriage campaign and the potential impact of the *Marriage Amendment (Definition and Religious Freedoms) Act 2017* (Cth). The paper will then directly consider the introduction of a RFA by outlining the arguments that have been made in favour of a RFA in Part III, and then identifying some of the potential problems with this proposal in Part IV. An alternative response focused on reforming anti-discrimination laws will be considered in Part V, with the paper concluding that the key issue here is one of *conflict* rather than *recognition*. When the issue is framed in this way, then the introduction of a RFA can be seen as a solution that doesn't actually address the ultimate underlying problem.

Part I: Existing Status of Freedom of Religion in Australia

The fundamental importance of freedom of religion should be beyond question. It is 'the essence of a free society',[8] and 'the bedrock for every human right and … a sturdy foundation for limited government'.[9] As described by Lord Nicholls in R *v Secretary of State for Education, ex parte Williamson*:[10]

Religious and other beliefs and convictions are part of the humanity

---

7   The Religious Freedom Roundtable was an initiative established by Tim Wilson during his term as the Human Rights Commissioner. The Roundtable was established following a national consultation on rights and responsibilities conducted between August and December 2014 and a public submission process in September 2015. The inaugural meeting of the Roundtable was held on 5 November 2015, however the initiative stalled following Tim Wilson's resignation as the Human Rights Commissioner in February 2016. See, Australian Human Rights Commission, *Religious Freedom Roundtable* (5 November 2015 - 19 February 2016).

8   *Church of the New Faith v Commissioner of Pay-Roll Tax (Victoria)* (1983) 154 CLR 120, 130 (Mason ACJ, Brennan J).

9   Jennifer A Marshall, *Why Does Religious Freedom Matter?* (The Heritage Foundation, 2010) 8.

10   [2005] UKHL 15, [15] (Lord Nicholls).

of every individual. They are an integral part of his personality and individuality. In a civilised society individuals respect each other's beliefs. This enables them to live in harmony. This is one of the hallmarks of a civilised society.

Indeed, at the recent Ministerial to Advance Religious Freedom, the United States Ambassador to the United Nations, Nikki Haley, emphasised the overarching significance of this freedom for all people across the world, stating that 'defending religious freedom makes for a safer and more peaceful world for all of us'.[11]

Freedom of religion is theoretically protected under both the *Australian Constitution* and broader Australian legal framework. Indeed, it is one of the few individual human rights to receive express protection under the *Australian Constitution*, with s 116 providing that the Commonwealth 'shall not make any law for establishing any religion, or for imposing any religious observance, or for prohibiting the free exercise of any religion, and no religious test shall be required as a qualification for any office or public trust under the Commonwealth.'

Despite this, the legal protection that is actually provided for religious freedom in Australia is, in practice, much more limited than its constitutional status might otherwise suggest.[12] There are a number of reasons for the failure of s 116 to have delivered on its promise of constitutional protection.

First, in contrast to the American doctrine of incorporation, the constitutional provision only binds the Commonwealth and not the States. The question of whether s 116 applies to the Territories has not been definitively settled,[13] although the integrationist approach favoured by the

---

[11] Nikki Haley, US Permanent Representative to the United Nations (Speech delivered at Ministerial to Advance Religious Freedom, United States Holocaust Memorial Museum, Washington D C, 26 July 2018).

[12] See, eg, Joint Standing Committee on Foreign Affairs, Defence and Trade, Parliament of Australia, *Legal Foundations of Religious Freedom in Australia (Interim Report)* (2017), viii. ('*Interim Report*')

[13] See, for example, *Kruger v Commonwealth* (1997) 190 CLR 1 where the issue was considered by a number of Justices, but with different views being expressed. Justice Dawson noted that various views had previously been expressed about whether s 116 had any application to laws made under the 'territories power' found in s 122, and reached the conclusion (with which Justice McHugh agreed) that it did not. Justices Toohey, Gaudron and Gummow reached the opposite conclusion, holding that s 116 is applicable to an exercise of power under s 122.

majority in *Wurridjal v The Commonwealth*[14] suggests that the preferred approach will likely be that s 116 applies to the Territories when the Commonwealth exercises the 'territories power' found in s 122.[15]

Secondly, the constitutional provision is drafted in restrictive language, particularly when compared to the broader constitutional protections provided in other countries such as the United States ('US') and Canada. Given the differences in wording between the American and Australian provisions ('Congress shall make no law respecting an establishment of religion' as against 'the Commonwealth shall not make any law for establishing any religion'), only a law that is for the *purpose* of establishing religion is a law that violates the Australian establishment clause in s 116. The inclusion of the preposition 'for' was done only for the sake of grammatical structure. And yet, such seemingly innocuous variation has assumed substantive significance in Australia.[16]

Thirdly, s 116 has been interpreted narrowly by the High Court of Australia, as evidenced by the restrictive purposive test applied in relation to the free exercise clause in *Kruger v Commonwealth* ('*the Stolen Generations Case*').[17] In relation to this final point, there is a strong argument to be made that this interpretation should be re-visited by the High Court and that a more natural reading of the free exercise clause would lead to it having a greatly expanded scope.

There have been a growing number of examples in recent years that demonstrate religious freedoms being undervalued and eroded in Australia,

---

[14]   (2009) 237 CLR 309. See also, Robert French, 'The Northern Territory – A Celebration of Constitutional History' (Speech delivered at the Centenary of the Northern Territory Supreme Court Kriewaldt Lecture, Darwin, 23 May 2011).

[15]   Section 122 of the *Australian Constitution* provides: The Parliament may make laws for the government of any territory surrendered by any State to and accepted by the Commonwealth, or of any territory placed by the Queen under the authority of and accepted by the Commonwealth, or otherwise acquired by the Commonwealth, and may allow the representation of such territory in either House of the Parliament to the extent and on the terms which it thinks fit.

[16]   Tony Blackshield, 'Religion and Australian Constitutional Law', in Peter Radan, Denise Meyerson and Rosalind F Croucher (eds), *Law and Religion: God, the State and the Common Law* (Routledge, 2005), 85. See also, Luke Beck, 'The Case against Improper Purpose as the Touchstone for Invalidity under Section 116 of the *Australian Constitution*' (2016) 44 *Federal Law Review* 506.

[17]   *Kruger v Commonwealth* (1997) 190 CLR 1. See also, Australian Law Reform Commission, above n 6, *ALRC Report 129*, [4.21]; Beck, above n 16, 506; Alex Deagon, 'Liberal Assumptions in Section 116 Cases and Implications for Religious Freedom' (2018) 46 *Federal Law Review* 113.

despite its ostensible status as a freedom expressly protected under the *Australian Constitution*. There are numerous examples that can be pointed to, but in particular there have been a growing number of complaints made against individuals or groups who have sought to promote traditional marriage as an expression of their religious faith. This has occurred particularly in the context of the debate in Australia surrounding the legalisation of same-sex marriage, with examples including:

- The complaint lodged with the Tasmanian Anti-Discrimination Commission against the Catholic Archbishop of Hobart, Julian Porteous, after he authorised the distribution of a booklet entitled 'Don't Mess with Marriage' at Catholic schools and churches;[18]

- The complaint made to the Queensland Anti-Discrimination Commission against Dr David van Gend relating to an article he wrote for *The Courier-Mail* that opposed same-sex marriage;[19]

- The numerous complaints lodged against conservative political activist Bernard Gaynor by gay-rights activist Gary Burns;[20]

- The controversy surrounding the 'Keeping it Light' video produced by the Bible Society and initially linked with Coopers Brewery;[21] and

- The Mercure Sydney Airport Hotel cancelling a planned meeting at the hotel by four major Christian groups in September 2016 after complaints and threats by marriage-equality advocates.[22]

These examples will most likely multiply in the coming years following the legalisation of same-sex marriage in Australia. The particular danger that lies in these examples is the chilling effect that such intolerance has on public debate and discussion. As was noted by Angela Shanahan:[23]

> If people ... are forced to appear before an Anti-Discrimination Commission ... then this is a threat to one of Australia's greatest

---

18   'Anti-discrimination complaint 'an attempt to silence' the Church over same-sex marriage, Hobart Archbishop says', *ABC News* (Online) 28 September 2015.

19   Angela Shanahan, 'Discrimination police indulging in gay abandon', *The Australian*, (Online), 15 October 2011.

20   Nicola Berkovic, 'Same-sex marriage opponents tongue-tied by the thought police', *The Australian*, (Online) 28 November 2015 .

21   Paige Cockburn, 'Coopers Brewery distances itself from Bible Society's same-sex marriage video, faces backlash', *ABC News*, (Online) 15 March 2017.

22   David Crowe, 'Same-sex marriage event off: threats to hotel staff', *The Australian*, (Online) 17 September 2016.

23   Angela Shanahan, 'Yes Side in Marriage Debate Ignores the Implications for Freedoms', *The Australian*, (Online) 3 September 2017.

freedoms, the right to free speech. This is a major disincentive to people making a contribution to debate across Australia. Anti-discrimination bodies should not be used as star chambers by those who simply don't like what someone else says.

Of course, while freedom of religion is absolute in relation to the right to *hold* a belief, it is accepted that there are legitimate restrictions that may be applied to the right to *exercise* that belief. For example, religious beliefs never provide an excuse for violence or intimidation of others. Indeed, the High Court has stated that religious freedom must remain 'subject to powers and restrictions of government essential to the preservation of the community' or 'subject to [such] limitations [...] as are reasonably necessary for the protection of the community and in the interests of the social order'.[24]

It is important to note however that such restrictions should not be imposed lightly, and must leave the greatest possible scope for the freedom to operate. For example, Article 18(3) of the *International Covenant on Civil and Political Rights ('ICCPR')* allows the freedom to manifest one's religion or beliefs to be subject 'only to such limitations as are prescribed by law and are necessary to protect public safety, order, health, or morals or the fundamental rights and freedoms of others'.[25]

To obtain a realistic understanding of the status of religious freedom in Australia it is necessary to consider the intersection between religious freedom and other human rights, particularly anti-discrimination laws. Indeed, the Joint Standing Committee on Foreign Affairs, Defence and Trade recently found in its Interim Report, *Legal Foundations of Religious Freedom in Australia* that '[a]n imbalance between competing rights and the lack of an appropriate way to resolve the ensuing conflicts is the greatest challenge to the right to freedom of religion'.[26]

Striking an appropriate balance is a challenging exercise, and often controversial. When considering this balance, it is important to recognise that discrimination *per se* is simply a recognition of difference and can be practised for justified reasons. Determining *when* discrimination should be appropriately

---

[24]   *Adelaide Company of Jehovah's Witnesses Inc v Commonwealth* (1943) 67 CLR 116, 149 (Rich J), 155 (Starke J).

[25]   *International Covenant on Civil and Political Rights*, opened for signature 19 December 1966, 999 UNTS 171 (entered into force 23 March 1976).

[26]   Joint Standing Committee on Foreign Affairs, Defence and Trade, above n 12, *Interim Report*, viii.

exercised, and when legal limits should be enforced, is the critical question. As we observed in our recent Submission to the Parliamentary Joint Committee on Foreign Affairs, Defence and Trade Human Rights Sub-Committee:[27]

> In contemporary society, it is fair to say that 'discrimination' now has an inherently negative connotation. No one wants to be thought as discriminating against anyone or anything. However, humans discriminate all the time between what they think is good or bad for them. This is an inevitable consequence of having the capacity for conceptual thought. A person who prefers to drink water over bleach is exercising discrimination, that is, discerning that water is better to drink than bleach. The real issue, especially when determining thresholds for legal liability, is *when* discrimination can be exercised. In our view, South Africa's adoption of the standard of 'unfair discrimination' in its discrimination laws has much merit to it. This standard recognises that discrimination occurs, but there are circumstances when doing so warrants legal intervention.

This has parallels to an observation made by Justice Sachs from the Constitutional Court of South Africa concerning the meaning of equality:[28]

> [E]quality should not be confused with uniformity; in fact, uniformity can be the enemy of equality. Equality means equal concern and respect across difference. It does not presuppose the elimination or suppression of difference. Respect for human rights requires the affirmation of self, not the denial of self. Equality therefore does not imply a levelling or homogenisation of behaviour but an acknowledgment and acceptance of difference.

There is presently an unjustifiable imbalance between religious freedoms and anti-discrimination laws in Australia, with the balance weighted far too strongly in favour of the latter. All too often, religious freedom is treated as a 'secondary' right that is not given equal weight with other human rights, in particular equality rights. This was, again, evident during the debate surrounding same-sex marriage in Australia, where Prime Minister Turnbull declared that he believed in religious freedom 'even more strongly' than same-sex marriage, but went on to leave the question of protecting religious freedoms as an after-thought to be dealt with only once same-sex marriage had already been

---

[27] Joshua Forrester, Augusto Zimmermann and Lorraine Finlay, Submission No 179 to the Parliamentary Joint Committee on Foreign Affairs, Defence and Trade Human Rights Sub-Committee, *Inquiry into the Status of the Human Right to Freedom of Religion or Belief*, June 2017, 38. (*'Submission No 179'*)

[28] *National Coalition for Gay and Lesbian Equality v Minister of Justice* [1998] ZACC 15 (9 October 1998).

legislated.[29]

At the very least, religious freedom needs to be accorded equal weight with other human rights. In fact, there is a strong argument that the constitutional foundation provided for religious freedom in Australia actually means that what is required is not that a balance be struck between religious freedom and anti-discrimination laws, but instead that there is 'a constitutionally required preference for religious liberty.'[30]

Religious freedom is not sufficiently protected when it exists merely as a narrow exemption that is grudgingly accepted in anti-discrimination legislation. This implicitly undervalues the importance of religious freedom, with the consequence that it is consigned to a secondary role and is left vulnerable to removal at a later date. This has been highlighted recently, with a number of senior parliamentarians and major political parties openly canvassing the removal of existing anti-discrimination exemptions.[31] Freedom of religion should not be considered as an exemption. It is a fundamental freedom that deserves to be protected in a positive sense. In our view, it is a fundamental freedom that is being subject to increasing pressure in Australia, and needs to be more robustly protected.

Part II: Potential Impact of 'Marriage Amendment (Definition and Religious Freedoms) Act'

Nowhere has this growing pressure been more starkly illustrated than in the context of the same-sex marriage debate. Marriage is '[p]erhaps the most prominent example of a practice for which there are secular laws but which has a clear spiritual dimension …'.[32] The recent introduction of same-sex marriage in Australia through the *Marriage Amendment (Definition and Religious Freedoms) Act 2017* (Cth), and the postal plebiscite campaign that preceded it, both gave rise to significant concerns in terms of how the legalisation of same-sex marriage would impact upon religious freedom. These concerns are not fictitious or far-

---

[29]   'Marriage legislation puts religious freedom in doubt', *The Australian*, (Online) 8 December 2017.

[30]   Reid Mortensen, 'Rendering to God and Caesar: Religion in Australian Discrimination Law' (1995) 18 *University of Queensland Law Journal* 208, 231.

[31]   See, eg, Paul Karp, 'Greens promise to end religious exemptions to Sex Discrimination Act', *The Guardian*, (Online) 17 May 2016. See also, Department of the Attorney-General and Justice Northern Territory Government, *Discussion Paper: Modernisation of the Anti-Discrimination Act* (September 2017)

[32]   Forrester, Zimmermann and Finlay, above n 27, *Submission No* 179, 43.

fetched, but are instead based on the real experiences of persons who support traditional marriage in Australia, and also in jurisdictions that have introduced same-sex marriage. This was recognised in the *Supplementary Explanatory Memorandum* to the *Marriage Amendment (Definition and Religious Freedoms) Bill 2017* which observed that '[t]here is substantial experience of discrimination and intimidation against persons and entities who support traditional marriage in Australia and in jurisdictions that have legislated for same-sex marriage, in areas like employment, education, professional accreditation and commercial boycotts'.[33]

An insight into the potential legal impact of redefining marriage, and its impact on religious freedom, can be seen by considering the examples from Canada and the US. Since the legalisation of same-sex marriage in these jurisdictions there have been numerous legal complaints made against organisations and individuals who have not wanted to provide services for same-sex weddings, ranging from a religious organisation being fined for refusing to rent their hall to a same-sex couple to use for a reception following their marriage[34] to individual bakers, florists and photographers being found guilty of discrimination when they refused (because of their religious beliefs) to provide services for same-sex weddings.[35]

It is important to note here that religion 'extends to faith and worship, to the teaching and propagation of religion, and to the practices and observances of religion'.[36] The exercise of religion therefore extends well beyond attendance at a place of worship, and may be exercised by both organisations and individuals.

It is also important to note here that freedom of speech and freedom of association are inextricably linked to religious freedom. In a broader sense, the ability to discriminate on the basis of an organisation's core commitments and values is central to the democratic freedoms of our nation. For example, when recruiting staff or appointing officeholders, a political party could be expected

---

[33] Parliament of Australia (House of Representatives), *Marriage Amendment (Definition and Religious Freedoms) Bill 2017 Supplementary Explanatory Memorandum and Supplementary Statement of Compatibility with Human Rights* (2017), [5].

[34] *Smith and Chymyshyn v Knights of Columbus and Hauser and Lazar* (2005) BCHRT 544.

[35] See examples provided by Augusto Zimmermann, *A Legal Opinion on the Potential Impact on Religious Freedom if the Marriage Act is Amended (to allow same-sex couples to marry)*, 5 September 2017.

[36] *Adelaide Company of Jehovah's Witnesses Inc. v Commonwealth of Australia* (1943) 67 CLR 116, 156 (McTiernan J).

to display discrimination resembling that practiced by religious bodies. It is reasonable, for example, that a politician from the Left of the Labor Party might discriminate against individuals with conservative views when recruiting staff for their office team. Likewise, environmental advocacy bodies such as Greenpeace or the Australian Conservation Foundation might reasonably be expected to discriminate against those sceptical about the science and policy responses regarding anthropogenic global warming when appointing scientists to their Scientific Advisory Committees.

This also necessarily includes the freedom to disassociate from practices inconsistent with one's religious beliefs. If individuals are not allowed to express their religious beliefs in public or to live in a way that is consistent with those beliefs, or if they are forced to participate in practices that are antithetical to those beliefs, then they are effectively being denied the opportunity to observe their religious faith. This is where the intersection between religious freedom and anti-discrimination laws creates complexities. For example, ordinarily the idea that an individual should not be refused goods or services because of their sex, sexuality, race, colour, ethnicity, nationality, age or other innate characteristics is unproblematic. However, when anti-discrimination laws prevent an individual from disassociating from practices that are antithetical to their religious beliefs, this obviously creates significant difficulties for individuals wishing to exercise their religious freedoms.

It was for this reason that there were attempts to amend the new marriage laws in Australia while they were being considered by the Australian Parliament to allow for conscientious objection where someone may otherwise be forced by law to knowingly and materially contribute to a same-sex marriage ceremony, and to ensure that freedom of speech was protected in a way that allowed people to speak freely in support of traditional marriage even after same-sex marriages became legal. The freedom of religion encompasses the freedom to disassociate from spiritual practices not in keeping with one's religious beliefs, and to speak in favour of one's own religious beliefs. As noted above, marriage is an example of a practice that has a clear spiritual dimension. As we have previously noted in our Submission to the Parliamentary Joint Committee on Foreign Affairs, Defence and Trade Human Rights Sub-Committee, '[e]nforcing anti-discrimination laws with respect to providing goods or services to homosexual marriage or commitment ceremonies puts members of a number of religions in a quandary'.[37] This is because such a requirement is inconsistent with their religious beliefs, including being 'squarely at odds with God's instruction that marriage is a union of a man and a woman'.[38]

The Australian Parliament declined to adopt amendments of this nature. Instead, the new law provides only a narrow exemption that allows a 'minister of religion' or a 'religious marriage celebrant' to refuse to solemnise a marriage because of their religious belief. This same right of conscientious objection does not extend to any other celebrant, or for that matter to any other wedding service provider, who might have a religious objection to providing services for a same-sex marriage ceremony.[39]

It was in recognition of these concerns about the impact that legalising same-sex marriage might have on religious freedoms that the Prime Minister announced the creation of an Expert Panel to conduct a religious freedom review. This was announced on 22 November 2017, after the results of the same-sex marriage postal plebiscite were known and at the same time that the Australian Parliament was considering the *Marriage Amendment (Definition and Religious Freedoms) Act 2017* (Cth). The Expert Panel was established to 'examine and report on whether Australian law (Commonwealth, State and Territory) adequately protects the human right to freedom of religion'.[40] The Expert Panel received more than 15,500 submissions during a two-month public consultation period,[41] providing a clear indication of the potency of this issue in Australia at the present time. The report of the Expert Panel was formally delivered to the Prime Minister on 18 May 2018.

Ultimately, however, the creation of the Expert Panel, and the response to its report, serves to highlight the inferior status granted to religious freedom in Australia when compared to other human rights (and, in particular, equality rights). The Expert Panel was announced as an afterthought in the same-sex marriage debate, only once the issue of religious freedoms began to attract public attention during the postal plebiscite campaign. The introduction of same-sex marriage laws was not delayed to allow for the Expert Panel report

---

[37] Forrester, Zimmermann and Finlay, above n 27, *Submission No 179*, 44.

[38] Ibid 44.

[39] See, *Marriage Amendment (Definition and Religious Freedoms) Act 2017* (Cth).

[40] Department of the Prime Minister and Cabinet, *Religious Freedom Review Terms of Reference*, (14 December 2017).

[41] See, Department of Prime Minister and Cabinet, above n 4, *Religious Freedom Review*.

to be considered, or for its recommendations to be potentially incorporated into the draft legislation. Rather, the protection of religious freedom was considered after the fact, with protective measures to be added, if necessary, to the legislation at a later date. It has now been well over a year since the *Marriage Amendment (Definition and Religious Freedoms) Act 2017* (Cth) was passed by the Parliament and came into effect in Australia. However, after receiving the Expert Panel report on 18 May 2018, the Government took almost seven months to release it publically and provide a response, and was unable to deliver any substantive reform to strengthen religious freedom during the term of the 45th Parliament. The secondary status afforded to religious freedom as a human right in Australia is no better illustrated than by this example.

Part III: Introducing a 'Religious Freedom Act' in Australia

Among the submissions that have been published by the Expert Panel and that took the view that religious freedom is currently insufficiently protected in Australia, a common response was to propose the introduction of a *RFA*. This proposal was made in submissions put forward by academics,[42] barristers and legal groups[43] religious bodies,[44] faith-based organisations[45] and public policy think tanks.[46] While there were some variations in the precise form of the *RFA* that was proposed by each of these groups, the general consensus within these submissions seemed to be that a future *RFA* should formally

---

[42]   See, for example, submissions made to the Expert Panel by Associate Professor Neil Foster (Submission Number 14570); Associate Professor Keith Thompson (Submission Number 14157); and Professor Greg Craven (Submission Number 14665). All submissions can be accessed at: Department of the Prime Minister and Cabinet, *Religious Freedom Review – Submissions.*

[43]   Ibid. For example, see submissions made by Neville Rochow SC (Submission Number 2539); the Victorian Christian Legal Society Inc (Submission Number 9984); and the Wilberforce Foundation (Submission Number 6435).

[44]   Ibid. For example, see submissions made by the Australian Catholic Bishops Conference (Submission Number 11901); Catholic Archdiocese of Hobart (Submission Number 15057); the Church of Jesus Christ of the Latter-Day Saints (Submission Number 9913); Anglican Church Diocese of Sydney (Submission Number 7482); Presbyterian Church of Australia (Submission Number 4008); and Uniting Church in Australia Assembly (Submission Number 3428).

[45]   Ibid. For example, see submissions made by the Australian Christian Lobby (in conjunction with the Human Rights Law Alliance) (Submission Number 14932); Australian Baha'i Community (Submission Number 14836); and the Australian Federation of Islamic Councils (Submission Number 2832).

[46]   See, eg, submissions made by Freedom For Faith (Submission Number 2520); and the Centre for Independent Studies (Submission Number 14929).

implement the right to freedom of thought, conscience and religion that is outlined in Article 18 of the *ICCPR*, a treaty that Australia ratified nearly forty years ago.

This is not a new proposal. Indeed, back in 1998 the Human Rights and Equal Opportunity Commission recommended the introduction of a *RFA* which would cover the full range of rights and freedoms recognised in both Article 18 of the *ICCPR* and Articles 1, 5 and 6 of the *Declaration on the Elimination of All Forms of Intolerance and of Discrimination Based on Religion or Belief ('UN Religion Declaration').*[47] More recently, the Joint Standing Committee on Foreign Affairs, Defence and Trade noted in the Interim Report that it produced as part of its *Inquiry into the Status of the Human Right to Freedom of Religion or Belief* the evidence that it had received with regards to the need for some form of *RFA* to be introduced at the national level in Australia.[48]

> There has been general agreement about the need to formally implement the right to freedom of religion or belief, if not the *ICCPR* in its entirety. Australia is rare among modern liberal democracies in its lack of a federal bill of rights instrument. There are various arguments in support of and opposing the implementation of such an instrument at federal level. Some contributors favour a Religious Freedom Act directly implementing Article 18 in federal law. Others have suggested protecting religious freedom through federal anti-discrimination law, either in a separate act or by consolidating anti-discrimination law into a single act. The Sub-Committee notes the strengths and weaknesses in each of the suggestions proffered.
>
> The Sub-Committee notes that the preponderance of evidence from all sides of the issue support the claim that religious freedom should be specifically protected in Commonwealth law, however this is achieved.

The overriding argument that is put in support of the introduction of a *RFA* is the increasing vulnerability of religious freedom in modern Australia. It is difficulty to argue against the truth of this proposition. There have, as outlined above, been numerous examples in recent years highlighting a growing intolerance towards religious activities and expressions of religious faith in Australia. Further, this is occurring in an environment where the existing legal protections for religious freedom are limited. While recognising

---

[47]   Human Rights and Equal Opportunity Commission, *Article 18: Freedom of religion and belief* (July 1998).

[48]   Joint Standing Committee on Foreign Affairs, Defence and Trade, above n 12, *Interim Report*, [6.31]-[6.32].

that 'Australia has long enjoyed religious freedom without robust legal protection'[49] the submission made to the Expert Panel by Freedom for Faith identifies a number of changes in Australian law and society over the past few decades that threaten religious freedom and have resulted in the need for more robust protections. These include the expansion of anti-discrimination laws (particularly the inclusion of a greater range of protected attributes), the 'persistent campaign to remove religious exemptions in anti-discrimination law', a changed culture that no longer holds religious freedom as a shared Australian value and, finally, increasing evidence of 'hatred against people of faith across the secular western world'.[50]

The introduction of a RFA is seen by proponents as offering enhanced protection to religious freedom, both directly through the protection that the terms of the law would itself provide but also indirectly through its symbolic elevation of religious freedom from a 'mere exemption' in existing anti-discrimination laws to a human right with an independent status that is worthy of positive protection in its own name. Some of the existing limitations of the current legal framework are seen as being potentially addressed through the introduction of a RFA, not only by directly strengthening the protection of religious freedom at the federal level but also through the impact that a federal RFA may potentially have on the laws of the States and Territories through the operation of the inconsistency clause in s 109 of the *Australian Constitution.*

There is overwhelming evidence to support the claim that religious freedoms are increasingly vulnerable in Australia today. It is also clear that the existing legal protections are both limited and patchwork in their application. Given this, there is clearly a case to be made for the introduction of a RFA as a way of seeking to address these issues. The question to consider then is whether this is the best way of addressing the need to strengthen the protection of religious freedom in Australia, or whether there may be unintended consequences that are best avoided. To make this point clear, in our view the discussion is not about *whether* religious freedom should be protected in Australia. Rather, it is about whether the RFA is the best mechanism for doing so.

---

[49]   Freedom for Faith, Submission No 2520 to the Religious Freedom Review Expert Panel, *Religious Freedom Review*, 29 January 2018.

[50]   Ibid.

Part IV: Potential Dangers of a RFA

While we strongly believe that religious freedom is not sufficiently protected in Australia, we do not believe that this is necessarily best corrected by introducing new legislative measures, whether focused specifically on religious freedom or dealing more generally with human rights. At one end of the spectrum there are some, like Professor George Williams, who have gone beyond the submission that there should be a stand-alone RFA and have instead argued that it does not make sense to privilege one right over another and that '[t]he right way forward is to protect religious freedom in a law that also recognises other fundamental rights. Only a broader human rights law of this kind can ensure proper and measured protection for religious interests.'[51] Professor Williams notes that Australia stands alone 'in being the only democracy without some form of national human rights act or bill of rights incorporating protection of freedom of religion.'[52]

We hold serious concerns about the potential introduction of a Charter of Rights – whether constitutionally entrenched or statutory – into Australia. The key concern is that a Charter of Rights would not itself avoid questions arising about the balance to be struck between conflicting human rights. All that it would achieve would be to shift such questions from the elected parliaments to a judiciary that is both unelected and unaccountable. Given that such questions are potentially highly divisive, and also engage both personal values and community standards, they are much better suited to being decided by our elected parliamentary representatives who are ultimately responsible to the people, rather than unelected judges who are not. Shifting the responsibility for contentious social policy decisions from the Parliament to the Court would be a significant and undesirable change.

In addition, a broad Charter of Rights that entrenches a suite of general human rights may have the opposite of its intended effect by actually, in practice, further diminishing freedom of religion. As Patrick Parkinson has previously observed, a Charter of Rights inevitably raises questions about how different rights are to be reconciled and balanced when they conflict against one another, with experience showing that ' ... the secular

---

51 George Williams, Submission No 3 to the Religious Freedom Review Expert Panel, *Religious Freedom Review*, 14 December 2017, 3.

52 Ibid 3.

liberal interpretation of human rights charters will tend to relegate Article 18 to the lowest place in an implicit hierarchy of rights established not by international law but by the intellectual fashions of the day.'[53] Professor Greg Craven identifies this as the 'nub of the problem if we proceed to implement a religious freedom statute in Australia. We need to develop a framework that will ensure that the right to religious freedom within a secularist society is interpreted in a way that is sensitive to the needs of religious adherents as well as the premises of a secular society.'[54] The introduction of a broad-based Charter of Rights in Australia may not ultimately enhance the protection afforded to religious freedom *vis-à-vis* (for example) equality rights, as religious freedom may instead continue to be afforded a secondary or inferior status in the hierarchy of rights established by the judicial interpretation given to any Charter.

There is a long history in Australia of religious groups expressing concerns about the potential introduction of a Charter of Rights.[55] For this reason, many of the submissions to the Expert Panel from faith-based groups that supported the introduction of a RFA were quick to emphasise that what they were proposing was not 'a mini-human rights Act nor a Charter of Rights by the back door'.[56] For example, the Freedom for Faith submission emphasised that their proposal for a RFA was 'different in character and much more limited than some human rights charters'.[57]

It is difficult, however, to see an actual substantive difference. The wording of a proposed RFA that effectively legislated the terms of Article 18 of the *ICCPR* would essentially replicate, for example, the terms of the protection given to religious freedom in the *Human Rights Act 1988* (UK). So the proposed language is not substantively different to the language used in comparable Charters in other jurisdictions. Admittedly, the statutory

---

[53] Patrick Parkinson, 'Christian concerns about an Australian Charter of Rights' (2010) 15(2) *Australian Journal of Human Rights* 83, 87.

[54] Greg Craven, Submission No 14665 to the Religious Freedom Review Expert Panel, *Religious Freedom Review*, 2 February 2018, 20.

[55] See, eg, Parkinson, above n 53, 83; Brigadier Jim Wallace, 'Why should Christians be Concerned about a Bill of Rights' in Julian Leeser & Ryan Haddrick (eds), *Don't leave us with the Bill: the case against an Australian Bill of Rights* (Menzies Research Centre, 2009) 251.

[56] Freedom for Faith, above n 49, 82. See also Catholic Archdiocese of Hobart, Submission No 15057 to the Religious Freedom Review Expert Panel, *Religious Freedom Review*, 13 February 2018, 9.

[57] Freedom for Faith, above n 49, 91.

basis of a proposed *RFA* would lessen concerns about the diminution of parliamentary sovereignty and the shift in power from the Parliament to the judiciary. But it does not remove this concern entirely. While in theory the Parliament would retain the capacity to overrule judicial interpretations that did not match community standards or expectations, experience shows us that, in practice, this is much more easily said than done.

Any time that a statutory basis for human rights is established it inevitably hands the interpretation of those rights to the judiciary, and yet this is a task that they are not ideally suited to. As Patrick Parkinson has observed:[58]

> When it comes to balancing different rights, or choosing which one should take priority over the other and to what extent people who equally respect human rights in principle, may come to quite different conclusions. Balancing rights, freedoms and responsibilities is not particularly a legal task. The law speaks typically in binary language – of winning and losing, of entitlement and absence of entitlement, of lawfulness and unlawfulness. The process of politics are far better suited to working out the balances between conflicting rights and claims.

Judges do not have the training or skills to engage in wider debates about social policy and public morality. Besides, the courts are not appropriate institutions to carry out and evaluate the research needed for such a role.[59] There is an obvious potential here for a partisan administration of justice. Such partisan interpretation of laws, as well as creating flawed court decisions, has the power to change pre-existing legislation to conform to these subjective judicial rulings.[60] Because this creates an unstable legal environment, as even long-standing laws may be amended or even overruled, Jeffrey Goldsworthy concludes:

> The traditional function of the judiciary ... does not sit altogether comfortably with the enforcement of a bill of rights. In effect, it confers on judges a power to veto legislation retrospectively on the basis of judgements of political morality ... This involves adding to the judicial function, a kind of power traditionally associated with

---

58 Patrick Parkinson, 'Christian Concerns with the Charter of Rights' (Research Paper No 09/72, Sydney Law School, 31 August 2009).

59 John Gava, 'We can't trust judges not to impose their own ideology', *The Australian*, (Online) 29 December 2008.

60 Gabriël A Moens, 'The Wrongs of a Constitutional Entrenched Bill of Rights' in M A Stephenson and Clive Turner (eds), *Australia: Republic or Monarchy?: Legal and Constitutional Issues* (The University of Queensland, 1994) 236.

> the legislative function, except that the unpredictability inherent in
> its exercise is exacerbated by its retrospective nature. That is why, on
> balance, it may diminish rather than enhance the rule of law.[61]

Indeed, many proponents of the RFA submit that one of the reasons
the RFA is necessary is due to the limitations of the constitutional guarantee
provided under s 116 of the *Australian Constitution*, which is at least partially due
to the narrow interpretation that the clause has been given by the High Court
of Australia. Why do we assume that religious freedom will be interpreted any
more favourably in a RFA?

Similarly, it is increasingly recognised that the core issue here lies in the
growing conflict between religious freedom and anti-discrimination laws.
Indeed, this very point was recently made by the Joint Standing Committee
on Foreign Affairs, Defence and Trade who described the 'greatest challenge'
to freedom of religion as being 'an imbalance between competing rights and
the lack of an appropriate way to resolve the enduring conflicts'.[62] The key
to strengthening the protection of religious freedom does not, therefore, lie
simply in providing for greater legal recognition of this right, but instead in
finding a way of managing conflicts between religious freedom and other
rights that doesn't inevitably result in religious freedom being treated as a
human right of secondary importance. Many of the submissions before the
Expert Panel that supported the introduction of a RFA acknowledged that
there are necessarily limits to religious freedom and that these rights must
at times be balanced with other rights. For example, the Freedom for Faith
submission suggested that the proposed RFA 'could helpfully provide a way
of balancing rights and freedoms without having a Charter of Rights'.[63] The
key difficulty with this is that, ultimately, a RFA leaves the question of how
that balance is struck in any particular case to the courts, raising again all of
the issues that have been described above concerning the transfer of power
from the parliament to the judiciary.

Associate Professor Neil Foster has suggested that this concern 'can be
met by adoption of clear guidelines for judicial decision-making (rather than

---

61   Jeffrey Goldsworthy, 'Legislative Sovereignty and the Rule of Law', in T Campbell,
      K D Ewing and A Tomkins (eds), *Sceptical Essays on Human Rights* (Oxford University
      Press, 2001), 75.

62   Joint Standing Committee on Foreign Affairs, Defence and Trade, above n 12,
      Interim Report, viii.

63   Freedom for Faith, above n 49, 13.

leaving open-ended discretions to judges), by legislating clear and workable "balancing clauses" to ensure that the religious freedoms of different groups are reasonably accommodated, and by fully (not partially) implementing the narrow "limitations" provisions of art 18(3) *ICCPR*.[64] This would reduce the problem, and if a *RFA* is introduced it is essential that it is drafted in a way that reflects these types of concerns. However, there must be doubts about whether even the clearest guidelines would be any match for an activist judge, determined to impose their own moral viewpoint on the world and unconstrained by anything as troublesome as democratic accountability.

A related issue here is that the introduction of statutory protections alters the community perception of how those rights are to be perceived and, in particular, whose responsibility it is to protect them. The onus shifts from civil society to the courts as human rights become primarily a matter of dispute and litigation. It changes the way that we think about the nature of rights and removes our own individual responsibility, creating a society where litigated rights are prioritised over moral responsibilities. This should not be mistaken for an argument in favour of no laws at all. Rather, it is simply a reminder that legal mechanisms are not the only way to protect human rights and, moreover, are often not the best way to protect them. In our view, the greatest realm of freedom for each individual is secured by fewer laws, not more.

The limitations of 'paper rights' has previously been emphasized by the-then Chief Justice of Queensland, Paul de Jersey, who observed that a Bill of Rights does not, in itself, guarantee the protection of the rights it specifies, noting that 'Australians arguably enjoy more secure rights protection than citizens of many countries which have bills of rights'.[65] He considered the first step that was necessary in any society to ensure the observance of core human rights was 'a government and a society which respect them, including the rights of minorities.'[66]

That presupposes educating the people about their own rights, and how their exercise impacts on others' rights, and governments adhering to the

---

[64] Neil Foster, Submission No 14570 to the Religious Freedom Review Expert Panel, *Religious Freedom Review*, 31 January 2018, 3.

[65] Paul de Jersey, 'A Reflection on a Bill of Rights' in Julian Leeser & Ryan Haddrick (eds), *Don't leave us with the Bill: the case against an Australian Bill of Rights* (Menzies Research Centre, 2009) 9.

[66] Ibid 9-10.

international standards to which the state is bound'.[67] In de Jersey's view, 'strong democratic institutions which can take practical steps to curb governmental abuses, and an educated populace tolerant of minority groups'[68] are much more valuable in the actual protection of human rights than any bill of rights. Indeed, because the effectiveness of human rights legislation is dependent on the socio-political context in which it operates, the impressive bills of rights passed in places such as Cuba, Rwanda, Cambodia and the Sudan have proved no barrier to multiple human rights abuses committed in those countries. According to Sir Harry Gibbs, formerly Chief Justice of the High Court of Australia,

> The most effective way to curb political power is to divide it. A Federal Constitution, which brings about a division of power in actual practice, is a more secure protection for basic political freedoms than a bill of rights ... Anyone who has seen the film 'The Killing Fields' will know that the fact that Khmer Republic had adopted a bill of rights did not assist the inhabitants of that unhappy country. We are all familiar with the abuses that have occurred in Uganda: that country had a bill of rights on the European model, and had judges that bravely tried to enforce it, but were unable to resist the forces of lawlessness.[69]

To this end, it is worth noting that the concerns expressed in Australia about the growing threat to religious freedom are also being expressed in other Western liberal democracies that have purported to enshrine the protection of religious freedom in a national Charter of Rights. Os Guiness has identified this as an emerging trend across the Western world:[70]

> The menace to religious freedom is no longer just the age-old evils of authoritarian oppression and sectarian violence around the world, but a grave new menace from within the West itself. For we are seeing an unwitting convergence between some very different Western trends that together form a perfect storm. One trend is the general disdain for religion that leads to a discounting of religious freedom, sharpened by a newly aggressive atheism and a heavy-handed separationism that both call for the exclusion of religion from public life. Another is the overzealous attempt of certain activists of the sexual revolution to treat freedom of religion and belief as an obstruction to their own rights

---

[67]   Ibid 9.

[68]   Ibid 10.

[69]   Harry Gibbs, 'A Constitutional Bill of Rights', in K Baker (ed), *An Australian Bill of Rights: Pro and Contra* (Institute of Public Affairs, 1986) 325.

[70]   Os Guiness, *The Global Public Square: Religious Freedom and the Making of a World Safe for Diversity* (InterVarsity Press, 2013) 17-18.

that must be dismantled forever. Yet another is the sometimes blatant, sometimes subtle initiatives of certain advocates of Islam to express their own claims in ways that contradict freedom of religion and belief, and freedom of speech as it has been classically understood. (Current Western forms of hate speech, for example, operate in a similar way to the blasphemy laws put forward on behalf of Islam, and they are equally misguided). Each of these trends represents a serious crisis in itself. But when considered together, and especially in light of the generally maladroit governmental responses, they are also a window into the decline of the West.

The existence of legal protections for religious freedom (whether statutory or even constitutional) that are far more robust and comprehensive than those currently existing in Australia have not stopped this trend in other Western countries. For example, the express protection afforded to the freedom of conscience and religion under the *Canadian Charter of Rights and Freedoms* did not prevent Trinity Western University from being denied accreditation for a proposed law school based upon its requirement that students adhere to a covenant that reflects its evangelical Christian principles. Indeed, in his Canada Day Message delivered on 1 July 2018 the Most Reverend Archbishop Shane B Janzen of the Anglican Catholic Church of Canada spoke of the 'growing threat of militant secularism and its impact on our fundamental rights and freedoms' and used the Trinity Western University example as evidence of a 'growing trend lending credence to the idea that freedom of religion, and the free exercise of belief, are obstructions to other more politically correct rights, and therefore must be discounted and dismantled'.[71] If strengthened legal protections have not prevented or reversed this trend in other comparable Western liberal democracies, why do we think it will have this outcome in Australia?

In this light, the introduction of a *RFA* may assist in making it look as though our Parliament is doing something to protect religious freedom, and may even be effective in the short-term in masking some of the symptoms, but it does not solve the underlying problem, namely the steady erosion of the respect and value that we accord to religious faith and practices in our society. This can be illustrated by considering the submission made by *Freedom for Faith* to the Expert Panel. As noted above, the submission identified four key changes that have occurred in Australia over the last twenty years and that

---

[71]   Archbishop Shane B Janzen, *Canada Day Message* (1 July 2018) Anglican Catholic Church of Canada.

have resulted in the need for better protection for religious freedom. These are the expansion of anti-discrimination laws, persistent attempts to remove religious exemptions in anti-discrimination laws, religious freedom no longer being a shared cultural value in Australia, and increasing evidence of hatred being expressed towards people of faith across the secular Western world. At best, a RFA may lessen the impact of the first two of these factors, although this will depend almost entirely upon the interpretive approach ultimately adopted by the courts. It will not, however, have any impact on the final two factors, and may actually aggravate the problem by transforming religious freedom into an issue of litigation that is to be dealt with by the courts. The introduction of a RFA is in no way a panacea for the growing challenges that religious freedom faces in Australia.

Part V: Conclusion: Resolving Conflicts between Human Rights

If it is accepted that religious freedom is increasingly vulnerable in Australia, but there are doubts about the introduction of a RFA, then what is the solution? The first thing to note is that there is no single or easy solution. The ultimate problem here is a deeper, cultural malaise in Australian society reflected by changing attitudes towards the role that religion and faith should play in our nation. This is a problem being experienced in all Western liberal democracies, and one that simply cannot be fixed solely by changes to laws or the legal system.

That does not mean, however, that there is no value in attempting to strengthen the protection afforded to religious freedom through the legal system. In our view, the introduction of a RFA is not the preferred option. A much better way to proceed would be to look at amending the existing anti-discrimination laws in Australia (at both the State and federal levels) so that they strike a better balance between conflicting human rights. This could be done by redefining what is actually meant by discrimination through the introduction of a general limitations clause of the kind identified by the Australian Law Reform Commission in its 2012 *Freedoms Report*.[72]

Such a clause would be inserted into anti-discrimination laws and 'would clarify that conduct which is necessary to achieve a legitimate objective,

---

[72]   Australian Law Reform Commission, above n 6, *ALRC Report 129*, [5.108]-[5.114]. See also, Joint Standing Committee on Foreign Affairs, Defence and Trade, above n 12, *Interim Report*, [7.34]-[7.35].

including freedom of religion, and is a proportionate means of achieving that objective, is not discrimination'.[73] An example can be seen in the general limitations clause previously proposed by Patrick Parkinson and Nicholas Aroney:[74]

1. A distinction, exclusion, restriction or condition does not constitute discrimination if:

(a) It is reasonably capable of being considered appropriate and adapted to achieve a legitimate objective; or

(b) It is made because of the inherent requirements of the particular position concerned; or

(c) It is not unlawful under any anti-discrimination law of any state or territory in the place where it occurs; or

(d) It is a special measure that is reasonably intended to help achieve substantive equality between a person with a protected attribute and other persons.

2.   The protection, advancement or exercise of another human right protected by the International Covenant on Civil and Political rights is a legitimate objective within the meaning of subsection 2(a).

The effect of a general limitations clause is to re-calibrate the relationship between conflicting human rights, but it does so by using language that does not suggest that the freedom of religion is an inferior or secondary right that is only granted as a limited exception to freedoms from non-discrimination. Admittedly, there is still a risk that the same problems of judicial activism identified above would also apply to the interpretation of a general limitations clause, and may ultimately undermine any attempt to strengthen protections for religious freedom. However, in our view, this risk is minimised through a general limitations clause because of the way that it actually redefines the concept of discrimination and, in this way, tackles the problem from the opposite direction.

This approach is to be preferred as it doesn't introduce entirely new (and potentially conflicting) laws but instead recalibrates existing laws in a way that strengthens the protection of religious freedom and, in fact, attempts to ensure that the widest scope of freedom is maintained when balancing conflicting human rights. It also avoids the complexities and dangers that would arise

---

[73]   Australian Law Reform Commission, above n 6, *ALRC Report 129*, [5.108]-[5.114].

[74]   Ibid, [5.111]. See also, Joint Standing Committee on Foreign Affairs, Defence and Trade, above n 12, *Interim Report*, [7.35].

from the introduction of a mini-Charter of Rights (as outlined above).

The insertion of a general limitations clause reinforces the point that discrimination itself is not an inevitable wrong, but rather a recognition of difference that can be appropriately exercised in many circumstances. The key question is to determine when discrimination becomes unfair such that legal intervention is warranted. This is consistent with the position adopted by the United Nations Human Rights Committee in relation to non-discrimination under the *ICCPR*, observing in General Comment No 18 that '… not every differentiation of treatment will constitute discrimination, if the criteria for such differentiation are reasonable and objective and if the aim is to achieve a purpose which is legitimate under the Covenant'.[75]

We would strongly agree with the claim that religious freedom is not sufficiently protected in Australia. We do, however, have serious doubts about whether this is best remedied through the introduction of a national RFA. More to the point, it is important to realise that the debate about legal protections – whilst important – is ultimately a debate about symptoms rather than cause. The ultimate issue is the growing marginalisation of religion and faith from public life across Western liberal democracies. Until this is addressed, it is unlikely that any legal reform - not least a *RFA* – will actually be successful in protecting religious freedom from the growing pressures that it faces, not only in Australia but across the entire Western world.

Bibliography

Adelaide Company of Jehovah's Witnesses Inc. v Commonwealth of Australia (1943) 67 CLR 116

Archbishop Shane B Janzen, *Canada Day Message* (1 July 2018) Anglican Catholic Church of Canada <http://www.anglicancatholic.ca/wp-content/uploads/2013/06/Canada-Day-Message-2018-ACCC.pdf>

Australian Constitution

Australian Human Rights Commission, *Religious Freedom Roundtable* (5 November 2015 - 19 February 2016) <https://www.humanrights.gov.au/our-work/rights-and-freedoms/projects/religious-freedom-roundtable>

Australian Law Reform Commission, *Traditional Rights and Freedoms - Encroachments by Commonwealth Laws* (2 March 2016) <https://www.alrc.

---

[75]   Human Rights Committee, *General Comment No 18: Non-Discrimination*, 37th sess, UN Doc HRI/GEN/1/Rev.9 (Vol. I) (10 November 1989), [13].

gov.au/publications/freedoms-alrc129>

Author Unknown, 'Anti-discrimination complaint 'an attempt to silence' the Church over same-sex marriage, Hobart Archbishop says', *ABC News* (Online) 28 September 2015 <http://www.abc.net.au/news/2015-09-28/anti-discrimination-complaint-an-attempt-to-silence-the-church/6810276>

Author Unknown, 'Marriage legislation puts religious freedom in doubt', *The Australian*, (Online) 8 December 2017 <https://www.theaustralian.com.au/opinion/editorials/marriage-legislation-puts-religious-freedom-in-doubt/news-story/ce9ec86ca4a6f93aadafab5ba283fee1>

Beck Luke, 'The Case against Improper Purpose as the Touchstone for Invalidity under Section 116 of the *Australian Constitution*' (2016) 44 *Federal Law Review*

Berkovic Nicola, 'Same-sex marriage opponents tongue-tied by the thought police', *The Australian*, (Online) 28 November 2015 <https://www.theaustralian.com.au/news/inquirer/samesex-marriage-opponents-tonguetied-by-the-thought-police/news-story/f4b1faf0bb7421ddf757b4e503d1dd27>

Blackshield Tony, 'Religion and Australian Constitutional Law', in Peter Radan, Denise Meyerson and Rosalind F Croucher (eds), *Law and Religion: God, the State and the Common Law* (Routledge, 2005)

Catholic Archdiocese of Hobart, Submission No 15057 to the Religious Freedom Review Expert Panel, *Religious Freedom Review*, 13 February 2018

Church of the New Faith v Commissioner of Pay-Roll Tax (Victoria) (1983) 154 CLR 120

Cockburn Paige, 'Coopers Brewery distances itself from Bible Society's same-sex marriage video, faces backlash', *ABC News*, (Online) 15 March 2017 <http://www.abc.net.au/news/2017-03-14/coopers-brewery-not-involved-gay-marriage-video/8351894>

Craven Greg, Submission No 14665 to the Religious Freedom Review Expert Panel, *Religious Freedom Review*, 2 February 2018

Crowe David, 'Same-sex marriage event off: threats to hotel staff', *The Australian*, (Online) 17 September 2016 <https://www.theaustralian.com.au/news/nation/samesex-marriage-event-off-threats-to-hotel-staff/news-story/d45bd0f9e9a774fc3e3d0741f176da13>

Deagon Alex, 'Liberal Assumptions in Section 116 Cases and Implications for Religious Freedom' (2018) 46 *Federal Law Review*

Department of the Attorney-General and Justice Northern Territory

Government, *Discussion Paper: Modernisation of the Anti-Discrimination Act* (September 2017) <https://justice.nt.gov.au/__data/assets/pdf_file/0006/445281/anti-discrimination-act-discussion-paper-september-2017.pdf>

Department of the Prime Minister and Cabinet, *Religious Freedom Review* <https://www.pmc.gov.au/domestic-policy/religious-freedom-review≥

Department of the Prime Minister and Cabinet, *Religious Freedom Review Terms of Reference*, (14 December 2017) <https://www.pmc.gov.au/resource-centre/domestic-policy/religious-freedom-review-terms-reference>

Department of the Prime Minister and Cabinet, *Religious Freedom Review – Submissions* <https://www.pmc.gov.au/domestic-policy/religious-freedom-review/review-submissions>

Forrester Joshua, Augusto Zimmermann and Lorraine Finlay, Submission No 179 to the Parliamentary Joint Committee on Foreign Affairs, Defence and Trade Human Rights Sub-Committee, *Inquiry into the Status of the Human Right to Freedom of Religion or Belief,* June 2017

Foster Neil, Submission No 14570 to the Religious Freedom Review Expert Panel, *Religious Freedom Review,* 31 January 2018

Freedom for Faith, Submission No 2520 to the Religious Freedom Review Expert Panel, *Religious Freedom Review,* 29 January 2018.

French Robert, 'The Northern Territory – A Celebration of Constitutional History' (Speech delivered at the Centenary of the Northern Territory Supreme Court Kriewaldt Lecture, Darwin, 23 May 2011)

Gava John, 'We can't trust judges not to impose their own ideology', *The Australian*, (Online) 29 *December 2008* <http://www.theaustralian.news.com.au/story/0,25197,24850259-7583,00.html>

Gibbs Harry, 'A Constitutional Bill of Rights', in K Baker (ed), *An Australian Bill of Rights: Pro and Contra* (Institute of Public Affairs, 1986)

Goldsworthy Jeffrey, 'Legislative Sovereignty and the Rule of Law', in T Campbell, K D Ewing and A Tomkins (eds), *Sceptical Essays on Human Rights* (Oxford University Press, 2001)

Guiness Os, *The Global Public Square: Religious Freedom and the Making of a World Safe for Diversity* (InterVarsity Press, 2013)

Haley Nikki, US Permanent Representative to the United Nations (Speech delivered at Ministerial to Advance Religious Freedom, United States Holocaust Memorial Museum, Washington D C, 26 July 2018)

Human Rights and Equal Opportunity Commission, *Article 18: Freedom of religion and belief* (July 1998) <https://www.humanrights.gov.au/sites/default/files/content/pdf/human_rights/religion/article_18_

religious_freedom.pdf>

Human Rights Committee, *General Comment No 18: Non-Discrimination*, 37th sess, UN Doc HRI/GEN/1/Rev.9 (Vol. I) (10 November 1989)

International Covenant on Civil and Political Rights, opened for signature 19 December 1966, 999 UNTS 171 (entered into force 23 March 1976)

Jersey de Paul, 'A Reflection on a Bill of Rights' in Julian Leeser & Ryan Haddrick (eds), *Don't leave us with the Bill: the case against an Australian Bill of Rights* (Menzies Research Centre, 2009)

Joint Standing Committee on Foreign Affairs, Defence and Trade, Parliament of Australia, *Legal Foundations of Religious Freedom in Australia (Interim Report)* (2017)

Karp Paul, 'Greens promise to end religious exemptions to Sex Discrimination Act', *The Guardian*, (Online) 17 May 2016 <https://www.theguardian. com/australia-news/2016/may/17/greens-promise-to-end-religious-exemptions-to-sex-discrimination-act>

Kruger v Commonwealth (1997) 190 CLR 1

Marriage Amendment (Definition and Religious Freedoms) Act 2017 (Cth)

Marshall A Jennifer, *Why Does Religious Freedom Matter?* (The Heritage Foundation, 2010) 8

Moens A Gabriël, 'The Wrongs of a Constitutional Entrenched Bill of Rights' in M A Stephenson and Clive Turner (eds), *Australia: Republic or Monarchy?: Legal and Constitutional Issues* (The University of Queensland, 1994)

Mortensen Reid, 'Rendering to God and Caesar: Religion in Australian Discrimination Law' (1995) 18 *University of Queensland Law Journal*

National Coalition for Gay and Lesbian Equality v Minister of Justice [1998] ZACC 15 (9 October 1998)

Parkinson Patrick, 'Christian Concerns with the Charter of Rights' (Research Paper No 09/72, Sydney Law School, 31 August 2009) <https://papers. ssrn.com/sol3/papers.cfm?abstract_id=1465125>

Parkinson Patrick, 'Christian concerns about an Australian Charter of Rights' (2010) 15(2) *Australian Journal of Human Rights*

Parliament of Australia (House of Representatives), *Marriage Amendment (Definition and Religious Freedoms) Bill 2017 Supplementary Explanatory Memorandum and Supplementary Statement of Compatibility with Human Rights* (2017)

Parliament of Australia, *Inquiry into the Status of the Human Right to Freedom of Religion or Belief* <https://www.aph.gov.au/Parliamentary_Business/Committees/Joint/Foreign_Affairs_Defence_and_Trade/

Freedomofreligion>

R v Secretary of State for Education, ex parte Williamson [2005] UKHL 15

Shanahan Angela, 'Discrimination police indulging in gay abandon', *The Australian,* (Online), 15 October 2011 <https://www.theaustralian.com. au/opinion/discrimination-police-indulging-in-gay-abandon/news-story/c1457f01388bc4f3b1fe0a1a974f82fd?sv=722e7dd39f14bfa10db6 9189e9be1cf9>

Shanahan Angela, 'Yes Side in Marriage Debate Ignores the Implications for Freedoms', *The Australian,* (Online) 3 September 2017 <https:// www.theaustralian.com.au/news/inquirer/yes-side-in-marriage-debate-ignores-the-implications-for-freedoms/news-story/b119dbc7f7cad9f77 3f7f8ac7eef926d>

Smith and Chymyshyn v Knights of Columbus and Hauser and Lazar (2005) BCHRT 544

Wallace Jim Brigadier, 'Why should Christians be Concerned about a Bill of Rights' in Julian Leeser & Ryan Haddrick (eds), *Don't leave us with the Bill: the case against an Australian Bill of Rights* (Menzies Research Centre, 2009)

Williams George, Submission No 3 to the Religious Freedom Review Expert Panel, *Religious Freedom Review,* 14 December 2017

Wurridjal v The Commonwealth (2009) 237 CLR 309

Part 3:

Specific Topics in Religious Liberty

6

A CHRISTIAN FRAMEWORK FOR RELIGIOUS DIVERSITY IN POLITICAL DISCOURSE[1]

ALEX DEAGON

Religious Perspectives and Public Policy

Many scholars and politicians argue that excluding religious perspectives from political decision-making is the only way to guarantee genuine neutrality, freedom and equality. This has been most recently exposed in the 2017 Frank Walker Memorial Lecture, delivered by Federal Labor Senator Penny Wong.[2] Senator Wong argued that the problem with 'conflating religious concepts of marriage with secular concepts of marriage' is 'the application of religious belief to the framing of law in a secular society. And in societies where church and state are constitutionally separate, as they are in Australia and the United States ('US'), this leads not only to confusion, but also to inequity'.[3] This addresses the common view that religion should not directly influence public policy and law because it can be sectarian and divisive. In this secular state, the liberal ideals of freedom, neutrality and toleration are preserved by removing religious perspectives from political discussion because of their so-called particularist and divisive nature. Religious reasons or arguments in public discourse should not form the basis

---

[1] This paper was given at the 2018 *Freedom for Faith* Conference and contains some material from a forthcoming article in the *Journal of Law and Religion* titled 'Reconciling Milbank and Religious Freedom: "Liberalism" through Love'.

[2] See, eg, Penny Wong, 'The Separation of Church and State – The Liberal Argument for Equal Rights for Gay and Lesbian Australians' (Speech delivered at NSW Society of Labor Lawyers Frank Walker Memorial Lecture, 17 May 2017).

[3] Ibid

for political decisions resulting in coercive laws.[4] Instead, universally accepted non-religious reasons and perspectives are provided. John Rawls and Robert Audi are exponents of this laicist, separationist perspective which argues that excluding religion from politics results in genuine neutrality, freedom and equality.[5] For Rawls it is through 'public reason' (reason which is not based on a reasonable comprehensive doctrine but instead represents part of an overlapping consensus between doctrines) and for Audi it is through explicitly 'secular' reason (excluding religious reasons).

However, non-religious or secular reasons and a secular state are not quite as neutral as Rawls and Audi would have us believe. In my book *From Violence to Peace: Theology, Law and Community* I argue two basic propositions in this respect.[6] First, secular liberalism is not neutral between faith perspectives. It is a kind of faith. More significantly, it is an approach which relies on violence. Second, Christian theology provides an alternative framework which relies on peace rather than violence, and this is the 'law of love'. I make this argument in the context of a foundation for legal community. However, the book does not directly address religious freedom or diversity in political discourse. So the aim of this chapter is to apply the two propositions to make the case for Christianity as the most desirable framework for religious diversity in political discourse, arguing in particular that the neutrality, freedom and equality sought by liberalism cannot be sustained by liberalism, and are actually better fulfilled in Christianity.

Parts II and III of the chapter theologically critique secular liberalism by exposing the liberal faith in reason, the character of liberalism as a faith perspective, and the violence of liberalism. Part IV proposes an alternative Christian framework of persuasion through revelation, governed by the law of love. In this approach, as explained in Part V, interactive political discourse

---

4   See John Rawls, *Political Liberalism: Expanded Edition* (Columbia University Press, 2011); Robert Audi, 'The Place of Religious Argument in a Free and Democratic Society' (1993) 30 *San Diego Law Review* ('*The Place of Religious Argument*'); Robert Audi, *Religious Commitment and Secular Reason* (Cambridge University Press, 2000) ('*Religious Commitment and Secular Reason*'); Robert Audi, *Democratic Authority and the Separation of Church and State* (Cambridge University Press, 2011).

5   Cecile Laborde, 'Political Liberalism and Religion: On Separation and Establishment' (2013) 21(1) *Journal of Political Philosophy*. For a more detailed exposition of Rawls and Audi, see Alex Deagon, 'Liberal Secularism and Religious Freedom: Reforming Political Discourse' (2018) 41(3) *Harvard Journal of Law and Public Policy*.

6   See Alex Deagon, *From Violence to Peace: Law, Theology and Community* (Hart Publishing, 2017) ('*From Violence to Peace*').

is framed as being in loving community. The remaining parts defend the Christian framework against a series of objections, claiming in the final analysis that Christianity is the most desirable perspective and in fact facilitates genuine religious diversity by redeeming and transforming liberal political discourse. The purpose of the chapter, therefore, is not to simply abolish liberalism, but to produce genuine religious freedom in a framework which paradoxically transcends and fulfils the ideals of freedom, equality and tolerance that secular liberalism proclaims but can never attain.

Secular Liberalism as a Theology

The key claim is that the secular contingently originated from within the Christian theological framework, and is predicated on theological assumptions surrounding the nature of being and knowledge. The secular is not inevitable; rather, like many religious sects, it was in effect created as a result of theological and philosophical disagreement. This indicates the secular can be viewed as a type of faith in the sense that it is composed of particular assumptions and beliefs which are heterodox rejections or alterations of Christian theology.[7] This corresponds with the significant literature distinguishing between 'traditional', usually monotheistic religion such as Christianity, Islam and Judaism, traditional non-theistic religions such as Buddhism, and 'non-traditional', non-theistic 'beliefs' such as Agnosticism, Atheism and Secularism.[8] As such secular liberalism can be categorised as a faith perspective as distinct from a religion.[9]

In particular the fact that the secular elevates or has faith in pure, autonomous reason indicates that it can be viewed as a faith perspective. The idea of faith comes from the New Testament use of the Greek term *pistis*, which means to have a conviction or trust in, and its root means to be persuaded. Faith

---

[7]   Ibid 83-100 for the full version of the argument.

[8]   See, eg, Paul Copan, 'The biblical worldview context for religious liberty' in Angus Menuge (ed), *Religious Liberty and the Law: Theistic and Non-Theistic Perspectives* (Routledge, 2018); Katya Kozicki and William Pugliese, 'Religious liberty in Brazil: Piecing the puzzle together through contemporary decisions' in Angus Menuge (ed), *Religious Liberty and the Law: Theistic and Non-Theistic Perspectives* (Routledge, 2018); Alex Deagon, 'Secularism as a Religion: Questioning the Future of the "Secular" State' (2017) 8 *The Western Australian Jurist* 31; Ronald Dworkin, *Religion Without God* (Harvard University Press, 2013); John Calvert, '*Kitzmiller's* Error: Defining "Religion" Exclusively Rather Than Inclusively' (2009) 3 *Liberty University Law Review* 213.

[9]   See Iain Benson, 'Notes Towards a (Re)Definition of the "Secular"' (2000), 33(3) *University of British Columbia Law Review* 519.

includes both the affective element of trust, and the intellectual element of persuasion through reasons. [10] Perhaps counter-intuitively, this kind of faith is central to the legal system of the secular state. There is a type of religious soteriology implied in law, even its most 'secularised' iterations:

> Great hope is placed in law, properly understood and administered, as a vehicle for the transformation of society. Most movements for modern reform accept without question law's account of itself as autonomous, universal, and above all, secular – meaning, in the first instance, religiously neutral, but also, more strongly, paradigmatically rational ... law's claim to the universal resembles – indeed arguably derives its power from – the universalism that is claimed by ... Christianity.[11]

Similarly, it might even be claimed that every legal system needs a transcendent source to give authority to its contents – even if, in lieu of a 'higher source', that transcendent source is law itself.[12] If it is accepted that there is no transcendent source attracting people's trust, law becomes the entity that people trust. 'To work effectively law must rely on more than coercive sanctions ... it must attract people's trust and commitment. Quite simply, citizens must ... place their faith in it'.[13] Law encourages belief in its own sanctity in order to encourage obedience.[14]

The secular assumption is that there is nothing transcendent, particularly when it comes to the functioning of the state. However, the secular liberal state creates a *de facto* 'God' by placing its faith in the 'god' of law together with its components of reason and rationality.[15] As such, even secular reason, which claims to be pure reason or autonomous reason apart from faith, is actually a type of faith, similar in some respects to 'religious' faith. Such faith is not necessarily apart from reason or unreasonable, and it is distinct

---

[10]   John Milbank, 'Sublimity: The Modern Transcendent' in R Schwartz (ed) *Transcendence: Philosophy, Literature and Theology Approach the Beyond* (Routledge, 2004) 230; John Milbank, *The Future of Love: Essays in Political Theology* (Cascade Books, 2009) 150-153.

[11]   W Fallers-Sullivan, R Yelle, and M Taussig-Rubbo, 'Introduction' in W Fallers-Sullivan, R Yelle, and M Taussig-Rubbo (eds) *After Secular Law* (Stanford University Press, 2011) 2-3.

[12]   Ibid. See, eg, Jacques Derrida (1989) 'Force of Law: The Mystical Foundation of Authority' (Paper presented on *Deconstruction and the Possibility of Justice*, Cardozo Law School).

[13]   Rex Ahdar, 'The Inevitability of Law and Religion: An Introduction' in R Ahdar (ed) *Law and Religion*, (Ashgate, 2000) 5.

[14]   Ibid

[15]   See Fallers-Sullivan, Yelle and Taussig-Rubbo, above n 11, 2-3; Ahdar, above n 13, 5.

from 'religious' faith, but faith is involved nonetheless. The idea of pure or secular reason implies that 'reason cannot impact on issues of substantive preference', but in reality reason has to make certain assumptions and trust in the reasonableness of reality. 'Reason has always to some degree to feel its way forward'.[16] Reason should recognise that it operates within strict limits and is therefore not competent to pronounce final judgement against other metaphysical or religious positions. A certain stance of faith is always involved.[17] So secular reason, despite its claims to the contrary, is actually based in faith. The structure of the secular, in the sense that it intrinsically has faith in reason, possesses a faith object similar to the way that many religions possess a faith object.

In addition to the general argument about the secular being a faith perspective, other work already provides detailed arguments for the faith (or at least non-neutral and metaphysical) character of liberalism.[18] This section strengthens those arguments with further examples and analysis because establishing secular liberalism as a non-neutral theological perspective is an essential premise for the argument that Christianity is the most desirable framework to peacefully govern what is in fact a co-existence of different public theologies and faiths. An initial but important point is the liberal virtues of equality and toleration are fundamentally based in Christian theology. In particular, the inherent dignity and equal value of all persons, with the corresponding mandate for equal treatment, derives from the idea of their special creation by God and their possessing of the *Imago Dei*.[19] However,

---

[16]   John Milbank, 'The Double Glory, or Paradox Versus Dialectics: On Not Quite Agreeing With Slavoj Žižek' in C Davis (ed) *The Monstrosity of Christ: Paradox or Dialectic?* (MIT Press, 2009) 277.

[17]   John Milbank, 'Hume vs Kant: Faith, Reason and Feeling' (2011) 27 *Modern Theology* 276-277.

[18]   See, eg, Alex Deagon, 'Liberal Secularism and Religious Freedom: Reforming Political Discourse' (2018) 41(3) *Harvard Journal of Law and Public Policy* 923-925 ('*Liberal Secularism and Religious Freedom*'); Raymond Plant, 'Religion in a Liberal State' in G D'Costa et al (eds), *Religion in a Liberal State* (Cambridge University Press, 2013) 19, 22; Stanley Fish, 'Liberalism Doesn't Exist' (1987) *Duke Law Journal*. See also, Rex Ahdar and Ian Leigh, *Religious Freedom in the Liberal State*, Oxford University Press, 2nd ed, 2013) 17-18; 57-58 and references contained there.

[19]   See, eg, Perez Zagorin, *How the Idea of Religious Toleration Came to the West* (Princeton University Press, 2003); Bruce Ward, *Redeeming the Enlightenment: Christianity and Liberal Virtues* (Eerdmans, 2010); John Witte Jr and Frank Alexander (eds) *Christianity and Human Rights* (Cambridge University Press, 2010); Yuval Noah Harari, *Sapiens: A Brief History of Humankind* (Harvill Secker, 2011).

these principles have become secularised and distorted:

> On this reading, any overlaps between these theological principles and those of liberalism are to be explained by the "fact" that the values of liberalism are themselves secularized distortions of Christian insights. So, for instance, the liberal commitment to human equality is a secular distortion of the theological truth that all human beings are created in the image of God and, as such, are equal in the sight of God. Likewise, the liberal commitment to the toleration of plurality and difference is a secular distortion of Christian universalism, which subsumed but did not abolish difference.[20]

The theological character of liberalism is not merely genetic. For example, Kozinski argues that philosophy alone cannot resolve the political problem of religious pluralism. Any solution must be theologically informed, a cooperation between political philosophy and political theology – and despite claims to the contrary by political liberals such as John Rawls, their own solution also incorporates theology. Rawls serves as a good example in proving the futility of liberalism's reliance on an encompassing public reason (which ends up relegating traditional religions to the private sphere) in the sense that Rawls ends up relying on non-public (religious) reasons anyway.[21] Kozinski critiques Rawlsian public reason as 'undergirded by an exclusivist comprehensive doctrine with not only metaphysical but also theological premises'.[22] The Rawlsian framework, as a 'freestanding yet morally based overlapping consensus in a milieu of deep pluralism requires a foundation in an exclusive, particular comprehensive doctrine'.[23] 'Since his nonfoundationalist, pragmatic methodology logically precludes such premises, there is a major contradiction at the heart of his project'.[24]

The Rawlsian emphasis on the use of objective reason and moral intuitions formed through experience, combined with the *a priori* nature of the original

---

[20]   Gavin Hyman, 'Postmodern Theology and Modern Liberalism' (2009) 65 *Theology Today* 469. Hyman is referring to John Milbank's reading without necessarily endorsing it.

[21]   See Rawls, above n 4.

[22]   Thaddeus Kozinski, *The Political Problem of Religious Pluralism: And Why Philosophers Can't Solve It* (Rowman and Littlefield, 2010) xiii. For other more detailed engagement with Rawls with similar arguments see Deagon, *Liberal Secularism and Religious Freedom*, above n 18.

[23]   Kozinski, above n 22, xxii.

[24]   Ibid

position, indicates a reliance on Kantian metaphysics.[25] Furthermore, the logic of the Rawlsian position demands that 'public political culture possesses the absolute and exclusive authority to determine the commonly held conception of justice that is the focus of any overlapping consensus'.[26] Any reasonable comprehensive doctrine acceptable for public reason must be 'reconcilable with or foundational for' that conception of justice. This is what Kozinski calls the 'meta-idea'.[27] Kozinski persuasively contends that this meta-idea is actually an empirical fact for Rawls which is justified by its political value. Rawls does present an argument for its value, but this argument is based on Rawls' own privately held reasonable comprehensive doctrine:

> Rawls must argue for the meta-idea in an unRawlsian manner, because the is of the meta-idea, its factual existence in public political culture, cannot become a politically authoritative ought without some sort of foundationalist, metaphysical, or otherwise non-political justificatory argument.[28]

More importantly, Kozinski shows that Rawlsian political liberalism subscribes to theological premises. Rawls excludes any religious comprehensive doctrine that 'does not conform to his understanding of the inferior and thoroughly privatised and de-politicised place of religious belief and obligation in the political order'.[29] The attending theological assumption is either that God has not revealed any authoritative prescriptions regarding the political order, or if He has, they are not binding in the modern liberal democratic state. This 'theological judgment' 'would attenuate severely the religious freedom of those who deny it'.[30] Thus, Rawlsian political liberalism precludes the possibility of pursuing a Christian political community. It is essentially a work of political theology.

---

[25]   Ibid 6. Kantian metaphysics here is shorthand for the intellectual tradition of modern enlightenment political philosophy which has its culmination in Kant's transcendental idealism: that there exists an *a priori* knowing subject who uses objective reason to evaluate thought and arrive at objective truth, and moral intuitions formed through experience to evaluate conduct and arrive at objective justice. Consequently in this sense the Rawlsian project is purportedly foundationalist and deontological.

[26]   Ibid 26.

[27]   Ibid.

[28]   Ibid 31.

[29]   Ibid 38.

[30]   Ibid. See also Ahdar and Leigh, above n 18, 99.

Secular Liberalism as Violent

Here the term 'violence' means the following, as I define it in my book: 'violence exists in the sense that it establishes categories and draws boundaries around people (alienation) under the assumption of purely rational self-interest and atomistic individuality (antagonism)'.[31] Secular liberalism is violent firstly due to its Hobbesian and Lockean presuppositions – that we are all atomistic, purely rational individuals with conflicting wills. This radical individualism without feeling or faith results in a clash of all against all, or an intrinsically violent 'state of nature'. On this view law suspends the violence by regulating our relationships between each other and the state, but this is merely suspended violence rather than peace. Furthermore, the suspension itself occurs through coercion; as such, the violence of the state of nature is just replaced (and exacerbated) by the greater violence of the state.[32]

Hobbesian ontology in particular is fundamentally characterised by antagonism, a clash of wills. For example, Hobbes states that 'the condition of man ... is a condition of war of every one against every one, where everyone is governed by his own reason'.[33] Contractual relationships between the members of humanity are also paramount for Hobbes. These are presumably predicated on the priority of the will to make agreements.[34] Hobbes proceeds to argue that there must then be some external power or authority to compel people to fulfil their obligations:

> Even though the origin of justice is the making of covenants, until the fear of the other not performing is taken away, there can be no injustice. But while men are in the natural condition of war, taking away this fear cannot be done. Before the names of "just" and "unjust" can have a place, there must be some coercive power to equally compel men to the performance of their covenants. This can be done by the terror of some punishment greater than the benefit they expect by the breach of their covenant ... there is no such power before the erection of a commonwealth.[35]

So with will as paramount, human relationships are characterised by the clash of these wills, and contracts to restrain these wills. However, according

---

31   Deagon (2017a), p 3.
32   See John Milbank and Adrian Pabst, *The Politics of Virtue: Post-Liberalism and the Human Future* (Rowman and Littlefield, 2016); Deagon, *From Violence to Peace*, above n 6.
33   Thomas Hobbes, *Leviathan* (Longman, 2008) 86-87.
34   Ibid 91.
35   Ibid 96.

to Hobbes, there is only one way to construct a state power that will ultimately protect the citizens from actual or threatened internal or external violence and forsaking of covenants:

> This way is to confer all of their power and strength upon one man, or upon an assembly of men, that will reduce all of their wills, from a plurality of voices into one will … Everyone thereby submits their wills to his will, and their judgments to his judgments … when this is done, the multitude is united in one person that is called a commonwealth … This is the generation of that great Leviathan, or rather, to speak more reverently, of that immortal god, to which we owe our peace and defense under the immortal God. By the authority given him by every particular man in the commonwealth, he has the terror derived from so much power and strength conferred on him, that he is enabled to perform the wills of all of them … the essence of the commonwealth consists in this: By mutual covenant with one another, a multitude have made by their individual authority one person who can act for the ends of using his strength and any means he thinks is expedient for the multitude's peace and common defense.[36]

So on the basis of a (fictional) state of nature characterised by violence, Hobbes proposes a contract between the members of this state of nature to submit all of their wills to one mammoth will, the Leviathan, which is charged with the protection of the society and its members through absolutely sovereign coercive force, or violence. Hobbes consequently attempted to build social theory 'solely upon the rational calculation of self-interest', and the public interest is 'mostly confined to the securing of the private interests of life, property and contract'.[37] It is precisely this presupposition of the violent fictional state built to constrain the selfish, atomistic, rational individual which warrants critique.

Therefore, the main reason for the preference of classical Christianity over the modern, liberal secular is the ontologically violent nature of secular liberalism. In addition to the presuppositions just described, there are a number of modern examples in the legal space which are identified by and to some extent participated in by Cover and Derrida.[38] More generally, Plant

---

[36]   Ibid 116.

[37]   John Milbank, *Theology and Social Theory: Beyond Secular Reason* (Blackwell, 2nd ed, 2006) 29-30 ('*Theology and Social Theory*').

[38]   Deagon, *From Violence to Peace*, above n 6, 3, 6, 67-77, 102-107. See especially Robert Cover, 'Violence and the Word' (1986) 95 *Yale Law Journal* 1601; Derrida, above n 12.

has noted a general movement from ethos to rules in religious freedom.[39] The movement from ethos (or unbounded principles) to rules produces the problem of juridification. 'Legalising' or 'systemising' renders the principle into a rigid code which becomes inflexible and formal. Specifically, drawing boundaries around people and categorising them with respect to religion and non-religion, contexts where freedom and coercion are privileged or marginalized, alienates members of the community. Such a move invites transgression by articulating itself in terms of formal boundaries which alienate; in other words, such a law is intrinsically violent.[40]

One further example of violence in the context of religious freedom is the liberal distinction between the public and private realm, where religion is deemed 'lesser' and typically placed into the private dimension and excluded from the public. As McGhee argues, this liberal approach is a myth which constructs an alienating space (distinction between 'public' policy and 'private' religion) that is enforced through legal power, and therefore coerced by violence:

> The spatialization that accompanies this designation of different types of activities into their "public" and "private" realms is not merely the neutral act of facilitating an ideal forum for "rational debate" … this spatialisation and separation sets up an exclusionary space which is articulated by power'.[41]

This also exposes the religious 'myth of liberalism.[42]

Gedicks similarly argues that 'public' and 'private' are subjectively constructed and socially contingent categories. Liberalism's relegation of religion to private life is an exercise in power by controlling ways of naming and knowing:

> Secularism…does not mark any natural or inevitable distinction between private and public life. The confinement of religion to private life reflects the exercise of contingent power, not the disinterested discovery of essential meaning or self-existent reality.[43]

---

[39] Plant, above n 18, 11-12.

[40] See Alex Deagon, 'Rendering to Caesar and God: St Paul, the Natural Law Tradition, and the Authority of Law' (2014) 13(3) *Law, Culture, and the Humanities*, 469-492, where this problem has been identified. (*'Rendering to Caesar and God'*).

[41] Derek McGhee, 'Moderate Secularism in Liberal Societies' in G D'Costa et al (eds) *Religion in a Liberal State* (Cambridge University Press, 2013) 119.

[42] Ibid.

[43] Frederick Gedicks,'Public Life and Hostility to Religion' (1992) 78 *Virginia Law Review* 681.

Fish describes this as an 'intellectual/political apartheid' which has the effect of 'honouring religion by kicking it upstairs and out of sight'.[44] Thus, the mythical and contingent construction of a private/public distinction which excludes religion from the public space is a theological exercise of power which produces violence by alienating religious members of the community. As Milbank and Pabst observe:

> Liberalism legitimates the limitless expansion of the power of the more skilled, opportunistic and ruthless, so long as this proceeds in accordance with contractual agreement and the supposedly "neutral" expansion of one's own domain. And yet the expansion of private resources of all kinds in reality affects through influence of usage the environment and scope of free action for others.[45]

Thus, liberal secularism is a faith perspective and its structure ideologically and violently undermines religious freedom. Where liberal secularism proclaims neutrality while excluding and alienating other theological views incompatible with it, my approach acknowledges its own theological bias while demonstrating secular liberalism, and consequently all other approaches, include a theological bias. The idea is this provides in effect a level playing field which facilitates true religious freedom by creating a political space for different theological perspectives to peacefully coexist, and persuasion to the good or most desirable perspective is through revelation and governed by the law of love.

A Christian Framework: The Law of Love

Historically, Christians have always understood that the beliefs grounding their ethics are matters of faith, or persuasion (rhetoric).[46] In particular, as the glory of Christ is revealed to the mind, the mind is persuaded, which is the same as saying the mind appropriates this revelation by peaceful persuasion or rhetoric, rather than the violent coercion of secular reason. As the mind is transformed by faith, it participates in the glory of Christ by imitating Christ and then loves one's neighbour as a reflection of the Trinitarian relations. So the truth of Christianity in the divine structure of the Trinity exists in perfect love and peace despite difference, and this is

---

[44]   Stanley Fish, 'Are There Secular Reasons', *The New York Times* (Online) 22 February 2010.

[45]   Milbank and Pabst, above n 32, 16.

[46]   John Milbank, *Theology and Social Theory: Beyond Secular Reason* (Blackwell, 1990) 329.

revealed in the person and work of Christ as the law of love.[47]

In short, the love and peace inherent in the Trinitarian relations are *revealed* (truth-as-*aletheia*) through the Incarnation of Christ and *persuade* (faith-as-*pistis*) members of the community to 'love your neighbour as yourself' – the law of love articulated by the Apostle Paul in the New Testament.[48] This fulfils the codified law since 'love does no wrong to a neighbour'.[49] Law can be understood as a principle or set of principles which govern individual relationships within a community. Love, as defined above and modelled by Christ, involves the voluntary sacrifice of oneself for another. So the law of love, to 'love your neighbour as yourself', is the voluntary giving of oneself for another as the principle which governs individual relationships within a community.[50]

This law of love, modelled on and enabled by the Incarnation and crucifixion of Christ, consequently encourages love for one's neighbour in terms of humility and sacrifice. Importantly, this is not forced or coerced (for that would necessitate violence), but rather freely volunteered as an imitation of Christ in trust that the action will be reciprocated, for each member of the community participates by faith as their mind is persuaded by the revelation of love and peace in the Trinity.

Redeeming Political Discourse: A Peaceful Co-existence of Difference

The liberal framework for political discourse involves, at least in principle, a free and equal dialogue between different perspectives. The respective validity of these perspectives is determined by whether these perspectives are viewed as rationally persuasive in the sense of being motivated and justified by secular or public reason. If a perspective is rationally persuasive and generally comprehensible it represents a genuine consensus and therefore it should be legally implemented.[51] However, faith perspectives in political discourse are excluded these perspectives are deemed to be incompatible with the secular liberal framework of purely rational persuasion and general

---

[47] Deagon, *From Violence to Peace*, above n 6, 172, 183-186.

[48] Romans 13:9 (English Standard Version is used unless otherwise indicated).

[49] Ibid 13:10.

[50] Deagon (2017a), p 7.

[51] See Rawls, above n 4; Audi, *The Place of Religious Argument*, above n 4; Audi, *Religious Commitment and Secular Reason*, above n 4. Cf Bryan McGraw, *Faith in Politics: Religion and Liberal Democracy* (Cambridge University Press, 2010).

comprehensibility. Moreover, where particular perspectives are classed as faith perspectives and therefore irrational, they are violently alienated from public discourse and relegated to a contingently constructed 'private' realm.

With the vision of Christ who gives life through resurrection, violent alienation through incompatible difference is no longer authoritative.[52] Christianity consequently provides a more peaceful framework which does not merely 'permit' the expression of different perspectives if they meet arbitrarily imposed criteria, but creates a space for the harmonious co-existence of differing perspectives. The particular nature of divine gift(s) allows difference to be harmonised and promoted, producing peace through virtue in the body as Paul described in 1 Corinthians 12.[53] This is the 'reconciliation of virtue with difference'.[54] Persuasion in Christianity is peaceful because it comes from faith in the divine revelation of truth – specifically, the law of love.

It is in this sense Augustine argues that when a person is persuaded by faith, they will fulfil the law in accordance with the everlasting law (to love your neighbour as yourself) for the good and peace of the society.[55] Through the paradigm of the law of loving your neighbour as yourself, which is the unity and diversity in the community of the Trinity, a model is provided from Christian theology which allows harmonious relationship between the individuals and the society, one which avoids the violence of antagonism and alienation, and provides for a peaceful community which privileges one's neighbour as an individual and therefore strengthens the community as a composite of unique individuals.[56]

The above is a general approach in relation to the legal community. This chapter addresses the more specific question of what the law of love looks like in terms of regulating the public expression and debate of faith perspectives in a religious freedom context. Fundamentally, the 'law of love' approach seeks to create a harmonious space where a person can freely express, debate and choose faith perspectives without being subject to state, community or

---

[52]   John Milbank, 'Paul Against Biopolitics' in J Milbank et al (eds) *Paul's New Moment: Continental Philosophy and the Future of Christian Theology* (Brazos Press, 2010) 42-43. ('*Paul Against Biopolitics*')

[53]   Ibid

[54]   Milbank, *Theology and Social Theory*, above n 37, 332-333.

[55]   Augustine, *Concerning the City of God Against the Pagans* (Penguin, 2008) 873; Cf Deagon, *Rendering to Caesar and God*, above n 40.

[56]   Deagon, *From Violence to Peace*, above n 6, 8-9.

individual antagonism and alienation (violence). There should not be arbitrary legal or political constraints on the expression of perspectives. Charity (love) or 'doing good' requires going beyond boundaries or precedents, something 'creative'.[57] As Milbank exhorts, 'to act charitably we must break through the existing representation of what is our duty towards our neighbour and towards God', and 'break through the bounds of duty which "technically" pre-defines its prescribed performance'.[58]

In particular, we need to go beyond mere legal duty (for example, to just avoid hate speech, blasphemy or vilification) and selfish interest (the aggressive pursuit of our own agenda without due consideration for alternative views, or the prideful need to be seen as right), desiring to truly act with humility, love and sacrifice just like Christ did in humbling himself to death on a cross for our forgiveness:

> Do nothing from selfish ambition or conceit, but in humility count others more significant than yourselves. Let each of you look not only to his own interests, but also to the interests of others. Have this mind among yourselves, which is yours in Christ Jesus, who, though he was in the form of God, did not count equality with God a thing to be grasped, but emptied himself, by taking the form of a servant, being born in the likeness of men. And being found in human form, he humbled himself by becoming obedient to the point of death, even death on a cross.[59]

In this practical sense, love of neighbour means properly listening and engaging rather than judging, interpreting expressed views charitably and asking questions to clarify and learn rather than assuming or misrepresenting the views of others, and not engaging in malicious or contemptuous conduct. Love of neighbour in political discourse eschews 'anger, wrath, malice, slander' and lying, and pursues 'kindness, humility, meekness and patience' with honesty, forbearance, compassion and forgiveness.[60] Most importantly, perspectives should be adopted by means of peaceful persuasion rather than coercion. A public discourse regulated by the law of love may be manifested as the substantive (fully inclusive) and harmonious coexistence of different theological perspectives of varying electability and desirability, with freedom to choose any particular perspective.

---

[57] John Milbank, *The Word Made Strange: Theology, Language, Culture* (Blackwell, 1997) 134 ('*The Word Made Strange*').

[58] Ibid 134. See Deagon, *From Violence to Peace*, above n 6, 188-193.

[59] See Philippians 2:3-8.

[60] See Colossians 3:8-9, 12-13.

Objection 1: Breaking Trust

This new law of the Spirit both produces and is apprehended by faith. In this sense the Apostle Paul promotes a polity governed by faith or trust, persuasion by *aletheia* or the divine revelation of truth. He also stresses that this rule of trust constitutes a more fundamental mode of eternal law.[61] Such trust is a 'vertical' trust that God is just to an eminent and infinite extent that we cannot begin to fathom and a trust that this justice will eventually triumph so that a harmony of peace and order will embrace humanity.[62] It is also a 'horizontal' trust and mutual dependence between each member of the community, which provides a structure for harmonious existence and the embrace of difference without assimilation or alienation. Milbank reasons:

> It may appear that trust is weak recourse compared to the guarantees provided by law, courts, political constitutions, checks and balances, and so forth. However, since all these processes are administered by human beings capable of treachery, a suspension of distrust, along with the positive working of tacit bonds of association, is the only real source of reliable solidarity for a community. Hence to trust, to depend on others, is in reality the only reliable way in which the individual can extend his or her own power... the legitimate reach of one's own capacities, and also the only reliable way to attain a collective strength.[63]

The proposal for sacrifice, trust and humility to characterise public discourse might be viewed as problematic due to the unscrupulous. What if people selfishly take advantage of the humility and sacrifice offered? Paradoxically obvious yet strange, the Christian answer is located in the crucifixion of Christ, who voluntarily allowed himself to be taken advantage of as part of his act of sacrifice.[64] As Milbank observes,

> Most forms of persuasion (and if we eschew violence, but still want to encourage virtue, only persuasion is left) are thoroughly coercive. We need in consequence to find a language of peace, and this is presumably why we point to *one* drama of sacrifice in particular. Truth and persuasion are circularly related. We should only be convinced by rhetoric where it persuades us of the truth, but on the other hand truth *is* what is persuasive, namely what attracts and does not compel. And Christians

---

[61]   Milbank, *Paul Against Biopolitics*, above n 52, 49-50.

[62]   Ibid 53.

[63]   Ibid.

[64]   See Deagon, *From Violence to Peace*, above n 6, 127-132.

only see this *entire* attraction in the figure on the cross, a specific and compelling refusal to return evil for evil.[65]

So truth is most effectively revealed and people most ably persuaded by what attracts, namely Christ's refusal of violence which draws people to the peace of Christianity. Jesus himself said 'when I am lifted up from the earth, [I] will draw all people to myself', and he 'said this to show by what kind of death he was going to die'.[66] There is something irresistible (in the sense of peaceful persuasion) about the steadfast maintenance of humility, love, trust and sacrifice even in the midst of the most horrific mistreatment. Jesus cried out 'Father, forgive them! For they know not what they do'; he called upon the Father to forgive the ones who were at that moment crucifying him.[67] The answer to the question posed is, therefore, indicative of the radical and paradoxical nature of Christianity. The Christian response to people taking advantage of humility, sacrifice, trust and forgiveness is to continue offering that humility, sacrifice, trust and forgiveness as the concretely instantiated revelation of Christ, the truth. As people see this truth revealed, their minds are transformed through the common grace of the Spirit of Christ and they are peacefully persuaded to do likewise.

Here resides the desirability of Christianity: the law of love reveals the nature of Christ and peacefully persuades individuals in a community to act in accordance with it, hence in Christianity truth persuades to the good without coercion. The Church as persuading rather than coercing is important, for this allows the proclamation of a new political event: that of the cross, which replaces the sovereign power of the secular state with a different type of power or strategy of governance.[68] Paradoxically, the power of the cross is in its complete lack of sovereign power – Christ refuses to exert the power he possesses, instead resisting violent rule and establishing peace through service and the sacrifice of self; this in itself is far more powerful, and through Christ we can envisage the possibility of a similarly loving space for the expression of different perspectives.[69]

It might further be objected that this framing of the Christian approach fails to take proper account of Romans 13:1-7. In this passage it seems

---

[65]   Milbank, *The Word Made Strange*, above n 57, 250.
[66]   John 12:32-33.
[67]   Luke 23:34.
[68]   Milbank, *The Word Made Strange,* above n 57, 251.
[69]   Deagon, *From Violence to Peace,* above n 6, 183.

that Paul is invoking some kind of threat of physical violence to justify obedience to the civil authorities. In this context obedience to the good is effectively coerced by the state through violence, which is problematic in light of the preceding argument that a Christian approach persuades to the good without coercion and violence. There is insufficient space here to provide a comprehensive response, but I can briefly indicate a possible resolution.[70] First, Romans 13:1-7 must be contextualised by Romans 13:8-10, which grounds coerced obedience to the civil authorities in the law of love.[71] Second, there are contexts where violence might be appropriate yet compatible with ontological peace grounded by the law of love. Violence may be 'allowed' to 'facilitate educational redemption and ultimate peace'.[72] In a fallen world where there are some recalcitrant individuals, 'coercive action to prevent a person damaging themselves or others can be redeemed through their retrospective acceptance of the means taken to reach this final goal of peace'.[73] The reality of evil in the world necessitates a 'redeeming violence' in the pursuit of final, perfect peace.[74] Yet this violence is not the 'unrestrained and evil' violence which presupposes conflict as an ontological and inevitable necessity and 'detracts from the good', but violence 'that is gift or strengthening' and which 'communicates some substantive good'.[75]

Thus, the solution is to view the violence described in Romans 13:1-7 as a 'redeeming violence' necessary to bring about the substantive good of peaceful co-existence as a function of the law of love articulated in Romans 13:8-10. Instantiating the law of love fulfils the law by peaceful persuasion to the good. However, in a fallen world where evil exists, redeeming violence may be necessary on the path to achieving the good and perfect peace, on the condition that this violence is a last resort for extreme circumstances and recognised as redemptive and contingent. This approach also addresses the problem of practical application. The law of love persuades to the good without coercion, but where ultimate good and perfect peace is endangered protection in the form of redeeming violence may be necessary. Of course, this is not to say people will be persuaded by 'redeeming violence' to accept the

---

[70]   See Alex Deagon, "'It's Not Just Courtesy, it's the Law': (Not) Giving Way to Alienation' (2018) 9 *The Western Australian Jurist* 208 for the complete argument.

[71]   See Deagon, *From Violence to Peace*, above n 6,141-142.

[72]   Ibid 176.

[73]   Ibid 185.

[74]   Ibid 185-186.

[75]   Ibid 180-181.

Christian perspective. To truly preserve religious freedom perspectives must be freely chosen or rejected. Redeeming violence would only be necessary to prevent coercion to any particular perspective and to protect all perspectives from disruptive, antagonistic violence.

Objection 2: 'Establishing' Christianity and the Limits of Religious Freedom

This raises the further question of how this framework might regulate the expression of particular perspectives, especially odious or violent ones. Is there complete freedom to express all kinds of perspectives? What about perspectives which incite violence? An initial point is religious freedom is not absolute. When one considers the wide array of religious and non-religious perspectives, and the implications for public conduct and public policy, it is clear there must be some limit.[76] The point of dispute is not the fact there must be a limit, but where exactly that limit lies. The work of Rawls, Audi and their interlocutors investigates precisely this question. A second point is determination of whether a particular perspective is 'odious' or unworthy of expression is largely a moral question which is evaluated on the basis of one's own perspective. Therefore, disqualification of perspectives on such a basis would amount to privileging some perspectives over others through an evaluation of merits constructed by a particular perspective. Genuine religious freedom must allow the possibility for articulation of perspectives potentially viewed as offensive. These perspectives can then be freely evaluated by people and rejected on their merits rather than by state *fiat*.

Thus the limit cannot be based on the content of the perspective as such. Rather, the limit on religious freedom must be based on the capacity of the perspective to undermine the virtues which underpin religious freedom, particularly the ability to freely express, debate and choose particular perspectives. If a particular perspective involves coercion to that or other perspectives, such a perspective is incompatible with religious freedom in the Christian framework. Recall the law of love as the governing principle of political discourse. The law of love has, at its foundation, revelation producing persuasion and the rejection of violence through coercion. Hence the law of love internally regulates the different perspectives comprising political discourse to manifest the refusal to engage in violence. In this way the refusal

---

[76]   See, eg, Ahdar and Leigh, above n 18, 127.

of violence prevents coercion and facilitates persuasion, or true freedom.

This argument raises a further and very powerful objection. The objection might be framed as follows. This article advocates for the adoption of a Christian framework to produce genuine religious freedom. However, Christianity is itself a religious perspective. Therefore, the article is effectively arguing for the establishment of Christianity as the state religion, for it is Christian doctrine (The Trinity, Revelation, Incarnation, the law of love) which informs and governs the political apparatus facilitating political discourse. And the establishment of a particular religion as a state religion in this way by definition undermines religious freedom because people have to engage in the Christian framework using Christian virtues to participate. Following from this, it is disingenuous to claim this framework allows religious freedom because the framework itself is a religious perspective: Christianity.

A cogent and consistent response to this objection is critical for the framework proffered in this chapter. First, it would be a mistake to conclude that this article is advocating for the establishment of Christianity as a state religion, or that the framework would result in the establishment of Christianity as a state religion. The polity envisaged is not a theocratic society based in something like canon law. Rather, it is both the model for an ideal society and a way of living within a given society, characterised by love. The aim, ultimately, is to exist harmoniously within a community of difference.[77] This chapter is advocating for a Christian ontology within a state – a Christian approach which may redeem and transform conceptions of political discourse. The fact one can redeem the other implies there is still a distinction between the two – Jesus' kingdom is not of this world, it is a heavenly peace which may be brought to the earth of political discourse to the extent that we participate in the divine being in the way explained above.[78] Hence, again, this chapter does not advocate for the legal establishment of the Christian religion. It argues that if people practice the Christian virtues which constitute the law of love this will result in the peaceful co-existence of different perspectives, and therefore these virtues should govern religious diversity in political discourse. This 'democratisation of virtue' means all people can accept and practice these

---

[77]   Deagon, *From Violence to Peace*, above n 6, 170.

[78]   Ibid 145. This affirmation of different kinds of communities and associations within the 'state' is what Milbank calls 'complex space', in contrast to the 'simple space' of liberalism with a centralised state controlling individuals. See Milbank, *The Word Made Strange*, above n 57, 276-284.

virtues even if they are not Christian.[79]

Relatedly, the second important point to recall is the argument that all perspectives are theological. The objection as framed assumes there is some 'neutral' perspective which can form the foundation for governance in contrast to the religious 'Christian' perspective. Though some have claimed secular liberalism is such a perspective, it has been explained above that secular liberalism is in fact a theological perspective. In short, there is no neutral perspective and therefore this aspect of the objection loses much of its force. There must, nevertheless, be some governing perspective or framework for regulating human interactions and political discourse. The question is consequently not which perspective is neutral (for there is none), but which perspective is most desirable in the sense that it will result in true religious freedom. This chapter has contended the answer to that question is Christianity. Without imposition of the Christian religion on others, a Christian framework uniquely allows the peaceful coexistence of difference, including different views.

As indicated earlier, the Christian perspective produces a space for political discourse which is characterised by the 'fruit of the Spirit': 'love, joy, peace, patience, kindness, goodness, faithfulness, gentleness, self-control'; for 'against such things there is no law'.[80] The Christian virtues are beyond law and yet fulfil the law by their nature, and therefore abide the desirability of peace without the violence of coercion.[81] Manifesting this alternative framework for political discourse, governed by love beyond mere legal requirements, will persuade people there is another way to true peace and it is desirable.[82] This process can also indicate a way in which those who come from a secular perspective may be equally treated in this Christian framework, rather than existing in a space of alienation or antagonism which would perpetuate the violence we are attempting to avoid. The virtues of secular liberalism can peacefully co-exist in this space of differing perspectives. As such, there is no need to finally alienate the secular in articulating the theological.[83]

The desirability of Christianity is further entrenched by its unique ability

---

[79] See John Milbank, *Beyond Secular Order: The Representation of Being and the Representation of the People* (Blackwell, 2013) 264. ('*Beyond Secular Order*')

[80] Galatians 5:22-23.

[81] Deagon, *From Violence to Peace*, above n 6,141, 194. See also Milbank, *Beyond Secular Order*, above n 79, 228-236.

[82] Deagon, *From Violence to Peace*, above n 6, 194.

[83] Ibid 145, 148.

to recognize and accommodate difference by peaceful rather than violent means.

> Christianity ... pursued from the outset a universalism which tried to subsume rather than merely abolish difference: Christians could remain in their many different cities, languages, and cultures, yet still belong to one eternal city ruled by Christ, in whom all "humanity" was fulfilled.[84]

Following this Augustinian aspect however, Christianity does not

> ... imply mere mutual tolerance, far less any resignation to a regulated conflict ... while it is open to difference ... it also strives to make of all these differential additions a harmony ... true community means the freedom of people and groups to be different, not just to be functions of a fixed consensus, yet at the same time it totally refuses *indifference*.[85]

In this way, Christianity acknowledges the necessity of difference. Rather than trying to deny difference or regulate it with violence, at the ontological level Christian theology seeks a universal harmony of difference through incorporating the virtues contained in a faith united with reason, thereby enabling a community of peace at the political level.[86] Christianity can propose its own metanarrative as one option among many, yet as the most desirable one since it can instantiate peace – the harmonious ordering of difference, rather than the violent striving between differences.[87]

Objection 3: Christianity and Violence

It might be objected that Christianity has also imposed itself through violence in history through the Crusades, Inquisition and other such events. This cannot be overlooked. None of the above is to say Christianity has not been complicit in violence and coercion through political means, nor to exonerate Christianity's crimes in this respect.[88] In such a sense one could even rely dogmatically on the law of love in an ironically 'unloving' way, particularly given the ambiguities of applying love in terms of absolute rules, defining standards and values, and the balance of rationality and emotion. The law of love in this frame could be used to justify almost

---

[84]   Milbank, *Theology and Social Theory*, above n 37, 267-268.

[85]   Ibid 268.

[86]   Deagon, *From Violence to Peace*, above n 6, 17.

[87]   Ibid 67.

[88]   Timothy Shah, 'The Roots of Religious Freedom in Early Christian Thought' in Timothy Shah and Allen Hertzke (eds), *Christianity and Freedom Volume I: Historical Perspectives* (Cambridge University Press, 2017) frankly acknowledges this.

anything, including to undermine religious freedom.[89]

To address these objections the law of love as the foundation for religious freedom has been defined as clearly as possible to mean the harmonious co-existence of difference. Peace, patience, generosity, understanding and forgiveness are its virtues. These virtues, informed by the Christian framework of the intrinsic dignity of the individual, imply freedom should be maximized and not undermined by violence or coercion. As mentioned above, the only criteria for restricting freedom in this context is if the particular conduct or speech somehow undermines these virtues. Furthermore, as Cavanaugh persuasively argues, it is worth recalling the violent imposition that has regrettably occurred in the past may well be inconsistent with the essence of Christianity and represents a misappropriation of Christian theology for politically nefarious purposes such as military expansion and consolidation/centralization of state power.[90] Just as any other perspective can be misused by those in power to further their own agenda without invalidating that perspective, the political misuse of Christian theology to suppress or marginalize other doctrines in other contexts is no reason to reject the orthodox political application of Christian theology as argued here, which is to fully and equally allow the free and peaceful co-existence of different perspectives.[91] This is especially so when one bears in mind the ancient Christian origin for the concept of religious freedom for all perspectives.

Recent scholarship setting out the Christian pedigree of religious freedom on the basis of key theological doctrines such as intrinsic human dignity through God's creation of humans in his image, and Christ's assumption of human nature though the Incarnation, underscores this point.[92] There is insufficient space to examine this in any great detail but

---

[89] See, eg, Joseph Fletcher, *Situation Ethics: The New Morality* (Westminster John Knox Press, 1966); Reinhold Niebuhr, *An Interpretation of Christian Ethics* (Westminster John Knox Press, 2013).

[90] William Cavanaugh, *The Myth of Religious Violence: Secular Ideology and the Roots of Common Conflict* (Oxford University Press, 2009).

[91] See Deagon, *From Violence to Peace*, above n 6, 55-57, 142-143, 176-179.

[92] See especially, Timothy Shah and Allen Hertzke, *Christianity and Freedom Volume I: Historical Perspectives* (Cambridge University Press, 2016) and the chapters contained in there. Milbank too addresses some of the historical Christian justifications for religious liberty in John Milbank, 'The Decline of Religious Freedom and the Return of Religious Liberty' (Lecture delivered at the Religion and the Public Sphere Lecture Series, London School of Economics, 2017).

a brief outline will serve my purpose. It is not the task of this chapter to specifically set out the Christian pedigree of religious freedom, but acknowledging this historical fact is a supporting aspect of the more general normative argument for the desirability of Christian law of love as a governing framework. For example, Shah traces the development of arguments for universal religious freedom in some of the early patristic writers, including Justin Martyr, Athenagoras, Tertullian and Lactantius. He notes Tertullian in particular advocated for religious freedom (and first coined the term 'religious liberty') and in an unprecedented, universal way, claiming it is a fundamental human right or privilege of nature that a person should be able to worship according to their convictions without religion being compelled.[93] Wilken agrees, and more significantly in the context of relying on the law of love, emphasises that the ultimate source for Tertullian was the Bible. Tertullian's approach reflects the biblical view of the dignity and worth of a human being as the *Imago Dei*, clearly articulated in Genesis 1:26-27.[94]

Fundamentally, Christianity requires freedom of religion because love does not compel belief, and Christianity requires non-establishment for the same reason. While liberal secularism could be seen as establishing the religion of secularism, Christianity does not establish religion in this context because it is a meta-legal approach which facilitates the state creating a space for the harmonious and equal existence of different beliefs, governed by the law of love and the other theological virtues. Even if one assumes Christianity is true with both temporal and eternal implications, it does not follow that Christianity must be compelled, because coerced religion is not true religion and therefore it is impotent. It is mere externality or legalism and this is far worse than non-faith. Thus Christianity advocates belief as persuasion through revelation, not violent coercion by law or other means.

Objection 4: Is Christianity Inclusive?

This finally returns us to the issue of how this Christian framework equally includes those perspectives which are not Christian, such as secular liberalism.

---

[93]   See Shah, above n 88.

[94]   See Robert Wilken, 'The Christian Roots of Religious Freedom' in Timothy Shah and Allen Hertzke (eds) *Christianity and Freedom Volume I: Historical Perspectives* (Cambridge University Press, 2016).

Is it fair, equal and free that those who are not Christians are asked to participate in political discourse through Christian virtues? Does this not merely reinscribe the problem of alienating and subordinating other religious and non-religious traditions by elevating Christianity? Many scholars have done work in this space of critiquing secular liberalism as political order, much of it cognizant of Milbank's critique without explicitly advocating a Christian framework as an alternative or response. Instead these broadly propose a more neutral approach which eschews institutional privileging of any perspective for the same reason they reject secularism.[95]

This is broadly addressed above. The article is not advocating official establishment or institutionalization in a theocratic sense. But some form of codification or institutionalisation is usually necessary for practical effectiveness.[96] A possible solution is the law of love can be privileged without the state 'officialising' or 'institutionalising' it. It can be implemented by inculcating and democratizing the practice of virtue, as will be outlined more fully below. This allows the law of love to be instantiated in political practice without being 'legally' established, and avoids the twin problems of codifying (i.e. limiting) charity and alienating non-Christian views.

The promotion of Christian virtue as governing political discourse does not alienate or restrict the freedom of those who are not Christians. Such virtues (humility, kindness, sacrifice, forgiveness, love etc) are universally desirable and universally achievable regardless of one's particular perspective. Rather than Christianity undermining religious freedom in a democracy, it ensures it by promoting practices that facilitate genuine religious freedom and genuine democracy – fundamentally, the refusal of coercive violence and the use of peaceful persuasion. Milbank calls this the 'democratisation of virtue', where 'the most important human goods are in principle achievable by all', which 'is

---

[95]   See, eg, Talal Asad, *Formations of the Secular: Christianity, Islam, Modernity* (Stanford University Press, 2003); William Connolly, *Why I Am Not a Secularist* (University of Minnesota Press, 1999); Charles Taylor, *A Secular Age* (Harvard University Press, 2007); Craig Calhoun et al (eds), *Rethinking Secularism* (Oxford University Press, 2011); Michael Warner et al (eds), *Varieties of Secularism in a Secular Age* (Harvard University Press, 2010); Brian Black et al, *Confronting Secularism in Europe and India: Legitimacy and Disenchantment in Contemporary Times* (Bloomsbury, 2014); Rowan Williams, *Faith in the Public Square* (Bloomsbury, 2012).

[96]   John Milbank, 'A Closer Walk on the Wild Side: Some Comments on Charles Taylor's A Secular Age' (2009) 22 *Studies in Christian Ethics* 103. Cf Taylor, above n 95, 743.

itself also a Christian legacy'.[97] Milbank argues 'that the viability of democracy itself depends upon a continued constitutional commitment to "mixed government"', which is a blend of 'the life and implicit wisdom of the social many with the guidance of the virtuously rational few and the unifying artifice of the personal one, under the orientation of all to the transcendent Good and final vision of the Godhead'.[98] Moreover, the 'Christian democratisation of virtue as charity [love] implies a transfigured version of mixed government that newly promotes the creative flourishing of all and the combined shaping of an earthly city that might remotely image the eternal.'[99]

In other words, genuine democracy entailing true religious freedom promotes the individual and communal good so that the earthly polity might echo the eternal one. Such democracy is premised upon the universal practice of virtue, particularly love, which peacefully persuades the community to the good. As Milbank later clarifies, 'virtue is democratic because its practice is open to all, especially the supreme virtues of love, trust, hope, mercy, kindness, forgiveness and reconciliation, which we have all in the West, whether avowedly Christians or not, inherited from the teachings of the Bible'.[100] In short, promotion of the theological virtues in Christianity does not restrict or alienate those who do not subscribe to the Christian perspective. True promotion of the theological virtues actually necessarily incorporates and redeems the virtues of secular liberalism.

Reconciling Christianity and Liberalism

As we have seen, secular liberalism produces violence by proclaiming non-religious neutrality, freedom and equality while simultaneously promoting and enforcing a non-neutral quasi-religious perspective, undermining freedom and equality. Secular liberalism therefore holds out a standard it can never attain by its very nature. Conversely and paradoxically, the theological law of love fulfils the liberal virtues of religious freedom, neutrality and equality, in conjunction with the Christian virtues of faith, hope, love, humility, sacrifice, by transcending them and acknowledging that all perspectives, including Christianity and secular liberalism, are non-neutral theological perspectives

---

97   Milbank, *Beyond Secular Order*, above n 79, 264.
98   Ibid 10.
99   Ibid.
100   Milbank and Pabst, above n 32, 7.

which can be equally articulated and freely chosen. Indeed, if the liberal virtues of equality, tolerance and respect for difference are distorted forms of Christian virtues, that indicates the liberal virtues can be redeemed, removed from their secular framework and (re)placed into their proper theological framework in a way which paradoxically enhances both their Christian and liberal nature. As Hyman puts it, 'modern liberalism has played a positive role in the unfolding of Christian truth in bringing to light elements of the Christian ethical tradition that had previously, for whatever reason, been obscured'.[101]

This redeemed liberalism can become part of or even facilitate a theologically grounded public political discourse, and this is not inconsistent with Milbank's own thoughts. Indeed, in the preface to the second edition of *Theology and Social Theory*, Milbank acknowledges the debt an honest Christian theology must pay to the liberal insight:

> The careful reader will realize that throughout the book the attitude towards "secular reason" is never as negative as it appears to be on the surface. For it is viewed not as what it primarily proclaims itself to be, namely the secular, but rather as disguised heterodoxy of various stripes, as a revived paganism and as a religious nihilism. In each case my attitude cannot be simply oppositional, since I regard Catholic Christianity as fulfilling the best pagan impulses ... It follows that there remains truth in all these distortions and even that ... the [liberal] distortions develop better certain aspects of orthodoxy which orthodoxy must then later recoup.[102]

It is then possible to 'align one's loyalties both to modern liberalism and to Christianity', for as modern liberalism correctly emphasises the importance of reason and the distinction between reason and revelation, so Christianity provides the background which indicates immanent (modern, liberal) political structures point towards the transcendent and are informed by eternal virtues.[103]

Therefore the better approach is a loving community of expression grounded in virtue which will produce religious freedom through peace rather than

---

[101] Hyman, above n 20, 470. This also strengthens the claim made above in relation to the imposition of Christianity through violence. The contingent development of enlightenment liberalism out of Christianity actually privileged ultimately Christian virtues obscured in medieval Christianity.

[102] Milbank, *Theology and Social Theory*, above n 37, xiv-xv.

[103] Milbank, *Beyond Secular Order*, above n 79, 115-116.

violence.[104] This is a 'politics of virtue' which eschews selfish, Machiavellian modes of discourse in favour of charity, humility and sacrifice. We need to act with

> more receptive gratitude, more communicated generosity, and in such a way that in turn opens up the possibility of trust and further self-giving on the part of others ... Deeds must be publicly enacted and *offered*, and the highest outcome of virtuous practice is the reciprocal giving that is friendship, upon which ... the human city is founded.[105]

'Thus politics is a shared demand for a manifest mutual recognition and regard, since justice and friendship are co-original and inseparable', and the politics of virtue is then really a superfluous phrase – to act virtuously is really to truly act politically.[106] So, just as love does not dispense with the law but rather fulfils it, so the redeemed liberalism does not categorically reject liberalism but 'recoups' its better aspects to facilitate a more loving, virtuous and peaceful democratic community, and specifically a more loving and virtuous democratic discourse around religious freedom.

'... and the desire of all nations shall come'[107]

Christianity is not a neutral approach to regulating religious freedom and the expression of religious perspectives. But it has never claimed to be. Christianity is a theological approach but in this context is not theocratic or an attempt to establish Christianity or a state religion. This paper does not advocate for divine kingship or the rule of God in the political sphere in terms of authority in the way that, for example, O'Donovan does.[108]

However, it is not sufficient to simply assert in response that Christianity is not fit for the task because of its partisan nature. Indeed, as this chapter has shown, secular liberalism too is not a neutral approach even when its proponents say it is. There is no neutral approach, for all approaches are burdened by metaphysical and theological assumptions. The question must then move from neutrality, which is impossible, to desirability. This chapter has argued

---

[104] John Milbank, 'Against Human Rights: Liberty in the Western Tradition' (2012) 1(1) *Oxford Journal of Law and Religion* 232-234.

[105] Milbank and Pabst, above n 32, 6-7.

[106] Ibid 7.

[107] Haggai 2:7 (King James Version).

[108] Oliver O'Donovan, *The Desire of the Nations: Rediscovering the Roots of Political Theology* (Cambridge University Press, 1996).

secular liberalism is not in itself desirable because it does not acknowledge the fact it is merely a faith perspective, and actually rejects expressions of faith in political discourse. Secular liberalism's rejection of faith, including any faith in ultimate reason, actually renders itself as unreason. Thus, it has no option but to enforce its version of orthodoxy through violence and coercion.

Conversely, Christianity is an eminently desirable and appropriate framework for religious freedom and the regulation of different perspectives because its method of governance is informed by the sacrificial love of Christ:

> Love is patient and kind; love does not envy or boast; it is not arrogant or rude. It does not insist on its own way; it is not irritable or resentful; it does not rejoice at wrongdoing, but rejoices with the truth. Love bears all things, believes all things, hopes all things, endures all things. Love never fails.[109]

This rule of Christ as gift, or governance through the law of love, is the desire of all nations for a harmonious community. Christianity is more desirable because it regulates by peace rather than violence. Christianity is honest in acknowledging that it is a faith perspective (while simultaneously exposing the hypocrisy of perspectives equally theological but less forthcoming), though it is actually rational because of its faith in ultimate divine reason. Thus, Christianity peacefully persuades through revelation, particularly the revelation of truth in Christ: the law of love.

Peaceful persuasion by revelation through the law of love necessarily entails religious freedom, which is the ability to choose between different faith perspectives of varying electability and desirability existing in a harmonious, non-coercive space. The law of love, consisting of the Christian virtues such as honesty, kindness, humility, sacrifice and forgiveness, creates and regulates this harmonious space for substantive existence and discussion of differing perspectives. These virtues are Christian in foundation but can be universally practiced or democratised, and in this way Christianity does not exclude non-Christian perspectives. For example, Christianity recognises and redeems the important contributions of secular liberalism by fulfilling and transcending the liberal virtues of freedom and equality. Therefore, Christianity enables a redeemed liberalism through love and is the most desirable framework for genuine religious freedom.

---

[109] 1 Corinthians 13:4-8.

Bibliography

Ahdar Rex (2000) 'The Inevitability of Law and Religion: An Introduction' in R Ahdar (ed) *Law and Religion*, Ashgate

Ahdar Rex and Ian Leigh, *Religious Freedom in the Liberal State*, (Oxford University Press, 2nd ed, 2013)

Asad Talal, *Formations of the Secular: Christianity, Islam, Modernity* (Stanford University Press, 2003)

Audi Robert 'The Place of Religious Argument in a Free and Democratic Society' (1993) 30 *San Diego Law Review*

Audi Robert, *Democratic Authority and the Separation of Church and State* (Cambridge University Press, 2011)

Audi Robert, *Religious Commitment and Secular Reason* (Cambridge University Press, 2000)

Augustine, *Concerning the City of God Against the Pagans* (Penguin, 2008)

Benson Iain, 'Notes Towards a (Re)Definition of the "Secular"' (2000) 33(3) *University of British Columbia Law Review*

Black Brian et al, *Confronting Secularism in Europe and India: Legitimacy and Disenchantment in Contemporary Times* (Bloomsbury, 2014)

Calhoun Craig et al (eds), *Rethinking Secularism* (Oxford University Press, 2011)

Calvert John, '*Kitzmiller's* Error: Defining "Religion" Exclusively Rather Than Inclusively' (2009) 3 *Liberty University Law Review*

Cavanaugh William, *The Myth of Religious Violence: Secular Ideology and the Roots of Common Conflict* (Oxford University Press, 2009)

Connolly William, *Why I Am Not a Secularist* (University of Minnesota Press, 1999)

Copan Paul, 'The biblical worldview context for religious liberty' in Angus Menuge (ed), *Religious Liberty and the Law: Theistic and Non-Theistic Perspectives* (Routledge, 2018)

Cover Robert, 'Violence and the Word' (1986) 95 *Yale Law Journal*

D'Costa Gavin et al (eds), *Religion in a Liberal State* (Cambridge University Press, 2013)

Deagon Alex, 'Rendering to Caesar and God: St Paul, the Natural Law Tradition, and the Authority of Law' (2014) 13(3) *Law, Culture, and the Humanities*

Deagon Alex, *From Violence to Peace: Law, Theology and Community* (Hart Publishing, 2017a)

Deagon Alex, 'Secularism as a Religion: Questioning the Future of the "Secular" State' (2017b) 8 *The Western Australian Jurist*

Deagon Alex, "'It's Not Just Courtesy, it's the Law': (Not) Giving Way to Alienation' (2018a) 9 *The Western Australian Jurist* 208

Deagon Alex, 'Liberal Secularism and Religious Freedom: Reforming Political Discourse' (2018b) 41(3) *Harvard Journal of Law and Public Policy*

Derrida Jacques, 'Force of Law: The Mystical Foundation of Authority' (Paper presented on *Deconstruction and the Possibility of Justice*, Cardozo Law School, 1989)

Dworkin Ronald, *Religion Without God* (Harvard University Press, 2013)

Eberle Christopher, *Religious Conviction in Liberal Politics* (Cambridge University Press, 2002)

Fallers-Sullivan W, R Yelle, and M Taussig-Rubbo, 'Introduction' in W Fallers-Sullivan, R Yelle, and M Taussig-Rubbo (eds), *After Secular Law* (Stanford University Press, 2011)

Fish Stanley, 'Liberalism Doesn't Exist' (1987) *Duke Law Journal*

Stanley Fish, 'Are There Secular Reasons', *The New York Times* (Online) 22 February 2010 <https://opinionator.blogs.nytimes.com/2010/02/22/are-there-secular-reasons/>

Fletcher Joseph, *Situation Ethics: The New Morality* (Westminster John Knox Press, 1966)

Gedicks Frederick, 'Public Life and Hostility to Religion' (1992) 78 *Virginia Law Review*

Harari Noah Yuval, *Sapiens: A Brief History of Humankind* (Harvill Secker, 2011)

Hobbes Thomas, *Leviathan* (Longman, 2008)

Hyman Gavin, 'Postmodern Theology and Modern Liberalism' (2009) 65 *Theology Today*

Kozicki Katya and William Pugliese, 'Religious liberty in Brazil: Piecing the puzzle together through contemporary decisions' in Angus Menuge (ed), *Religious Liberty and the Law: Theistic and Non-Theistic Perspectives* (Routledge, 2018)

Kozinski Thaddeus, *The Political Problem of Religious Pluralism: And Why Philosophers Can't Solve It* (Rowman and Littlefield, 2010)

Laborde Cecile, 'Political Liberalism and Religion: On Separation and Establishment' (2013) 21(1) *Journal of Political Philosophy*

McConnell Michael, 'Why Protect Religious Freedom' (2013) 123(3) *Yale Law Journal*

McGhee Derek, 'Moderate Secularism in Liberal Societies' in G D'Costa et al (eds) *Religion in a Liberal State* (Cambridge University Press, 2013)

McGraw Bryan, *Faith in Politics: Religion and Liberal Democracy* (Cambridge

University Press, 2010)

Milbank John, *Theology and Social Theory: Beyond Secular Reason* (Blackwell, 1990)

Milbank John, 'Postmodern Critical Augustinianism: A Short *Summa* in Forty-Two Responses to Unasked Questions' in G Ward (ed) *The Postmodern God: A Theological Reader* (Blackwell, 1997a)

Milbank John, *The Word Made Strange: Theology, Language, Culture*, (Blackwell, 1997b)

Milbank John, *Being Reconciled: Ontology and Pardon* (Routledge, 2003)

Milbank John, 'Sublimity: The Modern Transcendent' in R Schwartz (ed) *Transcendence: Philosophy, Literature and Theology Approach the Beyond* (Routledge, 2004)

Milbank John, *Theology and Social Theory: Beyond Secular Reason* (Blackwell, 2nd ed, 2006)

Milbank John, 'The Double Glory, or Paradox Versus Dialectics: On Not Quite Agreeing With Slavoj Žižek' in C Davis (ed) *The Monstrosity of Christ: Paradox or Dialectic?* (MIT Press, 2009a)

Milbank John, *The Future of Love: Essays in Political Theology* (Cascade Books, 2009b)

Milbank John, 'A Closer Walk on the Wild Side: Some Comments on Charles Taylor's *A Secular Age*' (2009c) 22 *Studies in Christian Ethics*

Milbank John, 'Paul Against Biopolitics' in J Milbank et al (eds) *Paul's New Moment: Continental Philosophy and the Future of Christian Theology* (Brazos Press, 2010)

Milbank John, 'Hume vs Kant: Faith, Reason and Feeling' (2011) 27 *Modern Theology*

Milbank John, 'Against Human Rights: Liberty in the Western Tradition' (2012) 1(1) *Oxford Journal of Law and Religion*

Milbank John, *Beyond Secular Order: The Representation of Being and the Representation of the People* (Blackwell, 2013a)

Milbank John, 'What lacks is feeling: mediating reason and religion today' in G D'Costa et al (eds) *Religion in a Liberal State* (Cambridge University Press, 2013b)

John Milbank, 'The Decline of Religious Freedom and the Return of Religious Liberty' (Lecture delivered at the Religion and the Public Sphere Lecture Series, London School of Economics, 2017)

Milbank John and Adrian Pabst, *The Politics of Virtue: Post-Liberalism and the Human Future* (Rowman and Littlefield, 2016)

Niebuhr Reinhold, *An Interpretation of Christian Ethics* (Westminster John Knox Press, 2013)

O'Donovan Oliver, *The Desire of the Nations: Rediscovering the Roots of Political Theology* (Cambridge University Press, 1996)

Plant Raymond, 'Religion in a Liberal State' in G D'Costa et al (eds), *Religion in a Liberal State* (Cambridge University Press, 2013)

Rawls John, *Political Liberalism: Expanded Edition* (Columbia University Press, 2011)

Shah Timothy, 'The Roots of Religious Freedom in Early Christian Thought' in Timothy Shah and Allen Hertzke, *Christianity and Freedom Volume I: Historical Perspectives* (Cambridge University Press, 2017)

Shah Timothy and Allen Hertzke, *Christianity and Freedom Volume I: Historical Perspectives* (Cambridge University Press, 2016)

Taylor Charles, *A Secular Age* (Harvard University Press, 2007)

Ward Bruce, *Redeeming the Enlightenment: Christianity and Liberal Virtues* (Eerdmans, 2010)

Warner Michael et al (eds), *Varieties of Secularism in a Secular Age* (Harvard University Press, 2010)

Wilken Robert, 'The Christian Roots of Religious Freedom' in Timothy Shah and Allen Hertzke, *Christianity and Freedom Volume I: Historical Perspectives* (Cambridge University Press, 2017)

Williams Rowan, *Faith in the Public Square* (Bloomsbury, 2012)

Witte Jr John and Frank Alexander (eds), *Christianity and Human Rights* (Cambridge University Press, 2010)

Penny Wong, 'The Separation of Church and State – The Liberal Argument for Equal Rights for Gay and Lesbian Australians' (Speech delivered at NSW Society of Labor Lawyers Frank Walker Memorial Lecture, 17 May 2017). <https://www.pennywong.com.au/speeches/the-separation-of-church-and-state-the-liberal-argument-for-equal-rights-for-gay-and-lesbian-australians-nsw-society-of-labor-lawyers-frank-walker-memorial-lecture-2017>

Woodhead Derek, 'Liberal Religion and Illiberal Secularism' in G D'Costa et al (eds) *Religion in a Liberal State*, (Cambridge University Press, 2013)

Zagorin Perez, *How the Idea of Religious Toleration Came to the West* (Princeton University Press, 2003)

7

THE RELIGIOUS ROOTS OF "SEPARATION OF CHURCH AND STATE": CONSTITUTIONAL IMPLICATIONS FOR MODERN AUSTRALIA

AUGUSTO ZIMMERMANN[*]

First Considerations

The idea of separation between church and state has its own historical roots in traditional Christian philosophy. In Western history the concept of church-state separation was institutionalised between the 11th and 13th centuries. In 1075, Pope Gregory VII declared the church's total independence from 'secular control', thus freeing the church from dependence on the civil authority.

But time has passed and things have changed. In today's Western societies the understanding of an entirely secular public square has achieved significant political support.[1] Broadly speaking, the idea implies that everyone ought to support their positions about law, politics, and public policy on solely non-religious grounds.[2]

In this sense, the Establishment Clause found in s 116 of the *Australian Constitution* has sometimes been identified as evidence that Australia should be regarded as an entirely 'secular' country. However, in no way does the provision imply the exclusion of 'religious' perspectives from the political process and the support of government towards religious organisations.

---

[1]   Paul Horwitz, *The Agnostic Age* (Oxford University Press, 2011) 10-21.

[2]   See Stephen L Carter, *The Culture of Disbelief: How American Law and Politics Trivialise Religious Devotion* (Anchor Books, 1993) 54–55; Michael W McConnell, 'Religious Freedom at Crossroads' (1992) 59 *University of Chicago Law Review* 115, 122–25.

Proponents of the religiously neutral public square appear to believe that it is possible to detach citizens from their personal convictions, that their reasoning is capable of being exercised in a religiously neutral manner.[3] For them religious beliefs must be kept to one's self and their devotions done in private so as not to disturb the public square. Religion's communal aspects must also be kept private or within the four walls of a church.[4]

However, this chapter endeavours to demonstrate how it is deeply erroneous, although increasingly popular, to assert that the anti-establishment clauses in the United States ('US') and Australian Constitutions were aimed at ensuring a rigid separation between church and state. The reality is that both the context behind the drafting of the clauses, and the religious roots of the concept of separation of church and state, combine to negate the proposition that either the Australian or American Constitutions were intended to do any such thing.

Religious Roots of the Modern Concept of Church-State Separation

The idea of separation between church and state has its own historical roots in traditional Christian philosophy. There was no significant distinction between sacred and secular in pre-Christian Western societies. Ancient Greek and Roman societies, clearly, were not secular, but were deeply religious.

In Ancient Rome, the worship of the state in the person of the divine Emperor was the ideology that unified the Roman Empire. Roman law, and the resulting persecution of religious dissidents, corroborates that the only religions permitted in Rome were those licensed and approved by the state. As the law from the Twelve Tables (5th century BC) determined, 'Let no one have gods on his own, neither new ones nor strange ones, but only those instituted by the State.' Later, writes David Daintree,

> … it was typical of the ambitious politician to claim some kind of divine ancestry: Julius Caesar, for example, relied on a claim to be descended from the goddess Venus, and following the overthrow of the Republic, the practice arose quite quickly of pretending (and no doubt in many cases actually believing) that deceased emperors had been deified and

---

3   Carter, above n 2, 56.
4   Or any other paradigmatically religious institution (e.g., monastery, synagogue, or mosque).

assumed into the pantheon of heaven.[5]

Thus a form of "civil religion" began to emerge that was linked with the worship of the emperor as an expression of the allegiance to the Roman state. During that time, Alister M McGrath explains,

> A dead emperor who was held worthy of the honor could be voted a state divinity (Latin: divus), and be incorporated into the Roman pantheon. Refusal to take part in this imperial cult was regarded as an act of treason … This is probably understood as a highly elevated view of the Roman emperor, which resulted from the remarkable achievements of Augustus. It was no longer possible to regard Augustus simply as an outstanding ruler; he was widely regarded as a *divus*, being invested with some form of supernatural or transcendent significance. It was not regarded as necessary for imperial figures to be dead before they were accorded some form of divine status; there is ample evidence to indicate that at least some members of the imperial family (such as Julius Caesar) were treated as divine during their lifetimes.[6]

As for ancient Greece the polis was a church-state and there was no such a thing as the separation between church and state. Statecraft was soul-craft and this is precisely why the philosopher Socrates ended up being executed by his fellow Athenian citizens. According to the public indictment by his three accusers, Socrates 'was guilty of not believing in the gods that the city believed in, and that he brought into the city other new divinities. Further, he is guilty of corrupting the young'.[7] In his 2012 book, *In Defence of Freedom Speech*, Chris Berg notes that religion and politics were inseparable in ancient Greece.[8] As Berg points out,

> Athens was not just a city of men but a city of gods and men. And the 'gods' that Socrates brought into the city, as per the indictment, existed outside the democratic polity. There was nothing special about introducing gods into Athens, but Socrates' gods were personal gods, not collective gods. They were a power outside the regulatory control of the [state].[9]

Others suffered similar fates that were reserved to those who defied the

---

5   David Daintree, *Soul of the West: Christianity and The Great Tradition* (Connor Court, 2015) 15.

6   Alister E McGrath, *Christian History: An Introduction* (Willey-Blackwell, 2013) 17-19.

7   Diogenes Laertius, cited in Arlene W Saxonhouse, *Free Speech and Democracy in Ancient Athens* (Cambridge University Press, 2006) 130.

8   Chris Berg, *In Defence of Free Speech: From Ancient Greece to Andrew Bolt* (Institute of Public Affairs, 2012) 11.

9   Ibid.

gods of the Greek or Roman states, which the respective definitions of law confirmed. Religious language and terminology were deeply infused in these definitions.[10] An example of this infusion is the definition of natural law by the celebrated Roman jurist, Cicero: 'To curtail this law is unholy, to amend it illicit, to repeal it impossible; ... and God, its designer, expounder and enactor, will be as it were the sole and universal ruler and governor of all things.'[11] In his seminal book, *The Ancient City* (1866), French historian Fustel de Coulanges (1830–1889) commented:

> It is a singular error to believe that in the ancient cities men enjoyed [religious] liberty. They had not even the idea of it. They did not believe that there could exist any right as against the city and its gods ... The ancients, particularly the Greeks, always exaggerated the importance, and above all, the rights of society [at the expense of the individual]; this was largely due, doubtless, to the sacred and religious character [with] which society was clothed in the beginning.[12]

Whereas the idea of a "secular state" was unknown to the people of ancient civilizations, there is substantial evidence tracing the concept of church-state separation directly to the Bible. Indeed, the concept can be traced not just to Scripture but also to the teachings of Jesus Christ more directly. In Matthew 22:21, Christ declares that citizens must 'render unto Caesar the things that are Caesar's, and to God the things that are God's.' Because some things are due to God alone, one must conclude that the state's claim upon human existence is limited.[13] This naturally implies a separation of power between the spiritual role of the church and the temporal role of the state.

These teachings of Christ are deeply revolutionary and they still speak to us today. They are the original roots of religious freedom in all our modern western societies. As above mentioned, the Greeks and Romans knew absolutely nothing about the separation of religion and state. Religion served for them mainly as an accessory of statecraft. And yet, the advent of Christianity changed everything because Christ did not equate the "Kingdom of God" with any specific form of government, which makes it more possible

---

10   Marcus Tulius Cicero, *De Republica*, II. 22.23

11   Ibid.

12   Fustel de Colanges, *The Ancient City: A Study of the Religion, Laws and Institutions of Greece and Rome* (Dover Publications, 2006) 223.

13   Harold O J Brown, 'The Christian American Position', in Gary Scott Smith (ed), *God and Politics: Four Views on the Reformation of Civil Government* (Presbyterian and Reformed Publishing Co, 1989) 146.

to establish a jurisdictional separation of church and state. Further, Christianity approaches human redemption and virtue ultimately as the products of God's supernatural activity. As such, the state can be transformed into an administrator of justice under God's law, and people are to render to Caesar only those things that are Caesar's and to God what is God's.[14]

The advent of Christianity set new forces into motion that freed religious energies from a preoccupation with parochial loyalties. Indeed, early Christians challenged the state cult of imperial Rome by refusing obeisance to Caesar as their lord or master. They sought 'immunity from the religious laws and had to endure periods of official persecution while defending their distinct identity and way of life.'[15] Of course, Jesus's dictum that what belongs to God should not be given to Caesar comes here as an important constraint to tyranny. His words communicated a powerful message that political power has to be limited so that 'Caesar could not demand worship that belonged to God.'[16] And since Rome rejected Christ's challenge to its claim to ultimate power, it retaliated by persecuting Christians. As Dinesh D'Souza points out:

> For the ancient Greeks and Romans, the gods a man should worship were the gods of the state. Each community had its own deities—it was a polytheistic age—and patriotism demanded that a good Athenian make sacrifices to the Athenian gods and a good Roman pay homage to the gods of Rome. The Christians, Celsus fumed, refused to worship the Roman gods. They did not acknowledge the Roman emperor as a god, even though Caesar had been elevated by the Roman Senate to divine status. Instead the Christians insisted on worshiping an alien god, putting their allegiance to him above their allegiance to the state.[17]

Although Christ was, perhaps, the first person ever to articulate the principle of separating religion and government, there was a certain division of jurisdictional functions between civil and ecclesiastical powers in Ancient Israel. The Jewish king had authority to enact civil laws, but no authority was given to him to legislate on religious matters. Not only was he prohibited from creating canon law, but the high priest was obliged by the law to remind

---

14   Gary Amos, 'The Philosophical and Biblical Perspectives that Shaped the Declaration of Independence', in H W House (ed), *The Christian and American Law: Christianity's Impact on America's Founding Documents and Future Direction* (Kregel Publications, 1998) 56.

15   Steven Alan Samson, 'Faustian Bargains: Entanglements Between Church and State in America' (2011) 2 *The Western Australian Jurist* 61, 88-9.

16   Vishal Mangalwadi, *The Book that Made Your World: How the Bible Created the Soul of Western Civilization* (Thomas Nelson, 2011) 342.

17   Dinesh D'Souza, *What's so Great About Christianity* (Regnery, 2007) 46.

the monarch of his constitutional duties under Mosaic Law. This contributed to a principle of constitutional governance based on the division of powers. 'By appointing Saul as king, the Israelites established political authority independent of religious authority, by regulations codified by Moses.'[18] Max Dimont comments on this important aspect of the legal code of the Old Testament:

> The Mosaic Code laid down the first principles for a separation of church and state, a concept not encountered again in world history until three thousand years later, during the Enlightenment in the eighteenth century of our era. In the Mosaic Code, the civil authority was independent of the priesthood. Though it is true that the priesthood had the right to settle cases not specifically covered by Mosaic law (Deuteronomy 17:8-12), that did not place it above the civil government. The priesthood was charged with the responsibility of keeping this government within the framework of the Mosaic law ... Moses also laid the foundation for another separation, which has since become indispensable to any democracy. He created an independent judiciary.[19]

At least from the time of Moses down to the Babylonian captivity, most of the kings of Israel came from one particular tribe (Judah), whereas normally the priests came from another tribe (Levi). This established a clear division of powers, although both political and ecclesiastical authorities were ultimately subject to the Mosaic Law. Of course, abuses occurred from the very beginning and the first appointed king was also the first to break jurisdictional boundaries, which had been created in order to constitutionally protect the people of Israel from tyranny. Accordingly, the Old Testament (1 Samuel 13) reports the episode when King Saul grew impatient as he had to wait for the prophet Samuel. He decided to ignore the prophet's presence and offer religious sacrifices personally. The king was then accused of overstepping his proper authority by attempting to fulfil a constitutional role exclusively designated for the religious leader. In addition, 1 Chronicles 26:20 explains that the Levites were the only ones in charge of the temple and the gifts devoted to God. By law, the religious activities limited their sphere of activity and they were not directly responsible for the affairs of the state. This is not to say that there were no competing claims to the king's priesthood. In Psalm 110, which is a 'Coronation Psalm', the king is described 'as a priest forever according to the supreme order of Melchizedek.'

---

[18] Mangalwadi, above n 16, 341.
[19] Max I Dimont, *Jews, God and History* (Signet, 2nd ed, 2004) 85-6.

Be that as it may, relying on the teachings of Christ in the 11th century the church started to demand further protections against the 'secular control'. Initiated by Pope Gregory VII in 1075, such a "Papal Revolution" records the important episode *gave birth to the modern Western concept of church-state separation*, which demanded the end of all government interference over the church's doctrinal and ecclesiastic affairs. According to the celebrated Harvard professor of legal history, Harold Berman, the "Papal Revolution" laid down 'the foundation for the subsequent emergence of the modern secular state by withdrawing from emperors and kings the spiritual competence which they had previously exercised.'[20]

Inspired by these scriptural lessons the American Founders envisaged the institutional separation between church and state in the US.[21] The US Constitution, unlike any other early document in American legal history, lacks overtly religious content but its protection of the church from government intervention was truly a revolutionary idea. As Steve Samson points out:

> [F]rom the earliest days of the church, monarchs had often claimed authoritative powers in matters of church doctrine and government. The authority of the Roman emperor as the supreme pontiff over the state religion was maintained to some degree even as the empire became nominally Christian, though it was expressly repudiated by the Christian emperor, Gratian.'[22]

Of course, the first American colonists were Christian pilgrims who had been harshly persecuted on account of their religious convictions. In the hopes of freely practising their religious faith, they fled England and persecution from the established Church. It is therefore unsurprising that those American Founders dreaded the influence of ecclesiastical powers in political matters; a fear which their ancestors brought with them from the parent country. To ensure that the plight of their ancestors would be fully heard, the *First Amendment* was included and it reads: 'Congress shall make no law respecting an establishment of religion, or prohibiting the free exercise thereof [...]'.

The *First Amendment* is the most well-known provision in the American *Bill of Rights*. It combines five civil liberties condensed in the various proposals from the state ratifying conventions. These liberties are designed to limit

---

[20]   Harold J Berman, *Law and Revolution: The Formation of the Western Legal Tradition* (Harvard University Press, 1983) 115.
[21]   Amos, above n 14, 56.
[22]   Samson, above n 15, 69.

the power of the federal parliament. The first liberty to be protected in this amendment received a special attention: 'Congress shall make no law respecting an establishment of religion, or prohibiting the free exercise thereof'. As can be seen, the provision limits only the federal legislature (i.e. Congress) so that the individual States are fully exempt and so they could, if their individual legislatures so desired, create laws establishing an official church. As Robert A Destro points out,

> The First Amendment was necessary to assure the critics of the new Constitution that Congress would not use its express or implied powers (such as commerce, taxation or spending) to make laws infringing State or individual prerogatives regarding religion. Necessarily included in this prohibition were federal attempts to establish a national religion or dis-establish the established religions of the States which had them, and to enact or enforce laws which sought to burden religious belief or practice.[23]

The American Founders created a political system not derived from any statement of religious doctrine, although it was predominantly Christian in its legal assumptions, moral values, and religious sympathies. They certainly did not intend to suppress religious argument from political debates. On the contrary, the vast majority of them strongly believed in the intrinsic connection between politics and faith, since this was considered a particularly important thing for both public morality and good governance. 'Our Constitution was made only for a moral and religious people. It is wholly inadequate to the government of any other', said John Adams in 1798.[24] Although the American *Constitution* does not make an explicit tribute to God, in his *The American Commonwealth* James Bryce commented that 'Christianity [was] in fact understood to be, though not the legally established religion, yet the national religion.'[25]

---

[23] Robert A Destro, 'The Structure of the Religious Liberty Guarantee' (1995) 11 *Journal of Law & Religion* 371. Professor Destro also explains (at 359):
> Though there was some dispute among the framers, the States, and the antifederalists concerning the extent to which the enumerated powers of the federal government could be utilized to set national policy respecting establishments of religion and religious liberty, there was little dispute among them about the core of the matter: the powers granted the federal government did not include a specific supervisory jurisdiction over either religious matters generally, or the relationship of religion and religious institutions to the political communities of the Nation.

[24] BeliefNet, *Message from John Adams to the Officers of the First Brigade of the Third Division of the Militia of Massacusetts*

[25] James Bryce, *The American Commonwealth – Volume 2* [1888] (Liberty Fund, 1995) 1376.

In this sense, the first federal legislature which enacted the *First Amendment* took special care to re-enact the Northwest Ordinance of 1787, permitting the federal government to promote religious education in all public schools in the Northwest Territory: 'Religion, morality and knowledge, being necessary to good government and the happiness of mankind ... shall be forever encouraged.'[26] Because public morality and the promotion of religion were seen as going hand in hand, the first House of Representatives, on the next day the *First Amendment* was passed, on 24 September 1787, it passed also (by a substantial two-to-one majority) a resolution calling for a National Day of Prayer and Thanksgiving.

Above all, none of the American Founders advocated for anything like a rigid wall of separation between church and state. On the contrary, they thought that States and localities should encourage religion. They agreed also that the new nation should not have an established federal church, but even at the federal level the Founders supported such things as the hiring of congressional and military chaplains, and requesting President Washington to issue a Thanksgiving Proclamation. In no way does the amendment inhibit the power of the States to decide on religious matters. What is more, the individual American States would remain free to decide, and most actually had either an established church or a strict religious test for office holders.[27] As noted by Stephen Carter,

> [t]he legislative history leaves little doubt that the Clause, in all of its incarnations, was designed by the Founders to embody 'the jurisdictional concern of federalism' – to ensure that 'civil authority in religious affairs resided with the states, not the national government' ... Perhaps the best evidence of this original understanding is the fact that the established churches lingered on in the New England states long after the First Amendment was adopted.[28]

James Madison's original draft of what is now the Establishment Clause, introduced in the House of Representatives on 7 June 1789, reads: 'nor shall any national religion be established'. The final Senate version, prior to conference with the House, reads: 'Congress shall make no law establishing articles of faith

---

[26]   See John Baker, 'Establishment of Religion', in Edwin Mase III et al (eds), *The Heritage Guide to the Constitution* (Regnery, 2005) 302.

[27]   Brion McClanahan, *The Founding Fathers' Guide to the Constitution* (Regnery Publishing, 2012) 184.

[28]   Carter, above n 2, 298.

or a mode of worship'.[29] And yet, the Christian deity was fully acknowledged in all the state constitutions by the time of constitutional ratification. The establishment clause meant only to affect the federal legislature, 'placing no inhibition on the States, and leaving the whole subject to their uncontrolled discretion, though subject to the general guarantees against oppression.'[30] That so being, after declaring that 'all men are equally entitled to the free exercise of religion, according to the dictates of conscience', Article 16 of *Virginia Declaration of Rights* of 1776 stated: 'It is the mutual duty of all to practice Christian forbearance, love, and charity towards each other.' As James Bryce explained:

> The early constitutions of several states recognized what was virtually a state church, requiring each locality to provide for and support the public worship of God. It was not till 1818 that Connecticut in adopting her new constitution placed all religious bodies on a level, and left the maintenance of churches to the voluntary action of the faithful. In Massachusetts a tax for the support of the Congregationalist churches was imposed on all citizens not belonging to some other incorporated religious body until 1811, and religious equality was first fully recognized by a constitutional amendment of 1833. In Virginia, North and South Carolina, and Maryland, Protestant Episcopacy was the established form of religion till the Revolution, when ... because the Anglican clergy were prone to Toryism (as attachment to the British connection was called) ... all religious distinctions were abolished and special ecclesiastical privileges withdrawn. [31]

The leaders of the American Revolution did not work to eliminate Christian influences on the nation. They certainly made no attempt to change the state constitutions that recognised the supremacy of God's law. Curiously, even after the Revolution, the American States of New Hampshire, Massachusetts, Connecticut, South Carolina, and Maryland continued to have tax-supported established churches.[32] Most of these state constitutions adopted a great degree of religious freedom although only a few Americans would conceive a civil order not explicitly acknowledging the supremacy of God's law.[33] Even

---

[29] All the drafts of the Clause appear as Appendix A in Edwin S Gaustad, *Faith of Our Fathers: Religion and the New Nation* (Harper & Row, 1987) 157-58.

[30] Ibid, 1370.

[31] Ibid, 1372.

[32] Forrest McDonald, *Novus Ordo Seculorum: The Intellectual Origins of the Constitution* (University Press of Kansas, 1985) 43.

[33] Cobb, above n.283, pp.409-507.

Pennsylvania, which had been one of the more liberal colonies in matters of religion, 'required that officeholders take an oath declaring the belief in the divine inspiration of the whole of the Bible'.[34]

As can be seen, the *First Amendment* in no way denies the importance of religion in society. In most of American history, the main purpose of the Establishment Clause has been to protect religious freedom against a secular government.[35] In this context of religious pluralism and tolerance, such amendment was crafted to permit maximum freedom of religion. Since this is actually an anti-establishment clause, it 'does not mean that people whose motivations are religious are banned from trying to influence government, nor that the government is banned from listening to them.'[36] The anti-establishment clause is therefore self-consciously theistic in its origin, a fact that the celebrated Harvard professor of Political Theory, Samuel Huntington, succinctly explained:

> At the end of the eighteenth century, religious establishments existed throughout European countries and in several American states. State control of the church was a key element of state power, and the established church, in turn, provided legitimacy to the state. The framers of the American Constitution prohibited an establishment of a national church in order to limit the power of government and to protect and strengthen religion. The 'separation of church and state' is the corollary to the identity of religion and society.[37]

As can be seen, the original intention behind the amendment is not to establish freedom *from* religion, but to create freedom *for* religion. It explicitly prohibits a federal church to be established and it is primarily designed to secure religious liberty, or what Thomas Jefferson famously called 'the most inalienable and sacred of all human rights.'[38] Hence, when Roger Williams wrote about the 'wall of separation between the garden of the Church and the wilderness of the world', he was simply expressing 'an ideal of toleration and religious plurality' that is reflected in 'the ability of the believer to worship without the interference of the state.'[39] This should operate as a constitutional

---

[34] McDonald, above n 32, 42.

[35] Carter, above n 2, 108.

[36] Ibid, 106.

[37] Samuel Huntington, *Who are We? America's Great Debate* (Free Press, 2005) 85.

[38] Thomas Jefferson, 'Freedom of Religion at the University of Virginia', in Saul K Padover (ed), *The Complete Jefferson* (Duell, Sloan & Pierce, 1943) 958.

[39] Carter, above n 2, 116

limitation on the legislative branch of federal government. In *The General Principles of Constitutional Law*, a work completed in March 1880 by the celebrated Thomas Cooley, when he was the Law Dean at Michigan University (later he became Justice of the Supreme Court of Michigan), the following comments are made:

> By establishment of religion it was never intended … that the government should be prohibited from recognizing religion, or that religious worship should never be provided for in cases where a proper recognition of Divine Providence in the working of government might seem to require it, and where it might be done without drawing any invidious distinctions between different religious beliefs, organizations, or sects. The Christian religion was always recognized in the administration of the common law; and so far as that law continues to be the law of the land, the fundamental principles of that religion must continue to be recognized in the same cases and to the same extent as formerly.[40]

Above all, the American Establishment Clause should be interpreted against this historical background. It in no way implies that the US should be governed by a 'secular government' devoid of any religious influence.[41] Ever since 1947, however, when the Supreme Court decided the case of *Everson v Board of Education*, a doctrine of rigid separation of state and church has pushed religious freedom and observance out of public schools and public affairs generally. This long series of controversial decisions, beginning in the 1950s – against prayer in public schools, Bible reading, quotation of certain religious passages from public documents, display of the Decalogue on school walls – have exerted a chilling effect on religious freedom in the United States.[42]

These judicial rulings violate the original meaning of the *Amendment*. We may observe in passing that this abuse of judicial process is not uncommon amongst radical organisations that oppose the presence of religious values or symbols in the public sphere. As it has been stated, 'when they cannot stop

---

[40]   Thomas M Cooley, *Principles of Constitutional Law* (Little Brown & Co, 1898) 224.

[41]   Ibid.

[42]   Interestingly enough, as Russell Kirk reminds,
Formal schooling was commenced by churches. Ultimate questions cannot be answered except by religious doctrines – unless we are prepared to embrace the dialectical materialism of the Marxists. Congress has chaplains and support religious services. Every president of the United States has professed his belief in divine wisdom and goodness. Yet certain judges deny the right of young Americans to pray in the public schools – even as an act of 'commencement' concluding their twelve or thirteen years of school. (Russell Kirk, *Rights and Duties: Reflections on our Conservative Revolution* (Spence Publishing Company, 1997) 159).

a bill from being passed by the Legislature and approved by the Executive, or when they find in the statutes laws they do not like, the next recourse is usually the courts.'[43] By contrast, when Founders like Thomas Jefferson, John Marshall and Patrick Henry studied law, 'common-law study was in its nature historical and theoretical. Familiarity with the history of England was essential to it.'[44] As noted by Michael P Schutt,

> The study of law was reserved for the person of virtue and character because the law was a subject of dignity and import. Moral reality – distinguishing between right and wrong, conserving natural rights and duties – is central to its very nature. That is why the student was expected to study Scripture, philosophy, writings on human nature, rhetoric, and ethics.[45]

Many of today's American judges and politicians maintain an entirely different meaning of the first clause of the *First Amendment*. They persist in fancying that somehow or another the US *Constitution* speaks of a 'wall of separation' between church and state. But, of course, no such phrase appears in any American legal document. Those words concerning a hypothetical 'wall' of separation that has provoked much controversy, occur merely in a letter written in 1802 by Thomas Jefferson, addressed to an assembly of Baptists. And yet, when American judges have turned to the Founding Era to shine light on the meaning of the religion clauses, they have relied on an ahistorical approach based on the personal views of Jefferson. Such an approach is unreliable for numerous reasons, primarily because Jefferson was not involved in the draft (and ratification) of the *First Amendment*. Further, the original understanding of 'church-state separation' was certainly intended to create freedom *for* religion and be against undue governmental intervention.

Church-State Separation in Australia

Although Christianity played a vital role in originally shaping Australian society, this does not mean that people from other religions were not welcomed, nor does it mean that there was any obligation for those living in the land to necessarily belong to the Christian religion, or indeed any religion. The

---

[43]   Dayton McKean, 'State, Church, and Lobby', in James Ward Smith and A Leland Jamison (eds), *Religious Perspectives in American Culture* (Princeton University Press, 1961) 129.

[44]   Kevin R C Gutzman, *The Politically Incorrect Guide to the Constitution* (Regnery Publishing, 2007) 173.

[45]   Michael P Schutt, *Redeeming Law: Christian Calling and the Legal Profession* (Il: IVP Academic, 2007) 26.

remarkable climate of religious tolerance and open-mindedness was stressed in the very first sermon preached on Australian soil on Sunday, February 3, 1788. On that special occasion, the Rev Richard Johnson began his sermon with the following remarks:

> I do not address you as Churchmen or Dissenters, Roman Catholics or Protestants, as Jews or Gentiles ... But I speak to you as mortals and yet immortal ... The Gospel ... proposes a free and gracious pardon to the guilty, cleansing to the polluted, healing to the sick, happiness to the miserable and even life for the dead.

One of the fundamental issues facing Australians during the early period of the nation's existence was not that of securing the removal of religion from public life, but rather that of managing religious pluralism.[46] As noted by Greg Melleuish and Stephen Chavura, a primary concern 'was to ensure that religious difference did not turn into religious conflict, thereby creating a social order riven by violent ... activities'.[47] They dismiss the claim that Australia is somehow an uniquely secular nation as an 'illusion, brought on by an inadequate understanding of what religion, and the religious condition, mean, together with a dash of wishful thinking'.[48] Indeed, as Alex Deagon points out,

> Many of the framers did not desire a secular society which rejected the public display and discourse of religion. The historical and culture context of the development of s 116 was a general endorsement of religion and a climate of tolerance based on a concern for the advancement of religion.[49]

Historians highlight the fact that the *Australian Constitution* originated at the Conventions in the 1890s, which featured strong competition between different interests, including clashes 'between free-traders and protectionists, nationalists and imperialists, and big and small colonies'.[50] These differences

---

[46] Peter Kurti, Religion and the New Sectarianism: Countering the Call for Silence', in James Allan (ed), *Making Australia Right: Where to from Here?* (Connor Court Publishing, 2016), 171.

[47] Greg Melleuish and Stephen Chavura, 'Utilitarianism contra Sectarianism', in William Coleman (ed), *Only in Australia: The History, Politics, and Economics of Australian Exceptionalism* (Oxford University Press) 65.

[48] Ibid 63.

[49] Alex Deagon, 'Secularism as a Religion: Questioning the Future of the 'Secular' State' (2017) 8 *The Western Australian Jurist* 31, 59.

[50] John McMillan, Gareth Evans and Haddon Story, *Australia's Constitution: Time for Change?* (George Allan & Unwin, 1983) 40.

of perspective on nation-building issues such as roads, rivers, railways, and revenue distribution fostered sharp disputes during the proceedings. An overriding concern among the constitutional framers was to implement a system to prevent the new Commonwealth government from monopolizing economic life.[51] Consequently, the framers included in the *Constitution* the principle that:

> Government, and particularly the national government, should be modest and unobtrusive ... The prevailing view of delegates to the 1890s Conventions was that governments existed essentially to hold the ring for a laissez-faire economy: their job was to provide a stable and peaceful environment for the operation of free market forces.[52]

This anti-monopolistic attitude also guided the Australian Founders as they drafted s 116, the part of the *Constitution* that deals with religious life. Remember that the *Australian Constitution* originated in a social environment with different branches of the Christian church competing strongly for cultural influence. It is likely that a majority of the framers maintained at least a formal affiliation with major Protestant groups, although the views of Roman Catholics and Jews were also included.[53] It is against this historical background that s 116 must be interpreted. This section, which the American *First Amendment* obviously inspired, provides that:

> The Commonwealth shall not make any law for establishing any religion, or for imposing any religious observance, or for prohibiting the free exercise of any religion, and no religious test shall be required as qualification for any office or public trust under the Commonwealth.[54]

Recognising the potential for religious bodies to exploit the federal system, s 116 then guards against a situation in which members of one denomination might dominate Federal Parliament, thus introducing legislation to establish their own body as the National Church, or introducing religious tests to favour admission of individuals from their own body to the Commonwealth bureaucracy. And yet, the provision does not amount to a complete rejection of the people's religious sentiments; quite the contrary. After all, the *Australian Constitution* itself openly recognises the legitimacy of religion in the public square when, in its Preamble, it declares that the Australian people are 'humbly

---

[51]   Ibid 47.

[52]   Ibid.

[53]   See Geoffrey Blainey, *A Shorter History of Australia* (Random House, 1994) Chapter 11.

[54]   *Constitution of the Commonwealth of Australia 1900* (Cth) s 116.

relying on the blessings of Almighty God'.

It is profoundly erroneous, although increasingly popular, to assert that the Establishment Clause in the *Australian Constitution* was aimed at enshrining secularism. Far from seeking to banish religion from government and society, the Australian Founders intended a laissez-faire environment that ensured no particular religious body would enjoy unfair advantage on account of a federal endorsement. An accompanying benefit is that s 116 also protects religious bodies in Australia against unwanted intrusions of the Commonwealth government. Thus s 116 limits only the federal tier of government to legislate with respect to religion. The High Court in the *Jehovah's Witnesses Case* in 1943 expressed this quite clearly when Chief Justice Latham declared that '[t]he prohibition in s 116 operates not only to protect the freedom of religion, but also to protect the right of a man to have no religion. No *federal law* can impose any religious observance' (emphasis added).[55] An accompanying benefit is therefore that s 116 protects religious bodies against unwanted intrusions of the federal government. As Nicholas Aroney points out:

> [T]he High Court has very explicitly affirmed that the non-establishment clause does not prohibit governmental assistance being given to religious bodies, and it certainly has never held that s 116 somehow prohibits the enactment of federal laws or the execution of government policies that are supported, either in whole or in part, on the basis of religious considerations or reasons ... In the United States, the equivalent provision contained in the First Amendment has been interpreted, at times, to prohibit virtually all forms of state assistance; but in Australia, state aid to religious schools has been upheld. To suggest that the non-establishment principle makes religious considerations entirely irrelevant to federal law-making and policy-formation is simply beyond the pale—particularly in Australia, but even in the United States.[56]

In other words, the main object of this constitutional guarantee is to preserve religious freedom from federal encroachment, which is entirely different, of course, from having a government expressly prohibiting the promotion of religious values and principles. The provision clearly does not inhibit the government from identifying itself with the religious impulse as such or from authorizing religious practices where all could agree on their desirability. Dr Michael Hogan, Research Associate in Government and

---

[55] *Adelaide Company of Jehovah's Witnesses v Commonwealth* (1943) 67 CLR 116, 123.

[56] Nicholas Aroney, "The Constitutional (in)Validity of Religious Vilification Laws: Implications for their Interpretation" (2006) 34 *Federal Law Review* 287, 301-302.

International Relations at Sydney University, put it this way:

> Australia does not have a legally entrenched principle, or even a vague set of conventions, of the separation of church and state. From the appointment of Rev. Samuel Marsden as one of the first magistrates in colonial New South Wales, to the adoption of explicit policies of state aid for denominational schools during the 1960s, to the two examples mentioned above, Australia has had a very consistent tradition of cooperation between church and state. 'Separation of church and state', along with 'the separation of powers' or 'pleading the Fifth', are phrases that we have learned from the U.S., and which merely serve to confuse once they are taken out of the context of the American Constitution.[57]

To fall afoul of s 116, the Commonwealth Parliament would have to go so far as to establish an official denomination, or to value one denomination over the others. In other words, what the guarantee means is that this particular Parliament is not authorised to set up a state religion on the lines of the Church of England. This is after all an anti-establishment clause. Besides, the real purpose of this provision is to effectively limit the role of the federal government (thus affirming the legislative rights of the states), and not to limit the role of the church or any other religious grouping. As Nicholas Tonti-Filippini pointed out:

> Having come from a society where the king nationalised religion and made the church a department of state under parliamentary control, persecuting and marginalising those whose religious opinions differed from those of the state, it is not surprising that the founders wanted a constitution which would allow maximum freedom of religion. Where religion is concerned, it is the church that needs protection from the hubris of politicians and not vice versa. The church did not impose religion upon England. England imposed its views on the church ... The Australian Constitution does not exclude religious arguments, religious people, or the Churches from public debate. The opposite is true. People are not to have their religious freedom infringed by the state and are to be permitted to express their religious opinions in the public square.[58]

Unfortunately, s 116 of the *Australian Constitution* is generally interpreted

---

[57]   Cited in Nicholas Tonti-Filippini, 'Religion in a Secular Society' (2008) 52(9) *Quadrant Magazine* 83-84. For a comparative analysis of church and state relations in Australia and the United States, see: Gabriël A Moens, 'Church and State Relations in Australia and the United States' (1996) 4 *Brigham Young University Law Review* 787-813. See also, Gabriël A Moens, 'The Action-Belief Dichotomy and Freedom of Religion' (1989) (12) *Sydney Law Review* 195-217.

[58]   Tonti-Filippini, above n 57, 83.

by those who deny and denounce the Judeo-Christian roots of the Australian law as evidence that the document should be regarded as an entirely secular document. As seen above, nothing could be further from the truth. In reality, the framers prohibited the establishment of a national church because they wished to limit the power of central government so as to protect and strengthen religion. The enduring role of religion in our laws and customs may be regarded by some as a mere relic of the past, and soon to be overtaken by the rise of secularism and 'social progress', but Australia's Christian heritage is irrefutable. Those who wish to advance 'secularism' may opt for being indifferent to the enduring role of religion in our legal system, but they have no right to rewrite history in order to advance their arguments.

Judicial Interpretation of the Australian Establishment Clause

It is appropriate now to discuss the approach taken by the High Court when interpreting the Establishment Clause. In 1981, the High Court, in the *DOGS* case, offered its first significant decision regarding the interpretation of the Establishment Clause.[59] The case involved the validity of federal financial support for religious schools by means of a series of grants to the States. Most of the private schools benefiting from this aid were religiously affiliated schools, and the Australian Council for the Defence of Government Schools ('DOGS') challenged the grants, arguing that government funding of church schools amounted to an 'establishment' of religion.

The argument was rejected in a six-to-one decision. First, the majority emphasized the differences between the US and Australian establishment clauses and refused to follow the lead of the US courts. The majority then held that s 116 does not prohibit federal laws from assisting the practice of religion, or from providing financial support to religious schools on a non-discriminatory basis. The Court made it clear that the federal government can indirectly give benefits to religion as long as the purpose is not to establish an official state church. To fall afoul of s 116, the Court said the Commonwealth would have to go so far as to effectively establish an official church or to value one particular Christian denomination over all the others.

In his majority ruling, Justice Wilson contended that a 'narrow notion of establishment' is necessary not only to preserve traditional practices and

---

[59] *A-G (Vic) (ex rel Black) v. Commonwealth* (1981) 146 CLR 559 ('*DOGS Case*').

legal provisions, but also to make sense of other legal provisions that are contained in s 116.[60] As he put it, if the Establishment Clause were to be read so broadly as to require 'strict separation' between church and state, then it is hard to see what room would be left for the operation of traditional practices in the country such as the coronation oath and the opening prayers at several of our nation's State and Federal Parliaments, not to mention the explicit acknowledgment of 'Almighty God' in the Preamble of the *Constitution*.

Justice Mason took a similar view, arguing that establishment required only 'the concession to one church of favours, titles and advantages [that] must be of so special a kind that it enables us to say that by virtue of the concession the religion has become established as a national institution, as, for example, by becoming the official religion of the State'.[61] Justice Stephen concurred with him, noticing that the precise language of s 116 precludes a wide interpretation of the word 'establish'. Justice Stephen said:

> The very form of s 116, consisting of four distinct and express restrictions upon legislative power … cannot readily be viewed as the repository of some broad statement of principle concerning the separation of church and state … On the contrary by fixing upon four specific restrictions of legislative power, the form of the section gives no encouragement to the undertaking of any such distillation.[62]

Justice Gibbs concurred with the majority and explained that the Establishment Clause simply requires the Commonwealth to 'not make any law for conferring on a particular religion or religious body the position of a state (or national) religion or church'.[63] According to Gibbs, 'the natural meaning of the phrase *establish any religion* is, as it was in 1900, to constitute a particular religion or religious body as a state religion or state church'.[64] Chief-Justice Barwick agreed that the word *establishment* 'involves the identification of the religion with the civil authority so as to involve the citizens in a duty to maintain it and the obligation of, in this case, the Commonwealth to patronise, protect, and promote the established religion'.[65] Thus Barwick stated that 'establishing religion involves its adoption as an institution of the Commonwealth, part of

---

[60]   Ibid, 653 (Wilson J).
[61]   Ibid 612 (Mason J).
[62]   Ibid 609 (Stephen J).
[63]   Ibid 604 (Gibbs J).
[64]   Ibid 597 (Gibbs J).
[65]   Ibid 582 (Barwick CJ).

the Commonwealth 'establishment'.[66]

Justice Murphy was the only Justice to disagree in that six-to-one decision. He based his dissent on controversial US Supreme Court decisions which have required a 'wall of separation' between church and state. In particular, he explicitly referred to the opinion of US Justice Black in the first American Establishment Clause case, *Everson v. Board of Education*.[67] In that decision Black J stated: 'No tax in any amount, large or small, can be levied to support any religious activities or institutions, whatever they may be called, or whatever form they may adopt to teach or practice religion'.[68] This opinion is premised on Black's controversial view that the *First Amendment* has erected a rigid wall between church and state. 'That wall must be kept high and impregnable. We could not approve the slightest breach', he stated.[69] Relying on Black's opinion in *Everson*, Murphy claimed that s 116 should be interpreted so as to prohibit any financial assistance by the Commonwealth government to religious schools.[70]

In contrast, the majority considered that American precedent to be utterly irrelevant for Australia. Given the differences in wording between the American and Australian constitutional provisions ('Congress shall make no law respecting an establishment of religion' as against 'the Commonwealth shall not make any law for establishing any religion'), all the High Court judges apart from Justice Murphy held that only a law that is effectively *for* the establishment of a national religion is a law that violates s 116 of the *Australian Constitution*. As Chief Justice Barwick stated:

> [B]ecause the whole expression is '*for* establishing any religion', the law to satisfy the description must have that objective as its express and, as I think, single purpose. Indeed, a law establishing a religion could scarcely do so as an incident of some other and principal objective. In my opinion, a law which establishes a religion will inevitably do so expressly and directly and not, as it were, constructively.[71]

The inclusion of the preposition 'for' was done only for the sake of grammatical structure. And yet, as can be seen, such seemingly innocuous variation of the American wording has assumed substantive significance in

---

[66]   Ibid.

[67]   *Everson v. Board of Education*, 330 US 1 (1947).

[68]   Ibid 16.

[69]   Ibid 18.

[70]   *A-G (Vic) (ex rel Black) v. Commonwealth* (1981) 146 CLR 559, 565 (Murphy, J).

[71]   Ibid 559 (Barwick CJ).

Australia.[72] As noted by Tony Blackshield,

> The argument depends on a heightened lexical contrast. In the United
> States, it is said, the First Amendment's exclusion of any 'law ...
> prohibiting the free exercise' of religion extends to any law 'respecting'
> an establishment of religion casts its net even wider, to catch any law
> which might touch upon or relate to the idea of establishment in any way.
> By contrast, it is said, the Australian wording narrows the prohibition to
> laws which are *for* the establishment of religion or the impairment of
> its free exercise: that is, to laws of which that is the explicitly intended
> *purpose*. Thus, laws which might offend the American provision because
> they might tend to have the practical *effect* of establishing a *purpose*.[73]

Interestingly, a referendum held in 1988 sought to amend s 116 to make
it also applicable to the Australian States. If approved, the proposal would
have eliminated the word 'for' so as to make the Section provide in part: 'The
Commonwealth, a State or a Territory shall not establish any religion'. The
proposal also sought to extend the scope of s 116 by covering all government
acts rather than just legislation. The proposal failed to obtain popular approval.
Only 30 per cent of the Australian citizens voted in favour of the amendment,
and the proposal did not achieve a majority in any state.[74]

Overwhelmingly rejecting the changes to s 116 reflected a general
satisfaction about the existing constitutional arrangements. Also, it reflected a
community antipathy towards judicial activism that is particularly concerned
with funding for religious schools. Activist judges like Lionel Murphy argued,
in large part on the basis of controversial US case-law, that financial aid to
religious institutions was a form of establishment of religion. He even held
that non-preferential sponsoring of or aiding religion is still 'establishing'

---

[72]   Tony Blackshield, 'Religion and Australian Constitutional Law', in Peter Radan,
Denise Meyerson and Rosalind F Croucher (eds), *Law and Religion: God, the State and
the Common Law* (Routledge, 2005) 85.

[73]   Ibid 86.

[74]   'The question submitted to referendum in 1988 included a proposal to amend s
116 so that the protection it confers against Commonwealth legislation would also
avail against State and Territory legislation. Incidentally, it was also proposed that
the amended provision should eliminate the world 'for', instead providing simply
that "The Commonwealth, a State or a Territory shall not establish any religion,
impose any religious observance or prohibit the free exercise of religion ...". The
entire amendment was therefore opposed, most strenuously by representatives of
the Roman Catholic Church, on the ground that it might undermine the reasoning
in DOGS Case. The referendum failed in all States.' (Blackshield, above n 72, 102)

religion.[75] The idea was to undermine the reasoning in the *DOGS* case and to reopen the debate about government funding of religious schools. The proposal was soundly defeated in all the Australian States, perhaps because the citizens knew very well that, in the US, federal courts have dramatically restricted the State rights by regularly placing the establishment and free-exercise of religion clauses in some form of mutual tension.

The meaning and scope of church-state separation was again tested in the High Court in a challenge to the validity of the National Schools Chaplaincy Program ('NSCP').[76] In 2006 the Commonwealth created the program as a voluntary program under which schools sought financial support from the Commonwealth to establish or enhance chaplaincy services for school communities.[77] Schools choose the chaplains that best meet their needs, with a funding agreement supporting the position. The High Court, in delivering its decision in *Williams v Commonwealth* (2012),[78] did not satisfy the plaintiff's expectation that the chaplaincy program would be deemed an unconstitutional violation of church-state separation. Instead, by a six-to-one majority the High Court simply ruled that the executive power, found in s 61 of the *Constitution*[79] did not authorize federal officials to enter into funding agreements or authorize payments for it from the Consolidated Revenue Fund.[80] In sum, the Court invalidated the federal funding for all such programs without explicit statutory authorization, without recourse to any argument relying on a violation of the

---

75   *Attorney General (Vic); Ex Rel Black v Commonwealth* (1981) 146 CLR 559, 624 (Murphy
      J). 'Before being appointed to the High Court, Justice Murphy had been a minister
      under a progressive [i.e. left-wing] Labor government and was often accused by his
      enemies of political, results-oriented decision-making'. (Carolyn Evans, 'Religion as
      Politics not Law: the Religious Clauses in the Australian Constitution' (2008) 36(3)
      Religion, State and Society 294).

76   See *Williams v Commonwealth* (2012) 288 ALR 410.

77   Under NSCP, chaplains offered 'general religious and personal advice to those seeking
      it;' and would '[work] in a wider spiritual context to support students and staff of
      all religious affiliations and not [seek] to impose any religious beliefs or persuade an
      individual toward a particular set of religious beliefs.' (*Williams v Commonwealth (No
      1)* (2012) 288 ALR 410, [305] (Heydon J, citing the NSCP guidelines).

78   *Williams v Commonwealth* (2012) 288 ALR 410 ('*Williams*')

79   Section 61 reads: 'The executive power of the Commonwealth is vested in the
      Queen and is exercisable by the Governor-General as the Queen's representative,
      and extends to the execution and maintenance of this Constitution, and of the laws
      of the Commonwealth'.

80   See also the case notes: Benjamin B Saunders, 'The Commonwealth and the
      Chaplains: Executive Power after *Williams v Commonwealth*.' (2012) 23 *Public Law
      Review* 153; Amanda Sapienza, 'Using Representative Government to Bypass
      Representative Government' (2012) 23 *Public Law Review* 161.

Establishment Clause.[81]

The primary argument motivating Mr Williams's objection to the chaplaincy program – that the Commonwealth could not financially support a chaplaincy program because there was a constitutional separation of Church and State – was entirely rejected. The court, however, upheld his argument that the chaplaincy program was constitutionally invalid since it was an executive scheme undertaken by way of grants, guidelines and contracts, with the appropriation of the relevant funds by the Commonwealth Parliament being the only aspect of legislation involved.[82] And yet, the High Court had already decided in *Pape v Commissioner of Taxation* (2009) that such an appropriation is really not enough – there must be a head of Commonwealth power to support expenditure.[83] As law professor Anne Twomey explains:

> In *Williams No 1* the Court built on this finding by holding that not only must there be a head of legislative power, but in many cases there must be actual legislation to support the expenditure. The Court, in reaching this conclusion, placed reliance on the principle of federalism, the importance of parliamentary scrutiny of executive action and the fact that it is 'public money' that is being expended, so that proper scrutiny and care is important.[84]

The outcome of the case led the Commonwealth to introduce amendments to the *Financial Management and Accountability Act 1997* (Cth), giving statutory validation and authorising expenditure that fell within any of more than 400 programs described in the regulations. One such authorised program is Program 407.013 – 'National School Chaplaincy and Student Welfare Program'. In short, the Commonwealth rushed through new legislation to ensure that the chaplaincy program would continue to be implemented (together with more than 400 programs presently amounting to as much as AU$37 billion, or up to 10 per cent of all federal expenditure).

The plaintiff, Ron Williams, was not happy with the government solution.

---

[81]   In response to *Williams*, the Commonwealth enacted emergency legislation in the form of the *Financial Framework Legislation Amendment Act (No 3) 2012* (Cth), which purports to validate all such expenditures by it and which allows the NSCP to continue.

[82]   Anne Twomey, 'Williams Revisited: The Commonwealth Constrained but Chaplains Resurrected' (2014) 26 *Upholding the Australian Constitution* (Samuel Griffith Society) 1.

[83]   See *Pape v Commissioner of Taxation* (2009) 238 CLR 1, [8] and [111] (French CJ); [178]-[183] (Gummow, Crennan and Bell JJ); [320] (Hayne and Kiefel JJ) and [601]-[602] (Heydon J).

[84]   Twomey, above n 82, 2.

He challenged the constitutionality of those regulations authorised by the new legislation. He contested the government's authority to draw money from consolidated revenue funds in regard to matters that are beyond the powers of the Commonwealth.[85] Although Williams won again, the court did not address the complaint on the basis of church-state separation principles. Instead, the focus was on a federalism concern about the ability of the federal government to fund programs which do not have a clear legislative mandate to be executed. Hence, in *William No. 2* the court unanimously decided that the federal law was constitutionally invalid because no head of power can be found in order to support the chaplaincy program.[86] To continue operating in schools across the nation, the chaplaincy scheme would have to be replaced by conditional grants to the Australian States under s 96 of the *Commonwealth Constitution*, and, of course, assuming that the States accept the grants offered. As one prominent constitutional law professor put it, 'Mr Williams may have won two battles in the High Court but he appears to have lost the war'.[87]

The challenge in the second *Williams* case was not if the chaplaincy program breached the Establishment Clause.[88] This argument had failed when the chaplaincy scheme was first challenged. Rather than dealing with matters of church-state separation, *Williams No. 2* was solely related to the constitutionality of the federal government to fund programs under specific legislation.[89] This is about the constitutional validity of statutory provision that was rushed through both houses of Parliament, giving the stamp of approval to funding schemes in one piece of federal legislation.[90] In a unanimous decision, the court held that certain aspects of the legislation were constitutionally invalid. Rather than striking it down as completely invalid, the court opted for invalidating certain aspects of the funded program which were not attached to a prescribed head of Commonwealth power. In other words, the federal government could still continue sponsoring the chaplaincy program, but the money would have to be sent to the State governments in the form of a 'grants scheme', instead of having it go directly to the schools where the

---

85   See *Williams v Commonwealth (No 2)* (2014) 309 ALR 41 ('*Williams No. 2*')

86   Ibid.

87   Twomey, above n 82, 4.

88   *Williams v Commonwealth (No 2)* (2014) 309 ALR 41

89   Ibid.

90   The legislation allowed for funding of a wide range of programs that comprise up to 10 per cent of federal expenditure, including accommodation for asylum seekers offshore, the national counterterrorism committee.

program had been implemented.

Since s 116 operates only as a fetter upon the exercise of federal legislative power, it might be important to ask whether the provision applies to executive and administrative acts of the federal government.[91] Commenting on the Establishment Clause, the then Chief Justice Garfield Barwick once explained that, although the relevant provision is directed only at the legislative power of the Commonwealth, if a federal executive act comes 'within the ambit of the authority conferred by the statute, and does amount to the establishment of religion, the statute which supports it will most probably be a statute for establishing a religion and therefore be void as offending s 116'.[92] Above all, however, s 116 operates primarily as a limitation of the legislative power of the Commonwealth and the Australian States are not affected by the provision. As Professor Aroney points out:

> [N]othing in s 116 prevents a State from making a law that establishes any religion, imposes religious observance, prohibits the free exercise of religion, or imposes a religious test as qualification for the public office. Second, s 116 prohibits the 'making of laws'. Thus, the provision directly restricts the exercise of legislative power, but not executive and judicial power. The latter are only indirectly affected by virtue of the fact that s 116 limits the kinds of laws that the Parliament can enact, including laws which confer functions, powers or jurisdictions upon executive agencies and, most probably, the courts. Third, the specific prohibitions in s 116 (e.g., against establishing any religion or prohibiting the free exercise of any religion) appear to be 'purposive' in the sense that a law will only be found to contravene s 116 if it was enacted for one of these prohibited purposes. This leaves open the possibility that laws which are enacted for a constitutionally legitimate purpose (or purposes) will not be struck down, even if in practical effect they establish a religion or prohibit the free exercise thereof'.[93]

---

91   Moens, above n 57, at 787-88.

92   *Attorney-General of Victoria ex rel. Black v Commonwealth* (1981) 146 CLR 559, 551 ('*DOGS Case*'). Although this statement has been made in the context of the Establishment Clause, 'there appears no reason why his observation should not equally apply to the free exercise guarantee of s 116.' (Moens, above n 57, 788).

93   Nicholas Aroney, 'Freedom of Religion as an Associational Right' (2014) 33 (1) *University of Queensland Law Journal* 155-6.

Final Considerations

Although Christianity played a central role in the development of the Australian legal system,[94] the religious foundations of our system now appear to be increasingly doubted. As a result, some of Christianity's values and principles are suppressed and even denied as Western democracies move away from Christianity towards 'secularism.'

And yet, it is worthwhile to observe how significant Western legal-institutional concepts, including the idea of church-state separation, can be traced back to traditional Christian teachings, in particular Christ's admonition to 'render therefore unto Caesar the things which be Caesar's, and unto God the things which be God's.'[95] As the American law professor, Steven Smith, correctly reminds, '[t]he commitment to church-state separation and the derivative commitment to freedom of conscience arose in—and acquired their sense and their urgency from—a classical, Christian world view in which the spiritual and temporal were viewed as separate domains within God's overarching order'.[96]

In the prevailing modern framework, it should not be a surprise that s 116 is generally interpreted as evidence that the Australian Constitution should be regarded as an entirely secular document. However, as seen above, nothing could be further from the truth. In reality, the concept carries within it an undeniably religious background and the Australian Framers did not intend religion to be disregarded and divorced from society, let alone the law. On the contrary, they were largely protective of religion, Christianity in particular.

This religious influence is no less illustrated through the original purpose of s 116 of the *Australian Constitution*. The intention behind, and effect of, this Establishment Clause does not support a rigid church-state separation; quite the contrary. Those who wish to advance such a radical 'secularism' – or a more 'rigid' church-state separation – may opt for being dismissive of the enduring role of religion in our society and its laws, but certainly they have no right to rewrite history in order to advance their arguments.

---

[94] See, Augusto Zimmermann, 'Constituting a Christian Commonwealth: Christian Foundations of Australia's Constitutionalism' (2014) 5 *The Western Australian Jurist* 123-151.

[95] Luke 20:25 (King James Version)

[96] Steven D Smith, 'Discourse in the Dusk: The Twilight of Religious Freedom?' (2009) 122 *Harvard Law Review* 1869, 1887.

Bibliography

A-G (Vic) (ex rel Black) v. Commonwealth (1981) 146 CLR 559

Adelaide Company of Jehovah's Witnesses v Commonwealth (1943) 67 CLR 116

Amos Gary, 'The Philosophical and Biblical Perspectives that Shaped the Declaration of Independence', in H W House (ed), *The Christian and American Law: Christianity's Impact on America's Founding Documents and Future Direction* (Kregel Publications, 1998)

Aroney Nicholas, 'Freedom of Religion as an Associational Right' (2014) 33 (1) *University of Queensland Law Journal*

Baker John, 'Establishment of Religion', in Edwin Mase III et al (eds), *The Heritage Guide to the Constitution* (Regnery, 2005)

BeliefNet, *Message from John Adams to the Officers of the First Brigade of the Third Division of the Militia of Massacusetts* <http://www.beliefnet.com/resourcelib/docs/115/Message_from_John_Adams_to_the_Officers_of_the_First_Brigade_1.html>

Berg Chris, *In Defence of Free Speech: From Ancient Greece to Andrew Bolt* (Institute of Public Affairs, 2012)

Berman J Harold, *Law and Revolution: The Formation of the Western Legal Tradition* (Harvard University Press, 1983)

Blackshield Tony, 'Religion and Australian Constitutional Law', in Peter Radan, Denise Meyerson and Rosalind F Croucher (eds), *Law and Religion: God, the State and the Common Law* (Routledge, 2005)

Blainey Geoffrey, *A Shorter History of Australia* (Random House, 1994)

Brown O J Harold, 'The Christian American Position', in Gary Scott Smith (ed), *God and Politics: Four Views on the Reformation of Civil Government* (Presbyterian and Reformed Publishing Co, 1989)

Bryce James, *The American Commonwealth – Volume 2* [1888] (Liberty Fund, 1995)

Carter L Stephen, *The Culture of Disbelief: How American Law and Politics Trivialise Religious Devotion* (Anchor Books, 1993)

Cicero Tulius Marcus, *De Republica*

Colanges de Fustel, *The Ancient City: A Study of the Religion, Laws and Institutions of Greece and Rome* (Dover Publications, 2006)

Constitution of the Commonwealth of Australia 1900 (Cth)

Cooley M Thomas, *Principles of Constitutional Law* (Little Brown & Co, 1898)

D'Souza Dinesh, *What's so Great About Christianity* (Regnery, 2007)

Daintree David, *Soul of the West: Christianity and The Great Tradition* (Connor Court, 2015)

Deagon Alex, 'Secularism as a Religion: Questioning the Future of the

'Secular' State' (2017) 8 *The Western Australian Jurist*

Destro A Robert, 'The Structure of the Religious Liberty Guarantee' (1995) 11 *Journal of Law & Religion*

Dimont I Max, *Jews, God and History* (Signet, 2nd ed, 2004)

Evans Carolyn, 'Religion as Politics not Law: the Religious Clauses in the Australian Constitution' (2008) 36(3) *Religion, State and Society*

Everson v. Board of Education, 330 US 1 (1947).

Financial Framework Legislation Amendment Act (No 3) 2012 (Cth)

Gaustad S Edwin, *Faith of Our Fathers: Religion and the New Nation* (Harper & Row, 1987)

Gutzman R C Kevin, *The Politically Incorrect Guide to the Constitution* (Regnery Publishing, 2007)

Horwitz Paul, *The Agnostic Age* (Oxford University Press, 2011)

Huntington Samuel, *Who are We? America's Great Debate* (Free Press, 2005)

Jefferson Thomas, 'Freedom of Religion at the University of Virginia', in Saul K Padover (ed), *The Complete Jefferson* (Duell, Sloan & Pierce, 1943)

Kurti Peter, Religion and the New Sectarianism: Countering the Call for Silence', in James Allan (ed), *Making Australia Right: Where to from Here?* (Connor Court Publishing, 2016)

Mangalwadi Vishal, *The Book that Made Your World: How the Bible Created the Soul of Western Civilization* (Thomas Nelson, 2011)

McClanahan Brion, *The Founding Fathers' Guide to the Constitution* (Regnery Publishing, 2012)

McConnell W Michael, 'Religious Freedom at Crossroads' (1992) 59 *University of Chicago Law Review*

McDonald Forrest, *Novus Ordo Seculorum: The Intellectual Origins of the Constitution* (University Press of Kansas, 1985)

McGrath E Alister, *Christian History: An Introduction* (Willey-Blackwell, 2013)

McKean Dayton, 'State, Church, and Lobby', in James Ward Smith and A Leland Jamison (eds), *Religious Perspectives in American Culture* (Princeton University Press, 1961)

McMillan John, Gareth Evans and Haddon Story, *Australia's Constitution: Time for Change?* (George Allan & Unwin, 1983)

Melleuish Greg and Stephen Chavura, 'Utilitarianism contra Sectarianism', in William Coleman (ed), *Only in Australia: The History, Politics, and Economics of Australian Exceptionalism* (Oxford University Press)

Moens Gabriël A, 'Church and State Relations in Australia and the United States' (1996) 4 *Brigham Young University Law Review*

Moens Gabriël A, 'The Action-Belief Dichotomy and Freedom of Religion'

(1989) (12) *Sydney Law Review*

Pape v Commissioner of Taxation (2009) 238 CLR 1

Russell Kirk, *Rights and Duties: Reflections on our Conservative Revolution* (Spence Publishing Company, 1997)

Samson Alan Steven, 'Faustian Bargains: Entanglements Between Church and State in America' (2011) 2 *The Western Australian Jurist*

Sapienza Amanda, 'Using Representative Government to Bypass Representative Government' (2012) 23 *Public Law Review*

Saunders B Benjamin, 'The Commonwealth and the Chaplains: Executive Power after *Williams v Commonwealth.*' (2012) 23 *Public Law Review*

Saxonhouse W Arlene, *Free Speech and Democracy in Ancient Athens* (Cambridge University Press, 2006)

Schutt P Michael, *Redeeming Law: Christian Calling and the Legal Profession* (Il: IVP Academic, 2007)

Smith D Steven, 'Discourse in the Dusk: The Twilight of Religious Freedom?' (2009) 122 *Harvard Law Review*

Tonti-Filippini Nicholas, 'Religion in a Secular Society' (2008) 52(9) *Quadrant Magazine*

Tonti-Filippini Nicholas, 'Religion in a Secular Society' (2008) 52 *Quadrant*

Twomey Anne, 'Williams Revisited: The Commonwealth Constrained but Chaplains Resurrected' (2014) 26 *Upholding the Australian Constitution* (Samuel Griffith Society)

Williams v Commonwealth (No 1) (2012) 288 ALR 410.

Williams v Commonwealth (No 2) (2014) 309 ALR 41

Zimmermann Augusto, 'Constituting a Christian Commonwealth: Christian Foundations of Australia's Constitutionalism' (2014) 5 *The Western Australian Jurist*

8

WHERE WOULD THE CONSTITUTIONAL SPACE BE LOCATED? FORB EFFORTS IN PARTNERSHIP WITH INTERFAITH DIALOGUE

BRIAN ADAMS

Location of Constitutional Space

When I think about the theme of this conference, Creating the Constitutional Space for Other Fundamental Freedoms, I immediately think of attendant conceptual and social spaces related to the constitutional space. In short, where would this space be located? Where does it fit?

To answer this, it is useful to understand that this theme suggests a social norm where Freedom of Religion and Belief is expected or respected. Taking that view, I would like to lay out a model of social institutional relationships that is key to influencing or strengthening social norms in society. Keeping this heuristic model in mind assists identification of strategic partners that can help achieve Freedom of Religion and Belief ends in otherwise impossible contexts. This is the underlying model informing the shape and objectives of the G20 Interfaith Summit. Once I sketch this model, I then introduce interfaith dialogue ('ID') as one potential partner. This proposition is supported through cases in the United Arab Emirates ('UAE'), China and Saudi Arabia.

Definers, Defenders and Developers

In this model there are three institutions or groups that should work, if not in concert, then at least in respectful communication with one another to effect the generation of social norms.

The first of these three are the definers. Definers are those who work to articulate and envision social norms. Depending on the country or culture, these may include legislators and policymakers.

The second group is made up of defenders. These are they who enforce the articulation of the norms and adjudicate disputes. Again, depending on the country or culture, these may include the judiciary, policing bodies, or human rights commissions.

The third group is made of the developers of social norms. This is the civil society space where social norms are tested, applied, evolved and challenged.

A few comments are necessary before I situate the work of this conference in relation to this model. It should be clear that these groups overlap. Further, this model does not exactly fit every country and culture. For example, in some countries, civil society makes a very limited contribution to norm development. In other countries, civil society groups can have legislative or judicial roles or they may perform both roles in a combined body.

One final note is the importance of communication channels between civil society groups. If it is desirable that these groups work together towards positive and dynamic social change, there must be some way to have them on the same page.

My perception is that this conference sits solidly in the defenders' sphere of this model, with significant ties into the developers' sphere. The value of identifying constitutional space is that it also identifies potential partners, which broadens the tent of support. Identifying constitutional space also helps partners identify other points of influence and impact.

Identifying potential partners and opportunities for influence in newly recognised constitutional space, may require further discussion and communication about the work involved in advancing Freedom of Religion and Belief. Such discussions would focus on articulating the foundations of Freedom of Religion and Belief. For example, what are the principle objectives of Freedom of Religion and Belief initiatives? Clarifying objectives would help identify partners from other spheres whose foundational objectives overlap or align in some areas. Identification of similarities is only a start, because successful partnerships are dependent upon successful communications between partners. There must be efforts to rework articulation of them in terms that are inclusive of potential partners. The first of these is very natural for scholarly work, while the second is almost antithetical to scholarly pursuits.

Interfaith Dialogue Case Studies

That is enough abstract description. I now turn to case studies which illustrate what I am proposing, namely that there is value in finding partners from other social spheres to help achieve ends that would be difficult to obtain otherwise. These case studies are all drawn from the ID work in which I am engaged. More specifically, these examples address:

1) efforts to officially recognise particular faith groups;
2) efforts to broaden space for public religious practice; and
3) shaping a nation's official acknowledgment of religious plurality.

The first example I will draw upon is a current instance of official recognition of a religious community in the UAE. The UAE is a loose confederation of seven highly autonomous emirates where the relationship between non-Muslim religions and the state vary greatly. Non-Muslim religious groups are seen as foreign belief systems. There are clear ethnic, cultural, national and political differences between Emiratis and those who belong to other religious groups. Nor does the official recognition of a non-Muslim religious group in one emirate mean recognition in another. The acceptability of religious practice without official recognition also varies markedly between emirates.

Our centre has been working with various governmental ministries and religious communities in the UAE since the lead up to the first G20 Interfaith Summit in 2014. In fact, the first officially branded event in the G20 Interfaith Summit initiative was a regional pre-conference held in the UAE earlier that year under the patronage of Sheikh Nahyan, then Federal Minister for Youth and Culture. With his blessing, we began to work with various religious groups to build interfaith relationships. This effort took off when Surender Singh Kandhari, chairman of the Gurunanak Dabar Sikh temple in Dubai, and other religious community leaders began to collaborate on humanitarian projects in the country. The success of these projects attracted the attention of Dubai leaders who noted that one of the participating Christian communities was not officially recognised in Dubai and sought clarification on their work. This clarification included a meeting with Surender who strongly supported that community's contribution to Dubai's social harmony. His support led to an invitation from the Dubai government to that Christian group to begin the application process. The fact that this is an ongoing process and given the sensitivities on the part of both parties in the process, I have chosen not to name this group publicly.

The second example I would like to present is a hypothetical instance on the potential to broaden space for public religious practice in China. Unlike the UAE, the increasing religious plurality in China is domestic rather than foreign. That is, Chinese nationals are choosing new religions. China has a varied relationship with religious and philosophical communities. The last century has seen great swings in this relationship. The most recent swing during the last two years, has seen some religious groups are accepted in society, if they, *inter alia*, express support for the Communist Party. While this recognition allows some space for practice, a number of religious and philosophical groups are not officially recognised and are restricted in their religious practice and expression.

In short, many would agree that the Chinese government has not opened its doors to 'Western' human rights in a constitutional sense. However, this should not be seen as an unwillingness to recognise religious identity or a variety of expressions of that identity. Indeed, the Chinese government appears to be open to harnessing the civil benefits of religious practice, which include community cohesion, civil obedience and the personal discipline inherent in many traditions. But there is room for increased freedom of religious practice and expression.

So how could partnership with ID efforts yield fruitful developments in this context? One important, often overlooked, aspect of ID is its generative capacity. Bringing together people of different perspectives, wisdoms, worldviews, or social frameworks in a collaborative setting can generate social value in the form of increased community strength, innovative solutions, and strengthened economic development. This is not to propose that these communities become greater instruments of the government. Rather, it is possible to show by ID's generative aspect, the value of *increasing* the participation of diverse, value-bringing, religious and philosophical communities. Broadening public religious practice and participation could increase religious representation in officially recognised public space.

The third case is an aspirational example set in Saudi Arabia. Saudi Arabia's government, unlike that of the UAE or China, is a monarchy that bases its governing legitimacy firmly upon religious authority. The government's religious authority frames other religious interpretations or traditions as heretical. Other traditions are perceived as threats to its rule. However, there has been a stunning change in the last few months. While I have not seen any articulation of Freedom of Religion and Belief by Saudi clerics or government bodies, I have seen significant discussion of religious plurality and an openness to the redefinition of the Saudi relationship with faiths inside and outside of Saudi Arabia. A pithy illustration is that just recently (14 February 2018), a well-known, though somewhat controversial, Saudi cleric, Imam al-Ghambi, announced that it was fine for Muslims to celebrate Valentine's Day.

This changing relationship presents an opportunity to strengthen acceptance and understanding between the Saudi government and the religiously plural population. It also opens the door to the possibility of official recognition of religious plurality in the kingdom. Our centre is beginning work in the space this change offers.

Conclusion

In this presentation I have presented what I hope is a heuristic model to help locate the constitutional space for Freedom of Religion and Belief in a broader social context of social norms development. This model of Definers, Defenders and Developers, highlights the importance of recognising other participants/contributors to this development and suggests that identifying these partners can help achieve otherwise impossible ends.

Some of those who are engaged in ID will be able enter into areas or engage in issues not otherwise accessible to those who only approach constitutional Freedom of Religion and Belief on an academic basis. The cases presented describe actual and hypothetical outcomes where ID involvement was the vehicle which strengthened Freedom of Religion and Belief.

9

THE ECONOMIC IMPACT OF RELIGIOUS VOLUNTEERING AND DONATION

A. KEITH THOMPSON

The Aim of the Paper

The purpose of this paper is to draw the attention of third sector researchers to an econometric study commissioned by an interfaith group which quantifies in monetary terms, the contribution to the Australian economy made by religious volunteers working outside their faith communities. While Australia's National Charities Commission does produce literature detailing the overall contribution made to the national economy by the charitable sector, there is no existing literature which seeks to measure in monetary terms, the difference that religiosity makes to the volunteering and donation behaviour of every day Australians. To that extent, the research described in this paper breaks new ground. Because there is no directly relevant Australian literature, the paper acknowledges that existing sociological research identifies some of the good that religiously motivated people do in Australian society, but then moves on to discuss this new economic research and briefly situates it in the context of work that Professor Ram Cnaan at the University of Pennsylvania has pioneered in the United States. However, this is not a paper about methodology or econometric science. There are references and links to the formal reports which it explains, but this paper does not explain the modelling that was developed and used to analyse the survey data. The paper does explain how the data was quantified, but it does not set out the detailed empirical analysis. It points to the data and empirical analysis in identified on-line sources.

The paper suggests that even though religion in the West in the 21st century is not viewed as favourably as in the past,[1] there is still significant evidence that demonstrates religious people in Australia do more good in society than those who have no religion.[2] This paper recognises that whether you accept the existence of that good depends on whether you think caring for the sick and needy without payment and donating to non-religious environmental and education purposes are human goods. The paper proceeds on the assumption that you do accept that religiously motivated people spending their time in caring for the aged and destitute and donating to causes beyond their particular faith tradition is something that ought to be fostered. The paper also infers that research that identifies what motivates religiously observant people and what they do beyond the walls of their churches, is worth understanding and is probably worth bottling. The paper directly responds to the questions - how significant is that volunteering and donation? And, can it be measured, and if so how?

Introduction

In 2013, an inter-faith think tank now named SEIROS (The Study of the Economic Impact of Religion on Society),[3] undertook to try and measure that impact in economic terms – that is, to reduce the identification of that

---

1   "Global views on religion", Ipsos, 2017 (<www.ipsos.com>).

2   For example, Hughes P and Black A 2002, 'The impact of various personal and social characteristics on volunteering', *Australian Journal on Volunteering*, Vol. 7, No. 2, 59-69; Leonard R and Bellamy J 2006, 'Volunteering within and beyond the congregation: A survey of volunteering among Christian church attendees', *Australian Journal of Volunteering*, Vol. 11, No. 2, 16-24 and Lyons M and Nivison-Smith I 2006, 'The relationship between religion and volunteering in Australia', *Australian Journal on Volunteering*, Vol. 11, No. 2, 25-37.

3   The author is a member of the Board and serves as Secretary of SEIROS. He works as Professor of Law and Associate Dean at The University of Notre Dame Australia's Sydney School of Law.

human good to dollars and cents. SEIROS is comprised of representatives of the major Christian faiths in Australia but has board members representing Judaism, Buddhism, the Sikh Community, the Baha'i faith and its observer members include representatives of Islam and Hinduism. Its work took up where a Deloitte Access Economics (DAE) scoping study in 2013 left off. DAE had responded to an inquiry as to whether there was existing economic data available in Australia from existing government and private research sources, that would enable measurement of the economic impact of religion on society. Their analysis confirmed that existing data primarily collected for sociological purposes, would enable some economic analysis, but advised that new and focused research would be required to produce convincing econometric analysis.[4] They also identified a large field of econometric research that could be undertaken (see figure 1 below). After considering the field DAE identified, SEIROS decided that it would begin with research to identify the economic impact of religiosity on volunteering and donation in Australian society, with a specific focus on religious volunteering and donation by people of faith beyond their own religious communities.

Those results are now in and have been analysed. The initial analysis of the resulting data has again been done by DAE. They focused on identifying the economic impact of volunteering and donation on only those who converted to religious faith as adults. DAE's chosen slice from the survey sample was small reflecting ABS census data which suggested that adult converts to religion are few in number. But even that focus has identified a very large annual benefit to the Australian economy - $481 million dollars using DAE's conservative numbers.

---

[4]   Deloitte Access Economics, "The economic impact of religion - a scoping study" prepared for The Church of Jesus Christ of Latter-day Saints, July 2013.

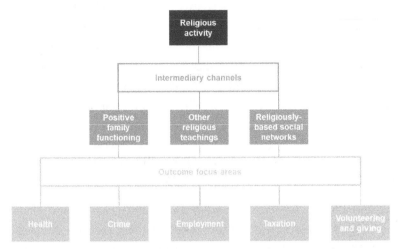

Figure 1 – Religious activities and government fiscal outcomes – focus areas

This paper discusses the research methodology and findings in accessible lay terms. It does that in three parts. In the first part, it discusses the existing Australian sociological literature which has confirmed that religiously minded people are more likely to volunteer and donate than those without religion. It also confirms existing sociological evidence that their time and hard-earned cash generosity does not stay within the four walls of their parish churches. Volunteering at church seems to teach people how to help others in need wherever they may be found.

In the second part, the scope of the DAE recommendations in 2013 is identified along with the focus of the research that SEIROS has here undertaken, the peer reviewed survey questions that were used, the data the survey produced and the negative hypotheses which DAE used to analyse the data. In the third part, the DAE findings are discussed. Though DAE have been careful to confirm that they have not proven that religiosity causes volunteering or donation since that was not the focus of the survey, still they have identified significant correlations. But perhaps what is most impressive is what is not said. That includes the positive economic impact of volunteering and donation outside their faith communities by people who have always been religious (ie not those converted as adults as in the DAE analysis), and the positive economic impact of volunteering and donation by religious people within their faith communities. Anecdotal evidence suggests that the overall positive contribution of religion on society may be larger than the mining and retail sectors combined.

This article concludes with the suggestion that this field of study is both important and worthwhile. If we can separate the good and bad effects of religion and encourage the good, the positive reputation of third sector organisations may be significantly enhanced. The wisdom of the precautionary principle suggests that we should not be reforming the tax sector of the economy until we understand some of its most important ticking parts.

PART ONE – WHAT THE EXISTING SOCIOLOGICAL LITERATURE PROVES

Hughes and Black (*Australian Community Survey* 2002), Lyons and Nivison-Smith (*Giving Australia Survey, ACOSS 2004*, 2006) and Leonard and Bellamy (*National Church Life Data Survey 2001*, 2006) all confirm "that church attendance is associated with higher levels of volunteering than in the general community".[5] Though church affiliation and attendance continue to decline,[6] volunteering is increasing within those churches.[7] Leonard and Bellamy reported in 2009 that

> the percentage of respondents who reported volunteering, either within or beyond the congregation, increased from 54% in 2001 to 57% in 2006. While these rates of volunteering are much higher than those reported by the ABS (2008) for the general population, 32% in 2000 and 35% in 2006, they nonetheless show a similar increase.[8]

While those authors said that the volunteering numbers they observed from the NCLS data were higher than reported by the ABS at about the same time, the NCLS numbers did synch with the *Giving Australia* survey conducted by the Australian Council of Social Services (ACOSS) in 2004. They observed that the non-ABS results might be skewed because the church attendees reporting were older and more likely to be female, even though the ABS put the increase that they observed down to raised community awareness of the

---

5   Rosemary Leonard, John Bellamy and Richard Ollerton, "Volunteering among Christian Church Attendees, 1991-2006", *Australian Journal on Volunteering*, 14 (2009) 7, 2. Referring to Hughes and Black, Lyons and Nivison-Smith and Leonard and Bellamy, above n 1.

6   Rosemary Leonard, John Bellamy and Richard Ollerton, above n 2, 1-2 comparing results in the 1991 and 2006 Censuses conducted by the Australian Bureau of Statistics (ABS). The 2016 Census confirmed the trends noted by these authors ten years previously.

7   Ibid 4.

8   Ibid.

many forms that volunteering could take during the intervening period.

For this paper's purposes, Leonard, Bellamy and Ollerton's most significant finding was that "[t]hose who did volunteer within their congregation were more likely to volunteer beyond their congregations".[9] This seems likely to be because they learn how to do social welfare and social justice work within their congregations then take their skills outside their church communities and help people with similar needs wherever they find them. This increased volunteering and giving, also correlates with Christian teachings about helping others in need. But according to the surveyors, the correlation is not statistically connected with leader direction or the desire to evangelise more members. Statistical differences between denominations evaporated when demographics were factored in. Some congregations volunteered more than others, but that was because their congregations were older and possibly had more available time because of retirement. While "there may be some inward-looking groups that support themselves but not the wider community, this is clearly not the dominant trend."[10]

These conclusions were also consistent with similar research that Bellamy had undertaken earlier again in partnership with Leonard[11] but also separately with Kaldor.[12] Those who attended church volunteered more, though middle-aged and older people volunteered more than young adults.[13] Church volunteering outside the congregation extended to "development and human rights; environment or local action groups; trade unions or political parties" and it also included education and youth work.[14]

PART TWO – THE ECONOMIC RESEARCH WORK OF SEIROS

The sociological insights of the authors discussed in Part One, confirm that religious attendance is correlated with increased service to people in need in the Australian community. But those researchers do not quantify the value of that service in economic terms. The SEIROS Board noted that research that

---

[9]   Ibid 7.
[10] Ibid 2.
[11] Rosemary Leonard and John Bellamy, "Volunteering within and beyond the congregation: A survey of volunteering among Christian church attendees", *Australian Journal on Volunteering*, 11 (2006) No. 2, 16-24.
[12] Bellamy J and Kaldor P 2002, *Initial impressions 2001*, Openbook, Adelaide.
[13] Leonard and Bellamy, above n 10, 23.
[14] Ibid 18-19.

quantified that value was possible since related economic research had been conducted in the United States by Professor Ram Cnaan at the University of Pennsylvania. He introduced a "Literature Review on the Impact of Religion on Quality of Life" in 2013 by observing that despite the view that "religion is a force that fuels hatred and brings about violence, aggression, and repression"[15] and is manipulable "by political regimes or by a few fanatic, charismatic leaders [,]…religion is largely the force behind performing good deeds and living healthier lifestyles."[16] His examples include the fact that many organised religions "call for avoidance of or strong moderation in the use of alcohol and other mood-altering substances…and call for delaying gratification and the willingness to give to others" which are a "force that is essential in maintaining civil society" as well as "the force behind many acts of compassion and care."[17] But then he makes what SEIROS has seen as an economic connection. He has written:

> It is an easy step [from understanding these 'well established connections between religion and quality of life'] to show that if religion helps with enhancing quality of life then it saves taxpayers millions of dollars. For example, if members of congregations smoke less than the rest of society and we know the cost of illness of an average smoker; we can then calculate the savings. However, this paper will be limited to a few quality of life measures and the impact of organized religion over these.

Cnaan has suggested that since US studies have shown better quality of life outcomes in 17 areas of study including the prevention of suicide, crime prevention, ending drug dependence and immigrant naturalisation, then similar studies ought to be possible in Australia.[18] Though the reasons for the correlation between "active engagement in religious activities" documented from "hundreds of studies [during]…the last 30 years" ranged from "instilling healthier and more pro-social values to the theory of 'hellfire'", there was no doubt that "in Western democracies…engagement in organized religion produces socially desired outcomes."[19]

DAE reviewed Cnaan's insights and summarised the Australian position

---

[15]   Ram A Cnaan, "Literature Review on the Impact of Religion on Quality of Life", xxx 1 (used with permission).
[16]   Ibid.
[17]   Ibid
[18]   Ibid 2.
[19]   Ibid 17.

as follows:

> Australia's not-for-profit (NFP) sector plays a crucial role in promoting social inclusion and enhancing the wellbeing of all Australians, especially the most vulnerable in our community. The sector works in tandem with government to: provide social and community services that substitute for services provided by government directly; promote social inclusion; and enhance the productivity of Australia's economy.

> The Australian government confers a range of tax concessions on NFPs, subject to various conditions. For instance, donors to organisations with deductible gift recipient (DGR) status are entitled to claim income tax deductions…

> Overall, the rationale for tax concessions, including income tax deductibility for donors, is that activities of eligible NFPs directly or indirectly reduce the demand for government services or otherwise improve the fiscal position of the Commonwealth.

> Religious organisations, like other NFPs, are income tax exempt and eligible for DGR status in respect of those activities that substitute for services otherwise provided by government. These include donations to various social welfare programs and contributions towards buildings used for educational purposes, for example.

> However, donations which support the core function of religious organisations, i.e., conducting religious services of worship and pastoral care of congregations, are not eligible for DGR status. Hence monies taken up as collections each week from members of church congregations do not qualify for income tax deductions.[20]

DAE then concluded that while "the impact of religion on various aspects of quality of life is well established…there is little empirical evidence available in the Australian context".[21] While data sets exist that could be used to estimate the results observed in international contexts, most of that information did not include questions enabling the identification of links between religious participation and attendance. Even though good data existed to show how much Australian governments had to spend on people with various health ailments or who were involved in criminal activity or

---

[20] Deloitte Access Economic, "The economic impact of religious activities – Scoping Study" prepared for The Church of Jesus Christ of Latter-day Saints, July 2013, i (used with permission).

[21] Ibid 36.

who were unemployed, there was little data in Australia to show the benefits between religion and quality of life.[22] For this reason, DAE suggested that the lacuna in the Australian data could be cured by survey research of the general Australian population that enabled links to be drawn between religious activity and desirable social outcomes along US lines. Analysis of such data "could identify causal linkages by separating those who grew up attending church from those who joined later in life."[23]

The SEIROS Board debated where it should start its research for some time. The DAE analysis had confirmed worthwhile economic research could be conducted to determine Australian religion's contribution to the reduction of government expenditure and the improvement of general health outcomes; the reduction of crime and the rehabilitation of offenders; the alleviation of general unemployment and the enhancement of the employability of the existing work force; the reduction of taxation generally because of religion's provision of substituted services at reduced cost and the effect of religiosity on volunteering and giving in Australian society. Ultimately volunteering and giving was identified as a starting point since sociological research had demonstrated an existing connection between religious observance and volunteering and giving behaviour in Australian society. With well-constructed peer-reviewed survey questions and in accordance with DAE's recommendations, the SEIROS Board considered that connection should be readily quantifiable.

Because of the established expertise of Melbourne's Christian Research Association (CRA), Dr Philip Hughes, the Senior Research Officer of that organisation, was contracted to design the survey for peer review by DAE. The settled form of the survey is available on the website of the Sydney School of Law of the University of Notre Dame Australia. Though there were methodological differences between CRA and DAE about how questions to determine behaviour over a period of time should be framed (whether responders should be asked to quantify their volunteering and giving behaviour during the last four weeks or during the preceding year), the ultimate form of those questions was DAE's choice since it was intended that they would analyse the resulting data looking for economic insight and they would prepare a report on that basis. The Project Shop in Melbourne

---

[22]   Ibid.
[23]   Ibid 38.

was contracted to collect data online and surveyed over 8000 adult Australians across the country from their database of over 900,000 people who had agreed to receive surveys.[24] When the incomplete surveys were stripped away, more than 7754 complete surveys informed DAE's analysis. CRA found that this sample

> represent[ed] people of all age groups 18 years and older from all states and territories in Australia. For a more accurate representation, the data was weighted by gender, age and state in which people lived to resemble the Australian population at the 2011 Census. It was noted that there were some small biases remaining in the sample with higher proportions being Australian born and having diplomas or degrees...Religious people were identified as those who indicated that they followed a religious faith and attended services of worship monthly or more often.[25]

CRA's preliminary sociological analysis of the data suggested:

- More religious people chose their occupations because of a desire to help others

- More religious people measured their success in life according to the differences they made in the lives of others

- More religious people provided care and assistance to family members and others beyond their own homes, and

- More religious people were involved in unpaid work for a variety of voluntary groups.

CRA's analysis confirmed the earlier sociological findings of Leonard and Bellamy, and Bellamy and Kaldor,[26] that the voluntary work of religious people outside their religious communities covered a spectrum and included volunteering for business, professional and union organisations, ethnic and cultural organisations, welfare and community services, youth children and

---

[24] Christian Research Association, "The Economic Impact of Religion in Australian Society: Report on the Impact through the lives of Individual", April 2016, 3 and 19.

[25] Ibid. For example, CRA noted that 76% of the people who responded to this survey had been born in Australia versus 70% in the 2011 ABS Census. Further, "[i]n the weighted data, 8 per cent had post-graduate degrees and 17 per cent had a bachelor's degree, compared with 6 per cent and 14 per cent respectively in the Australian population. In the weighted data 52 per cent were in the work force, compared with 58 per cent in the Australian population." But CRA concluded that though "these differences are relative small" they serve as a reminder that "sample surveys will not perfectly represent the population" (ibid 20).

[26] Above nn 10 and 11.

parenting organisations, with many of them being involved in education and training.[27] While the difference between the involvement of non-religious people and religious people in non-religious volunteering was statistically insignificant in this survey, CRA noted that "70 per cent of the hours [religious people] spent [volunteering] in their religious organisations was undertaken in projects for the benefit of the wider community".[28] CRA also noted

> evidence that people who had grown up attending religious services but who no longer attended, and people who were 'spiritual but not religious' had higher levels of involvement than those people who had never attended religious services or who described themselves as neither religious nor spiritual.[29]

Other sociological observations made in the CRA report were consistent with a 2010 study published by Kaldor, Hughes and Black that found "there were strong links between a religious approach to life and a personal sense of one's purpose, values of tolerance and concern for others, and informal helping and hours spent contributing as a volunteer".[30]

Because SEIROS wanted to undertake new and different research into the economic value of volunteering and giving in Australia, DAE's economic analysis started from completely different premises. DAE's research brief required the testing of two negative hypotheses using econometric data embedded in the survey answers. Those negative hypotheses were:

- Religious people are no more likely to volunteer for or donate to the broader community than non-religious people, all other things being equal; and

- Religious volunteers and religious donors do not contribute more time or donations to the broader community than non-religious volunteers and donors, all other things being equal.[31]

DAE explained the reason for this different analytical starting point by referring to their brief from SEIROS. SEIROS had asked DAE to

---

[27]   Christian Research Association, above n 23, 3.

[28]   Ibid 3-4.

[29]   Ibid 4.

[30]   Ibid 6 citing Kaldor, P, Hughes, P, & Black, A, *Spirit Matters: How Making Sense of Life Affects Wellbeing*, 2010, Mosaic Press, Melbourne, 143.

[31]   Deloitte Access Economics, "Economic value of donating and volunteering behaviour associated with religiosity", 2017, 6.

- Provide feedback on the design of a national survey

- Analyse data from this survey, to determine the statistical relationship between religiosity and donating and volunteering behaviour, controlling for a range of factors, and

- Quantify the economic value of any volunteering and giving or donating behaviour which is associated with religiosity.[32]

DAE explained the counterintuitive use of negative hypotheses by reference to Woolridge's authoritative work:

> Statistical analysis starts by assuming that there is no relationship between variables, and then seeks to ascertain whether this hypothesis can be disproved. We can only disprove this hypothesis if a statistically significant relationship is found after all other factors have been accounted for.[33]

The results of the DAE economic analysis are now set out.

PART THREE – THE DAE ANALYSIS

In their executive summary, DAE begin by observing that they cannot prove what causes volunteering and giving behaviour in adults because they cannot control for factors such as how a child was raised. But they affirm that "religious people are more likely to be volunteers and donors than non-religious people" and they quantify the minimum value of that difference in adults who converted to religion as adults.[34] They say that the reason why they limited their analysis to adults who converted to religion in adulthood, is that it is difficult to "untangle religiosity from other factors that might cause donating and volunteering behaviour", but limiting their analysis to this small subset of the collected data enables an affirmation of certain correlation.

To provide context for their economic analysis, they note as has this paper, that the link "between religiosity and volunteering within and beyond religious communities has…been extensively explored" and confirmed in Australia by previous research,[35] but without quantifying the economic value

---

[32] Ibid 5-6.
[33] Ibid 6 citing Wooldridge, Jeffrey M., *Introductory Econometrics: A Modern Approach*, South-Western Cengage Learning, Mason, Ohio, 2012.
[34] Ibid 4,
[35] Ibid 5.

of that activity. To quantify that value, they used an econometric framework to arrive at a causal interpretation "by exploiting differences between individuals that have experienced changes in religious status, and a counterfactual cohort [of]…individuals that have not experienced changes."[36]

They had reviewed the 48 questions that were intended to explore the "family life, informal contributions to society, unpaid work, giving, influences growing up, employment, income, health [plus] personal and household characteristics" of survey recipients before it was issued.[37] 95% of the 8154 people to whom the survey was sent, had responded at least partially, but responses were only used where there was enough relevant data provided. Those who had not answered "key questions were removed from the sample" as were those who gave extreme answers. This process meant 4961 volunteering responses were measured and 4381 responses in the giving analysis.[38] While religiosity is a "multi-dimensional variable involving belief, public and private practice, [as well as] salience and consequential dimensions"[39] which are difficult to measure, the survey responses provided attendance and frequency variables to enable such measurement as had other surveys including the 2013 Australian Census of Population and Housing, though ultimately DAE chose only to use the attendance data.

To further isolate volunteering and giving data that benefited society as a whole rather than responders' families or religious institutions, following the lead of the ABS, the DAE analysis used only formal volunteering data through an organisation or group that did not have a religious purpose.[40] Volunteering and giving to family and friends was also excluded.

The methodology section of the DAE report also explains how they isolated the effect of religiosity from other factors that might have influenced the analysis – including income, age, gender and family influences while the responder was growing up.[41] This process had followed 2017 recommendations of the Massachusetts Institute of Technology (MIT).

---

36   Ibid 6.
37   Ibid 7. For the full survey questionnaire, again see the appendix.
38   Ibid 8.
39   Ibid.
40   Ibid 9.
41   Ibid 7-8 (11-12).

THE DAE CONCLUSIONS

After noting that there appeared "to be a relationship between religiosity and the likelihood of volunteering and giving",[42] they found "specifically":

- that the average individual who is religious throughout both childhood and adulthood has an 11 percentage point higher likelihood of being a volunteer and a 20 percentage point higher likelihood of being a donor than the average individual who is unreligious throughout childhood and adulthood" but that other personal characteristics may have contributed to these results so that the correlations "cannot be interpreted causally.[43]

For this reason, DAE focused on individuals "who ha[d] gone from being non-religious to being religious" and found:

- that the average individual who becomes religious as an adult but is not religious in childhood has:

  o a 25 percentage point higher likelihood of being a volunteer that the average individual who remains unreligious throughout childhood and adulthood, and

  o a 23 percentage point higher likelihood of being a donor compared to the average individual who remains unreligious throughout childhood and adulthood.[44]

DAE then quantified the economic value of the differences they had found in their analysis. The "additional volunteering associated with religiosity [in Australia]…is around 30.5 million hours" and, using "opportunity cost methodology", this translated to an additional contribution of $339 million annually to the Australian economy.[45] Following the same economic analysis, the same cohort of people who became religious during adulthood had donated $142 million more than their non-convert peers in the general population.[46] The bottom line was that those who converted to religion during adulthood in Australia added $481 million to the national economy. DAE explained that this additional economic contribution came from only 180,000 people.[47]

DAE's analysis did not consider or quantify:

---

[42]   Ibid 24.
[43]   Ibid 24.
[44]   Ibid.
[45]   Ibid.
[46]   Ibid.
[47]   Ibid.

- how many Australians were religious throughout their lives

- whether Australians who were religious throughout their lives volunteered or donated more than their non-religious peers;

- the economic value of their volunteering and donation outside their religious communities; or

- the economic value of their volunteering and donation within their religious communities.

What the DAE analysis of the economic value of converts to religion does suggest, is that even though religion may not be regarded as favourably as in the past,[48] the volunteering and giving of its adherents has a large positive impact on the economy that merits further study.

FURTHER STUDY?

The DAE research breaks open an important area of research into the effects of religious behaviour on Australian society. If there is a significant positive impact, and DAE has found that there is, then the question that follows is what should governments' policy response be? Does the evidence of DAE favour encouraging religious activity or would this 'crowd out' secular volunteering and donation activity? These are difficult questions for a secular society to address, but it is submitted that this is an area where further research should contribute to the public debate.

Reasons for such further study include that:

- this influence should be understood so that it can be taken into account when national economic policy is set, and

- government might want to consider encouraging and enhancing religious activity generally with favourable non-economic policy.

SEIROS has envisaged a variety of further research projects that would enhance economic understanding. Those indicated on its website[49] include

1. Conducting religious institutional surveys in major regional areas to identify the direct economic contribution made by religious institutions to local economies with the prospect of gradually building a statistical compendium of the economic impact of religion in Australia,

---

[48]   See mention above n1.

[49]   <www.seiros.study>.

2. The development of an economic model of the not-for-profit and religious part of the economy to supplement research undertaken by the ABS Satellite National Accounts on the not-for-profit sector and research undertaken by the ACNC, and

3. Extension of the DAE analysis on volunteering and donation behaviour to include the traditionally religious cohort.

Consistent with Professor Cnaan's economic research in the United States referred to above,[50] DAE's analysis summarised in Figure 1 suggests that further economic research in Australia could include:

4. The impact of religion and religious observance on suicide and suicide prevention,

5. The comparative effectiveness of religiously affiliated subcontractors in helping people find employment or in improving their employment,

6. The economic benefit to Australia flowing from faith-based vocational improvement programs,

7. The economic savings that flow to Australia because of faith-based crime prevention teaching,

8. The primary and secondary economic benefits to Australia resulting from religious programs enabling prisoner rehabilitation and re-entry into the work force,

9. The economic savings to the Australia health system flowing from religious teachings about healthy life-styles,

10. The economic savings to the Australian economy as a whole that are the consequence of faith-based programs to end alcohol and drug dependency,

11. The economic uplift Australia receives because church run aged-care facilities enable their children to continue in paid employment,

12. The economic impact of faith-based programs that integrate immigrants into their new communities,

13. The economic impact of organised religion and religious teaching on the creation of relationships and networks,

14. The similar economic impact of organised religion and religious teaching in preventing the breakdown of relationships of many different kinds,

15. The economic benefits to the community when churches assist people escape from abusive relationships, and

---

[50] Nn 14-18 and supporting text.

16. The economic consequences of pro-social and civic behaviour taught to children and youth in church organisations.

CONCLUSION

The DAE report commissioned by SEIROS confirms that Australians converted to religion as adults are more likely to volunteer and donate to socially beneficial non-religious causes than their non-religiously observant peers. DAE quantified the benefit flowing to the Australian economy from their volunteering and donation at just under half a billion dollars annually.

That is a large number. But the DAE report is more impressive when one considers what it does not say. Current Australian census data confirm that religion in Australia is declining. Those still willing to confirm their religious affiliation to the Australian Bureau of Statistics in 2016 totalled only 59.9% of whom 52.1% identified as Christian.

It is reasonable to infer from that data, that despite DAE's large number, the converting adult cohort that DAE measured in their analysis is very small – at 3%, much less than the nearly 60% of Australians who were still willing to identify their religiosity in the 2016 census.

How much do the 57% contribute to causes beyond their identified religion? Clearly that answer is not as simple as multiplying half a billion dollars by 19. Indeed, that simple arithmetic would grossly understate the flow-on results of religious observance in Australia because it would not measure the good that religious people do within their own institutions or the good that those institutions themselves do within society.

The truth is that the survey material DAE analysed only scratches the surface of the universe of available data. But it does start the unfolding of a narrative about the contribution that religion and religious altruism makes in Australia's diverse and multi-cultural society. Clearly, we do not want to purge religion and religious observance from the public square. The majority of Australians still profess religious affiliation and even if they did not, we are slowly learning to celebrate the contributions of our minorities however they are constructed. The DAE report also infers that social policy responds to empirical data and analysis. The members of the SEIROS board and their contributors have responded to an obligation to give an account of the contribution they make to the life of the nation. The research explained here offers new and innovative insight into what constitutes the common good in 21st century Australia.

Bibliography

Bellamy J and Kaldor P (2002) Initial impressions 2001, Adelaide, Openbook

Christian Research Association (April 2016) The Economic Impact of Religion in Australian Society: Report on the Impact through the lives of Individual.

Deloitte Access Economics (July 2013) The economic impact of religion - a scoping study prepared for The Church of Jesus Christ of Latter-day Saints.

"Global views on religion", Ipsos, 2017 (<www.ipsos.com>).

<www.seiros.study>.

Hughes P and Black A (2002) The impact of various personal and social characteristics on volunteering, Australian Journal on Volunteering, Vol. 7, No. 2, 59-69.

Kaldor, P, Hughes, P, & Black, A (2010) Spirit Matters: How Making Sense of Life Affects Wellbeing, Melbourne, Mosaic Press.

Leonard R and Bellamy J (2006) Volunteering within and beyond the congregation: A survey of volunteering among Christian church attendees, Australian Journal of Volunteering, Vol. 11, No. 2, 16-24.

Leonard and Bellamy (National Church Life Data Survey 2001, 2006).

Lyons and Nivison-Smith (Giving Australia Survey, ACOSS 2004, 2006).

Lyons M and Nivison-Smith I (2006) The relationship between religion and volunteering in Australia, Australian Journal on Volunteering, Vol. 11, No. 2, 25-37.

Ram A Cnaan (June 2013) Literature Review on the Impact of Religion on Quality of Life.

Deloitte Access Economics (2017) Economic value of donating and volunteering behaviour associated with religiosity.

Hughes and Black (Australian Community Survey 2002).

Wooldridge, Jeffrey M (2012) Introductory Econometrics: A Modern Approach, Mason, Ohio, South-Western Cengage Learning

10

MEASURING THE ECONOMIC IMPACT OF RELIGIOSITY IN AUSTRALIA[1]

BRENDAN LONG

The debate on the role of religion in Australia has now become a central issue of public debate. This has not happened for many years. The nation has engaged in a difficult debate about legal recognition of same-sex relationships which has reopened the question of religious freedom and its protection by law. Other recent matters also focus thinking on the nature and scope of religious liberty protections: the troublesome question of funding models for religious schools as well as euthanasia and assisted suicide have also emerged as questions that raise religious liberty protections or lack thereof. With respect to euthanasia and assisted-suicide, as earlier with the abortion issue, the national and state/territory levels must deal with how religious health care providers can express conscientious objection to policies and procedures that are against their religious consciences. The appropriate way to manage expression of religious conviction in our national life has become a strong undercurrent in contemporary politics and remains a paramount consideration of policy at the highest levels in the Australian body politic.

The Research Question: How Does Religion Affect Other Aspects of Australian Society?

While the role of religion in Australian life has now come to occupy a central place in public policy debate there is a missing element in this national discussion.

---

[1]   This paper expands on the contribution in this book of Keith Thompson on the research by Deloitte Access Economics for the Study of the Economic Impact of Religion – a research body in which both contributors are members in a volunteer capacity.

This is the question of how religious commitment enhances the economic life of the nation for the common good of all Australians. This paper seeks to fill this gap in research by seeking to assess, in part, the extent to which the religious instinct to give is actualised for the sake of the others, for the sake of the common good of the Australian polity. Sophisticated economic and statistical analysis is presented. The question sought to be tested is whether religiosity of Australians makes any difference to the way we give in two ways, giving of time in volunteering and giving in money in terms of donations. Specifically, the paper seeks to assess if there are warrants to assert, on the basis of sophisticated statistical research, whether religious people in Australia give more time and money than non-religious people? Such activities have a measurable economic value which can benefit the Australian community as a whole. If religious Australians are more prone to giving time and money, then we can measure, at least in a partial way, the economic impact of religious life in Australia. We can also then ask if there should be a public policy position to support and encourage this contribution.[2]

---

[2]   A presentation by Daniel Payton of Deloitte Access Economics (DAE) to the 2018 Australian Conference of Economists indicated that tax concessions for donations increased donations more than the cost to the Budget of associated tax concessions in Australia, consistent with international research (The price elasticity of charitable donations, evidence from Australian tax file data, Daniel Payten, Deloitte Access Economics, paper presented to the 2018 Australian Conference of Economists, Canberra 2018). The financial aspect of the contribution of religion to a culture is simply one measure, and many would argue, a lesser measure than the many other benefits of religious adherence to a culture. The late Professor Dr Paul Reed, formerly Senior Social Scientist of Statistics Canada ('StatsCan') and Carleton University in Canada, showed in longitudinal studies in the 1990s that over a variety of indicia religious belief and "spirituality" figured strongly in relation to volunteering, membership and donating - all aspects important to the 20 per cent of those in any population who do 80 per cent of the charitable giving, volunteering and joining. The only other aspect that gave similar statistically significant measures to involvement was university education; religious belief and university education, therefore, being the most important aspects to indicate the likelihood of civic involvement in a culture and the distinction between the minority of citizens who make up the majority of those who volunteer, join and donate and those who do none of these things: income was, surprisingly, not a relevant factor in relation to charitable giving - spiritual and religious convictions and University education were the most influential factors. Dr Reed's work is discussed in greater detail below in relation to the definitions of "spirituality" and "religion" (Reed G Paul, 'An Emerging Paradigm for the Investigation of Spirituality in Nursing' (1992) 15(5) *Research in Nursing and Health*).

Taking Stock of Current Analysis of the Economic Impact of Religion in Australia

There can be little doubt that religious institutions play a very significant role in Australian life, including in activities that involve considerable economic resources. However, in Australian there is a paucity of data on the question of the economic footprint of religious institutions. There are three important sources of data that are relevant to this issue: published reports from the Australian Charities and Not-for-profit Commission ('ACNC'), the Australian Bureau of Statistics ('ABS') Non-Profit Institutions Satellite Account 2012-13, which is based on the ABS system of National Accounts, and the Giving Australia survey of religious identity and participation in religious services.

The ACNC publishes an annual report called the *Australian Charities Report*, the latest relating to 2016. Charities are required to file reports with the ACNC on expenditure and income and to specify their charitable purpose. According to the 2016 Charities Report, charities spent over $137 billion in 2016.[3] Of these charities, 30 per cent had a religious purpose (the highest category by a large margin).[4] The ACNC has also produced a report into the 'Economic contribution of the Australian charity sector' written by Deloitte Access Economics ('DAE').[5] However, the contribution of religious charities to education, health and social services is not specifically identified in the report. The data in the Charities Report of ACNC on the income and expenditure of charities could be mined to measure income and expenditure of religious charities as a whole. However, this data suffers from an inadequacy of aggregation in that the specific contribution of religious charities to economic aspects of their mission (such as health and education) are not readily identifiable from the charities' reporting to the ACNC and are hidden within the headline numbers often provided by peak associations reporting on behalf of member organisations. This makes the ACNC data on the economic component of religious charities' engagement rather opaque to the researcher.

The ABS Non-Profit Institutions Satellite Account, 2012-13 estimates that not-for-profit institutions contributed $79.2 billion to Gross Value Added

---

3   Australian Charities and Not-for-profits Commission, Parliament of Australia, *ACNC Annual Report 2016-17* (2017) 11.

4   Ibid 27.

5   See, Australian Charities and Not-for-Profits Commission, *Economic Contribution of the Australian Charity Sector* (December 2017).

('GVA') in the economy (a measure akin to GDP) at 3.8% of total GVA.[6] Again the majority of these institutions are religious in nature. The ABS approach also does not specifically measure the commitment of religious institutions in the areas of education, health and welfare which are the primary economic components of the religious organisations' activity.[7]

Unfortunately, neither of these two major measurement tasks by the Commonwealth Government capture the major form of economic activity of religious institutions. Furthermore, the ACNC and ABS approaches focus on direct expenditure and income of religious charities. As with all economic activity, expenditure in one sector stimulates activity in other sectors creating a multiplier effect. An example is that expenditure on employing persons in the religious sector leads to wage income expended that creates demand for other products like food and housing. Ideally, any measure of the economic impact of religious life would also calculate these multiplier effects. The report 'Economic contribution of the Australian charity sector', published by ACNC does model these wider economy impacts of charities but suffers from the problem that substantial engagement of religious charities in education, health and social services is subsumed within the aggregate measurement of the contributions of these sub-sectors. The economic impact of religious charities is reduced to more explicitly religious activity masking the real economic impact of religious charities. It is also important to consider the much higher cost that government would probably have to bear if it provided such services itself.

---

[6] Australian Bureau of Statistics, *5256.0 - Australian National Accounts: Non-Profit Institutions Satelite Account, 2012-13* (28 August 2015).

[7] Probably about a quarter of Australian children are educated in religious schools. Catholic schools educate one in five Australian children and there are many religious non-Catholic Schools: National Catholic Education Commission, *Catholic Schools in Australia* (2016). There is no measure of the proportion of health and aged care services that are provided by religious institutions, but the Catholic system delivers 10 per cent of these services and other Christian and religious charities are also major suppliers of these services: Catholic Health Australia, *Strategic Direction Statement 2020*. Christian welfare charities form a substantial part of social services delivery across a broad front of counselling, family support, poverty alleviation and homelessness programs and are also engaged with employment, disability and child care services. Churches are massive employers and operate as large corporations. This social welfare function of religious institutions is likely to be more significant economically than specifically religious functions associated with church functions of worship, baptism, marriage and funerals, however, this is another area where research is lacking.

Consequently, there is currently no aggregate measure of the economic impact of religious institutions in Australia.[8]

Turning to the question of giving, the focus of this paper, there is a third data source produced by Giving Australia which considers the contribution of religious persons and institutions to giving. In 2006, Lyons and Nivison-Smith published a significant study entitled, 'The relationship between religion and volunteering in Australia', in the *Australian Journal on Volunteering*, sponsored by Giving Australia.[9]   Their analysis used sophisticated logistic regression techniques to measure the impact of commitment on donation behaviour. The report showed that persons who regularly attended religious services indicate higher rates of giving and higher amounts of donations compared to the average population. The published data also shows religious people also gave to non-religious causes,[10] although as regularity of attendance increased to weekly attendance giving outside of religious causes decreased. Prior to the DAE analysis presented later in this report the Lyons and Nivison-Smith analysis presents the most sophisticated study of the correlation between religious activity and donation behaviour in Australia. It is based on survey data that is 12 years old. Giving Australia has published more recent data on giving

---

[8]   And this says nothing about the other less quantifiable aspects of religious membership and co-operation. The ethos of religious societies adds many aspects to society that are not at all quantifiable simply by economic measures. See, for an example of the nature and religious involvement in "life worlds": Iain T Benson, 'Pluralism, life worlds, civic virtues and civil charters' in M Christian Green and Pieter Coertzen (eds), *Religious Pluralism in Africa—Prospects and Limitations* (SUN Press, 2016) Chapter 17.

[9]   M Lyons and Nivison-Smith, 'The relationship between religion and volunteering in Australia' (2006) 41(4) *Australian Journal on Volunteering* 419-437.

[10]   Ibid 427, where Table 3 measures the giving rate and amount given by givers according to the measured level of religious participation. The measurements exclude donations to religious causes. The giving rate for persons with weekly religious participation is 81.3 per cent, for monthly religious participation is 86 per cent, for religious participation varying from monthly to annually at 87.5 per cent, and for those with less or no religious participation measured at between 81.4 per cent to 81.8 per cent. The rate of giving is collated with religious participation – religious participants tend to give more often. The average level of amounts given is highest for those with weekly participation, followed by those with monthly religious participation, and then roughly equal in other categories. The level of giving is also correlated with religious participation in this study.

behaviour,[11] however, this data does not provide information in relation to religious giving to non-religious causes, and therefore does not materially assist in pursuing the research question raised here.

The Theological Prerogative of Unselfish Giving

This phenomenon of religiously motivated giving is of interest to the sociologists of religion and the economist. It is also of interest to the public or practical theologian who seeks to examine, from a religious viewpoint, how faith commitment engages with society. Religious thinkers, especially if operating in the Christian tradition, would be interested to see if the strong economic presence of Christian charities translated into a change in social behaviour in general – including behaviour outside of the broadly Christian community. Essentially the public/practical theologian would expect to see two things: firstly, that religious behaviour would lead to increased giving of time and money from religious people, and secondly that this giving was not restricted to supporting religious communities themselves but was giving for the good of all – without an expectation of some return received by simply supporting the religious institution the religious person was associated with. In short, do religious people show a greater propensity for unselfish giving than non-religious persons in this nation?

The theological basis for the moral requirement of unselfish giving is a key element of most major religious faiths. In the Jewish and Christian faiths it is well grounded in the Old and New Testament accounts. In the Old Testament, foundational texts substantially shared by Jews and Christians, there is a constant tradition of the moral imperative of giving alms. Generosity to the poor and needy was required and praised in Old Testament works (Deuteronomy 15:11, Job 29: 11-16). Giving to the poor was seen as a form of 'righteousness' (Tobias 1:3) and could atone for sins (Daniel 4:24, Sirach 3.30 and Tobias 12.9). This is accentuated in the

---

[11]   The annual surveys of donation behaviour are commissioned by the Commonwealth of Australia, represented by the Department of Social Services. The Australian Centre for Philanthropy and Non-profit Studies ('ACPNS'), with the Centre for Social Impact ('CSI') Swinburne and the Centre for Corporate Public Affairs, have partnered to undertake this research project. The reports are made available through the Prime Minister's Community Business Partnership and accessible at: Prime Minister's Community Business Partnership, *Community Business Partnership*.

New Testament where giving is seen as an act of piety (Matthew 6:1-4 in the Sermon the Mount). In Luke, giving 'alms' is seen as an act of righteousness (Luke 11.41, 12:33), and Paul calls for Christian communities to provide for the poor in their midst (1 Corinthians 16.1-3, 2 Corinthians 8-9, Acts 24:17).

One of the key elements of this New Testament approach to giving is that the people of God in the Christian understanding are participants in the 'kingdom of God' – God's work in the world. As such, they act as a catalyst like yeast in bread, or in the biblical parlance 'the leaven'. The key quotation is in both the synoptic Gospels of Matthew and Luke flowing from the underlying oral tradition they draw on called 'Q'.[12] Here is the quotation from the New American Bible translation from Luke's version:

> To what should I compare the kingdom of God? It is like yeast that
> a woman took and mixed in with three measures of wheat flour until
> the whole batch of dough was leavened.[13]

The three measures represent an enormous volume, enough to feed a hundred. The principle is that the 'kingdom of God' starts from a small thing and expands in great abundance – a great good for many to enjoy. The Christian acts like the yeast as a catalyst. The catalyst is a small substance, not a strong spice, but a hidden element which through its innate chemical powers expands the bread so it can be consumed by many. The kingdom of God is like this, according to the biblical narrative, starting from a small element, it has an unseen capacity to create great benefits for all to share.

The disciples are called to be 'the salt of the earth' and 'the light of the world'. This theme of the disciples of Christ influencing the world for good by their actions is present in many parts of the synoptic gospels, but is neatly condensed in Matthew 5.13-16 where Jesus calls on his disciples to do 'good works'. These works 'shine before others'. Here is the quotation from Matthew from the New American Bible (although again the section is based on shared Q source with Luke in 14: 34-35 and 8:16):

---

[12]   Q comes the German Quelle meaning source. Defined in the Oxford Companion to the Bible as the 'hypothetical common source used by the Gospels of Matthew and Luke'. While it is 'hypothetical' as it is derived from redaction of biblical texts it is a well-established form of biblical critical analysis: see G Styler, 'Synoptic Problem', in Bruce *Metzger and Michael Coogan* (eds), *Oxford Companion to the Bible* (Oxford University Press, 1993) 724-727.

[13]   Luke 13:18-19 (New American Bible Version).

Just so, your light must shine before others, that they may see your good
deeds and glorify your heavenly Father.[14]

The theme is that the good works of the disciples must have a visible effect
on the world around them.

Why Measure the Economic Impact of Religiosity?

Applying these biblical concepts provides a test from which to assess the impact
of religiosity on contemporary Australian life. Satisfying this test, according
to its own stated standards, requires religious adherents to yield good works
which benefit others. The test can also be applied to religious activity in all
its myriad forms in contemporary Australian life. The question we can seek
to test is if religious people have a real positive impact on the life of the
Australian community. With such a large economic presence, thousands of
schools, many hospitals, aged care facilities and welfare programs, the public
or practical theologian and those interested in public policy would hope to
see such religious activity generate wider benefits for the whole community
and not just the membership of religious communities. If giving is restricted
just to the Christian polity then Christians risk reinforcing a 'ghetto mentality'
of self-serving fideism that risks being turned in on itself. This problem was
crystallised in the writings of the leading Protestant theologian Wolfgang
Pannenberg.[15] Theologians want to know if religious activity escapes this
'ghetto mentality' and produces real benefits for all which Christ called his
followers to achieve. If we can establish that there are social and economic
benefits of unselfish giving by Christians for the benefit of the whole
community, then Pannenberg's sceptical warning of the risks of a Christian
'ghetto mentality' are addressed.

However, non-religious public policy professionals may also be very
interested in this question for different reasons. Given that religious
institutions enjoy substantial tax concessions, and receive significant
public funding for education, health and welfare services, the public policy
researcher and bureaucratic adviser would presumably be interested to know

---

[14] Matthew 5:13-16 (New American Bible Version)

[15] Wolfganag Pannenberg, *Basic Questions in Theology* (Augsburg Fortress Publishing,
2008) Volume I, 16

what social benefits follow from the public investment.[16] This line of inquiry raises questions that appear reasonable to ask from the perspectives of both the religious researcher and the public policy professional.

Seeking to respond to this question is a key rationale for measuring the economic impact of religiosity. Social science researchers and theologians may want to ask if religious commitment does offer real benefits to the wider community and public policy analysts will be interested in arguments that give a pragmatic rationale for donations to religious projects. The standard way that economists have tended to consider religious activity is as a consumption choice of the individual or household. This perspective contends that expenditure on religious education or health, and donations to secure religious infrastructure, is simply consumption of a 'leisure good' like recreation. In this case, the good consumed is religious activity – akin to expenditure on a personal hobby or preferred form of recreation. The standard neo-classical economic model of Consumer Choice Theory[17] prescribes that the economic agent on the demand side of the economy, the person as a consumer, seeks to maximise consumption of preferred goods subject to his/her income constraint. Expenditure on religious activity in time or monetary donation is simply part of the consumption function of a consumer. Alternatively, if religious activity does generate benefits for the wider community, extending beyond its institutions and members and even beyond the religious population cohort, and is undertaken with this intention, then we may have a different paradigm in place. This paradigm offers the perspective that religious activity is undertaken in order to generate benefits for others altruistically, for the common good. Such a conclusion, if reasonably established, constitutes an effective rebuttal of the reductive and insufficiently explanatory view of religious activity as a consumption good that believers consume. It is a question that strikes at the very heart of the prevailing paradigm economics applies to "explain" religious behaviour. It

---

[16]   It should be noted, however, that as the public is made up of all citizens, religious and non-religious, it is important not to erroneously conflate the idea of "public" with the idea of "secular" meaning "separated from or not influenced by religion." Such an understanding of the "secular" as necessarily stripped of religion, in the manner of secularists, is not one that comports with the Australian understanding of "the co-operation of Church and State" as evidenced by the funding of many religious schools and health care initiatives (to name but two).

[17]   Consumer Choice Theory outlines how consumers seek to maximise utility based on consumption of preferred goods subject to the constraint of their budgets.

constitutes a question worthy of social scientific inquiry.

This paper presents research that seeks to sustain an argument in support of the perspective that religious life generates wider benefits for the Australian community. It seeks to achieve this by examining the volunteering and donating behaviour of religious people. If this cohort gives time and money outside their specific religious communities, from which they would derive some benefit, then it could be argued that there is an unselfish or altruistic element to their giving. This paper then seeks to measure this 'unselfish giving' in religious cohorts relative to non-religious cohorts.

Methodological Issues Associated with Measuring the Economic Impact of Religion

Econometric analysis remains a key focus of current theoretical and applied economic research endeavours, with the majority of newly published papers in leading journals involving some econometric component. One of the advantages of this genre of research is the capacity to 'control for' - or eliminate the effect of - a variety of influences on the ultimate variable to be measured. It is possible to control for age, gender, ethnicity, income and education to eliminate the impact of any effects these demographic elements of the model have on the final variable to be measured. This has the benefit of isolating the impact of a particular element of the model that it is desired to be tested. This approach has some promise for testing the economic impact of religiosity which is certainly implicated with a range of variables listed above.

There are challenges in capturing the specific impact of religious engagement on measured behaviour. The first challenge lies in the notion of religious behaviour itself. There is a mysterious element to it – a personal response to the sense of the transcendent. This response, by its very nature, is a behavioural response which is highly subjective. It involves personal moral action driven by a worldview that does not appeal solely to concrete "real world" factors. It is inspired by a perspective that transcends measureable "real world" behavioural responses.[18] Being religious is an a priori grounding

---

[18]   The term "real world" here is placed in quotation marks to indicate that, of course, what some understand as "real" is not what others understand by it. In other words, a reductive view of the world may well define as "unreal" that which simply is beyond its paradigms of measurement. Other measures, such as altruism here, are not captured by the metric but are nonetheless "real" even if missed by a reduced framework that fails to take it into account.

of the person as a person who looks beyond the here and now when forming the basis on how he or she decides to live. Unlike variables such as age, gender, education and income this subjective, individual 'transcendental' response is not itself directly measurable and therefore cannot be directly built into econometric models. There is, for good statistical reasons, no ABS series that measures responses to the transcendent. So how does the social scientific researcher approach the task of capturing the subjective religious behavioural response?

Although econometric analysis cannot directly measure the personal subjective, religious behavioural response, it can be deployed to measure the observed changes in behaviour that flow from being religious. The literature on this topic refers to something called a 'treatment effect'.[19] What is meant by a 'treatment effect' can be highlighted by reference to psychological approaches. There is a control group – a 'normal' or average sample which does not display the characteristic to be measured – in this case religiosity. The researcher can also examine a group that displays the specified characteristic - religiosity. Ideally, this would be a randomised trial. To illustrate the method of applying a 'treatment effect' we can refer again to methods in psychology. If we are measuring responses to depression, we can look at how non-depressed people behave (the control group) then look at how depressed people behave. The divergent behavioural response of depressed persons relative to the control group of non-depressed persons is identifiable and thus measurable. There is a 'treatment effect' of depression – how it affects behaviour. To make the issue even clearer, you can give depressed people a certain drug in one group and a placebo to another depressed control group and measure the 'treatment effect' of the drug on depressed persons. It is possible to measure the 'treatment effect' of religiosity on volunteering and donating behaviour. The incidence of volunteering and donating for religious people is compared to similar activity of the control group of non-religious people. It is also possible to measure this 'treatment effect' in a way that restricts additional giving of time and money by religious people to exclude volunteering and giving to religious communities.

A methodological problem becomes immediately evident. This problem is when to assess religiosity in a person's life experience. The question is whether we seek to measure religiosity in terms of persons being converted

---

[19]   Joshua Angrist, *Treatment Effects*, MIT Economics.

to religious faith in adult life or whether it is more important to focus on the behavioural response of persons who have been religious all of their lives. Conversion changes behaviour in measurable ways as you can measure the 'before conversion' and 'after conversion' effect. So focusing on behavioural responses of persons who experience conversion in adult life captures a 'treatment effect' of religiosity in a very clear way, in a more easily measureable way. However, as will be discussed below, the cohort of the 'converted' in adult life is a small part of the total religious cohort and represents some three per cent of the whole population. The critical methodological question in this research is how do you balance the impact of the 'treatment effect' of religious conversion in adult life against the slow, yet sustained, behavioural impact on volunteering and giving of the cohort who have been religious since childhood? Do we focus on the behavioural response of conversion or the behavioural response of people who have been religious since youth without a clear adult conversion event? The former emphasises the personal response, the latter the impact of long-term engagement and formation in a community of religious persons. The behaviour of both cohorts – the adult converted and the religious since youth group - appears to be important to get a more complete picture of the impact of religiosity on volunteering and giving. This is a complex problem and creates significant challenges in measuring the overall economic impact of the religious cohort.

This problem acknowledged, it is possible to measure the impact of religious behaviour in a partial sense by looking at the 'treatment effect' of adult conversion. We can observe the non-religious control group for a certain factor, observe the religious group behaviour for that factor and also net out the other influences on religiosity we know about econometrically. This is essentially the methodology adopted in some recent innovative research to which this paper now turns.

Discussion of the New Research into the Economic Impact of Religion in Australia

SEIROS is the acronym for a new research endeavour in Australia with the elongated title of 'The Study of the Economic Impact of Religion on Society'. It includes leaders and representatives from different religious traditions, academics and policy makers.[20] SEIROS has commissioned research from

---

[20] The author is a member of the SEIROS Board.

DAE to examine the economic impact of two aspects of religiosity - the propensity for giving of time and money. DAE examined the impact of religious engagement upon donating and volunteering behaviour outside of commitment to religious institutions. This captures the theological imperative discussed above of giving for the sake of the common good, genuinely altruistic giving.

In order to conduct empirical testing of religious behaviour there needs to be a reliable data source. Although there are some significant international surveys on religious status (like the World Values Survey) there is no published series on volunteering and donation behaviour which also measures religious commitment in Australia. Consequently, SEIROS decided to conduct its own survey working with the Christian Research Association ('CRA') which is an established social research institution with national best practice research methods in this area, conducted by Dr Phillip Hughes.[21] This survey based on 7756 observations used the frequency of survey respondents' attendance at a religious event as the measure of religiosity, and created a detailed profile of respondent characteristics including 48 questions covering eight topics across family life, informal contributions to society, unpaid work, giving, influences growing up, employment, education, income, health and personal and household characteristics. The survey also measured the level of commitment to volunteering inside and outside of religious events and the level of donations to Church based organisations and donations outside these organisations. This data was supplied to DAE who engaged in rigorous data cleansing to remove outlying data events and account for incomplete responses, and a weighting process to align the survey data set to match the population distribution of age, gender and state of residence from the ABS Census data. This resulted in a 'clean' data set of 4948 respondents for the cohort of respondents in the sub-sample who answered the questions on volunteering and 4381 respondents who answered questions on donation behaviour. It is important that the data set isolates volunteering and donating to religious causes. This allows the data set to inform econometric analysis of the element of giving time and money by religious people outside of religious causes. This avoids the theological concern mentioned above relating to altruism being beyond ones' own group. Still, in essence, giving is giving and elimination of religious giving of time and

---

21   The CRA survey analysed by DAE in its report for SEIROS has not been published at the time this paper has been prepared.

money introduces some conservatism to the analysis. On the other hand, such conservatism serves the goal of ensuring the capture of data which assists in rebutting the notion of the religious consumer paradigm of the neo-classical approach to religious economic behaviour discussed, and rejected, above.

DAE applied this 'cleansed' survey data set to econometric testing using a method called logistic regression. This method is useful when seeking to predict probabilities that individuals fall into two categories based on some explanatory variable like a positive or negative answer to a proposition. In this case, the propositions we are seeking to test is whether volunteering and donating is more prevalent amongst religious people. Logistic regression measures the relative likelihood of a person being a volunteer, or not being a volunteer, based on religiosity. This 'odds ratio' that falls out of the logistic model is the chance that any person who is a volunteer is also religious. The same method is also applied to the probability of persons who are donors being religious.

DAE tested four propositions in their logistic regression model. These propositions are:[22]

1. There is a statistically significant difference between religious and non-religious people, in terms of their likelihood of volunteering for non-religious purposes,

2. There is a statistically significant difference between religious and non-religious volunteers, in terms of the time devoted to volunteering for non-religious purposes,

3. There is a statistical difference between religious and non-religious people, in terms of the likelihood of giving for non-religious purposes,

4. There is a statistical difference between religious and non-religious donors, in terms of the value of their donation for non-religious purposes.

The first important element of the model to consider is how religiosity is established. The survey includes data on whether the respondent engaged in religious attendance when growing up or in adult life. The frequency of attendance was also measured. The modelling approach DAE adopted was to focus on attendance itself rather than frequency of attendance. The stated reason is that, upon testing, both these variables were highly correlated. Problems can arise in statistical analysis when variables that form part of

---

[22]   Deloitte Access Economics, *Economic value of donating and volunteering behaviour associated with religiosity* (31 May 2018) Analysis and Political Observatory, 34.

an estimation model are highly correlated (collinearity/multicollinearity). To avoid this collinearity problem DAE decided to measure religiosity in terms of current or historical attendance at a religious event - ignoring the frequency of such attendance. While the statistical imperative of avoiding collinearity is accepted, it is also noted that the incapacity to measure frequency of attendance reduces the explanatory power of the model. Surely, frequency of attendance at religious events is a superior measure of true religiosity than merely attending an event, potentially on a single occasion. It seems that the model would have been better specified if religiosity was based on frequency of attendance, but it is also noted that this would have increased the complexity of the analysis substantially. Because the logistic regression models test a binary proposition, a yes or no answer to a question, defining religiosity in terms of frequency of attendance would require specification of an arbitrary measure of what frequency of attendance would constitute an adequate measure of religiosity. When a person surveyed met a threshold level of attendance then they would be deemed religious. While the survey data empowered such analysis, DAE opted for the simpler test of assessing a positive response to religious status by mere self-identification of a survey respondent attesting to attending religious events rather than measuring religiosity in terms of frequency of attendance. There may be scope for further refinement of the model in the future to focus on frequency of attendance, or some other approach such as a self-evaluation of the degree of importance of religion or "spirituality" in the subject's life (as was done in Canada by the late Dr Paul Reed of StatsCan, referred to above).[23] Although it is also noted that DAE did explore the possibility of including frequency of religious attendance in the model specification this approach was rejected because of concerns over independence of the variables of frequency of attendance and identification of attendance.[24] Still,

---

[23]   Another recent discussion of the relationship between "spirituality" and "religion" and the influence of both on "resiliency" in a student population may be found in: Allison C Culey, 'An Analysis of Religious and Spiritual Beliefs and Behaviours in College Students' (Research Paper 304, St Catherine University, 2014) . This paper refers to an earlier study of Dr Paul Reed: P G Reed, 'An Emerging Paradigm for the Investigation of Spirituality in Nursing' (1992) 15(5) *Research in Nursing and Health*.

[24]   *DAE Report*, above n 22, 35-37. This element of the DAE analysis is problematical. If two variables are highly correlated, then there a case for not including both measures in a cognate measure of religiosity. However, just because two variables are likely to be correlated does not necessarily lead to a judgement that one variable (attestation of religious attendance) should be preferred over another (frequency of attendance). The case for choosing the former over the latter as the key measure of religiosity has not been well made in the *DAE Report*.

even if measuring religiosity in terms of frequency of attendance does not improve the specification of the model statistically, it would appear to increase the explanatory power of the model for the public theologian, public policy maker or sociologist of religion. Surely, it is more useful to measure religiosity as a continuous variable – something that is measurable in degree – rather than the discrete variable of whether attendance occurred or not. Here we encounter a constraint embodied in the use of the logistic regression technique with its requisite need for the respondent to make an 'either or', 'yes or no' response to the question being tested. Logistic regression, framed with the noted parameters, is not best suited to measuring religiosity in degrees. This is a downside of the use of this statistical method.

The second key element of DAE's econometric analysis is capturing the 'treatment effect' of religiosity. DAE had a choice as to how they would capture this effect. DAE could have looked at how people who identify as being religious at the time the CRA survey was conducted, measured as having attending a religious event in youth or adult life, and then examine volunteering and giving behaviour for this cohort compared to non-religious people with no history of religious engagement. DAE chose a different method. DAE chose to focus only on those who came to religious attendance in adult life, ignoring the cohort who demonstrated religiosity in youth or adult life. In effect, DAE chose to focus the econometric modelling on only the cohort who was converted to religiosity in adult life as demonstrated by the CRA survey data. This adult 'converted' status was chosen as the measure for testing the impact of religiosity on volunteering and donating behaviour. In Figure 1.1 contained in the Appendix, this is the third data line identified by the category of N-Y.

There are a number of interesting observations to be made from this survey set as categorized. Once we have purged the series of missing values on the religiosity question, we see that over half of all adults (52 per cent) do not indicate attendance at religious events and half of this subset attended religious services when young. Of the other half who answer yes to religious attendance (48 per cent, in fact), almost all (94 per cent) attended religious services in youth. The cohort that moves into attendance in adult life– the cohort where the 'treatment effect' is measured- is just three per cent of the population. The sample for the treatment effect is therefore very small at just 181 respondents and just 140 for the 'volunteering' sub-sample and 127 for the 'giving' sub-sample. The low size of this critical cohort is a little concerning, and with the benefit of hindsight, seems to call for a higher survey sample size to strengthen the statistical foundations of the econometric assessment of the treatment effect.[25]

In order to isolate the impact of religiosity on volunteering and giving, DAE needed to control for other factors that could be expected to affect volunteering and donating behaviour. DAE included a substantive list of control variables including:[26]

1. age range;
2. gender;
3. education level;
4. employment status;
5. income;
6. health status; and
7. in the case of volunteering if there is some life history of volunteering (from the person or their parents).

DAEs approach here is highly sophisticated. Some of these factors are highly correlated with volunteering and giving behaviour. Employment, education, higher incomes and a history of volunteering are correlated with volunteering behaviour. For giving behaviour, age, gender, income and health are significant (interestingly and curiously employment is not statistically significant). The model controls for these effects by adjusting the reported responses on volunteering and giving to net out these influences – a practice that available statistical modelling packages can achieve relatively easily.

The results of the modelling of the treatment effect of religiosity as defined are fairly clear. In the case of volunteering, the correlation with religiosity as measured by the 'adult converted' (N-Y) and the 'religious all their lives cohort' (Y-Y) are both statistically significant. This establishes two points. Firstly, that the defined 'treatment effect' of the 'adult converted' cohort is established – moving to religious attendance in adult life is correlated with increased volunteering. What is also established is that people who are religious all their lives also volunteer more. In terms of giving behaviour the same conclusions are also established. There is a caveat, however. The cohort who is religious in youth but not attending services in adult life is also correlated with increased giving. This is an issue that could be pursued in any further iteration of the

---

25   Ibid, Table A.3, 31.
26   Ibid 10.

modelling exercise. It is clear that the treatment effect as defined for religiosity positively influences whether a person is a volunteer or a giver. Propositions 1 and 3 listed above are affirmed. Future work, drawing on similar work in Canada, referred to above, should also analyse the religiosity/spirituality effect on "membership" as well since this is important to social scientists and public policy.

The results are less compelling when we look at the quanta of hours volunteered or the level of donations given. Here the measured treatment effect is not statistically significant although there is some evidence of statistical significance for increased hours of volunteering and the level of giving from the Y-Y cohort – those religious since youth. In strict terms, propositions 2 and 4 are not affirmed.

From this logistic regression model an estimate of national economic impacts of volunteering and giving from religious persons can be derived. Given that propositions 2 and 4 above are not affirmed, DAE assumes that the average level of hours volunteered and dollars donated is not affected by religiosity. However, the logistic regression model calculates that more people are likely to be volunteers or donors as a result of attending religious services in adult life (and not in childhood). It estimates that a person who becomes religious is 1.7 times more likely, on average, to be a volunteer than someone who has never been religious.[27] From this DAE calculates the increased total hours of volunteering associated with religiosity. How are these evaluated? There are two choices - opportunity cost or replacement cost. The price of the former is measured at 45 per cent of the wage rate and the latter is the market cost one would have to pay to employ a person to conduct the same service - the wage rate. These wage rates are multiplied by the mean additional hours of volunteering that a religious person demonstrates relative to the mean hours volunteered for non-religious people. The valuation of the benefit for the opportunity cost method is $339 million per annum and $918 million per annum for replacement cost.[28] Although DAE favour the lower rate, the work of leading Chicago economist Gary Becker in his seminal article, 'A Theory of the Allocation of Time',[29] would favour application of the prevailing wage rate

[27] Ibid 14. The N-N cohort has a 38% chance of being a volunteer compared to the N-Y cohort of 63% (63/38=1.7)

[28] Ibid 18.

[29] Gary S Becker, 'A Theory of the Allocation of Time' (1965) 75(299) *The Economic Journal* 493-517.

to measure the price of time forgone in volunteering. This is essentially the approach recommended in the ABS supporting documentation to the ABS Satellite NPI National Account.[30] In light of this research of high standing, the higher estimate of $918 million is preferred. The model estimates that individuals who transition to being religious are 1.5 times more likely to be donors than those who have never been religious, all else being equal.[31] Expansion of the donation base for religious donors leads to $142 million extra donations per year.[32] So DAE estimates that the positive impact of the treatment of religiosity on giving is from roughly $0.5 billion to $1.15 billion per annum.[33]

Developing the DAE Research Project

When SEIROS embarked on its goal of measuring the economic impact of religion in Australia it held a colloquium of academics at the Australian Catholic University in Melbourne in 2015. At that event the author questioned the approach favoured at that juncture of focusing on a survey of volunteering and donation behaviour. This survey has now become a central element of the SEIROS research endeavour in collaboration with DAE. The author is writing this paper in broad support of the DAE research with some critical observations. So what gave rise to the author's original concern? The author of this paper, as an economist, religious researcher and political professional sought to encourage a wider research endeavour that would ultimately lead to an aggregate estimate of the contribution of the religious community to the Australian economy as a GDP estimate. This should still be the ultimate goal of the SEIROS project. In prosecuting the argument the author appealed to a research methodology based on a pyramid model. The task is to measure the extent to which religious people, through following their religious faith commitment, enhance the life of the nation in measurable economic terms. It is a significant research endeavour building an argument from strong empirical foundations. The pyramid analogy advocated here for this research method can be seen to have three levels. The first level is the accumulation of relevant data sources like the survey of CRA applied by DAE. This is the foundation of the pyramid. The research pyramid narrows as data converges

---

30   Australian Bureau of Statistics, above n 6, Appendix 6.
31   *DAE Report*, above n 22, 21.
32   Ibid iii.
33   Ibid 23.

around the hypotheses that emerge from the data. The second level of the research pyramid is the identification of points at which convergence of data leads to the presentation of hypotheses that can be tested. The DAE research for SEIROS is an example of this second level of analysis. New hypotheses sharpen the analysis further, higher reflection in the analytical pyramid, which it is hoped will narrow further towards an apex. This apex is the third level of research when we arrive, it is hoped, at a summary measure of the real contribution to the economic life of the nation that religious people make. In short, it is a GDP estimate of the religious sector's contribution to the national economic project. This final estimate will include the benefits that religious people enjoy as part of economic engagement in religious service delivery from which religious people will enjoy some benefits important to them such as religious education of their children. However, such an estimate – the apex of the research pyramid, will also capture the aggregate benefits religious people make to the life of the nation, including the value of their altruistic commitments. This last component – the altruistic component – is difficult to measure but commitment to volunteering and donating outside religious communities by religious people will be a significant part of this altruistic commitment. The whole research project, the three levels of the pyramid research method, will evolve organically as the project unfolds. It is a major program of research with a life cycle of research engagement, but the holistic research pyramid methodological model outlined here aligns with the broad approach of the scientific research method researchers adopt in contemporary empirical social science research. It is also an approach that seeks to satisfy the stringent requirements of peer reviewed social science review methods.

Although the research process is necessarily heuristic, and will organically develop, some remarks can be offered to build more of the data foundation and the second analytical level. The data we have on religion in economic life is not as developed as could be expected given the size of the religious sector. If we look at the retail sector there are monthly volume estimates of trade, quarterly breakdowns to the sub-sectoral level, quarterly measures of consumer and wholesale price movements – a rich offering from the ABS. However, there is no ABS measure of religious economic commitment per se. The ABS Satellite NPI National Account for the not-for-profit sector includes a religious component but this relates to specifically religious activities and does not include the involvement of religious organisations in education, health and social services.[34] There is no ABS measure of the religious contribution to economic activity outside the specific provision of religious services. The ACNC published data does not fill this void.

So although we have some data that helps build the foundations of the pyramid it is far from sufficient. What is needed is a rigorous statistical atlas of the economic footprint of the religious community in the nation taking into account the role, as already essayed in Canada, of "spirituality" where that is relevant as well. This atlas could be built up through case studies and sectoral studies but the firmest foundations of the pyramid would require religious communities to report their income and expenditure in relatively disaggregated levels. Religious communities will need to cooperate in economic research projects by providing transparent access to data and underlying data sources. There are clear benefits to the common good for religious communities to cooperate as greater information can only enhance sound policy formulation. Why should not religious organisations seek to be ready to account for the achievement of the mission, the hope for the enhancement of the common good, they seek to serve?[35] On the other hand, why should "secular" society disregard, implicitly or explicitly, in its forms of analysis, the importance that religions and their communities play to the common good?

If we turn to the second analytical phase of the pyramid model, there is clearly scope for more work. DAEs analysis of the treatment effect of religion is only a partial economic analysis. The Y-Y cohort – those who remain religious throughout life - make up the vast majority of persons engaged in religious activity that has economic effects. While the approach of DAE to limit the measure to a 'treatment effect' may enhance measurement of causality between volunteering/donating and religiosity, it ignores the contribution of the remaining 28% of the measured population in the Y-Y continually religious cohort. The logistic regression model shows that the correlation between sustained religiosity and giving, volunteering and membership is statistically significant. This is an area of promising further research. We do not have to restrict the analysis of the impact of religiosity on volunteering and giving to a 'treatment effect' of adult conversion. If we seek to approach the question of the economic impact of religiosity holistically we should seek to measure the contribution all religious people make to the life of the nation beyond their

---

[34]   Australian Bureau of Statistics, above n 6, Table 4.

[35]   See, 1 Peter 3.15 (New American Bible Version).

own communities, and not restrict the analysis to the adult converted cohort.

In the research analysed here the first and second levels of the pyramid are being built up. We do not yet see the apex of the research pyramid. In fact, we don't really see that much of the foundations. The second level of analysis needs a firmer foundation in sound data to build a stable analytical structure to eventually come to the apex of the research effort. We are at the start of an interesting and innovative analytical project that is likely to take a decade to build, if all goes well. But in the CRA survey and the DAE econometrics we have a good beginning.

Conclusion

In this SEIROS research task we have found strong statistical evidence for positive effects of religious activity with volunteering and donating behaviour. Religious people give more time and money with economic effects that are calculated to be up to roughly $1.15 billion per annum.[36] These are benefits that are given outside of religious institutions for the benefit of the community. There is evidence of religious people being the leaven in the daily bread of Australian community life. However, this is just a partial analysis focusing solely on additional volunteering and donations from people who have come to religious commitment in adult life without prior religious engagement.

The question the researcher of religion, economics and public policy wants to ask is what is the final effect, the full contribution of the religious community to the life of the nation? Do religious communities as such large employers contribute as much to the economy as the retail sector? It seems that they might well make a contribution at least that significant. What is needed is an economic model of the religious community in Australia that captures its full commitment and also the flow on effects to the economy of persons employed in the religious sector and the savings that are made by providing services at a lower cost than could be offered by government. We need to look at the economic contribution of all religious people not just those that have come to religious faith in adult life. We also need to ask the important counterfactual question. If religious communities walked away from their religious commitment what would be the impact on the Australian economy? How much extra taxation would be needed for the government to

---

[36] Australian Bureau of Statistics, above n 6, Table 4.

fully fund the services that religious communities currently provide even if we assume, as we should not, that the kind of service would be of the same kind: here the ethos of the service needs also to be considered but is difficult to capture merely economically.

This paper contends that although the research presented here shows significant economic commitment of religious people, we can more completely measure the extent to which religious people act in ways of significant benefit to the common good. While research so far shows that the economic contribution of religious commitment is substantial, further research can be expected to show that it is much more significant than the published estimates to date have revealed. It is an important question of public policy, of religious, economic and social scientific research to more fully measure the extent to which the 'good works' of religious Australians enhance the life of the Australian people and should therefore be taken into account in policy formation in relation to matters (such as religious education funding, charitable status and so on) that could encourage or discourage religious involvements.

APPENDIX

Figure 1.1 – *Final sample size for the four religiosity cohorts.*

	Original sample	Volunteering sub-sample	Giving sub-sample	Original sample (excluding missing religiosity status)
N -> N	1494 (19%)	1233 (25%)	1081 (25%)	1494 (24%)
Y -> N	1711 (22%)	1439 (29%)	1288 (29%)	1711 (28%)
N -> Y	181 (2%)	140 (3%)	127 (3%)	181 (3%)
Y -> Y	2766 (36%)	2136 (43%)	1885 (43%)	2766 (45%)
missing	1604 (21%)	0 (0%)	0 (0%)	-
Total	7756 (100%)	4948 (100%)	4381 (100%)	6152 (79%)

Source: Deloitte Access Economics, *Economic value of donating and volunteering behaviour associated with religiosity* (31 May 2018) Analysis and Political Observatory, 31.

Bibliography

Australian Bureau of Statistics, *5256.0 - Australian National Accounts: Non-Profit Institutions Satellite Account, 2012-13* (28 August 2015)

Australian Charities and Not-for-Profits Commission, *Economic Contribution of the Australian Charity Sector* (December 2017) <www.acnc.gov.au/tools/reports/economic-contribution-australian-charity-sector>

Australian Charities and Not-for-profits Commission, Parliament of Australia, *ACNC Annual Report 2016-17* (2017) 11 <https://www.acnc.gov.au/sites/default/files/Download%20full%202016-17%20%20ACNC%20Annual%20Report%20%5BPDF%208.45MB%5D.pdf>

Becker S Gary, 'A Theory of the Allocation of Time' (1965) 75(299) *The Economic Journal*

Benson T Iain, 'Pluralism, life worlds, civic virtues and civil charters' in M Christian Green and Pieter Coertzen (eds), *Religious Pluralism in Africa—Prospects and Limitations* (SUN Press, 2016)

Catholic Health Australia, *Strategic Direction Statement 2020* <https://www.cha.org.au/images/2020_CHA_Strategic_Direction_Statement.pdf>

Culey C Allison, 'An Analysis of Religious and Spiritual Beliefs and Behaviours in College Students' (Research Paper 304, St Catherine University, 2014) <https://sophia.stkate.edu/msw_papers/304/>. Reed G Paul, 'An Emerging Paradigm for the Investigation of Spirituality in Nursing' (1992) 15(5) *Research in Nursing and Health*.

Deloitte Access Economics, *Economic value of donating and volunteering behaviour associated with religiosity* (31 May 2018) Analysis and Political Observatory <https://apo.org.au/node/174751>

Lyons M and Nivison-Smith, 'The relationship between religion and volunteering in Australia' (2006) 41(4) *Australian Journal on Volunteering*.

MIT Economics at https://economics.mit.edu/files/32) accessed at 1.30am 28 May 2019.

National Catholic Education Commission, *Catholic Schools in Australia* (2016) <https://www.ncec.catholic.edu.au/resources/publications/401-catholic-schools-in-australia-2016/file>.

Oxford Companion to the Bible, Metzger B and Coogan M (eds), Oxford University Press, Oxford, 1993.

Wolfganag Pannenberg, *Basic Questions in Theology*: Volume I, 16, Augsburg Fortress Publishing, (2008).

Payten D, 'The price elasticity of charitable donations, evidence from Australian tax file data, paper presented to the Australian Conference of Economists, Canberra, 2018.

Prime Minister's Community Business Partnership, Community Business Partnership <https://www.communitybusinesspartnership.gov.au>

11

RELIGIOUS FREEDOM UNDER THE 'AUSTRALIAN CONSTITUTION' AND RECOMMENDATIONS THAT RELIGIOUS CONFESSION PRIVILEGE BE ABOLISHED

A. KEITH THOMPSON

Introduction

The *Australian Constitution* provides limited protection for religious freedom. Part copied from the United States ('US') *First Amendment*, s 116 includes the provision that the Commonwealth cannot "prohibit the free exercise of religion". But the Royal Commission into Institutional Responses to Child Sexual Abuse ('Royal Commission') established by the Gillard government in 2012, recommended to the Turnbull government in 2017, that religious confession privilege ('RCP') should not apply in child sexual abuse cases. It did not directly recommend that RCP should be abolished by the Commonwealth but affirmed that the retention of RCP was inconsistent with the rights of children under international human rights instruments.

The reason why the Royal Commission did not directly recommend the abolition of RCP by the federal government, appears to be because religious confession is an "exercise of religion" and the federal government to which the Royal Commission reported, is constitutionally forbidden to legislate in a way that would prohibit any religious exercise, including confidential religious confession. But unlike the US, in Australia, that prohibition does not bind the states, so the Royal Commission was recommending that the states abrogate RCP even though it did not directly say that.

If that is correct, then the Royal Commission was recommending that

Australian governments implement its recommendations in a manner that would avoid possible challenge under the *Constitution*. That is an option that was specifically left open by those who framed s 116 of the *Constitution* in March and April of 1898 since the intention was to protect the continuing right of the states to regulate religious observance without impediment. The Royal Commission also said such state action was necessary to protect the rights of children in accordance with Article 18(3) of *International Covenant on Civil and Political Rights* ('*ICCPR*'), but that recommendation is ironic (since the *ICCPR* is not binding in Australian domestic law) and possibly dishonest since the Royal Commission's reports show that institutional child abuse was under control by the mid-1990s and that the enduring problem was to provide remedies to historical victims whose rights to sue in tort for their injuries had been foreclosed by state legislative action in the early-1990s.

Why was it possibly dishonest to recommend that the abolition of RCP by the Australian states was necessary to protect the rights of children? The *ICCPR* which the Commonwealth ratified for all the states in 1980, says that manifestations of religion should be free from any limitation unless it is 'necessary' to pass a formal law to protect public health and safety and the rights and freedoms of others. The Royal Commission's data suggests that institutional child sexual abuse declined after the 1980s and was almost extinct by the year 2000 when the State of Queensland passed innovative child protection legislation that has dried it up completely in that state. It is thus questionable whether the 'abolish RCP' recommendation was necessary or even reasonable.

There are other reasonable criticisms of the 'abolish RCP' recommendation. These include the insight from Dr Marie Keenan's research in Ireland to the effect that the perpetrators of child sexual abuse do not confess the details of their sins for a variety of reasons including that they do not think they are doing wrong. There is also the theological insight that a disclosure of abuse by a child victim of child sexual abuse to a minister of religion does not qualify for RCP protection since an innocent child does not commit sin when abused by another.

This article discusses these criticisms of the Royal Commission's 'abolish RCP' recommendation in the context of the *Constitution's* prohibition on legislation that interferes with the free exercise of religion.

It does that in three parts. Since the Royal Commission was a federal body which might have been expected to make legislative recommendations to the federal government, in Part One, I discuss the history and nature of the federal prohibition by comparing the 18th century protection words (free exercise) with the more modern idea that the 'manifestation' of religion should receive limited protection. That discussion also traverses the vexed question of where the line should be drawn between the absolute freedom of conscience which is enshrined in the *ICCPR* and the limited freedom of religious manifestation which is there afforded.

In Part Two, I analyse the Royal Commission's 'abolish RCP' recommendation in detail in light of the criticisms noted above, and in Part Three I suggest what the Royal Commission could have recommended in light of its data. I first draw attention to the complicity of Australian governments in institutional child sexual abuse since they were often the authorities that referred children to the institutions where the abuse took place, even if they did not operate those institutions. That insight and the decline of institutional child sexual abuse since 1980, suggests that the problem the Royal Commission should have addressed was how the trauma caused by historic child sexual abuse in institutions should be treated. And I suggest that Nelson Mandela's 'Truth and Reconciliation' model from South Africa, would have been more helpful than allowing churches and particularly, the Catholic Church, to be blamed for almost everything that went wrong.

I conclude that while the Royal Commission was assigned a horrible task and that it is difficult to direct the media to underlying truth when sensation sells, the victims of historic institutional child sexual abuse and Australia generally would have been better off if the Royal Commission had focused on reconciliation and healing rather than on blame and compensation.

Part One – "Free Exercise" of Religion Under the 'Australian Constitution'

The phrase, "free exercise of religion" was copied into the *Australian Constitution* from the US *First Amendment* at the instance of H B Higgins representing Victoria during the Australian Constitutional Convention debates between February and March 1898. His various draft clauses responded to Patrick Glynn's successful introduction of words acknowledging "Almighty

God" in the Preamble,[1] but also to petitions which had been tabled at the Convention on April 6, 7, 12 and 20 the previous year.[2] In accordance with one of those petitions, Higgins' first draft, proposed that the states in the new Commonwealth should be prohibited from passing laws which prohibited the free exercise of religion. After debate, that draft was amended to prohibit both states and Commonwealth from passing such laws, but he ultimately settled upon a formula denying that legislative power only to the Commonwealth so that the power to moderate dangerous religious activity could be reserved to the states. Because there is considerable debate in contemporary Australia as to whether religious freedom should receive more protection than is provided in the federal *Constitution* and in the common law, I have taken time to explain the nature of the protection for religious freedom that is provided by the federal *Constitution*. The Royal Commission has made its recommendation that the states abolish RCP in child sexual abuse cases in the light of the current position.

The "free exercise" language chosen in Australia, was language that had been the subject of similar debate before it was used in the US *Bill of Rights* 120 years earlier. But coming before the 20th century human rights instruments which more specifically differentiated the protection of religious belief and action, there was no other authoritative religious protection language available to Higgins when he made his recommendation to the Convention.[3] His final recommendation may have intended that the states (but not the Commonwealth) would be able to regulate religious activity but

---

[1]   *Convention Debates*, February 7, 1898, 655-657, February 8, 1898, 658-663 and then again on March 2, 1898, 1732-1779 and on March 17, 1898, 2474. See, Parliamentary Library, *Australasian Federation Conference: Third Session: Debates,* Parliament of Australia (1898).

[2]   On April 6, 1897, 1201 electors from Victoria, South Australia, Tasmania and New South Wales, prayed 'that neither the Federal Government nor any State Parliament sh[ould] make any law respecting religion or prohibiting the free exercise thereof'. On April 7, 1897, 1663 electors from Victoria, South Australia and New South Wales delivered a very similar petition. On April 12, 1897, 2606 residents of New South Wales, Victoria, South Australia and Tasmania prayed similarly. And finally on April 20, 1897, 2337 persons from New South Wales, Victoria, South Australia and Tasmania prayed that 'no state in the Commonwealth should be allowed to make any law respecting religion or prohibiting the free exercise thereof'. See, Parliamentary Library, *Australasian Federation Conference: First Session: Debates,* Parliament of Australia (1897).

[3]   Michael W McConnell, 'The Origins and Historical Understanding of Free Exercise of Religion' in Thomas C Berg (eds), *The First Amendment: The Free Exercise of Religion Clause, Its Constitutional History and the Contemporary Debate* (Prometheus Books, 2008) 86.

could not interfere with religious beliefs. If so, that would have aligned with the US Supreme Court's decision upholding legislation proscribing Mormon polygamy 20 years earlier in *Reynolds*.[4] But if Higgins' choice of the American 'free exercise language' intended only the protection of religious belief rather than religious manifestations in Australia, then it is ironic since most US state constitutions of the 18th century chose the 'exercise' word to stop their governments interfering with action motivated by religious belief. The Maryland and Rhode Island state constitutions went further and protected respectively 'religious practice' and 'religious concernment' from government legislative action.[5]

James Madison's engagement with the need for formal protection of religious freedom parallels the Australian Convention debate as to whether formal protection was necessary at all. As one of the original authors of *The Federalist Papers*, Madison originally did not think a *Bill of Rights* was necessary because the states had their own constitutions and as a government of limited powers, the proposed US federal government would not be able to exercise powers that it had not been given.[6] During earlier debate about the free exercise provision in the *Virginia Bill of Rights* of 1776, he had asserted that free exercise of religion must be protected 'unless under color of religion the preservation of equal liberty and the existence of the State [we]re manifestly endangered' instead of George Mason's idea that religious exercise should be fully tolerated unless it 'disturb[ed] the peace, happiness or safety of society.'[7] But according to Vincent Blasi, Madison did not understand the protective importance of the US *Bill of Rights* that he authored until ten years later when

> … during the Washington administration,…he witnessed with dismay how [his *Federalist Papers*' co-writer and] Treasury Secretary Alexander Hamilton implemented a complex system of public finance that permitted him to consolidate power in the national government in such a way as to overwhelm Madison's carefully designed system of checks and balances.[8]

---

[4] *Reynolds v US* 98 US 145 (1878).

[5] McConnell, above n 3, 87.

[6] Berg, above n 3, Editor's Preface, 12. Note that this same reasoning characterises the debate between Barton, Higgins, Braddon, Symon and Cockburn in February and March of 1898 in Australia.

[7] As quoted in McConnell, above n 3, 87.

[8] University of Virginia School of Law, *First Amendment Author James Madison "Belated" in Discovering its Importance* (March 5 2004).

For David Little, Madison's early 'reservations about a bill of rights …
had nothing to do with a lack of conviction'. He was more concerned that
the inclusion of express freedoms 'as part of the national Constitution, might
suggest … that these rights were delegated by the government, rather than
possessed inalienably by the people'.[9] McConnell's analysis adds that the free
exercise formulation upon which both James Madison and George Mason
were agreed in 1776, included the idea that "full and free exercise of religion"
was exempt from general law except in cases of overriding importance.[10]

The meaning of the 'free exercise' phrase has not received a lot of
jurisprudential attention since. In its Australian context where it is the
core part of the third of four clauses identifying religious space where the
Commonwealth is prohibited from legislating,[11] it appears to protect what has
become known in the 20th century as the *forum externum*. That focus stands
in contrast to the focus of the fourth clause which prohibits religious tests
for public office and thus prevents the Commonwealth from some legislative
interference with the *forum internum*.[12] The US Supreme Court has suggested
that religious beliefs are completely protected by this *internum-externum*
dichotomy, but that acts done for religious reasons are not protected when
they would offend the requirements of generally applicable law,[13] though they
did not apply that standard from the 1960s until 1991.[14]

The dichotomy between the *forum internum* and the *forum externum* is
much clearer in 20th century human rights instruments, but those who have
considered the matter most carefully are agreed that it is a false and unhelpful

---

[9]   David Little, 'Theological Source of the Religion Clauses in Historical Perspective'
in James E Woods (eds) *The First Freedom, Religion and the Bill of Rights* (J.M. Dawson
Institute of Church-State Studies, Baylor University, 1990) 22-23.

[10]   McConnell, above n 3, 88.

[11]   *Australian Constitution* s 116.

[12]   The fourth subclause of s 116 prohibits the Commonwealth from making religious
tests 'a qualification for any office or public trust under the Commonwealth'.

[13]   See, eg, *Reynolds v US* 98 US 145 (1878); *Employment Division v Smith* 494 US 872 (1990).

[14]   See, eg, *Sherbert v Werner* 374 US 398 (1963) where the Supreme Court overturned a
State law which denied unemployment benefits denied to a Seventh Day Adventist
woman who would not work on Saturdays, and *Wisconsin v Yoder* 406 US 205 (1972)
where the Supreme Court held that the State's interest in educating Amish children
was outweighed by their parents' religious wish to continue their education after the
eighth grade outside the state school system.

distinction.[15] Both the *European Convention on Human Rights* ('*ECHR*')[16] and the *ICCPR* (which the Royal Commission invoked in its recommendation that RCP be abolished in child sexual abuse cases) state that it is absolutely impermissible for government to intrude into the internal beliefs of an individual no matter what justification may be present. But those instruments say that manifestations of religion may be limited by law where that is necessary 'to protect public safety, order, health or morals or the fundamental rights and freedoms of others'.[17]

The dichotomy is said to be unhelpful because a clear line between the *forum internum* and the *forum externum* cannot be identified in practice. When action follows thought, it cannot be separated from it. When separation is attempted, the *internum-externum* dichotomy results in minimal or non-existent protection for the *forum internum*.[18] Yet many completely harmless religious acts like personal prayer and church attendance - which the *forum internum* was surely intended to protect - are the almost automatic manifestation of what occurs first in the mind. To suggest that harmless acts that are inseparably connected with what happens inside someone's mind should only benefit from the lesser protection afforded to the *forum externum* under the *ECHR* and *ICCPR* trivialises what first happened in that mind. The conceptual difficulty is more obvious when it is suggested that the government can review and potentially outlaw all action that follows religious belief regardless of whether

---

[15]   See, eg, Carolyn M Evans, *Freedom of Religion or Belief under the European Convention on Human Rights* (Oxford University Press, 2012) chapter 5 and particularly 72-79; Paul M Taylor, *Freedom of Religion: UN and European Human Rights Law and Practice* (Cambridge University Press, 2005) chapter 3 and particularly 117-124.

[16]   *Convention for the Protection of Human Rights and Fundamental Freedoms*, opened for signature 4 November 1950, 213 UNTS 221 (entered into force 3 September 1953).

[17]   *International Covenant on Civil and Political Rights*, opened for signature 19 December 1966, 999 UNTS 171 (entered into force 23 March 1976), Article 18(3); *Convention for the Protection of Human Rights and Fundamental Freedoms*, opened for signature 4 November 1950, 213 UNTS 221 (entered into force 3 September 1953), Article 9(2). Article 9(2) of the *ECHR* expresses the same limitation similarly:
Freedom to manifest one's religion or beliefs shall be subject only to such limitations as are prescribed by law and are necessary in a democratic society in the interests of public safety, for the protection of public order, health or morals, or for the protection of the rights and freedoms of others.

[18]   Evans, above n 15 , 76-78; Taylor, above n 15, 115-117. See also Gabriel Moens, 'The Action-Belief Dichotomy and Freedom of Religion'(1989) 12 *Sydney Law* Review 195; Caroline Kayleigh Roberts, *The Other Side of the Coin? A Critical Examination of the Right Not to Manifest Religion or Belief in Article 9 of the European Convention on Human Rights* (LLM Thesis, Aberystwyth University, 2014) Chapter One and particularly 16-27.

it is harmful to others in society or not. For if, in the name of public safety, government is allowed to outlaw personal prayer when it is manifest in any external act, the *forum internum* has still been extinguished. Commentary also observes that the *forum internum-forum externum* dichotomy devalues human dignity to the extent it suggests human conduct is, or should be separable from human belief. The regulation of religious acts which are intimately connected with religious beliefs devalues human dignity because it ignores that the way of life most religious believers choose becomes a part of their identity as completely as their gender. Carolyn Evans summarised it this way:

> The wording of Article 9 [of the *ECHR*] itself does suggest that a distinction must be drawn between the general right to freedom of religion or belief and the right to manifest that religion or belief. Yet it is not clear that the first limb of Article 9 simply becomes irrelevant once some manifestation is in question. At some point, burdening external manifestations of belief must have serious implications for the internal realm.[19]

She then recites the facts of the famous *Wisconsin v Yoder*,[20] an Amish compulsory education case in the US and concludes:

> The Court held that th[e Amish] were entitled to [an exemption from the State requirement to leave their children in school till they turned 16] under the First Amendment. The outcome of that case was controversial but, whatever the merits of the decision, the reasoning shows up the extent to which the internal and external realms are intertwined. Religion for the Amish, was not 'merely a matter of theocratic beliefs' but a 'deep religious conviction' that pervaded their whole way of life. Interfering in the way of life would have the inevitable consequence of interfering with the belief. At some point, placing burdens on manifestation of belief must also be a breach of the basic right to freedom of religion or belief.[21]

The consequence of these insights is that religious belief and action are probably best understood as part of a conscience spectrum that should be considered in the context of other human rights demands. The essentiality of conscience and belief to human identity and dignity are manifest in the fact that the *ECHR* and *ICCPR* framers said that the internal part of religious belief and action should be inviolable or non-derogable. Whether actions taken for religious reasons should be protected is a matter of balance, how they are

---

19   Evans, above n 15, 76.
20   *Wisconsin v Yoder* 406 US 203 (1972).
21   Evans, above n 15, 76.

balanced depends upon how much those religious actions intrude into, or even violate the human rights and dignity of others. But the balancing that is done, must take into account the dignity of the religious believers involved, however unpopular or politically incorrect their belief choices may have become.

The Royal Commission did not discuss where the line should be drawn between the *forum internum* and the *forum externum* in Australia. No doubt it avoided that question because there is no jurisprudence in Australia which confirms what is protected by 'free exercise' under the federal *Constitution* and because the *ICCPR* is not binding in Australia despite ratification by the federal executive. If and when the meaning of 'free exercise' is litigated before the High Court, it will have to decide whether the constitutional words of absolute prohibition allow balancing against other human rights and that will likely depend on whether the *ICCPR* has yet been legislated into domestic law.[22] The Royal Commission seems to have accepted that the prohibition on the passage of Commonwealth laws that would interfere with the free exercise of religion is absolute, but as the framers discussed, the states can do anything they wish

---

[22] Though the meaning of 'free exercise' in s 116 of the *Australian Constitution* has never been authoritatively defined in Australian jurisprudence, various of the High Court's judgements in *Adelaide Company of Jehovah's Witnesses Inc v Commonwealth (Jehovah's Witnesses Case)* (1943) 67 CLR 116 suggest that legislation which intrudes into religious activity space is not absolutely forbidden. Latham CJ in particular said that freedom of religion was a relative concept and had to be balanced against obedience to law. Religion did not exempt people from a duty to obey the law and it was "for the court to determine, whether a particular law is an undue infringement of religious freedom" (ibid 131).

to do in religious exercise space.[23] While the states will also be committed to observance of Article 18 of the *ICCPR* if the Commonwealth follows up its ratification of that instrument with binding domestic legislation, the Royal Commission has reasoned the states would not breach any such future commitment by interfering with the practice of religious confession because that is necessary to protect the rights and freedoms of children. I will examine that necessity further in Part Two. For the purposes of this Part of this article, it suffices to say that the Royal Commission has not adequately balanced the competing rights when making its abolish RCP in child sexual abuse cases recommendation. That is, the Commission does not appear to have considered or respected the effect of its recommendation on the conscience and belief of thousands who exercise religion daily, including by religious confession, and who have nothing to do with child sexual abuse. Nor have the Commissioners balanced the human dignity of those thousands against the one or two who might benefit from the limited abrogation of RCP, though as we shall see in Part Two, even that alleged benefit is dubious.

What is a little surprising is that the Australian jurisdictions which have moved to implement the Royal Commission's 'abolish religious confession privilege' recommendation have not done so with direct amendments to their existing evidence legislation. Rather they have extended the scope of their existing mandatory child abuse reporting regimes. In the case of South

---

[23]   Note there is uncertainty as to how much scope the Australian Territories have in this space. That vexed question is beyond the scope of this article. It suffices to observe that the High Court has not been consistent in deciding the scope of the legislative power conferred on the Commonwealth for the Territories in s 122 of the *Constitution*, whether the Commonwealth is subject to the constitutional guarantees in ss 51(xxxi), 92 and by extension, s 116, when it makes laws for the Territories. Between 1969 (*Teori Tau v Commonwealth* (1969) 119 CLR 564) and 1997 (*Newcrest Mining (WA) Ltd v Commonwealth* (1997) 190 CLR 513). The answer seemed to be that s 51(xxxi) did not apply to the Territories but the decision in *Newcrest* in 1997 changed that. Similar uncertainty surrounds the applicability of ss 92 and 116 to the Territories because of obiter comments in the *Ansett Airlines* case in 1976 (*Attorney-General (WA) v Australian National Airways Commission* (1976) 138 CLR 492) and the *Stolen Generations* case in 1997 (*Kruger v Commonwealth* (1997) 190 CLR 1). But the question of whether the Commonwealth can repeal a law that it has passed to newly recognise a longstanding religious practice with previously uncertain protection (e.g. s 127 of the *Evidence Act 1995* (Cth) protecting religious confession privilege), has not arisen in Australian jurisprudence and may not ever arise if Australian legislators continue to respond to the Royal Commission's 'remove religious confession privilege' recommendation by changing mandatory reporting laws rather than by adjusting s 127 of their various expressions of the *Uniform Evidence Act*. This approach is discussed below in the final paragraph of this part.

Australia, s 30(1)(e) of the *Child and Young People (Safety) Act 2017* adds Ministers of Religion to those who must report if they 'suspect on reasonable grounds that a child or young person is, or may be at risk' under s 31 of the Act. And the Australian Capital Territory has created a new Reportable Conduct Scheme under a new Division 2.2A of the *Ombudsman Act 1989* to similar effect with minor consequential amendments to the *Children and Young People Act 2008* and the *Working with Vulnerable People (Background Checking) Act 2011* which allow information sharing between relevant government departments.[24] In Victoria, from 1 July 2017, s 327 of the *Crimes Act 1958* has been amended to require any adult to report suspected child abuse but again, there has been no amendment to s 127 of the *Evidence Act 2008* (Vic) which still protects communications received in religious confession.

Part Two – The Royal Commission's 'Abolish RCP' Recommendation

A *The Recommendation*

The Royal Commission made several recommendations concerning RCP. Most relevantly, recommendation 7.4 provides that:

> Laws concerning mandatory reporting to child protection authorities should not exempt persons in religious ministry from being required to report knowledge or suspicions formed, in whole or in part, on the basis of information disclosed in or in connection with a religious confession.[25]

Recommendation 35 also provided:

> Each state and territory government should ensure that the legislation it introduces
>
> to create the criminal offence of failure to report recommended in recommendation 33 addresses religious confessions as follows:

---

[24] Note that the ACT passed the *Royal Commission Criminal Justice Legislation Amendment Act 2019* with immediate effect from the 28 March 2019. It made further amendments to the *Children and Young Person Act 2008*, the *Crimes Act 1900*, the *Crimes (Sentencing) Act 2005* and the *Ombudsman Act 1989* but again did not touch the *Evidence Act 1995* and there are doubts about the constitutionality of this legislation in an Australian territory since it is doubtful that the Commonwealth can delegate power to "prohibit" religious practice which would count as "free exercise" within the meaning of s 116 of the federal *Constitution*.

[25] Commonwealth, Royal Commission into Institutional Responses to Child Sexual Abuse, *Final Report Recommendations* (2017) 17.

a. The criminal offence of failure to report should apply in relation to knowledge gained or suspicions that are or should have been formed, in whole or in part, on the basis of information disclosed in or in connection with a religious confession.

b. The legislation should exclude any existing excuse, protection or privilege in relation to religious confessions to the extent necessary to achieve this objective.

c. Religious confession should be defined to include a confession about the conduct[26] of a person associated with the institution made by a person to a second person who is in religious ministry in that second person's professional capacity according to the ritual of the church or religious denomination concerned. [27]

The Royal Commission also recommended that the Australian Catholic Bishop's Conference consult with the Holy See to establish whether information conveyed by a child during the sacrament of reconciliation was covered by the seal of confession,[28] and that other institutions with a rite of confession should implement policies requiring that the rite for children could only be conducted 'in an open space within the clear line of sight of another adult'.[29]

The Royal Commission justified all of its recommendations in relation to RCP by saying that it had 'heard evidence of a number of instances where disclosures of child sexual abuse were made in religious confession, by both victims and perpetrators,'[30] and because RCP can be abrogated without offending the *ICCPR* because such abrogation is necessary to protect children from child abuse.[31]

B   *Are Victims Of Child Sexual Abuse Sinners Who Need To Confess?*

Recommendation 16.26 demonstrates that the Royal Commission was alive to the theological argument that disclosures of sexual abuse against them by children do not amount to confessions because victims of sin are not sinners in need of religious confession in the absence of sin on their part. However,

---

[26]   See also Trigg, above n 86, 91-96, 151-152 on the need to identify religious belief and practice as an area of right which needs to be specially safeguarded from state coercion to accepted majority views and practices.

[27]   Ibid 102.

[28]   Ibid 55.

[29]   Ibid 59.

[30]   Royal Commission into Institutional Responses to Child Sexual Abuse, *Criminal Justice Report: Failure to report offence* (14 August 2017) ('*Criminal Justice Report*').

[31]   Ibid.

the Royal Commission suggested the Catholic Church seek clarification of whether communications by children with priests in confession were protected by the Catholic seal of confession. The point of that recommendation is that if a child victim of sexual abuse has not sinned, then Catholic priests and other clergy involved in confessional practice need to know that RCP does not protect such communications and that disclosures of such communications from a child do not breach canonical rules no matter how confidential they may have been in the mind of the child. There is little need for further comment on that recommendation to the Australian Catholic Bishop's Conference save to observe that the recommendation of the Irish Commission to Inquire into Child Abuse ('the Ryan Commission') which held that the interests of an affected child be taken into account, was much more sensitive and allowed responsible adults and mature children to veto the requirement for a police report.[32] Though the Irish Government has more recently passed the *Children First Act 2015* which does mandate clergy reporting when child protection concerns arise, the obligations in s 14 of that Act, arguably do not reach the generic confessions which Dr Marie Keenan says come to the clergy from sexual abusers.[33] As I explain below in more detail, her interviews suggest that when abusive clergy do disclose sexual sin in the confessional, they do not confess enough to alert the receiving priest that the partner in their sexual dalliance was a child.

C *Do The Perpetrators Of Child Sexual Abuse Confess To The Clergy?*

The Royal Commission's recommendations did not acknowledge the detail of Dr Keenan's research where Catholic priests were the perpetrators

---

[32]   While the Irish Minister for justice confirmed that the Cloyne and Ryan Reports had 'clearly demonstrated the need to strengthen our law in regard to the disclosure of information regarding offences against children' (Department of Justice and Equality, *Minister Shatter announced publication of Bill to further strengthen child protection* (25 April 2012), the *Criminal Justice (Withholding of Information on Offences against Children and Vulnerable Persons) Bill 2012* (now passed into law) which came three years after the Ryan Commission finished its work, exempted parents, guardians, doctors, nurses and many other persons working with children from disclosure, if for bona fide reasons they did not believe it was in the best interests of the child to report the matter. That Bill also provided that if children were mature enough to express the view that no report be made to the Garda (the Irish Police), then their views should be respected.

[33]   Marie Keenan, *Child Sexual Abuse and the Catholic Church: Gender, Power and Organizational Culture* (Oxford University Press, 2012) 163-164.

of child sexual abuse even though her research was taken seriously by the Ryan Commission. Rather, the Royal Commission relied on a summary that acknowledged that eight out of the nine former priests she interviewed in Irish prisons said they had gone to confession and had their guilt eased there. Although she railed against Catholic Church infrastructure as part of the reason why so much child sexual abuse had been perpetrated within its walls,[34] she confirmed that the Catholic priests who perpetrate child sexual abuse do not confess their crimes in detail in religious rites.[35] While she found that the confessional was a place of support for some of those she interviewed in prison, those priests never made enough disclosure in confession to invite guidance, counsel or reproof,[36] and since they minimized their offending and disclosed only the minimum required by the sacrament, it is doubtful that they identified the other party to their sexual sin as a child in need of protection.

Others have confirmed Keenan's insight including Australia's most famous abusive Catholic priest, George Risdale. He infamously told the Royal Commission that

… he never told anyone about his sexual abuse of boys, even during confession, because the 'overriding fear would have been losing the priesthood'. [37]

And Dr Karen Terry, who is well known for her research into child sexual abuse at the John Jay College of Criminal Justice, has stated that one of the principal reasons why child sexual abusers do not confess their criminality is because they do not accept that what they have done is either a sin or a crime; rather they believe that their relationships with children are of mutual benefit and perversely, that they educate and help the younger 'partner'.[38]

D   *The Royal Commission's Justification Of Its Recommendation*

Since the evidence suggests that the perpetrators of child sexual abuse do not confess their child sexual abuse in confession, and since child victims of sexual abuse are not sinners in most theologies, it is difficult to understand

---

34   Ibid xxv, xxx, 23-25, 42-43, 46-47, 51-53, 172-174.
35   Ibid 162-165.
36   Ibid 164.
37   Andrew Joubaridis, 'Vile paedophile Gerald Ridsdale will give evidence at Royal Commission today' *News Limited* (Online) 27 May 2015.
38   See, eg, Karen J Terry, *Sexual Offenses and Offenders, Theory, Practice and Policy* (Wadsworth Cengage Learning, 2nd edition, 2013) 106 and 113.

why the Royal Commission recommended that RCP should be abolished by the Australian states and territories in child sexual abuse cases. The Royal Commission's answer was simply that it had 'heard evidence of a number of instances where disclosures of child sexual abuse were made in religious confession, by both victims and perpetrators.'[39] The Royal Commission then justified its "abolish RCP recommendation" by saying that it was necessary to protect children from child sexual abuse and that manifestations of religion could be limited under the *ICCPR* in cases of necessity.[40]

E   *Other Reasons Why The Abolition Of RCP Is Not Necessary Within The Meaning Of The ICCPR*

The evidence above suggests that child discussions of abuse with clergy do not constitute confessions, and that perpetrator confession is rare, if it exists at all. But there are other reasons to doubt the Royal Commission's recommendation that the abolition of RCP is necessary.

The first is that the Royal Commission's own statistics suggest that child sexual abuse in institutions has been declining since the 1980s and the case studies they reported do not disclose evidence of abuse in religious institutions since 2000. The second reason is philosophical and dates back to Jeremy Bentham's 1827 assertion that the benefit to justice served by abolition of RCP would be rare if not non-existent. We will discuss those reasons in turn.

F   *The Royal Commission Did Not Uncover Any Cases Of Child Sexual Abuse In Church Institutions After The Year 2000*

Those who work in religious institutions are not the only people who potentially go to confession, but it is significant for the purposes of determining necessity within the meaning of Article 18(3) of the *ICCPR* and in the context of Royal Commission and media concern, that the Royal

---

[39]   Royal Commission, *Criminal Justice Report*, above n 29.
[40]   Ibid.

Commission's reported case studies involved less than ten cases after 2000.[41] The Royal Commission's own graph suggests that the rate of child sexual abuse in Australian institutions generally began declining shortly after 1980,[42] but there was no commentary about the reasons for that decline (see Figure 3 in the Appendix).

It may be that church institutions became alive to the problem and took effective internal steps to respond to the crisis before the Royal Commission was established. But it is not without significance that the State of Queensland initiated an innovative child protection scheme in 2000 that required all employees and volunteers who would work with children in the future in that state, to undergo comprehensive nationwide police background checking (the Blue Card Check) before they could be so engaged.[43]

---

[41]   In Case Study 6, the first allegation was reported by the parents of the children to the principal in 2007 (Commonwealth, Royal Commission into Institutional Responses to Child Sexual Abuse, *Report of Case Study No. 6: The response of a primary school in the Toowoomba Catholic Education Office to the conduct of Gerard Byrnes* (2015) 4-6 . In Case Study 12, up to six allegations were made in an independent school affiliated with the Anglican Church in Perth between 1999 and 2009 (Commonwealth, Royal Commission into Institutional Responses to Child Sexual Abuse, *Report of Case Study No. 12: The response of an independent school in Perth to concerns raised about the conduct of a teacher between 1999 and 2009* (2015) 10-12 . In Case Study 18, abuse was perpetrated against ALA between 2004 and 2006 in undisclosed Australian Christian and Pentecostal churches (Commonwealth, Royal Commission into Institutional Responses to Child Sexual Abuse, *Report of Case Study No. 18: The response of the Australian Christian Churches and affiliated Pentecostal churches to allegations of child sexual abuse* (2015) 10. And in Case Study 23, various allegations were made about sexual abuse occurring after the year 2000 within Knox Grammar School which is affiliated with the Uniting Church (Commonwealth, Royal Commission into Institutional Responses to Child Sexual Abuse, Report of Case Study No. 23: The response of Knox Grammar School and the Uniting Church in Australia to the allegations of child sexual abuse at Knox Grammar School in Wahroonga, New South Wales (2016) 20-22. However readers should note that the Royal Commission has not yet released a number of other reports for a variety of reasons including that court cases are pending in some of them.

[42]   Commonwealth, Royal Commission into Institutional Responses to Child Sexual Abuse, *Analysis of Claims of Child Sexual Abuse made with Respect to Catholic Church Institutions in Australia* (2017) 21, Figure 3.

[43]   *Working with Children (Risk Management and Screening) Act 2000* (Qld). Note that the Working with Children Check system is called the "Blue Card Check" in Queensland, but it is not known by that name in other states. For details of the schemes in other Australian states and territories, see the following footnote.

Other Australian states followed suit[44] and save for an egregious Families South Australia case,[45] there has been no new institutional case of child sexual abuse in a Blue Card Check state after the scheme was implemented.

G   The Blue Card Scheme

The heart of these working with children protection schemes in Australia, is police checking when someone applies to work with children to identify 'any national charge or conviction (including spent convictions and pending non-conviction charges) for an offence (even if no conviction was recorded).'[46] While some of these provisions offend the presumption of innocence, the author has not been able to identify any case where that point has been taken and observes that although the removal of the presumption of innocence is not explicit, it presents as a necessary implication of the underlying legislation.[47] But in the context of this article, the effectiveness of Queensland's Blue Card Check system belies the Royal Commission's justification of the abolition

---

[44]   The current legislation in the states and territories is: *Working with Vulnerable People (Background Checking) Act 2011* (ACT); *Child Protection (Working with Children) Act 2012* (NSW); *Care and Protection of Children Act 2007* (NT); *Working with Children (Risk Management and Screening) Act 2000*(Qld); *Children's Protection Act 1993* (SA); *Registration to Work with Vulnerable People Act 2013* (Tas.); *Working With Children Act 2005* (Vic.); *Working with Children (Criminal Record Checking) Act 2004*(WA). See, Australian Institute of Family Studies, *Pre-employment screening: Working With Children Checks and Police Checks* (May 2016).

[45]   Shannon Grant McCoole was sentenced to 35 years imprisonment for multiple child abuse offences between January 2011 and June 2014. Ken McGregor and Josephine Lim, 'Families SA paedophile Shannon McCoole sentenced to 35 years in jail for horrific sexual abuse of children in care' *The Advertiser* (Online) August 7 2015.

[46]   This explanation is taken from the Queensland Government's official child protection site. State of Queensland Department of Justice and Attorney-General, *About the blue card system* (29 November 2017) Blue Card Services.

[47]   The principle of legality holds that fundamental human rights established in the common law may not be taken away except by clear and unambiguous statutory words of by necessary implication. See, eg, *Bropho v West Australia* (1990) 171 CLR 1, 17-18 (per Mason CJ, Deane, Dawson, Toohey, Gaudron and McHugh JJ) and *Wentworth v New South Wales Bar Association* (1992) 176 CLR 239, 252 (per Deane, Dawson, Toohey and Gaudron JJ). Nor does the removal of the presumption of innocence by necessary implication in Queensland and in other 'blue card' states, offend the *ICCPR*'s mandate that manifestation of religion should not be taken away except by explicit law when that law is clearly necessary to achieve a wise state legislative objective. The reason this *ICCPR* principle is not offended by the removal of the presumption of innocence is because the presumption of innocence has nothing to do with the manifestation of religion.

of RCP as being necessary for the protection of the rights of children. The Frequently Asked Questions section of the Queensland Government's Blue Card system website indicates that Blue Card applications are considered against information obtained from authorised bodies in Queensland and 'similar interstate authorities such as the Police, the office of the Director of Public Prosecutions, the Department of Corrective Services, the Department of Justice and Attorney-General and the courts'.[48] Unlike general police checking, the Blue Card Check 'considers all relevant offences across a person's lifetime',[49] and spent conviction legislative protections do not apply.[50]

H   Limitation Of Religious Exercise Under The ICCPR

The Royal Commission said that it understood the importance of RCP to people of faith but observed that the right of a person to freely practise religion was not absolute under Article 18 of the ICCPR since that article says that freedom of religion may be limited when limitation is necessary to protect public safety and, in this case, the rights and freedoms of children.[51]

With respect, the Royal Commission's summary of the meaning of Article 18 is unsatisfactory. As I have explained earlier in the paper, Article 18 has two dimensions. The first provides absolute protection to freedom of conscience – the *forum internum*. And the second provides protection to manifestations of religion except when *necessary* limitations are enacted in law to protect public safety, order, health, morals or the rights and freedoms of others. The language of the limitation is purposely objective, and for the reasons stated earlier in Part Two, it cannot be maintained that the abolition of RCP is *necessary* in Australia or in any of her states and territories. But the Royal Commission's belief that RCP should be abolished in the interests of protecting the rights and freedoms of others, is not new. Such arguments were common between the 17th and 19th centuries when Roman Catholics were regularly accused of terrorism in the wake of the Gunpowder Plot and

---

48   See, State of Queensland Department of Justice and Attorney-General, *General FAQs* (29 November 2017) Blue Card Services.

49   Ibid.

50   The applicable spent convictions legislation in Queensland is the *Criminal Law (Rehabilitation of Offenders) Act 1986*. A proposed new *Spent Convictions Bill* in 2008 as Queensland's part of an effort by the Standing Committee of Attorneys-General to standardize spent conviction legislation across all Australian jurisdictions, has lapsed.

51   Royal Commission, *Criminal Justice Report*, above n 29.

in an age when English law still did not allow Roman Catholics to vote.

I *Bentham (1827) And Others – The Abolition Of RCP Will Benefit No One*

Despite his aversion to all other forms of privilege,[52] Jeremy Bentham responded to "abolish RCP" arguments in the 19th century by affirming the primacy of freedom of conscience. He believed that RCP was essential to that freedom.[53] He explained:

> [A] coercion ... is altogether inconsistent and incompatible [with any idea of toleration] ... The advantage gained by the coercion – gained in the shape of assistance to justice – would be casual, and even rare; the mischief produced by it, constant and extensive...this institution is an essential feature of the catholic religion, and ... the catholic religion is not to be suppressed by force ... Repentance, and consequent abstinence from future misdeeds ... are the well-known consequences of the institution.[54]

He continued that secrets harvested by forcing the clergy to disclose confessions would be short-lived since people would cease confessing their sins the moment the confidentiality of their confessions was compromised.[55]

In a sense, Bentham was making a futility argument. Justice L'Heureux-Dubé developed those arguments further in 1991 when the Supreme Court of Canada confirmed that an ecumenical religious communications privilege should be recognised in that country on a case-by-case basis in accordance with 'Wigmore's 1904 canons'.[56] In her minority concurring judgment, she said that RCP should be recognised in Canada on the same basis as legal professional privilege. She was concerned that the majority's case-by-case ruling would leave penitents up in the air and chill religious freedom generally in Canada.[57] Quoting Sir Robin Cooke from the New Zealand Court of Appeal (and later the English House of Lords), she said that no 'person should suffer temporal prejudice because of what is uttered under the dictates or influence of spiritual

---

52 J H Wigmore, *Evidence in Trials at Common Law* (Boston Little Brown revised ed, 1961) Vol 8, 877.

53 Jeremy Bentham, *Rationale of Judicial Evidence* (Garland Publishing Inc, 1978) (Reprint of the 1827 edition published by Hunt and Clarke) Vol IV, 586-592.

54 Ibid 589-590.

55 Father Frank Brennan made similar observations in his article entitled 'Breaking the seal of the confessional a red herring that will not save one child' in *The Weekend Australian*, December 3-4 2016.

56 *R v Gruenke* [1991] 3 SCR 263.

57 Ibid 311-312.

belief';[58] and quoting Chief Justice Warren Burger of the US Supreme Court, she added that human beings needed to be able to disclose their flawed acts and thoughts to a spiritual counsellor with an expectation of absolute confidence.[59] Society had an enduring interest in preserving both freedom of religion and individual privacy because they transcended the pursuit of truth at all costs.

Justice L'Heureux-Dubé also thought it impractical to try and compel Catholic priests to disclose confessions and suggested that such compulsion was so like 'admitting confessions made under duress to police that the idea should be expressly condemned by the common law'.[60]

But if there is no point to the abolition of RCP which the Royal Commission recommended, is there anything else that the Royal Commission could or should have done to improve social justice in Australia? If the free exercise of religion which the Australian framers wanted to protect is valuable, and if freedom of conscience and religion under the *ICCPR* is so essential that legislative interference is only allowed when there is no other way to protect other rights in society, what was the Royal Commission to do within its terms of reference? If RCP was the unnecessary target of a reform proposal absent evidence showing that it was being abused against the interests of children, what should the Royal Commission have recommended to protect the interests of those who testified that they had been sexually abused in the past?

The answer is of course, that the Royal Commission has made many other recommendations, but the media have chosen to focus only on those which are useful for commercial reasons. The consideration that follows suggests that the Royal Commission's focus on compensation and institutional reform as its primary response to the psychological trauma occasioned by historical child sexual abuse, was misdirected because of public hysteria fomented by the media. The Chief Royal Commissioner's final words hinted at this failure when he acknowledged that most of the 8000 witnesses from whom the Commission had heard, had never previously spoken to the Police even though they had all become persons of maturity and good sense.[61] At the Australia and New

---

58   R v Howse [1983] NZLR 246, 251

59   R v Gruenke [1991] 3 SCR 263, 297 quoting Chief Justice Burger in *Trammel v United States* 445 U.S. 40 (1980), 51.

60   Ibid 304, citing J N Lyon, 'Privileged Communications – Penitent and Priest' (1964-1965) 7 *Criminal Law Quarterly* 327.

61   Peter McClellan, *Final Sitting Opening Address* (14 December 2017) Royal Commission into Institutional Responses to Child Sexual Abuse.

Zealand Association of Psychotherapy Conference on 30 September 2017, Chief Commissioner McClellan said that the Commission had published 50 research reports investigating subjects 'ranging from preventing institutional child sexual abuse to improving responses to victims and survivors.'[62] He further said that the redress schemes recommended by the Royal Commission included three core elements – 'a direct personal response; counselling and psychological care; and monetary payments.'[63] He spoke about the need for psychological care to be provided by 'practitioners with the qualifications and expertise to work with clients with complex trauma' and of the Commonwealth Government's acceptance of the Royal Commission's recommendation 'that counselling should be made available to survivors on a flexible basis throughout their lives as the need arises.'[64] And he also acknowledged that '[j]ustice for survivors [wa]s not confined to [the] criminal conviction of their perpetrator' and that court processes needed to change so that victims could tell their stories without being re-traumatised.[65] But the reasons why so many victims and survivors had not told their stories till this Royal Commission was created or how many more had still not done so, was left unclear. Did victims and survivors raise their voices before this Commission because providing testimony there was a better way to be heard than at the Police Station, or were they crying out for something else? Certainly, they wanted justice, but they could have sought that through existing justice enforcement agencies long ago. Were they rather looking for some deeper sense of reconciliation and closure than compensation or blame could provide? And did those victims who said they had discussed their trauma with clergy in confidential circumstances want to abolish the confidentiality that surrounded confessional for all? Would they not have seen that recommendation as excessive and the closure of a useful counselling process to many others suffering in the community? Many of those who had appeared before the Royal Commission felt validated by the Commissioners,[66] but how significant a part of their healing was that or any validation? Was validation more important than compensation and if that was

---

[62] Peter McClellan, Speech delivered at the Australia and New Zealand Association of Psychotherapy 30th Anniversary Conference, Sydney NSW, 30 September 2017.

[63] Ibid.

[64] Ibid.

[65] Peter McClellan, 'Criminal Justice Issues for the Royal Commission' (Speech delivered at the 2017 ODPP Victims' Voices Conference: Making Stronger Connections, Sydney NSW, 2 August 2017).

[66] Melissa Davey, 'Royal Commission Chair Peter McClellan to Retire, Supported by Abuse Survivors', The Guardian (Online) 20 December 2017.

so, why was there not more research into the healing that different kinds of validation could provide?

Part Three – What Else the Royal Commission has Done, and What More it Could Have Done

Because media interests have focused on the shortcomings of religious institutions and the recommendations the Royal Commission made to remedy those problems including the abolition of RCP, it is easy to gloss over the many other recommendations the Royal Commission made.[67] Those recommendations dealt generally with making institutions child safe, and included out of home care recommendations, recommendations for schools, clubs and sporting organisations, recommendations for detention organisations, religious organisations, and recommendations for those working with children who manifest harmful sexual behaviours.[68] But there were also recommendations about the creation of a fund to compensate the victims of historic child sexual abuse outside the existing legal system without meeting the normal legal standards of proof. That compensation regime and the recommended waiver of normal standards of judicial proof following the Royal Commission's internal prohibition on cross-examination so as to protect vulnerable victims and encourage their forthright participation in Commission proceedings, have been and remain controversial.[69]

However, this article will now suggest that the Royal Commission's focus on monetary compensation as the primary remedy for the victims of historic child sexual abuse, distracted those Commissioners from exploring

---

[67]   Ibid. In his final pre-retirement address, Chief Commissioner McClellan said the Royal Commission had made 'more than 400 recommendations about what institutions and governments should do to better protect children and respond to survivors.'

[68]   Commonwealth, Royal Commission into Institutional Responses to Child Sexual Abuse, *Final Report: Preface and Executive Summary* (2017) 5-100.

[69]   See, eg, Richard Guilliatt, 'Child sex abuse Inquiry's stance on recovered memories raises fears as report release nears' *The Australian* (Online) 2 December 2017. The views for the approach taken by the Royal Commission are set out in the following papers: Martine Powell et al, *An Evaluation of How Evidence is Elicited from Complainants of Child Sexual Abuse* (August 2017) The Royal Commission into Institutional Responses to Child Sexual Abuse; Phoebe Bowden, Terese Henning and David Plater, 'Balancing Fairness to Victims, Society and Defendants in the Cross-Examination of Vulnerable Witnesses: An Impossible Triangulation?' (2014) 37 *Melbourne University Law Review* 539. See also, McClellan, 'ODPP Victims' Voices Conference', above n 64.

other constructive things they could have recommended in contemporary Australian society to validate and heal the victims who did come forward and share their experiences.[70] Arguably, innovative social justice solutions were a part of the Royal Commission's remit since its terms of reference referred to the need to 'reduce impediments'[71] to appropriate response, and to identify 'what institutions and governments should do to … ensur[e] justice for victims through the provision of redress by institutions'.[72]

While it is easy to consider redress only in monetary terms, under Nelson Mandela's direction when he was seeking to create a new and more socially just society in South Africa, his Truth and Reconciliation Commission chose to interpret the redress reference innovatively. He spoke of 'millions [who] ha[d] suffered deprivation for decades' and the need to bring them together in a spirit of redress and reconciliation. He did not want 'a façade of unity'; he wanted 'to heal the wounds of the past by also addressing the plight of the victims.' His Commission would need to ensure that 'such violations never take place again', but also to ensure that 'the dignity of victims' was restored as far as possible and that they be provided with 'some degree of reparation.' Like the Royal Commission, his Commission was not to 'be a Court … or Tribunal', but the reconciliation and healing he sought 'w[ould] remain shallow if it [wa]s not accompanied by thorough-going changes.' He envisaged 'an encompassing process of transform[ation]'.[73]

Mandela's speech was tailored to the healing of a nation and his Commission was necessarily charged with a much larger task than Australia's

---

[70] In his final address to the media before the Royal Commission ceased to operate, Chief Commissioner McLellan said that very few of the victims who had given evidence before the Commission had previously revealed the circumstances of their abuse to the Police. See, Davey, above n 65. The reasons why those victims had not previously disclosed were not discussed, and it is unclear how many of them and others will seek compensation from the fund that the Royal Commission has recommended be established. The reasons for victim reticence remain murky matters of speculation and it is unclear whether victims are or feel healed by compensation payments.

[71] Royal Commission into Institutional Responses to Child Sexual Abuse, *Terms of Reference* (11 January 2013), (c) Chief Commissioner confirmed that he considered the Royal Commission's terms of reference 'require us to address the issue of justice for victims' in his address to the Australia and New Zealand Association of Psychotherapy Conference on 30 September 2017. See, McClellan, 'Australia and NZ Psychotherapy Conference', above n 61.

[72] Royal Commission, 'Terms of Reference', above n 70, (d)

[73] Nelson Mandela, '100 Day Speech: Opening Address to Parliament – President's Budget Debate' (Speech delivered at Parliament, Cape Town, 18 August 1994).

Royal Commission. But his insights into the innovation required of a successful new institution that was not to function as a court or tribunal in the interests of reconciliation and healing, are transferable. He knew that his nation could not afford to fully compensate its victims in monetary terms that would satisfy the legal requirements imposed by courts of law. But he sensed that full monetary compensation was not what his nation or its victims required. Rather, there must be a focus on the restoration of the human dignity of the victims; an understanding of the recognition that would empower them so that they could hold up their heads and speak truth to power in the future, instead of cowering in helpless silence as they had been obliged to do for decades.

The Royal Commission subcontracted many expert reports, but it did not focus on the psychological rehabilitation of victims, though it did recognise that need and took considerable trouble to make sure that it accommodated victim and survivor needs when it heard evidence from them.[74] But when it came to redress, the Commission appears to have considered that a reparations scheme coupled with institutional apologies, limited counselling and the assurance that these abuses will never happen again, would rehabilitate the victims that trusted it with testimony. Any reports the Royal Commission obtained into how victim rehabilitation works, have not been the focus of the Royal Commission's media releases. The Commission has been content to allow the media to report its work in ways that did little more than vilify churches. There has been no discussion of how many victims are likely to make reparation applications, though early media releases about the scheme suggest concern about abuse by prison inmates who could take advantage of low proof thresholds.[75]

The Royal Commission has not reported on what its victims said they needed to be rehabilitated. Indeed, since those answers are absent, it seems reasonable to infer that the Commission's previously silent victims, were not asked those questions directly, and the Commission's subcontracted experts were not asked to identify the things that victims thought would rehabilitate them. It is submitted that it would have been useful to know what motivated

---

[74]   McClellan, 'Australia and NZ Psychotherapy Conference', above n 61.

[75]   See, eg, Rachel Baxendale, 'No payout for abuse survivors who've done time, Turnbull says' *The Australian* (Online) 15 December 2017; Riley Stuart and Phillippa McDonald, 'Royal commission: Decision to block redress for some prisoners put under microscope', *ABC News* (Online) 16 December 2017.

the Royal Commission's previously silent witnesses to come forward now and what those individuals thought would rehabilitate them and others who have still not come forward.

Conclusion

So should the Australian states abolish RCP in child sexual abuse cases as the Royal Commission has recommended? Is that legislative change necessary if the law in contemporary Australia is to protect the rights of children under the *ICCPR* as the Royal Commission has asserted? And does that mean that the protection the framers of the *Australian Constitution* intended for "the free exercise of religion" is out of date?

The answer to all of these questions is, no. International human rights instruments still endorse the need to absolutely protect freedom of religious belief and only allow intrusion into religious acts when there is proof that those acts are harming others in obvious ways. There is of course, no causal connection between religious confession and child sexual abuse. The abolition of RCP would not prevent child sexual abuse in a single case.[76] While the Royal Commission did hear that child sexual abuse had been discussed in some confessional circumstances, those rare discussions neither prove that a change in this law is necessary, nor that such a change in the law would protect the rights of children. The suggestion that child sexual abusers habitually provide the clergy with detailed accounts of their atrocities is simply not true. Those who sexually abuse children hide their crimes from everyone for a variety of reasons.

The problem to which Prime Minister Gillard responded in 2012 when she established the Royal Commission was the inability of the victims of historic child sexual abuse to get the help they needed to be healed. That problem had been exacerbated by state government limitation legislation in the early 1990s designed to prevent those states becoming complicit parties in most of those cases.

But the sad thing is that there is no proof that either litigation or compensation will heal those who have survived child sexual abuse. We do

---

[76] See, eg, Keith Thompson, 'Should religious confession privilege be abolished in child abuse cases? Do child abusers confess their sins?' (2017) 8 *The West Australian Jurist* 95, 106. See also, Frank Brennan, 'Breaking the seal of the confessional a red herring that will not save a single child', *The Weekend Australian*, December 3-4 2016.

not know why victims and survivors do not report child sexual abuse and the Royal Commission's reports did not address this question. The Royal Commission has speculated that victim silence is the result of shame, an expectation of unbelief and the desire to avoid the trauma of reliving abuse during the criminal process.[77] Yet many who had never spoken before, came forward during the Royal Commission's hearings. Why was that?

Nelson Mandela's Truth and Reconciliation Commission in South Africa addressed a completely different order of abuse. He recognised that his state could not afford a comprehensive redress scheme, but he sensed that the healing his nation needed was not about money. The redemption of South Africa was about 'addressing the plight of the victims' and restoring their dignity with limited compensation and apologies as an almost symbolic gesture. He strove to avoid monetising the necessary reconciliation because his own redemption had come without price as his human dignity was reinstated following his release from prison as the world validated his suffering.

It would have been wonderful if the Royal Commission had considered the rehabilitation of victims holistically. The Commission was capable of formulating holistic recommendations because it learned how to validate its witnesses by avoiding unnecessary legal formality in its process.[78] But the focus on redress rather than rehabilitation and healing is a missed opportunity.

---

[77] Commonwealth, Royal Commission into Institutional Responses to Child Sexual Abuse, *Final Report: Volume 4 – Identifying and Disclosing Child Sexual Abuse* (2017) 77-117. See also, McClellan, 'Australia and NZ Psychotherapy Conference', above n 61.

[78] See, McClellan, 'Australia and NZ Psychotherapy Conference', above n 61; McClellan, 'ODPP Victims' Voices Conference', above n 64.

Appendix

Figure 3: Claims of child sexual abuse by decade of first alleged incident (where known)

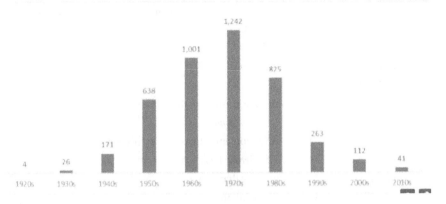

Figure 3 – Commonwealth, Royal Commission into Institutional Responses to Child Sexual Abuse, *Analysis of Claims of Child Sexual Abuse made with Respect to Catholic Church Institutions in Australia* (2017) 21, Figure 3.

Bibliography

Adelaide Company of Jehovah's Witnesses Inc v Commonwealth (Jehovah's Witnesses Case) (1943) 67 CLR 116

Attorney-General (WA) v Australian National Airways Commission (1976) 138 CLR 492)

Australian Constitution

Australian Institute of Family Studies, *Pre-employment screening: Working With Children Checks and Police Checks* (May 2016) <https://aifs.gov.au/cfca/publications/pre-employment-screening-working-children-checks-and-police-checks/part-overview>

Baxendale Rachel, 'No payout for abuse survivors who've done time, Turnbull says' *The Australian* (Online) 15 December 2017 <https://www.theaustralian.com.au/national-affairs/no-payout-for-abuse-survivors-whove-done-time-turnbull-says/news-story/00112d5aa468827bd7352dac40ec7613>

Bentham Jeremy, *Rationale of Judicial Evidence* (Garland Publishing Inc, 1978) (Reprint of the 1827 edition published by Hunt and Clarke)

Bowden Phoebe, Terese Henning and David Plater, 'Balancing Fairness to Victims, Society and Defendants in the Cross-Examination of Vulnerable

Witnesses: An Impossible Triangulation?' (2014) 37 *Melbourne University Law Review*

Brennan Frank, 'Breaking the seal of the confessional a red herring that will not save one child', *The Weekend Australian* (Online) December 3-4 2016

Bropho v West Australia (1990) 171 CLR 1

Care and Protection of Children Act 2007 (NT)

Child Protection (Working with Children) Act 2012 (NSW)

Children's Protection Act 1993 (SA)

Commonwealth, Royal Commission into Institutional Responses to Child Sexual Abuse, *Final Report Recommendations* (2017)

Commonwealth, Royal Commission into Institutional Responses to Child Sexual Abuse, *Criminal Justice Report: Failure to report offence* (14 August 2017) <https://www.childabuseroyalcommission.gov.au/getattachment/aa9249f1-b490-4b26-9772-a1ddb36e85d4/Failure-to-report-offence>.

Commonwealth, Royal Commission into Institutional Responses to Child Sexual Abuse, *Report of Case Study No. 6: The response of a primary school in the Toowoomba Catholic Education Office to the conduct of Gerard Byrnes* (2015) <https://www.childabuseroyalcommission.gov.au/sites/default/files/file-list/Case%20Study%206%20-%20Findings%20Report%20-%20Toowoomba%20Catholic%20school%20and%20Catholic%20Education%20Office.pdf>

Commonwealth, Royal Commission into Institutional Responses to Child Sexual Abuse, *Report of Case Study No. 12: The response of an independent school in Perth to concerns raised about the conduct of a teacher between 1999 and 2009* (2015) <https://www.childabuseroyalcommission.gov.au/sites/default/files/file-list/Case%20Study%2012%20-%20Findings%20Report%20-%20Perth%20Independent%20School.pdf>

Commonwealth, Royal Commission into Institutional Responses to Child Sexual Abuse, *Report of Case Study No. 18: The response of the Australian Christian Churches and affiliated Pentecostal churches to allegations of child sexual abuse* (2015) <https://www.childabuseroyalcommission.gov.au/sites/default/files/file-list/Case%20Study%2018%20-%20Findings%20Report%20-%20Australian%20Christian%20Churches.pdf>

Commonwealth, Royal Commission into Institutional Responses to Child Sexual Abuse, Report of Case Study No. 23: The response of Knox Grammar School and the Uniting Church in Australia to the allegations of child sexual abuse at Knox Grammar School in Wahroonga, New South Wales (2016) <https://www.childabuseroyalcommission.gov.au/sites/default/files/file-list/Case%20Study%2023%20-%20Findings%20Report%20-%20Knox%20Grammar%20School.pdf>

Commonwealth, Royal Commission into Institutional Responses to Child Sexual Abuse, *Analysis of Claims of Child Sexual Abuse made with Respect to Catholic Church Institutions in Australia* (2017) <https://www.childabuseroyalcommission.gov.au/sites/default/files/research_report_-_analysis_of_claims_of_made_with_respect_to_catholic_church_institutions_-_institutions_of_interest_0.pdf>

Commonwealth, Royal Commission into Institutional Responses to Child Sexual Abuse, *Final Report: Preface and Executive Summary* (2017)

Commonwealth, Royal Commission into Institutional Responses to Child Sexual Abuse, *Final Report: Volume 4 – Identifying and Disclosing Child Sexual Abuse* (2017)

Commonwealth, Royal Commission into Institutional Responses to Child Sexual Abuse, *Terms of Reference* (11 January 2013) <www.childabuseroyalcommission.gov.au/terms-reference>

Convention for the Protection of Human Rights and Fundamental Freedoms, opened for signature 4 November 1950, 213 UNTS 221 (entered into force 3 September 1953)

Criminal Justice (Withholding of Information on Offences against Children and Vulnerable Persons) Bill 2012

Criminal Law (Rehabilitation of Offenders) Act 1986

Davey Melissa, 'Royal Commission Chair Peter McClellan to Retire, Supported by Abuse Survivors', *The Guardian* (Online) 20 December 2017 <https://www.theguardian.com/australia-news/2017/dec/20/royal-commission-chair-peter-mcclellan-to-retire-supported-by-abuse-survivors>

Department of Justice and Equality, *Minister Shatter announced publication of Bill to further strengthen child protection* (25 April 2012) <http://www.justice.ie/en/JELR/Pages/PR12000117>

Employment Division v Smith 494 US 872 (1990)

Evans M Carolyn, *Freedom of Religion or Belief under the European Convention on Human Rights* (Oxford University Press, 2012)

Evidence Act 1995 (Cth)

Guilliatt Richard, 'Child sex abuse Inquiry's stance on recovered memories raises fears as report release nears' *The Australian* (Online) 2 December 2017 <https://www.theaustralian.com.au/.../d6deed03a1448507f6344b9bfe92358c>

International Covenant on Civil and Political Rights, opened for signature 19 December 1966, 999 UNTS 171 (entered into force 23 March 1976)

Joubaridis Andrew, 'Vile paedophile Gerald Ridsdale will give evidence at Royal Commission today' *News Limited* (Online) 27 May 2015 <http://www.news.com.au/national/courts-law/vile-paedophile-gerald-ridsdale-will-give-evidence-at-royal-commission-today/news-story/630 54c92d762e9c3d53629b8da59ccab>

Keenan Marie, *Child Sexual Abuse and the Catholic Church: Gender, Power and Organizational Culture* (Oxford University Press, 2012)

Kruger v Commonwealth (1997) 190 CLR 1

Little David, 'Theological Source of the Religion Clauses in Historical Perspective' in James E Woods (eds) *The First Freedom, Religion and the Bill of Rights* (J.M. Dawson Institute of Church-State Studies, Baylor University, 1990)

Lyon N J, 'Privileged Communications – Penitent and Priest' (1964-1965) 7 *Criminal Law Quarterly*

Mandela Nelson, '100 Day Speech: Opening Address to Parliament – President's Budget Debate' (Speech delivered at Parliament, Cape Town, 18 August 1994) <http://www.africa.upenn.edu/Govern_Political/Mandel_100.html>

McClellan Peter, 'Criminal Justice Issues for the Royal Commission' (Speech delivered at the 2017 ODPP Victims' Voices Conference: Making Stronger Connections, Sydney NSW, 2 August 2017) <https://www.childabuseroyalcommission.gov.au/speeches/2017-odpp-victims-voices-conference-making-stronger-connections>

McClellan Peter, *Final Sitting Opening Address* (14 December 2017) Royal Commission into Institutional Responses to Child Sexual Abuse <https://www.childabuseroyalcommission.gov.au/sites/default/files/final_sitting_opening_address_sydney.pdf>

McClellan Peter, Speech delivered at the Australia and New Zealand Association of Psychotherapy 30th Anniversary Conference, Sydney NSW, 30 September 2017 <www.childabuseroyalcommission.gov.au/speeches/australia-and-new-zealand-association-psychotherapy-30th-year-anniversary-conference>

McConnell W Michael, 'The Origins and Historical Understanding of Free Exercise of Religion' in Thomas C Berg (eds), *The First Amendment: The Free Exercise of Religion Clause, Its Constitutional History and the Contemporary Debate* (Prometheus Books, 2008)

McGregor Ken and Josephine Lim, 'Families SA paedophile Shannon McCoole sentenced to 35 years in jail for horrific sexual abuse of children in care' *The Advertiser* (Online) August 7 2015 <http://www.

adelaidenow.com.au/news/south-australia/families-sa-paedophile-shannon-mccoole-sentenced-to-35-years-in-jail-for-horrific-sexual-abuse-of-children-in-care/news-story/bcd114acaa40ff568ceb659f6685 e24f>

Moens Gabriel, 'The Action-Belief Dichotomy and Freedom of Religion'(1989) 12 *Sydney Law Review*

Newcrest Mining (WA) Ltd v Commonwealth (1997) 190 CLR 513

Parliamentary Library, *Australasian Federation Conference: First Session: Debates,* Parliament of Australia (1897) <http://parlinfo.aph.gov.au/parlInfo/search/display/display.w3p;adv=yes;orderBy=customrank;page=0;query=exercise%20religion%20Dataset%3Aconventions;rec=12;resCount=Default>)

Parliamentary Library, *Australasian Federation Conference: Third Session: Debates,* Parliament of Australia (1898) <http://parlinfo.aph.gov.au/parlInfo/search/display/display.w3p;adv=yes;db=CONSTITUTION;id=constitution%2Fconventions%2F1898-1103;orderBy=customrank;page=0;query=australasian%20federation%20conference;rec=8;resCount=Default>

Powell Martine et al, *An Evaluation of How Evidence is Elicited from Complainants of Child Sexual Abuse* (August 2017) The Royal Commission into Institutional Responses to Child Sexual Abuse <https://www.childabuseroyalcommission.gov.au/sites/default/files/file-list/research_report_-_an_evaluation_of_how_evidence_is_elicited_from_complainants_of_child_sexual_abuse_and_supplementary_-_government_responses.pdf>

R v Gruenke [1991] 3 SCR 263

R v Howse [1983] NZLR 246, 251

Registration to Work with Vulnerable People Act 2013 (Tas.)

Reynolds v US 98 US 145 (1878)

Roberts Kayleigh Caroline, *The Other Side of the Coin? A Critical Examination of the Right Not to Manifest Religion or Belief in Article 9 of the European Convention on Human Rights* (LLM Thesis, Aberystwyth University, 2014)

Sherbert v Werner 374 US 398 (1963)

State of Queensland Department of Justice and Attorney-General, *About the blue card system* (29 November 2017) Blue Card Services <https://www.bluecard.qld.gov.au/about.html>

State of Queensland Department of Justice and Attorney-General, *General FAQs* (29 November 2017) Blue Card Services <https://www.bluecard.qld.gov.au/faqs/general-faqs.html>

Stuart Riley and Phillippa McDonald, 'Royal commission: Decision to block redress for some prisoners put under microscope', *ABC News* (Online) 16 December 2017<http://www.abc.net.au/news/2017-12-16/royal-commission-government-criticised-for-blocking-jail-redress/9264970>

Taylor M Paul, *Freedom of Religion: UN and European Human Rights Law and Practice* (Cambridge University Press, 2005)

Teori Tau v Commonwealth (1969) 119 CLR 564

Terry J Karen, *Sexual Offenses and Offenders, Theory, Practice and Policy* (Wadsworth Cengage Learning, 2nd edition, 2013)

Thompson Keith, 'Should religious confession privilege be abolished in child abuse cases? Do child abusers confess their sins?' (2017) 8 *The West Australian Jurist*

Trammel v United States 445 U.S. 40 (1980)

University of Virginia School of Law, *First Amendment Author James Madison "Belated" in Discovering its Importance* (March 5 2004) <https://content.law.virginia.edu/news/2004_spr/blasi.htm>

Wentworth v New South Wales Bar Association (1992) 176 CLR 239

Wigmore H J, *Evidence in Trials at Common Law* (Boston Little Brown revised ed, 1961)

Wisconsin v Yoder 406 US 205 (1972)

Working with Children (Criminal Record Checking) Act 2004 (WA)

Working with Children (Risk Management and Screening) Act 2000 (Qld)

Working with Children (Risk Management and Screening) Act 2000 (Qld)

Working With Children Act 2005 (Vic.)

Working with Vulnerable People (Background Checking) Act 2011 (ACT)

12

SECTION 116 OF THE AUSTRALIAN CONSTITUTION IN THE CONTEXT OF FIRST WORLD WAR CONSCIENTIOUS OBJECTION

RICK SARRE

Abstract

In this paper I examine the purported right of persons to disobey conscription laws and claim that their religious beliefs preclude them from reporting for military service. In reviewing this issue in the context of Australian legal and political history, I will report that conscientious objectors were thrown a lifeline a century ago by the defeat of the two plebiscites called to determine whether conscription should be imposed during the First World War. Religion played a major role in the plebiscite debates. It was, indeed, a unique period in Australia's history.

Conscientious objection on religious grounds falls into the broad legal realm where religion and law intersect, and usually activates a discussion about one's freedom (or not) to observe one's religious beliefs and requirements in defiance of the law. The starting point for any discussion of freedom of religion is s 116 of the *Australian Constitution* which, on first reading, appears to guarantee such freedom by setting out a separation between church and state.[1] In the discussion below, I surmise that that guarantee is over-stated. Having said that, however, it is possible to conclude that there is a *de facto* right, or, better stated, a qualified right in Australian law regarding a person's choice to become a conscientious objector on the basis of his or her religious beliefs.

---

[1]   Paul Babie, 'National Security and the Free Exercise Guarantee Of Section 116: Time For A Judicial Interpretive Update' (2017) 45 *Federal Law Review* 351.

Introduction: The Inter-Relationship of Law and Religion

Before I begin an examination of the topic of freedom of religion in Australia (and, more specifically, the freedom an objector may claim in order to spurn compulsory military service), it is useful to trace briefly the way in which law and religion have traditionally intersected in Anglo-Australian legal history.[2] Until the mid-18th century, European scholarship was dominated by theologians. The legal scholars, and the colleges and universities where they were housed, were found predominantly within religiously-based orders. This is hardly surprising, given the history of the Christian church and its relationship with the state. From the 3rd to the 16th centuries in Britain, church autonomy was guaranteed by the church being co-sovereign with the state.[3] In medieval times, the church provided the forum for any announcement of official government policy. It occupied a central role in communities. Any attempt to question the church's authority was seen as tantamount to treason. Indeed, prior to the 17th century, there was a wide consensus that the English monarch ruled by 'divine right'. Nor was there any official doubt in law that God existed.[4] Until the end of the 18th century, arguments based upon scriptural interpretations of the Bible were acceptable as evidence in the English courts, and the Christian religion was part of the law of the land.[5]

The consequence of all of this was a mingling of theological and legal notions in the day to day running of the state. Even to this day, the King or Queen of England is the official head of the Church of England. The

---

2   This history informs what is referred to as the common law legal system. See James Thomson and Rick Sarre (eds), *Introduction to Law*, (Butterworths, 3rd edition, 2001) 19.

3   Marci Hamilton, *God Versus the Gavel: Religion and the Rule of Law* (CUP, 2005) 240-241.

4   See generally, Courtney Kenny, 'The Evolution of the Law of Blasphemy' (1922) 1(2) *Cambridge Law Journal* 127, 131. See also, Rick Sarre, 'Why theology should play a role in the criminological enterprise' in Emil Płwaczewski (ed), *Current Problems of the Penal Law and Criminology* (forthcoming, 2019).

5   Refer Court of King's Bench, Westminster, July 24, 1797, before Chief Justice Lord Kenyon and a special jury, in the case of *King v Williams*. Williams was on trial for publishing Thomas Paine's *The Age of Reason*. Lord Kenyon's charge to the jury went as follows:

> Gentlemen, we sit here in Christian assembly to administer the law of the land; and I am to take my knowledge of what the law is from that which has been sanctioned by a great variety of legal decisions. I am bound to state to you what my predecessors in Mr. Wollaston's Case (2 Strange, 834) stated half a century ago in this Court, of which I am an humble member, namely, that the Christian religion is part of the law of the land (at 14).

Queen's executive authority and her role as 'Defender of the Faith' remain inextricably mixed.

This tradition carried on into colonial times. It is noteworthy that religious leaders continued to hold the highest positions of societal authority for at least the first three centuries of the American colonies notwithstanding their victory in the War of Independence of 1776.[6] To the extent that the Queen is the head of the Executive under the *Australian Constitution*, Australians are obliged to accept her role today as Defender of the Faith too.

Does Australia Have Separation of Church and State?

The answer to this question is, not surprisingly, difficult to determine.[7] It is useful to begin with a recitation of s 116 of the *Australian Constitution* which reads as follows:

> The Commonwealth shall not make any law for establishing any religion, or for imposing any religious observance, or for prohibiting the free exercise of any religion, and no religious test shall be required as a qualification for any office or public trust under the Commonwealth.

This is, *prima facie*, a statement of separation of church and state or, more accurately, "co-operation" of church and state which recognises both the ability to cooperate alongside the fact of a jurisdictional separation. Yes, there is a separation in so far as no religion can demand that the state, or its people, act in a particular religious way, or observe some particular religious rites (as obtains, for example, in a theocratic nation such as Iran). And yes, there is a separation in so far as religions are protected from interference from the state. But this is a qualified separation. If a religious order were to allow child marriage, for example, or any other practice that were to be deemed unacceptable in modern Australia such as female genital mutilation, the state could intervene and ban such a practice.[8] Moreover, an Australian government could ban a religion if it were deemed to be, for example, a threat to the state.[9]

---

[6] E Digby Baltzell, *Puritan Boston and Quaker Philadelphia* (Free Press, 1979) 335.

[7] See generally Gary Bouma et al, *Freedom of religion and belief in 21st century Australia* (2011) The Australian Human Rights Commission.

[8] Luke Beck, 'Clear and Emphatic: The Separation of Church and State under the Australian Constitution' (2008) 27(2) *The University of Tasmanian Law Review* 2.

[9] The *Jehovah's Witnesses* case on this point is discussed below (i.e. *Adelaide Co. of Jehovah's Witnesses Inc v Commonwealth* (1943) 67 CLR 116).

True, the Commonwealth has never done, or attempted to do, any of the things specifically set out as proscriptions in s 116. But the separation is largely illusory. Indeed, in this country we find inextricable links between the Christian religion and the state. Religious organisations, and hence their members, from time to time and under specified legislation, get special privileges. For example, there are protections in the *Fair Work Act 2009* (Cth),[10] the *Migration Act 1958* (Cth) and the *Evidence Act 1995* (Cth) preventing, *prima facie,* the success of any anti-discrimination suits (launched by virtue of the significant raft of state and federal anti-discrimination legislation)[11] that may be brought against those exercising *bona fide* religious practices. A strict separation of church and state would not tolerate that. Moreover, religious groups as institutions pay no tax due to exemptions found in the *Taxation Administration Act 1953* (Cth). And by way of final example, donors for specified donations can claim tax deductibility under the *Charities Act 2013* (Cth) if the donations are for registered bodies including those that are formed for "the advancement of religion."[12]

There is more to add, too, in advancing the argument that the church and state in this country are in more of a symbiotic relationship than a bifurcated one. Observers point to the way in which governments in Australia provide religious schools with significant levels of state funding.[13] The law allows ordained ministers to perform weddings under the *Marriage Act 1961* (Cth) without the regulatory qualification that is required of non-religious celebrants. And what might surprise a lot of Australians who do not regularly listen to the live broadcasts of the Australian parliament is that all parliaments, State and Federal, start every parliamentary sitting day with

---

[10]   Unlawful workplace discrimination occurs when an employer takes adverse action against a person who is an employee or prospective employee because of the following attributes of the person: '[R]ace, colour, sex, sexual preference, age, physical or mental disability, marital status family or [a] carer's responsibilities, pregnancy, religion, political opinion, national extraction or social origin': *Fair Work Act 2009* (Cth), s 153.

[11]   Listed below n 18, 19.

[12]   Kerry O'Halloran, *Religion, Charity and Human Rights* (Cambridge University Press, 2014) 396.

[13]   Section 116 is not an impediment to state aid to religious schools. While s 116 precludes the legislature from creating a church or religious school, the federal legislature cannot be prevented from passing legislation that provides financial assistance to non-governmental religious schools. See *Attorney-General (Vic); ex rel Black v Commonwealth* (1981) 146 CLR 559 ('*DOGS case*').

a Christian prayer, followed by the Lord's Prayer.[14]

Moreover, Australian law provides some (albeit qualified) protection against discrimination that may be carried out against someone on the basis of their religious convictions.[15] In addition, so long as the educational curriculum is being taught, generally speaking, all religiously-based schools[16] can teach their unique religious precepts.[17]

Finally, religious bodies have the right to determine whom to hire on the basis of gender, sexuality and marital status by virtue of exemptions that

---

[14] The status of the prayer is currently the subject of a Senate Inquiry. See, Parliament of Australia, *Proposal to replace the parliamentary prayer with an invitation to prayer or reflection* (2018).

[15] As the Australian Human Rights Commission notes:
Discrimination on the basis of religion alone is not unlawful under federal anti-discrimination law. However, in some cases people have been found to be covered by the term 'ethnic origin' in the *Racial Discrimination Act*, and discrimination on this basis is against the law. ... Discrimination related to religion, religious conviction, religious belief or religious activity can be unlawful under the laws of the ACT, NT, QLD, Tasmania, Victoria and WA. In SA, discrimination on the basis of religious dress or appearance in work or study can be unlawful.
Moreover, '[s]ome people observe particular rules on clothing, appearance or jewellery for religious reasons. For example, some Sikh men wear a turban to adhere with their religious beliefs. Employers should not discriminate against a person in employment on the basis of their religious dress.' Australian Human Rights Commission, *Religion* (2018). See also, Renae Barker, 'Burqas and Niqabs in the Courtroom: Finding Practical Solutions' (2017) 91(2) *Australian Law Journal* 225.

[16] Emma Rowe, *Religion in Australian Schools: An historical and contemporary debate* (24 August 2017) The Conversation. See also, Marion Maddox, *Taking God to School: The End of Australia's Egalitarian Education?* (Allen & Unwin, 2014)

[17] The Australian Secular Lobby and the National Secular Lobby have argued that the commitment to secularism in state schools is being eroded. They point to the National School Chaplaincy Program that provides funding for schools to employ a chaplain; religious instruction classes are conducted during school hours in some schools; state funding for religious schools continues unabated; the teaching of 'creationism' occurs in some independent (religiously-based) schools. See, National Secular Lobby (2019).

are in the relevant federal legislation,[18] and state and territory equivalents.[19] These examples all support the fact of a co-operative rather than strictly "separationalist" model for church/state relations in Australia.

This is not to say that religious practitioners find themselves totally aloof from the scrutiny of the law. For example, church business practices involving the law of contract can be reviewed by the courts,[20] as can any claims casting doubt on any malfeasant religious leader's dubious financial practices.[21]

None of the above facts should raise alarm bells, however. Rex Ahdar usefully weighs up why we should respect certain religious exemptions generally — he cites principles of dignity, fairness, and the fact that religions have been a foil for totalitarianism — and why we should not.[22] Into this latter category he places the observation that all laws carry a burden for some people, and the religiously inclined should simply accept that fact. The state, Ahdar says, has the role of protecting the security of any person who may be affected by others' religious practices, public pronouncements and edicts.

---

[18]   See, eg, *Racial Discrimination Act 1975* (Cth); *Sex Discrimination Act 1984* (Cth); *Disability Discrimination Act 1992* (Cth); *Age Discrimination Act 2004* (Cth); *Human Rights Commission Act 1986* (Cth).

[19]   For example, the *Equal Opportunity Act (SA)* 1984, s 34(2) states:
This Division does not apply to discrimination on the ground of sex, sexual orientation, gender identity or intersex status in relation to employment or engagement for which it is a genuine occupational requirement that a person be a person of a particular sex, sexual orientation, gender identity or intersex status.
Moreover, see s 34(3):
This Division does not apply to discrimination on the ground of sexual orientation, gender identity or intersex status in relation to employment or engagement for the purposes of an educational institution
if — (a) the educational institution is administered in accordance with the precepts of a particular religion and the discrimination is founded on the precepts of that religion; … Also s 50(1) provides:
This Part does not render unlawful discrimination in relation to —
(a) the ordination or appointment of priests, ministers of religion or members of a religious order; or
(b) the training or education of persons seeking ordination or appointment as priests, ministers of religion or members of a religious order; or...

[20]   *Ermogenous v Greek Orthodox Community* (2002) 209 CLR 95.

[21]   Sean Fewster, 'Fugitive Agape cultist Rocco Leo fails to front court as ordered, $9 million lawsuit splits further as former parishioners lose faith,' *The Advertiser* (Online) 18 May 2017.

[22]   Rex Ahdar, 'Exemptions for Religion or Conscience under the Canopy of the Law' (2017) 5(3) *Journal of Law, Religion and State* 185.

The High Court, Section 116 and Conscientious Objection

For all of the concessions, exceptions and permutations listed above, there is not a great deal of joy to be found in s 116 for conscientious objectors. The High Court has consistently maintained, since 1912, that a person cannot object to compulsory military service on the ground of religious belief alone.[23] In the case of *Krygger v Williams*,[24] the High Court held that s 116 only protected religious observance from government interference; it did not permit a person to be excused from a legal obligation merely because that obligation (in this instance, the obligation to register, train or report for military service) conflicted with his or her religious beliefs. One could argue that the framers of the *Constitution* were intent on establishing religious freedom more as a 'shield' than as a 'sword.'[25]

There are two key cases that require some discussion here: litigation that involved, in the first case, members of the Jehovah's Witnesses, and the second involving the Church of Scientology.

A   *The Jehovah's Witnesses case*

The *Krygger v Williams* construction came up for review in a Second World War case regarding Jehovah's Witnesses.[26] In January 1941, acting pursuant to the *National Security (Subversive Organisations) Regulations 1940*, the Australian government declared, by regulation, that Jehovah's Witnesses were 'prejudicial to the defence of the Commonwealth' and to the 'efficient prosecution of the war.' This was because Witnesses profess that their allegiance to their God is superior to any allegiance to the government of the day, and, by extension, its laws. Witnesses, in other words, could not be relied upon (said the government) to be allies in wartime. Immediately after this declaration, police occupied the premises of the organisation's headquarters. Lawyers for the Witnesses challenged the regulations on a number of fronts, including the role that s 116 played in separating church and state. Eventually the matter came before the High Court. If one reads the outcome (in favour of the Witnesses), one might think that the s 116 argument succeeded, but that was not the case. The High Court struck out

---

[23] See generally, Tom Frame, *Church and State: Australia's Imaginary Wall* (UNSW Press, 2006).

[24] (1912) 15 CLR 366

[25] Babie, above n 1, 351.

[26] *Adelaide Co. of Jehovah's Witnesses Inc v Commonwealth* (1943) 67 CLR 116

the regulations as unconstitutional not because of any freedom of religion or because of any clear separation of religion and state, but because the regulations were deemed by the court to exceed the government's power over matters to do with 'defence.' Indeed, the court stated, *obiter*, that s 116 had *not* been infringed. The constitutional 'guarantee' of freedom of religion was interpreted (albeit by way of passing comment in this case) very narrowly.

It is clear, therefore, that if any Australian government wishes to, it can constrain freedom of religion if a religious group is going to foment disorder, or threaten the security of the country, especially in time of war.[27]

B   *The Scientology case*

Forty years later, the High Court offered another perspective on this topic. In *Church of the New Faith v Commissioner of Payroll Tax*,[28] the Church of Scientology scored a win that many legal commentators may not have expected.

The Victorian Tax Office wanted to tax Scientology as a business rather than as a church. A church enjoys, under Australian law as noted above, a largely tax-free status. A business does not. While Scientology refers to itself as the Church of Scientology (and officially as the Church of the New Faith), it was not enough to satisfy Crockett J in the Victorian Supreme Court (nor the Victorian Court of Appeal) that it was a religion. Crockett J held that 'religion is essentially a dynamic relation between man and a non-human or superhuman being'[29] and that the doctrines of Scientology were 'not sufficiently concerned with a superhuman, all powerful and controlling entity.'[30]

On appeal, however, the High Court determined that the Victorian Supreme Court was wrong. It held that the Church of Scientology *had* discharged the onus of showing that it had a 'religious' purpose. The Court

---

[27]   See generally James Richardson, 'The Sociology of Religious Freedom: A structural and socio-legal analysis' (2006) 67 *Sociology of Religion* 271; James Richardson, *Regulating Religion: Case Studies from Around the Globe* (Kluwer, 2004).

[28]   (1983) 154 CLR 120.

[29]   (1983) 1 VR 97, 111.

[30]   Ibid 110.

clarified the law.[31] The judgments offered a number of definitions of religion. Usefully adopted is the one propounded by Mason ACJ and Brennan J in their joint judgement:[32]

> Belief in a supernatural Being, Thing or Principle; and acceptance and observance of canons of conduct in order to give effect to that belief.

One needs to remember that this was a tax case and not a case decided in a time of war, but it is useful nevertheless for the purposes of determining who might legitimately claim an objection to military service based upon their religious beliefs.

Based upon the decision in *Church of the New Faith*, conscientious objectors, too, need not have deeply held religious beliefs, simply a belief in a supernatural being, thing or principle, while being accepting of and observing canons of conduct, in order to give effect to that belief.

Conscientious Objection: the Australian Position

Successive Australian governments, from the passage of Australia's first *Defence Act 1903* (Cth), have upheld the right of conscientious objectors to withdraw from military service generally so long as they satisfy the requirement that they hold legitimate religious beliefs.[33] Conscientious objection is relevant at any time when there is compulsory military registration for training, or a requirement of active service. Indeed, from 1911, compulsory registration and training was required of all men (aged 18-60) in Australia. Different groups sought conscientious objection status. Those claiming such status for religious reasons included members of the Society of Friends (Quakers), Christadelphians, Seventh Day Adventists, Brethren[34] and Jehovah's

---

[31] In *Church of the New Faith v Commissioner of Payroll Tax* (1983) 154 CLR 120, 136 Mason ACJ and Brennan J noted:
We would therefore hold that, for the purposes of the law, the criteria of religion are twofold: first, belief in a supernatural Being, Thing or Principle; and second, the acceptance of canons of conduct in order to give effect to that belief, though canons of conduct which offend against the ordinary laws are outside the area of any immunity, privilege or right conferred on the grounds of religion.

[32] Ibid. This definition has been adopted by the Australian Bureau of Statistics. See, Australian Bureau of Statistics, *1266.0 - Australian Standard Classification of Religious Groups* (18 June 2017).

[33] See Hugh Smith, 'Appendix A: Australia' in Charles Moskos and John Chambers II (eds), *The New Conscientious Objection: From Sacred to Secular Resistance* (OUP, 1993) 209.

[34] Various strands of Brethren have been able to satisfy the test for such status, but their members typically choose to serve in non-combatant roles.

Witnesses.[35] The government took its responsibility to keep potential enlistees in check very seriously. If a person was not able to satisfy the religious test, they were prosecuted in the magistrates' courts. While historical records are impossible to collate accurately on this subject, according to Bobbie Oliver some 27,749 prosecutions for failing to register and train had been launched by 30 June 1915.[36]

It is instructive to look at the issue of conscientious objection in a significant period in Australia's history: our involvement in the First World War, 1915-18. The question of conscription remained a highly charged and divisive political issue throughout.[37]

World War I

The Great War from 1914-1918 resulted in over 8.5 million military deaths and between 6.6 and 13 million civilian deaths across all fronts.[38] Australia entered the war in 1915 alongside Britain, as a loyal colony was expected to do. Australia had a population of about five million in 1915.[39] During the years 1915 to 1918, almost 417,000 Australian men enlisted voluntarily.[40] This represented 39 per cent of the Australian male population between the ages of 18 and 45,[41] and 332,000 were deployed overseas.[42]

Initially, Australian and New Zealand forces were deployed to the Gallipoli Peninsula, with an invasion that commenced on 25 April 1915.[43] The Gallipoli campaign, lasting eight months, resulted in horrendous loss of life for British, Irish, Australian, New Zealand, French, Canadian and Indian soldiers. Allied deaths totalled over 44,000 including 9,000 Australians.[44] When the invasion

---

[35] Bobbie Oliver, *Peacemongers: Conscientious Objectors to Military Service in Australia, 1911-1945* (Fremantle Arts Press, 1997) 40-46.

[36] Ibid 23.

[37] Ibid 23-45.

[38] Matthew White, *Source List and Detailed Death Tolls for the Primary Megadeaths of the Twentieth Century* (February 2011) Necrometrics. Civilian death estimates depend upon whether the Russian Civil War and the Armenian massacres are included.

[39] Year Book, 1916. Commonwealth of Australia, 91.

[40] Oliver, above n 35, 29

[41] Ibid..

[42] Ibid.

[43] Ibid. 31.

[44] Australian War Memorial, *Australian Fatalities at Gallipoli* (5 March 2017). The Ottoman Empire losses were put at almost 87,000 dead: NZ Ministry for Culture and Heritage, *Gallipoli Casualties by Country* (1 March 2016) New Zealand History.

was finally repulsed and the troops withdrew in early January 1916, Australian troops were re-directed to the Western Front.[45]

The losses in northern France and southern Belgium were even more horrendous. For example, in one day —1 July, 1916 —at Fromelles, France, 1,917 Australian troops died, and 3,146 were injured.[46] From July 23, 1916 to September 5, 1916, over 24,000 Australian men were killed, wounded or captured in the region known as the Somme.[47]

Given these losses, and given that Australian forces had been deployed with the understanding that the hostilities would be short-lived, enthusiasm for signing up for overseas duty began to wane.[48] It became increasingly evident that the promise of a quick war was vacuous.

By mid-1916, Australia was not meeting its recruitment target. Only around a third of eligible men were volunteering.[49] Labor Prime Minister Billy Hughes, who had assumed the role of Prime Minister in October 1915 when Andrew Fisher stepped down, determined that the only way to increase enlistment numbers was to impose conscription. He decided to hold a 'referendum' to be able to carry out his obligation to the Empire with the permission of the people.[50] He was not expecting a vociferous campaign for the 'no' vote.[51] He was wrong. There were many who opposed conscription, not just in Australia

---

[45] 80 per cent of all Australian overseas troops were deployed to the Western Front: Oliver, above n 35, 29.

[46] Peter Pedersen, *Anzacs on the Western Front* (John Wiley and Sons, 2012) 19.

[47] Ibid. xxiv.

[48] Robert Bollard, *In the Shadow of Gallipoli: The Hidden Story of Australia in WWI* (University of New South Wales Press, 2013) 71-72.

[49] Oliver, above n 35, 31. See also, Leslie Robson, *The First AIF: A Study of its Recruitment 1914-1918* (Melbourne University Press, 1970); Francis Hurley, *Compulsory Military Training and the Conscription Referendum in Victoria 1911-1916* (Melbourne University Press, 1972).

[50] A referendum is employed when a government wishes to amend a constitution. Since there was no constitutional amendment at stake, this is more correctly referred to as a 'plebiscite.'

[51] Indeed, he had no reason to suppose that conscription would be rejected because it was well-established in the Commonwealth and elsewhere. Of all the combatant nations in the Great War, South Africa and Australia were the only ones not to adopt it.

but in many other nations.[52] They formed a variety of religious and political alliances.

A *Irish Catholic Resistance to the War*

Archbishop Daniel Mannix (1864-1963, born Irish) was a leader in the Catholic Church in Melbourne.[53] He took a strong stand against conscription. In January 1917 Archbishop Mannix was quoted as asserting that the war was simply an economic battle between elite classes. 'The war,' he said, was 'just an ordinary trade war' that was driven by trade jealousy.[54] Conscription, he maintained, would simply reinforce the 'class versus class' social injustices that were evident in Australian society.[55] Indeed, Irish Catholics had good reason to resist. In April 1916, the Easter Rising (rebellion) in Ireland had been defeated by force by British troops.[56] About 3,500 people were taken prisoner by the British, and 1,800 of them were sent to internment camps or prisons. Most of the leaders of the Rising were executed following courts-martial in May 1916.[57]

B *Quaker Resistance*

Margaret Thorp, 1892-1978, a Quaker, was a strong vocal critic of the war. She was, moreover, critical of the support for the war by the mainstream

---

[52] David Boulton, *Objection Overruled: Conscription and Conscience in the First World War* (Dales Historical Monographs, 2014) 220-223. In fact, for a brief period ahead of the vote, by order of the Governor-General, conscription notices were sent, so confident was the government that a 'yes' vote would prevail. See, Oliver, above n 35, 31. See also, Cyril Pearce, Comrades in Conscience: *The Story of an English Community's Opposition to the Great War* (Francis Boutle Publishers, 2001); Andrew Bolton, 'Conscientious Objection as a Spiritual Path,' in Paul Babie and Rick Sarre (eds), *Bringing Religion to Life*, (Springer, 2019, forthcoming).

[53] Michael Gilchrist, *Daniel Mannix: Priest and Patriot* (Dove Communications, 1982).

[54] Ibid 39.

[55] There are a number of publications where Mannix and his views are presented and discussed including James Franklin, Gerry Nolan and Michael Gilchrist, *The Real Archbishop Mannix: From the sources* (Connor Court, 2015); Michael McKernan, *Victoria at War: 1914-1918* (NewSouth Publications, 2014) 181; Neville Meaney, *Australia and World Crisis 1914-1923, Vol 2* (Sydney University Press, 2009) 208; Michael Gladwin, *Captains of the Soul: A History of Australian Army Chaplains* (Big Sky, 2013).

[56] See generally, Séan Enright, *Easter Rising 1916: The Trials* (Merrion, 2014).

[57] There is a strong argument to be made that the failed Easter Rising and subsequent reprisals radicalized Mannix who had previously been a lukewarm Republican at best. See, Franklin, Nolan and Gilchrist, above n 55.

churches. She thus opposed the referendum. A member of the Anti-Military Service League, she later joined Emma Miller to start a branch of the Women's Peace Army which composed this anthem:

> I didn't raise my son to be a soldier,
> I brought him up to be my pride and joy,
> Who dares to put a musket on his shoulder,
> To kill some other mother's darling boy?[58]

C   Resistance by An Array of Women's Movements

At the time of the Great War, women's rights were almost non-existent in Britain. It was not until 1918 that the British Parliament passed an Act granting the vote to women over the age of 30,[59] but they had to be householders, the wives of householders, occupiers of property with an annual rent of £5, or graduates of British universities. However, Australian suffrage was well entrenched. By 1908, all Australian women who were British subjects, 21 years and older, were entitled to vote. Out of this strong movement emerged the Women's Peace Army.[60] They joined with the Sisterhood of International Peace in supporting the No-Conscription Fellowship.[61] Catherine Marshall and then Lilla Brockway took over the running of the No-Conscription Fellowship because many male leaders faced imprisonment for failing to register for training.[62]

D   The Labor Party and Union Resistance

The Labor Party officially campaigned against conscription too, notwithstanding their leader's advocacy for the 'yes' vote.[63] As Bollard explains, this was a sign that the labour movement was less inclined to follow their

---

[58]   The full song containing this verse may be found at: Hilda Moody and Mrs Bremner, *Women's Anti-Conscription Songs (1916)*, Australian Folk Songs.

[59]   *Representation of the People Act 1918* (UK).

[60]   See Michael Kazin, *War Against War – The American Fight for Peace 1914-1918* (Simon & Schuster, 2017) 48-56. Indeed, the International Congress of Women for a Permanent Peace met at The Hague, Holland, in 1915 to try to broker a peace settlement.

[61]   Peter Barberis, John McHugh and Mike Tyldesley, *Encyclopedia of British and Irish Political Organisations* (A&C Black, 2000) 341.

[62]   Oliver Haslam, *Refusing to Kill: Conscientious Objection and Human Rights in the First World War* (Peace Pledge Union, 2006) 22.

[63]   Museum of Australian Democracy at Old Parliament House, *Billy Hughes at War: Conscription during the First World War* (2018).

political masters. There had been a political 'sea-change.'[64]

> At the base of the labour movement, in the working class itself, patriotism
> no longer held the same force. Private fears and reservations ... were
> brought out into the open, and into open debate, by the referendum
> campaign. And as much as the leaders of the 'No' campaign were anxious
> to assure the public that they were opposed to conscription and not
> the war ... Moreover, the labour movement that those defiant officials
> represented was not in a mood to passively accept an attack. ... Many of
> the young working-class men who now faced the threat of conscription
> were members of trade unions, and many of them had recently been on
> strike and had won. If Hughes wanted to take on the trade unions, he
> would face more than a handful of recalcitrant officials, he would face a
> battle-hardened army.[65]

One particularly vocal union critic of the war was Tom Barker (1887-1970).[66]
He was an organiser of the Industrial Workers of the World. He decided to
campaign against the referendum with the use of a clever poster. He knew
that to advocate refusal of service was a serious offence. So he designed the
wording in a manner that highlighted that those who were losing their lives
were not the ones making the decisions:[67]

> To Arms!
> Capitalists, Parsons, Politicians, Landlords, Newspaper Editors and
> Other Stay-At-Home Patriots
> Your country needs YOU in the trenches!!
> WORKERS
> Follow your Masters

There was thought given by police to charging Tom Barker under s 30A of
the *Crimes Act 1914* (Cth). This section prohibited sedition. Sedition is defined
as any enterprise that is intended to bring the government into hatred or
contempt, with an intention to incite violence or to create public disturbance
or disorder.[68] Tom Barker had not done that. But the government of the day
had also passed the *Unlawful Associations Act 1916* (Cth) which had a much
lower proof threshold. Tom Barker was thereupon convicted for organising

---

[64]   Bollard, above n 48, 79.

[65]   Ibid 79-80. Later, Labor leader John Curtin, as Prime Minister in 1943 with the
fall of Singapore, caved in to political pressure and introduced a limited version of
conscription for overseas service, earning the condemnation of many in his own party.
See, Hazel Flynn (ed), *The Great War: Ten Contested Questions* (Harper Collins, 2015).

[66]   Eric Fry, *Tom Barker (1887-1970)* Australian Dictionary of Biography.

[67]   Ibid.

[68]   *Macquarie Concise Dictionary of Modern Law* (CCH, 1988).

a rally, and was deported on the first ship that was on offer. As it happened, a Chilean ship docked in Sydney Harbour in 1918.[69] Even though Tom Barker spoke no Spanish, he was put on the ship, headed out to sea, and sailed to South America.[70]

The 'Referendum' Ballot of October 1916

Military registration and training for all Australian men aged 18 to 60 serving in Australia had been compulsory since 1911.[71] The 'referendum' (or plebiscite) if carried, would have extended this requirement to active service overseas. Prime Minister Hughes put the conscription ballot to the vote on 28 October 1916.

The question that was posed for this vote was as follows:[72]

> Are you in favour of the Government having, in this grave emergency, the same compulsory powers over citizens in regard to requiring their military service, for the term of this War, outside the Commonwealth, as it now has in regard to military service within the Commonwealth?

With Catholics, Quakers, the Labor party, women's groups, socialists and unionists all opposing the proposition, the 'no' campaign prevailed - 1,160,033 voters voted against the proposal while 1,087,557 voted for it. It was thus defeated by a margin of 3.22 per cent.[73]

As Bollard writes:[74]

> [C]onscription had been beaten, and given the obstacles faced by the 'antis', theirs was a famous victory. But the victory had been narrow and uncertain. As long as the war lasted, and especially if the military situation deteriorated, it was likely that the question of conscription would arise again.

Following the ballot, Hughes was expelled from the Labor Party and formed a new party, the Nationalists.[75] This party prevailed in the election of May 1917 and Hughes thus maintained his position as Prime Minister.

---

[69] Fry, above n 66.

[70] Ibid. He later returned to England and in 1959 became Mayor of the Borough of St Pancras, London. He died in 1970.

[71] Smith, above n 33, 208-210.

[72] Oliver, above n 35, 44.

[73] Ibid.

[74] Bollard, above n 48, 98.

[75] Officially the party was known as "National Labor" from 14 November 1916, and then "Nationalist" from 17 February 1917 to the end of his term on 9 February 1923. National Museum of Australia, Billy Hughes, (14 August 2019).

The 'Referendum' Ballot of November 1917

In 1917, Britain sought a sixth Australian division for active service. Australia had to provide 7,000 men per month to meet this request, yet volunteer recruitment continued to lag.[76] On 20 December 1917, Prime Minister Hughes put another similar, yet shorter, 'referendum' question to the Australian people. The ballot question that was asked read:

> Are you in favour of the proposal of the Commonwealth Government
> for reinforcing the Commonwealth Forces overseas?[77]

It, too, was defeated, this time by a margin of 7 per cent.[78] The war continued to the end (eleven months later) with volunteers only.

By the end of the war, 59,342 Australian troops had been killed or died of wounds or illness (almost one in five of enlistees) and 152,171 had been wounded and/or gassed (nearly 45 per cent).[79] In all, there were 215,585 casualties, or 53 per cent of all enlistees. Only one out of every three Australians who enlisted got through physically unscathed.[80] Viewed this way, although casualties were higher in number for the British, Australia suffered the highest percentage of casualties of any allied nation.[81]

Conscription in Later Wars

Compulsory military service for duty within Australia was revived in 1939 once Australia had followed Britain in declaring war on Germany. The *Defence Act 1939* (Cth) had determined that conscientious objection status could be applied 'whether the beliefs are part of the doctrines of any religion.'[82] In February 1943, "Australia" was defined to include New Guinea and the adjacent islands. This obliged Australian men to sign up for service in the region. Of the over 250,000 people who were called to serve, 2,791 sought

---

[76] Oliver, above n 35, 45.

[77] Oliver, above n 35, 45

[78] Oliver, above n 35, 45. 1,181,747 voted 'no' and 1,015,159 voted 'yes'. Ibid.

[79] Ibid. 29.

[80] My grandfather Claude Sarre (1892-1982) arrived in France early in 1916, deployed as an engineer. He was formally discharged from the AIF on July 5, 1919. He served on the front line in France and Belgium for almost three years. He remained remarkably lucky, and returned with few obvious mental and physical scars.

[81] Pedersen, above n 46, xxiv.

[82] Act No. 38 of 1939 amended the *Defence Act 1903-1939* (Cth) by adding this phrase in a new sub-section 61 (3).

exemption.[83] Of these, 1,014 were granted full exemption on the grounds of conscientious objection, and 1,076 were referred to non-combatant duties, such as stretcher-bearers.[84]

Compulsory military service was introduced from 1965 as Australia followed the United States into war in Vietnam. Hence conscientious objection became a political issue again.[85] 50,000 men were called up from which 1,012 applied for conscientious objection status.[86] 72 per cent were granted total exemption. 14 per cent were exempted from combat duties while the remaining 14 per cent had their applications rejected.[87] Conscription was abolished three days after the election of the Whitlam Labor government on 2 December 1972.[88]

In 1991, the Hawke Labor government introduced laws to allow individual conscientious objection to *particular* wars although a year later that Bill was tabled indefinitely.[89] The law has not changed since World War II. In summary, conscientious objection today can be based on something other than deeply held religious belief so long as the objection is grounded in moral beliefs capable of being articulated intellectually. Indeed, while the High Court's conclusion in *Krygger v Williams* has been modified by the definitional shift in *Church of the New Faith*, a conscientious objector today would still find more joy from statutory fiat rather than s 116 of the *Constitution*.

Conclusion

Australia has seen a variety of political positions on conscientious objection based upon religious belief during the course of the 20th century. The law today allows conscientious objection for those who meet the 'religious belief' threshold, but it relies on government legislation and administrative decision-making. Section 116 is not particularly helpful to any person seeking to exercise this right.

History reveals that there was strong opposition to Australia's involvement in World War I as the war dragged on and as losses mounted. When two attempts to introduce conscription for military service overseas arose, there

---

[83] Smith, above n 33, 210-211.
[84] Ibid.
[85] See, Australian Society for the Study of Labour History, *A Conscription Story, 1965-69.*
[86] Smith, above n 33, 210.
[87] Ibid.
[88] Ibid.
[89] Smith, above n 33, 211.

were vociferous and successful challenges from the trade union movement, the Labor Party, and an active women's movement. Religions, too, found themselves well represented in the 'no' campaign ranks, with Catholics (predominantly Irish) and Quakers in the forefront of the campaigns. In the ranks of conscientious objectors and those opposed to compulsory military service at the time one can find many religiously-inspired advocates. Their stories reveal many dreadful practices meted out against them, not just in Australia but in New Zealand,[90] the United States and Britain.[91] They did not lack courage.[92] It is regrettable that Australia has, so far, no public memorial to them.

Bibliography

Adelaide Co. of Jehovah's Witnesses Inc v Commonwealth (1943) 67 CLR 116

Age Discrimination Act 2004 (Cth).

Ahdar Rex, 'Exemptions for Religion or Conscience under the Canopy of the Law' (2017) 5(3) *Journal of Law, Religion and State*.

Attorney-General (Vic); ex rel Black v Commonwealth (1981) 146 CLR 559.

Australian Bureau of Statistics, *1266.0 - Australian Standard Classification of Religious Groups* (18 June 2017) <https://www.abs.gov.au/ausstats/abs@.nsf/mf/1266.0>.

Australian Human Rights Commission, *Religion* (2018) <https://www.humanrights.gov.au/quick-guide/12091>.

Australian Society for the Study of Labour History, *A Conscription Story, 1965-69* <http://www.labourhistory.org.au/hummer/vol-2-no-4/conscription/>.

Australian War Memorial, *Australian Fatalities at Gallipoli* (5 March 2017) <www.awm.gov.au/articles/encyclopedia/gallipoli/fatalities>.

Babie Paul, 'National Security and the Free Exercise Guarantee Of Section 116: Time For A Judicial Interpretive Update' (2017) 45 *Federal Law Review*.

Baltzell Digby E, *Puritan Boston and Quaker Philadelphia* (Free Press, 1979).

Barberis Peter, John McHugh and Mike Tyldesley, *Encyclopedia of British and Irish Political Organisations* (A&C Black, 2000).

---

[90]   In the context of New Zealand (where conscription was enforced) see David Grant, *Field punishment No. 1: Archibald Baxter, Mark Briggs and New Zealand's Anti-Militarist Tradition* (Steele Roberts, 2008).

[91]   For a list of religious groups in other Allied armed forces and their sacrifices see: Bolton, above n 52.

[92]   Oliver, above n 35, 10.

Barker Renae, 'Burqas and Niqabs in the Courtroom: Finding Practical Solutions' (2017) 91(2) *Australian Law Journal*.

Beck Luke, 'Clear and Emphatic: The Separation of Church and State under the Australian Constitution' (2008) 27(2) *The University of Tasmanian Law Review*.

Bollard Robert, *In the Shadow of Gallipoli: The Hidden Story of Australia in WWI* (University of New South Wales Press, 2013).

Bolton Andrew, 'Conscientious Objection as a Spiritual Path,' in Paul Babie and Rick Sarre (eds), *Bringing Religion to Life*, (Springer, 2019, forthcoming).

Boulton David, *Objection Overruled: Conscription and Conscience in the First World War* (Dales Historical Monographs, 2014).

Bouma Gary et al, *Freedom of religion and belief in 21st century Australia* (2011) The Australian Human Rights Commission <https://www.humanrights.gov.au/sites/default/files/content/frb/Report_2011.pdf>.

Church of the New Faith v Commissioner of Payroll Tax (1983) 154 CLR 120

Disability Discrimination Act 1992 (Cth).

Enright Séan, *Easter Rising 1916: The Trials* (Merrion, 2014).

Equal Opportunity Act (SA) 1984.

Ermogenous v Greek Orthodox Community (2002) 209 CLR 95.

Fair Work Act 2009 (Cth).

Fewster Sean, 'Fugitive Agape cultist Rocco Leo fails to front court as ordered, $9 million lawsuit splits further as former parishioners lose faith,' *The Advertiser* (Online) 18 May 2017 <https://www.adelaidenow.com.au/news/law-order/fugitive-agape-cultist-rocco-leo-fails-to-front-court-as-ordered-9-million-lawsuit-splits-further-as-former-parishioners-lose-faith/news-story/aef9cf26ee1f91c7f77094c079787c06>.

Flynn Hazel (ed), *The Great War: Ten Contested Questions* (Harper Collins, 2015).

Frame Tom, *Church and State: Australia's Imaginary Wall* (UNSW Press, 2006).

Franklin James, Gerry Nolan and Michael Gilchrist, *The Real Archbishop Mannix: From the sources* (Connor Court, 2015).

Fry Eric, *Tom Barker (1887-1970)* Australian Dictionary of Biography <http://adb.anu.edu.au/biography/barker-tom-5131>.

Gilchrist Michael, *Daniel Mannix: Priest and Patriot* (Dove Communications, 1982).

Gladwin Michael, *Captains of the Soul: A History of Australian Army Chaplains* (Big Sky, 2013).

Grant David, *Field punishment No. 1: Archibald Baxter, Mark Briggs and New*

Zealand's Anti-Militarist Tradition (Steele Roberts, 2008).

Hamilton Marci, *God Versus the Gavel: Religion and the Rule of Law* (CUP, 2005).

Haslam Oliver, *Refusing to Kill: Conscientious Objection and Human Rights in the First World War* (Peace Pledge Union, 2006).

Human Rights Commission Act 1986 (Cth).

Hurley Francis, *Compulsory Military Training and the Conscription Referendum in Victoria 1911-1916* (Melbourne University Press, 1972).

Kazin Michael, *War Against War – The American Fight for Peace 1914-1918* (Simon & Schuster, 2017).

Kenny Courtney, 'The Evolution of the Law of Blasphemy' (1922) 1(2) *Cambridge Law Journal.*

Macquarie Concise Dictionary of Modern Law (CCH, 1988).

Maddox Marion, *Taking God to School: The End of Australia's Egalitarian Education?* (Allen & Unwin, 2014).

McKernan Michael, *Victoria at War: 1914-1918* (NewSouth Publications, 2014).

Meaney Neville, *Australia and World Crisis 1914-1923, Vol 2* (Sydney University Press, 2009).

Moody Hilda and Mrs Bremner, *Women's Anti-Conscription Songs (1916)*, Australian Folk Songs <http://folkstream.com/reviews/anticonscription.html>.

Museum of Australian Democracy at Old Parliament House, *Billy Hughes at War: Conscription during the First World War* (2018) <https://billyhughes.moadoph.gov.au/conscription>.

National Secular Lobby (2019) <www.nationalsecularlobby.org>.

NZ Ministry for Culture and Heritage, *Gallipoli Casualties by Country* (1 March 2016) New Zealand History <https://nzhistory.govt.nz/media/interactive/gallipoli-casualties-country>.

O'Halloran Kerry, *Religion, Charity and Human Rights* (Cambridge University Press, 2014).

Oliver Bobbie, *Peacemongers: Conscientious Objectors to Military Service in Australia, 1911-1945* (Fremantle Arts Press, 1997).

Parliament of Australia, *Proposal to replace the parliamentary prayer with an invitation to prayer or reflection* (2018) <https://www.aph.gov.au/Parliamentary_Business/Committees/Senate/Procedure/Parliamentaryprayer>.

Pearce Cyril, Comrades in Conscience: *The Story of an English Community's Opposition to the Great War* (Francis Boutle Publishers, 2001).

Pedersen Peter, *Anzacs on the Western Front* (John Wiley and Sons, 2012).

Racial Discrimination Act 1975 (Cth).

Representation of the People Act 1918 (UK).

Richardson James, 'The Sociology of Religious Freedom: A structural and socio-legal analysis' (2006) 67 *Sociology of Religion.*

Richardson James, *Regulating Religion: Case Studies from Around the Globe* (Kluwer, 2004).

Robson Leslie, *The First AIF: A Study of its Recruitment 1914-1918* (Melbourne University Press, 1970).

Rowe Emma, *Religion in Australian Schools: An historical and contemporary debate* (24 August 2017) The Conversation <https://theconversation. com/religion-in-australian-schools-an-historical-and-contemporary-debate-82439>.

Sarre Rick, 'Why theology should play a role in the criminological enterprise' in Emil Pływaczewski (ed), *Current Problems of the Penal Law and Criminology* (forthcoming, 2019).

Sex Discrimination Act 1984 (Cth).

Smith Hugh, 'Appendix A: Australia' in Charles Moskos and John Chambers II (eds), *The New Conscientious Objection: From Sacred to Secular Resistance* (OUP, 1993).

Thomson James and Rick Sarre (eds), *Introduction to Law,* (Butterworths, 3rd edition, 2001).

White Matthew, *Source List and Detailed Death Tolls for the Primary Megadeaths of the Twentieth Century* (February 2011) Necrometrics <http://necrometrics. com/20c5m.htm#WW1>.

13

EQUAL VOICE LIBERALISM AND FREE PUBLIC RELIGION: SOME LEGAL IMPLICATIONS

ALEX DEAGON

Abstract

This paper proposes some potential legal implications for free public religion in the context of 'equal voice liberalism'. Equal voice liberalism and its antecedent connections to priority for democracy are first outlined in conjunction with an analysis of free public religion. The paper subsequently argues that equal voice liberalism is a framework conducive to facilitating free public religion while preserving equality. In this context the paper attempts to give more analytical and evaluative precision to the commonplace ideas of freedom and equality in terms of proportionate, reasonable accommodation of difference. Finally, the paper argues in support of religious associations requiring the space to independently form and develop unique perspectives which they can contribute to public discourse, which in turn enhances the importance of freedom and equality.

Introduction: Law and Public Religion

Many scholars and politicians argue excluding religious perspectives from political decision-making is the only way to guarantee genuine neutrality, freedom and equality. This has been exposed in the 2017 Frank Walker Memorial Lecture, delivered by Federal Labor Senator Penny Wong. Senator Wong argued that the problem with 'conflating religious concepts of marriage with secular concepts of marriage' is 'the application of religious belief to the framing of law in a secular society. And in societies where church and state are constitutionally separate, as they are in Australia and the US, this leads not only to confusion, but also to inequity'.[1] This expresses the common view that religion should not contribute to public policy and law because it can be sectarian and divisive. In this secular approach, the liberal ideals of freedom, neutrality and toleration are preserved by removing religious perspectives from political discussion because of their so-called particularist and divisive nature. Religious reasons or arguments in public discourse should not form the basis for political decisions resulting in coercive laws.[2]

Senator Wong further argued that one of the foundations of liberal democracy is that human beings are equal to each other, and 'discrimination against people on the basis of an innate characteristic, like sexual orientation, is anti-liberal and anti-democratic'.[3] The implication is religious freedom should not be used as an excuse to discriminate in a liberal democracy.[4] This raises the problem of how to legally resolve what can be the competing imperatives of freedom and equality, particularly when the religious freedom in question is 'public' in nature and comes within the scope of anti-discrimination law.[5]

Conversely, there is a growing concern among some scholars that it is inconsistent and unfair to exclude religion from contributing to law and public policy when the distinction between religion and non-religion is not always clear, and deeply held non-religious convictions can play essentially the

---

[1] Penny Wong, 'The Separation of Church and State – The Liberal Argument for Equal Rights for Gay and Lesbian Australians' (Speech delivered at NSW Society of Labor Lawyers Frank Walker Memorial Lecture, 17 May 2017).

[2] See John Rawls, *Political Liberalism: Expanded Edition* (Columbia University Press, 2005); Robert Audi, 'The Place of Religious Argument in a Free and Democratic Society' (1993) 30 *San Diego Law Review* 677; Robert Audi, *Religious Commitment and Secular Reason* (Cambridge University Press, 2000); Robert Audi, *Democratic Authority and the Separation of Church and State* (Cambridge University Press, 2011).

[3] Wong, above n 1.

[4] Michael Kent Curtis, 'A Unique Religious Exemption from Anti-Discrimination Laws in the Case of Gays? Putting the Call for Exemptions for Those Who Discriminate against Married or Marrying Gays in Context' cited in Michael Kent Curtis (ed), *The Rule of Law and the Rule of God* (Palgrave Macmillan, 2014).

[5] See, eg, Anthony Gray, 'Reconciliation of Freedom of Religion With Anti-Discrimination Rights' (2016) 42(1) *Monash University Law Review* 72; Alex Deagon, 'Defining the Interface of Freedom and Discrimination: Exercising Religion, Democracy and Same-Sex Marriage' (2017) 20 *International Trade and Business Law Review* 239 ('*Freedom and Discrimination*').

same role as religious convictions.[6] This is not to say religious perspectives should be privileged above secular perspectives or given more merit than them, merely that religious perspectives should be publicly debated and critiqued equally alongside secular ones.[7] Excluding religious perspectives from the public sphere arguably presents serious challenges to holistic, inclusive public policy debate given Australia's religious diversity and the various religious and non-religious perspectives on important social issues. It would mean religious belief could not contribute to policy debate on issues such as same-sex marriage, abortion, euthanasia, offshore detention, poverty and climate change. In addition, being part of a public religious group is more than the simple expression of shared religious beliefs. It is an exercise in solidarity and community-building which mediates between the extremes of collectivism and individualism, strengthening both the individual and the community within liberal-democratic constitutionalism.[8] Thus, excluding the perspectives of religious individuals and communities effectively disenfranchises a significant portion of Australians and limits ways of thinking about how we can attain public good.

This chapter assumes the latter approach and seeks the free expression of all religious perspectives in the public sphere, to be considered and critiqued in the marketplace of ideas.[9] Here secularism, atheism, agnosticism, Christianity, and all other religions and non-religions are freely able to express and critique each other's views. Rather than a secularism which

---

[6]   See, eg, Paul Copan, 'The Biblical Worldview Context for Religious Liberty' in A Menuge (ed), *Religious Liberty and the Law: Theistic and Non-Theistic Perspectives* (Routledge, 2018) 15-18; Rex Ahdar and Ian Leigh, *Religious Freedom in the Liberal State* (Oxford, 2nd ed, 2011) 61-69.

[7]   See Michael McConnell, 'Why Protect Religious Freedom' (2013) 123 *Yale Law Journal* 770, 808; Linda Woodhead, 'Liberal Religion and Illiberal Secularism' in G D'Costa et al (eds), *Religion in a Liberal State* (Cambridge, 2013) 96.

[8]   See, eg, Angus Menuge, 'The Secular State's Interest in Religious Liberty' in A Menuge (ed), *Religious Liberty and the Law: Theistic and Non-Theistic Perspectives* (Routledge, 2018); Alex Deagon, 'On the Symbiosis of Law and Truth in Christian Theology: Reconciling Universal and Particular through the Pauline Law of Love' (2015) 23(4) *Griffith Law Review* 589; Veit Bader, 'Post-Secularism or Liberal-Democratic Constitutionalism?' (2012) 5(1) *Erasmus Law Review* 5 ('*Liberal-Democratic Constitutionalism*').

[9]   As such the chapter will not directly engage the likes of Rawls and Audi, or explore their similarities, differences and nuances. For a detailed critique of 'public reason' and 'secular reason', see Alex Deagon, 'Liberal Secularism and Religious Freedom in the Public Sphere: Reforming Political Discourse' (2018) 41(3) *Harvard Journal of Law and Public Policy* 901.

excludes religious views from public political discussion, or the simplistic substitution of atheism or agnosticism for traditional Christianity, what is required is a sensible balancing or proportionate accommodation of different claims, taking into account minority religions, majority religions, and no religion – what influential liberal-pluralist scholars such as Veit Bader and Nicholas Wolterstorff call 'priority for democracy' or 'equal voice liberalism' respectively.[10] This provides a framework for facilitating a culture where public religion (the pluralistic encounter of a collection of religions in the public sphere) is free, with the state allowing all views, religious and non-religious, to be freely and equally proposed and considered. This is just the true liberal democracy.[11]

More specifically, the chapter will suggest that priority for democracy, liberal-democratic constitutionalism, and equal voice liberalism are simply different terms for what is essentially the same pluralist concept of liberal democracy – all religious and non-religious perspectives are equally able to be heard and debated in the public sphere and contribute to democratically decided public policy within specified constitutional limits. On this foundation the chapter will argue this framework is conducive to free public religion while simultaneously preserving equality between religious and non-religious citizens. Such an analysis requires a more precise articulation of what is meant by 'preserving freedom and equality' in a liberal democracy, and this approach will then be used to inform a discussion of legal implications for public religion in associative contexts.

Part II of the chapter outlines the central concepts of priority for democracy and equal voice liberalism, pointing out the connections and consistencies between the frameworks to develop a single operating framework of 'equal voice liberalism', before turning to state the definition and principles associated with public religion. Part III consequently argues this equal voice liberalism provides a pluralist framework conducive to facilitating the free, equal, collective public encounter of religious (and

---

[10]   Veit Bader, 'Religious Pluralism: Secularism or Priority for Democracy' (1999) 27 *Political Theory* 597 ('*Priority for Democracy*'); Nicholas Wolterstorff, *Understanding Liberal Democracy: Essays in Political Philosophy* (Oxford University Press, 2012) 113-142.

[11]   See John Witte Jr., 'From Establishment to Freedom of Public Religion' (2004) 32 *Capital University Law Review* 499, 517 and the more detailed analysis of 'public religion' below.

non-religious) perspectives which constitutes 'public religion'. However, given the analytical and evaluative imprecision of terms like 'freedom' and 'equality', Part IV aims to develop a principle of proportional, reasonable accommodation of difference which can be used as the basis for preserving freedom and equality in the liberal-democratic context of public religion. Finally, Part V applies these principles in the process of considering legal implications for religious associations which operate at the interface of freedom and equality.

Central Concepts

Priority for Democracy

'Priority for Democracy' is a phrase coined and developed by Veit Bader, who characterises it as a principle which accounts for the intuition that liberal democracy is not neutral, and so it is 'always a shorthand for liberal democracy'.[12] Priority for democracy means all religious, philosophical and scientific voices (like votes) should be considered equally when it comes to decision-making.[13] As Bader contends:

> Instead of trying to limit the content of discourse by keeping all contested comprehensive doctrines and truth-claims out, one has to develop the duties of civility, such as the duty to explain positions in publicly understandable language, the willingness to listen to others, fair-mindedness, and readiness to accept reasonable accommodations or alterations in one's own view.[14]

So the focus is on creating a public space for free and fair discussion of contested views which are equally considered in the decision-making process. Allowing the opportunity for all views to be robustly proposed and debated in a civil manner is a primary feature of liberal democracy. One may of course disagree with what is expressed, but the nature of democratic discourse is that all kinds of views should be able to be proposed. It follows that a priority for democracy model would include all religious or non-religious perspectives compatible with the democratic process, leading to a pluralistic encounter of perspectives which will combine and contribute to policy-making and allow true liberal democracy – the freedom to equally express and decide between a

---

12   Bader, *Priority for Democracy*, above n 10, 612.
13   Ibid 612–13. Cf Jeremy Waldron, *Law and Disagreement* (Oxford, 1999).
14   Bader, *Priority for Democracy*, above n 10, 614.

full array of perspectives.[15]

As such, both religious authorities (as 'depositors of divine truth') and 'secular truths' must learn to accept the notion that when it comes to public, democratic decision-making, 'error has the same rights as truth'.[16] That is, contrary to the exclusivist specifications of Rawls and Audi, criteria such as religious or non-religious, true or false, rationality or irrationality, and comprehensive or minimalist cannot be used as a basis to exclude particular views from policy debate. Bader argues that to implement priority for democracy we must focus on 'civilised and decent ways of living with disagreement: liberal-democratic culture, attitudes or habits, virtues and traditions of good judgement, and good practice are crucial'.[17] These virtues include 'civic integrity' (principled consistency of speech and action) and 'civic magnanimity' (open-mindedness and mindfulness of the equal moral status of opponents in speech and action).[18]

In a later work Bader explicitly characterises the idea as the 'priority for liberal democracy' in contrast to secularism or the metanarrative of secularisation, which is 'unfair' when it comes to genuine democratic debate and 'implausible and tendentiously at-odds with freedoms of political communication and considered anti-paternalism'.[19] An extensive interpretation of freedom of political communication and of its anti-paternalism are 'core aspects' of priority for liberal democracy.[20] In terms of freedom of political communication, Bader argues genuine democratic debate 'requires and in turn strengthens a public arena in which the divergent opinions and proposals can be published, exchanged, discussed, negotiated and transformed, and in which new ones can emerge'.[21] Democratic constitutions guarantee crucial preconditions for proper democratic debate, including the various freedoms of opinion, information, media, assembly

---

[15] Deagon, *Freedom and Discrimination*, above n 5, 252-253; Cf Bader, *Priority for Democracy*, above n 10, 617.

[16] Bader, *Priority for Democracy*, above n 10, 613-614.

[17] Ibid 618.

[18] Ibid 618-619. As we will see, such ideas are also reflected in Wolterstorff's equal voice liberalism as a framework for free public religion in terms of a proportionate, reasonable accommodation of difference.

[19] Veit Bader, *Secularism or Democracy? Associational Governance of Religious Diversity* (Amsterdam University Press, 2007) 27 (*'Secularism or Democracy'*). See generally 93-126.

[20] Ibid 95, 110.

[21] Ibid 110-111.

and association. Bader further notes:

> It is a common understanding among constitutional lawyers that these freedoms do not, and should not, discriminate between secular and religious opinions. The public arena must be the place where the contest between all opinions or voices takes place, whether religious or secular.[22]

As articulated in Bader's earlier work, anti-paternalist decision-making is based around the idea that all views count equally as votes, even if 'paternalistic elites' count these voices as ill-informed, irrational, false or odious. The people must be sovereign such that 'defenders of absolute truth' must settle for popular decisions, and it is in this sense that 'error has the same rights as truth'.[23]

Finally, Bader specifies 'priority for liberal democracy' further to be 'liberal-democratic constitutionalism'.[24] Bader states that liberal-democratic constitutionalism is 'a meta-constitutional and meta-legal ideal containing the constitutional essentials' or 'core' of the various articulations of rights and principles in state constitutions, and is compatible with many competing theories of the Rule of Law and democracy.[25] Here he also reiterates the central aspects of freedom of political communication and anti-paternalism articulated in earlier work.[26]

In this context Bader develops an argument that 'associational governance' of religious diversity is the most appropriate mechanism of governance in conditions of increased religious pluralism and fragmentation of organised religion, especially compared to the more traditional secularist model which strictly separates 'state and politics from organised religions'.[27] This associative democracy is a 'specific variety of liberal-democratic institutional pluralism' which involves power-sharing through formally recognising and integrating the existing plurality of groups and organisations into the political process, along with a principle of decentralisation and self-determination. It supplements representative democracy and is 'driven by the conviction that all

---

[22]   Ibid.

[23]   Ibid 112. Cf Bader, *Priority for Democracy*, above n 10, 613-614.

[24]   Bader, *Liberal-Democratic Constitutionalism*, above n 8, 5.

[25]   Ibid 26.

[26]   Ibid 24. See also, Veit Bader, 'Included, Excluded or Foundational: Religion in Liberal-Democratic States' in Gavin D'Costa et al (eds), *Religion in a Liberal State* (Cambridge, 2013) 137-141 where Bader summarises these principles.

[27]   Bader, *Liberal-Democratic Constitutionalism*, above n 8, 18-19.

those relevantly affected by collective political decisions are stakeholders, and thus should have a say'.[28] 'This promotes strong interpretation of associational freedoms and the proposals to represent the interests of different minority groups in the political process'.[29] For example, all states (including those with strict-separation ideologies such as the US and France) 'recognise organised religions either legally or administratively, finance them either directly or indirectly (tax exemptions), and privilege freedoms of religion by granting them, and not others, many exemptions. They also finance faith based organisations in all sorts of care and social services and also in education, either directly or indirectly'.[30] Bader's fundamental point is secularist separation is neither desirable nor practical. A truly democratic society needs a system of governance which promotes equal representation of religious and non-religious perspectives in accordance with constitutional prescriptions.

Equal Voice Liberalism

'Equal voice liberalism' was coined by Nicholas Wolterstorff, who argues that liberal democracy is characterised by an 'equal right to full political voice within constitutional limits'.[31] Wolterstorff specifically states his 'equal political voice interpretation of liberal democracy' to be a 'commitment to the equal rights of citizens to full political voice, this voice to be exercised within an explicit or implicit constitution that imposes limits and guarantees on government, and within a legal order that protects citizens against impairment of their right to full political voice by their fellow citizens'.[32] This approach consequently emphasises an equal voice for all perspectives, which implies there should be no restrictions (e.g. public reason) on the type of political arguments that can be put forward.[33]

Wolterstorff believes the 'essence' of liberal democracy is citizens display a 'moral engagement' and 'civility', which means respectfully listening to the arguments of others and reconsidering your own if necessary, and accepting a

---

[28]   Ibid 18-19, footnote 86.

[29]   Ibid 19, footnote 86.

[30]   Ibid 19. See also Bader, *Secularism or Democracy*, above n 19, 175-262.

[31]   Wolterstorff, *Understanding Liberal Democracy*, above n 10, 125. See also Hans-Martien Ten Napel, *Constitutionalism, Democracy and Religious Freedom* (Routledge, 2017) 92.

[32]   Wolterstorff, *Understanding Liberal Democracy*, above n 10, 113, 125-126.

[33]   Ten Napel, above n 31, 92.

legitimate, democratic majority outcome where full agreement is not reached.[34] Since civility and moral engagement are only able to work to a certain point, Wolterstorff also advocates for constitutional limits in this framework, which are the constitutional protections of freedom of religion, speech, association and assembly. These rights set limits to political debate but are necessary to secure equal political voice (where the requirements of public reason, by contrast, are not necessary to secure equal political voice).[35]

All this implies that the priority for democracy and equal voice liberalism models provide the freedom for religious and non-religious alike to express their unique perspectives in a public space and contribute to public policy. They also allow a government to genuinely (neutrally) consider these different views as it articulates and implements policy, without establishing, promoting or excluding particular views.   Having this authentically neutral approach paradoxically involves acknowledging competing religious and non-religious perspectives while allowing the state to support religion and non-religion in a non-preferential and non-discriminatory way (that is, within constitutional limits) through prioritising a kind of equal voice democracy. Rather than a strict secular separationism, this concept follows the more accommodationist approach of preventing state adoption or promotion of any particular religion, and allowing the presence and contribution of all different perspectives through reasonable policy debate conducted within constitutional limits.[36]

The general idea might be as follows. In the Australian democratic system, voters form political opinions on religious, philosophical, moral or other perspectives, and vote for a government with policies which implement these perspectives. The elected government then, in principle, implements that policy platform as a function of representative democracy. These processes are guarded by constitutional limits such as freedom of political communication and freedom of religion. Thus, although the opinions undergirding the policy may well be religious in nature, the implementation of that policy occurs as part of the constitutionally prescribed and protected democratic system. It is

---

[34]   Ibid 92; Cf Wolterstorff, *Understanding Liberal Democracy*, above n 10, 138-139. Wolterstorff also broadens the idea of moral engagement to include political advocacy on the basis of one's judgement of what justice or the common good requires (148).

[35]   Ten Napel, above n 31, 92; Wolterstorff, *Understanding Liberal Democracy*, above n 10, 133.

[36]   Alex Deagon, 'Secularism as a Religion: Questioning the Future of the "Secular" State' (2017) 8 *The Western Australian Jurist* 31, 93-94.

therefore truly 'neutral' in the sense that it is just democracy in action, rather than the state deliberately or actually identifying with or preferring a particular religion.[37] All the state does is facilitate free, equal, collective engagement of different religious and non-religious perspectives in the development of policy which is democratically implemented.

Connecting Priority for Democracy and Equal Voice Liberalism

There are strong affinities between the concepts of priority for democracy, liberal-democratic constitutionalism, and equal voice liberalism. Billingham provides the tools for explicitly connecting priority for democracy (or now, liberal-democratic constitutionalism) and equal voice liberalism through his framework of 'argumentative democracy'. Billingham offers a straightforward overview of equal voice liberalism, or what he more broadly terms as 'argumentative democracy' in contrast to the strict separation of public reason liberalism.[38] This argumentative democracy has three features:

> First, citizens openly and honestly deliberate with one another, seeking to understand and respond to each other's reasons and arguments, whilst being open to persuasion. Second, decisions are made using democratic procedures, with citizens voting on the basis of their best judgement of the overall balance of reasons. Third, there are no restrictions on the reasons, values or principles that citizens are permitted to appeal to in public deliberation and to base their votes on.[39]

Billingham explicitly characterises Wolterstorff's equal political voice liberalism and Eberle's pluralist 'ideal of conscientious engagement' as

---

[37]   Ibid.

[38]   See Paul Billingham, 'Does Political Community Require Public Reason? On Lister's Defence of Political Liberalism' (2016) 15(1) *Politics, Philosophy and Economics* 20.

[39]   Ibid 23-24.

examples of argumentative democracy.[40] It is also plausible to view Bader's liberal-democratic constitutionalism (now comprising his earlier phrases 'priority for democracy' and 'priority for liberal democracy') as an example of argumentative democracy based on the features provided by Billingham. As detailed above, Bader also advocates an open, honest, civil debate between citizens seeking to understand and respond to various perspectives without any kind of public reason restrictions. Bader also agrees that decisions are subsequently made using popular democratic procedures where citizens vote based on their judgement of the positions and reasons provided.

In fact one can go even further than this and argue that 'priority for democracy', 'liberal-democratic constitutionalism', 'equal voice liberalism' and 'argumentative democracy' are actually just a host of different terms for the same pluralist conception of liberal democracy. This conception has three distinguishing criteria. First, an anti-paternalist approach which allows true equal voice between different perspectives. Second, this fully democratic process occurs within constitutional limits or with constitutional protections. Third, the democratic process necessarily involves principles of civility consisting of the civic virtues and a moral engagement between citizens. The following explains each of these criteria while also outlining how Bader, Wolterstorff and Billingham share these three criteria in the frameworks they respectively propose, which implies they are actually articulating the same pluralist framework broadly construed.

---

[40]   Ibid 24. See Christopher Eberle, *Religious Conviction in Liberal Politics* (Cambridge, 2002). Eberle's framework is not considered in this chapter for the sake of brevity but is further support for the idea that a liberal-pluralist approach facilitates free public religion. Eberle, against the likes of Rawls and Audi, compellingly defends the thesis that 'a citizen has an obligation sincerely and conscientiously to pursue a widely convincing secular rationale for her favoured coercive laws, but she doesn't have an obligation to withhold support from a coercive law for which she lacks a widely convincing rationale' (10). A citizen who has religious reasons for supporting a coercive law is allowed to publicly voice those reasons in policy debate. Rather than public reason which is effectively secular reason that excludes religious perspectives, Eberle advocates for sincerely and genuinely arriving at rationally justifiable views (where rationally justifiable includes reference to religious reasons), and respectfully engaging those with different views by articulating those reasons and receiving objections to learn from them, perhaps resulting in refinement of the view (104-106). Since it is unlikely there will be sufficient agreement between reasonable persons to provide a public justification for intrinsically contested values, the engagement results in a society of respectful citizens who are reasonably and rationally able to put forth their various religious and non-religious views, or a 'pluralist' society (215-216). And pluralism encourages religious vitality and facilitates freedom of religion (41-47).

Anti-paternalism and Equal Voice

As mentioned already, anti-paternalism and equal voice involves an approach which does not automatically exclude certain views because they are religious, irrational, misinformed or offensive as deemed by elites. Rather, each view is given an equal opportunity to present itself in the public sphere and be critiqued by other views. As a result of this free debate, citizens vote and the population accepts the majority result as a valid democratic outcome even if particular citizens disagree according to their stated perspective. Bader explicitly puts forward such a framework, adopting a 'considered anti-paternalism' which allows all perspectives to be equally proposed and counted for the purposes of democratic decision-making, rather than having some perspectives excluded based on prescriptive substantive requirements.[41] Similarly, Wolterstorff clearly characterises his view as an 'equal voice liberalism' which allows all views to be proposed equally and have full political voice, without any kind of public reason restrictions on the kind of arguments which can be provided.[42]

Finally, Billingham also adopts this idea as part of his 'argumentative democracy' framework. He states that citizens 'openly and honestly' deliberate, seeking to understand and respond to 'each other's reasons and arguments' with the debate ultimately resolved through equal democratic procedures.[43] This reference to honesty and the specific reasons of citizens implies Billingham rejects a public reason requirement and supports an anti-paternalist or equal voice approach. Indeed, he further states that 'the views of each person matter equally, such that decisions should be made democratically, giving each an equal vote and an equal influence over outcomes'.[44] Religious people 'can base their advocacy and votes on religious reasons' and 'citizens give one another equal political voice, despite believing that many have false views'.[45] Thus Bader, Wolterstorff and Billingham share the criteria of anti-paternalism and equal voice in their conception of liberal democracy.

---

[41]   See Bader, *Priority for Democracy*, above n 10, 612-614; Bader, *Secularism or Democracy*, above n 19, 110-112.

[42]   See Wolterstorff, *Understanding Liberal Democracy*, above n 10, 125-126, 133.

[43]   Billingham, above n 38, 23-24.

[44]   Ibid.

[45]   Ibid 24-26.

Constitutional Limits and Protections

The second criteria is equal voice and fully democratic decision-making must occur within constitutional limits and be regulated by constitutional protections in order to guarantee this equal voice. Bader alludes to the need for constitutional protections in his earlier work but makes it explicit in characterising his conception as liberal-democratic 'constitutionalism'.[46] In particular, Bader argues that 'democratic constitutions … guarantee crucial preconditions for actual democratic debate, the freedoms of political communication, i.e. freedom of opinion, of information, of print and other media of mass communication, of assembly, propaganda and demonstration, of association or organisation, and of petitions and hearings'.[47] Hence, equal voice democracy must be buttressed by robust constitutional protections to flourish. Wolterstorff agrees, claiming constitutional limits are necessary to secure equal political voice and outlining a similar raft of protections.[48]

Billingham too recognises that his version of argumentative democracy is 'liberal' in the sense that 'equal vote and equal influence over outcomes' does not imply one individual or group in society can 'impose their comprehensive doctrine upon others. Basic rights – to freedom of conscience, religion, speech, association and so on – should be given constitutional protection'.[49] Due to these constitutional protections, though religious citizens can advocate and vote on a platform of religious reasons, 'they are not permitted to force others to convert to their religion or to stop others from practising their own religion'.[50] Therefore Bader, Wolterstorff and Billingham all concur in saying that this pluralist conception of liberal democracy requires constitutional protection.

Principles of Civility

Finally, the third criteria involves principles of civility which consists of citizens displaying civic virtues and a moral engagement when they interact and discuss controversial policy issues. These principles of civility include attitudes and actions such as honesty and humility, serious attempts to argue

---

[46]   Bader, *Secularism or Democracy*, above n 19, 110-111; Bader, *Liberal-Democratic Constitutionalism*, above n 8, 24.

[47]   Bader, *Secularism or Democracy*, above n 19, 110-111.

[48]   Wolterstorff, *Understanding Liberal Democracy*, above n 10, 133.

[49]   Billingham, above n 38, 24.

[50]   Ibid 24.

one's position in an understandable way while duly considering alternative positions, preparation to accept reasonable refinements and accommodations to one's view, and acknowledging the equal dignity and status of all citizens even when you disagree with their views. Bader calls these the 'duties of civility', which includes being able to 'explain positions in publicly understandable language, the willingness to listen to others, fair-mindedness, and readiness to accept reasonable accommodations or alterations in one's own view'.[51] He also argues that implementing priority for democracy involves finding decent and civilised ways to live with disagreement, implementing 'civic integrity' and 'civic magnamity' (principled and consistent engagements acknowledging the equal dignity and moral status of those who disagree).[52] Wolterstorff, while acknowledging that 'civility' will always need to be backed by constitutional protections, also advocates for a 'moral engagement' between citizens as they engage in equal voice democracy, which entails substantively similar principles.[53] Billingham goes into much more depth on this criteria and characterises his argumentative democracy as realising 'valuable relationships between citizens'.[54] More specifically:

> Each citizen commits to understanding others' points of view and to engaging in public deliberation as to what decisions best promote justice and the common good. Each takes the arguments that others present seriously and seeks to grapple with those arguments and present defences of his/her own views. Citizens also recognize that the views of each person matter equally, such that decisions should be made democratically, giving each an equal vote and an equal influence over outcomes. These practices are rightly seen as embodying many important aspects of mutual respect and realizing certain goods of friendship and community.[55]

He goes on to explain how argumentative democracy is:

> ... based upon a set of shared commitments that enable citizens to realise a valuable form of community... Citizens should be committed to acting together based on democratic decisions, to subjecting their views to critical scrutiny, to seeking points of common cause with one another wherever they can be found and to each supporting what they

---

51 Bader, *Priority for Democracy*, above n 10, 614.
52 Ibid 618-619.
53 Wolterstorff, *Understanding Liberal Democracy*, above n 10, 138-139; Cf Ten Napel, above n 31, 92.
54 Billingham, above n 38, 23.
55 Ibid 23-24.

believe to be the best laws – those that best serve true justice and the common good. In this way, they ... develop a sense of shared identity and social unity. In other words, they enjoy civic friendship.[56]

Consequently, Billingham also advocates these principles of civility as an essential part of his argumentative democracy framework, emphasising the communal and civic friendship which results from understanding one's place in a democracy as an equal and valued contributor who genuinely engages with the views of others to seek the common good. In fact this 'civic friendship' (which is effectively advocated by Bader and Wolterstorff as well) is superior to that which is achieved under public reason liberalism because people 'openly engage with other people's beliefs' rather than spurious justifications paternalistically deemed as acceptable for public consideration.[57]

The preceding analysis therefore indicates Billingham's argumentative democracy can be characterised as Bader's priority for democracy and Wolterstorff's equal voice liberalism, where all people are heard equally without any public reason restrictions, offering whatever reasons they see fit with an equal voice and equal vote. It can also be characterised as Bader's priority for liberal democracy and liberal-democratic constitutionalism by including constitutional protection for basic rights like freedom of religion, association and speech in the midst of 'equal voice' deliberative democratic processes which are approached with principles of civility. Wolterstorff also explicitly connects this full, equal political voice in a democracy with constitutional limits and principles of civility, which he calls moral engagement.[58]

Hence 'argumentative democracy', 'liberal democracy', 'priority for democracy', 'priority for liberal democracy' and 'liberal-democratic constitutionalism' can be characterised as various manifestations of 'equal voice liberalism' operating democratically through equal voice procedures, according to principles of civility ,with constitutional protections. So for the remainder of this chapter this liberal-pluralist constitutional conception will be termed broadly as an 'equal voice liberalism' equivalent to the other conceptions, and the chapter will adopt this conception as the operative framework for the argument that equal voice liberalism is conducive to

---

56   Ibid 25-26.

57   Ibid 26.

58   Cf Rowan Williams, *Faith in the Public Square* (Bloomsbury, 2012) 135.

facilitating free public religion. The chapter now turns to outline the idea of 'free public religion'.

Free Public Religion

This outline of free public religion will focus on John Witte Jr.'s approach.[59] In particular Witte draws on John Adams (against Thomas Jefferson's secularist 'wall of separation' approach) to articulate a 'public religion' [sic] as 'some image and ideal of itself, some common values and beliefs to undergird and support the plurality of protected private religions'.[60] For Adams the notion that a state could be neutral and lack a public religion is a philosophical fiction, and absent any shared set of values and beliefs 'politicians would invariably hold out their private convictions as public ones. It was thus essential for each community to define and defend the basics of a public religion'.[61] The creed of this 'public religion' was:

> ... honesty, diligence, devotion, obedience, virtue, and love of God, neighbor, and self. Its icons were the Bible, the bells of liberty, the memorials of patriots, and the Constitution. Its clergy were public-spirited ministers and religiously committed politicians. Its liturgy was the public proclamation of oaths, prayers, songs, and election and Thanksgiving Day sermons. Its policy was state appointment of chaplains for the legislature, the military, and prisons; state sanctions against blasphemy, sacrilege, and iconoclasm; state administration of tithe collections, test oaths, and clerical appointments; and state sponsorship of religious societies, schools, and charities.[62]

Adams believed only a collective religion can establish freedom and a public religion is the foundation for free government and a flourishing human society.[63] However, while Jefferson advocated for robust free exercise and a separated church and state, Adams was concerned to limit what he deemed to be illegitimate religious freedom (resulting in 'depravity and license') through mild establishment.[64] Jefferson countered that to establish a public religion would be to threaten the development and sincerity of private religions. As

---

[59]   See Witte, above n 11. Cf Jose Casanova, *Public Religions in the Modern World* (University of Chicago Press, 2011); Wolterstorff, *Understanding Liberal Democracy*, above n 10, 329-352.

[60]   Witte, above n 11, 504.

[61]   Ibid.

[62]   Ibid.

[63]   Ibid.

[64]   Ibid 505.

Witte observes, 'somewhere between these extremes a society must strike its balance'.[65]

On one hand, the Adams approach 'sought to balance the general freedom of all private religions with the general patronage of one common public religion'.[66] In this way, basic freedoms of conscience, exercise and equality were granted to most religious groups and practices. Most religious individuals were able to assemble, speak, publish, parent, educate, travel and so forth on the basis of their religious beliefs. Most religious groups were able to incorporate, hold property, receive private donations, enforce religious laws, and maintain buildings, schools and charities for voluntary members. The corresponding patronage of a public religion (generally Protestant Christianity) meant government endorsement and public display of religious statements, symbols and ceremonies in the sense described above, including state aid to religious groups, government-sponsored chaplains appointed to public entities such as the military and hospitals, and religiously-based laws.[67]

However, religious minorities with low cultural conformity and high religious temperament were discriminated against and did not receive the full gamut of these freedoms.[68] As religious diversity increased and opportunities to emigrate to states more favourable to religious minorities decreased, patronage of a public religion became increasingly untenable. Eventually state governments began to clamp down on private religious dissenters and deny fundamental freedoms of non-conforming private religions.[69]

When the dissenters appealed to the Supreme Court for relief the Court responded by applying the Jeffersonian strict separation model, mostly to state patronage of education. The Court 'removed religion from public schools' by preventing schools from prayer and reading Scripture, and 'removed religious schools from state support' by preventing salary supplement, supply of resources, and tax exemptions.[70] However, more recent cases suggest the Supreme Court is revising this extreme approach,

---

[65]   Ibid.
[66]   Ibid 506.
[67]   Ibid 507.
[68]   Ibid 506.
[69]   Ibid 508-510.
[70]   Ibid 512.

and indicate a new, balanced way of defining and defending the legal place of public religion under the *First Amendment*.[71] On numerous occasions the Court has 'upheld government policies that support the public access and activities of religious individuals and groups – so long as these religious parties act voluntarily, and so long as non-religious parties also benefit from the same government support'.[72] For example, Christian clergy could run for political office, religious individuals and groups were able to access generally available funding for education or community purposes, and religious people could display their symbols as much as non-religious people.[73]

From these cases Witte delineates four themes for a free public religion in a modern liberal democracy. First, 'public religion must be as free as private religion', precisely because religious parties are religious and sometimes engage in divisive and counter-cultural practices. They 'provide leaven and leverage for the polity to improve' by taking a stand beyond the mainstream and so are essential for maintaining a flourishing difference.[74] Second, 'freedom of public religion sometimes requires the support of the state'.[75] The modern state is highly regulatory and it is practically impossible for religious bodies to avoid entanglement with state education, charity, welfare, family assistance, healthcare, taxation and so on. It is not preferential treatment when 'a general government scheme provides public religious groups and activities with the same benefits afforded to all other eligible recipients'.[76] Third, 'a public religion cannot be a common religion'. It must be:

> ... a collection of particular religions, not the combination of religious particulars. It must be a process of open religious discourse, not a product of ecumenical distillation. All religious voices, visions, and values must be heard and deliberated in the public square. All public religious services and activities, unless criminal or tortious, must be given a chance to come forth and compete, in all their denominational particularity ... that is how a healthy democracy works.[77]

Finally, 'freedom of public religion also requires freedom from public

---

[71] *United States Constitution*
[72] Witte, above n 11, 515–516.
[73] Ibid.
[74] Ibid 516.
[75] Ibid 517.
[76] Ibid.
[77] Ibid.

religion'.[78] The state should not compel participation in religious beliefs or practices, but they also cannot prevent participation in public ceremonies or programs just because they are religious. As Witte powerfully observes:

> It is one thing to outlaw Christian prayers and broadcasted Bible readings from the public school; after all, students are compelled to be there. It is quite another thing to ban moments of silence and private religious speech in these same public schools. It is one thing to bar direct tax support for religious education, quite another thing to bar tax deductions for parents who choose to educate their children in religious schools. It is one thing to prevent government officials from delegating their core police powers to religious bodies, quite another thing to prevent them from facilitating the charitable services of voluntary religious and non-religious associations alike. It is one thing to outlaw governmental prescriptions of prayers, ceremonies, and symbols in public forums, quite another thing to outlaw governmental accommodations of private prayers, ceremonies, and symbols in these same public forums.[79]

For Witte people who object to these things can simply choose a different school or charity, and choose not to look at the person privately praying or wearing the religious symbol. This kind of voluntary self-protection from public religion rather than state-enforced privatisation of religion 'will ultimately provide far greater religious freedom for all' and facilitate a much more effective democracy in terms of co-existing peacefully in the face of differing views.[80]

Equal Voice Liberalism as a Framework for Free Public Religion

This part draws upon the preceding discussion of equal voice liberalism to argue this framework is conducive to facilitating the kind of 'free public religion' for a modern democracy that Witte describes. To do this it will not be enough to simply copy the Adams approach. Public state patronage of a particular religion through mild establishment, even if accompanied by in-principle support for the freedom of other private religions and non-religions, would fail the 'constitutional limits' criterion. 'Mild' establishment is still establishment and explicit state support for a particular religion would contravene both the American and Australian establishment clauses. Furthermore, as Witte

---

78   Ibid.
79   Ibid 518.
80   Ibid.

outlines, the Adams approach in fact resulted in discrimination against the 'minority' religions and a curtailing of their religious freedom. This is not appropriate for the free and equal liberal democracy envisaged by the likes of Bader and Wolterstorff.

However, there are some aspects of the Adams approach which remain relevant. The insight that it is impossible for the state to be religiously or even philosophically neutral is one of the critiques of public reason liberalism proffered by those who advocate an equal voice liberalism approach, and this is the conceptual foundation for the view that the state should facilitate a public interaction of different views rather than one particular 'neutral' view.[81] The general freedom of private religions to believe, practice, publish and assemble is also a principle which should be maintained. These aspects are incorporated by Witte in his four themes of free public religion which constitute its nature for the purposes of this chapter.

Consequently, this part will apply the three criteria of equal voice liberalism articulated above to Witte's four themes of free public religion to more specifically argue that equal voice liberalism facilitates this conception of free public religion. To briefly recapitulate for more clarity in this analysis, the three criteria of equal voice liberalism are anti-paternalism as equal voice, with constitutional protections for freedom of religion, speech and assembly, conducted according to the principles of civility. The four themes of free public religion are that public religion is as free as private religion, can require support from the state, is a process of open religious discourse, and also requires freedom from religion.

First, anti-paternalism as equal voice supports free public religion. Witte explicitly identifies free public religion as requiring a collection of particular religions engaging in open public discourse and being free to be heard and debated in the public square. A healthy democracy works by allowing different perspectives to compete in all their particularity. Equal voice liberalism is clearly a favourable framework for this conception because it involves giving an equal voice to all perspectives, including religious perspectives, in public policy debate. Furthermore, equal voice liberalism by its nature facilitates equal freedom for private religion as well as public religion by allowing private religions to assemble and speak their views in a counter-

---

[81]   See, eg, Wolterstorff, *Understanding Liberal Democracy*, above n 10, 76-113; Bader, *Liberal-Democratic Constitutionalism*, above n 8.

cultural way.[82] As McGraw persuasively argues, the involvement of religion in politics actually results in a more free and democratic society.[83] It may be that society does not agree with these particular views and they are rejected according to a proper democratic process in a policy context, but equal voice liberalism provides the mechanism for private religions to contribute to a healthy democracy by being part of a flourishing public religion comprised of alternative views which may eventually become culturally accepted or at least contribute to pursuing the public good.[84]

Second, constitutional protections for basic freedoms supports free public religion. Witte argues that free public religion involves freedom of religion and freedom from religion (both public and private). In terms of freedom of religion, constitutional protections of religious freedom, freedom of speech, and freedom of assembly which are part of the liberal framework facilitate freedom of public religion by empowering religious individuals and organisations to publicly assemble and reasonably advocate for their particular political views based on religious convictions without fear of legal restriction or adverse consequence. Conversely, constitutional limits such as non-establishment and non-imposition clauses ensure freedom from public religion. Witte's version of public religion is not endorsement or establishment of a particular religion by the state. It does not entail imposed religious beliefs and practices. It may mean some state support for particular religious bodies offering public services, but this funding is generally available to all relevant organisations so this does not constitute discriminatory or preferential treatment which would contravene an establishment clause.[85] Hence constitutional protections as part of equal voice liberalism provide a robust environment for free public religion by enabling freedom of religion and freedom from religion.

Finally, the principles of civility support free public religion. This contention is not as straightforward as the previous two because Witte does not explicitly discuss principles of civility in his summation of free public

---

[82]   See Eberle, above n 40, 41-47.

[83]   See generally Bryan McGraw, *Faith in Politics: Religion and Liberal Democracy* (Cambridge, 2010).

[84]   See also Wolterstorff, *Understanding Liberal Democracy*, above n 10, 277-297.

[85]   As, for example, the Australian High Court found in *Attorney-General (Vic); Ex rel Black v Commonwealth* (1981) 146 CLR 559. See also Witte, above n 11, 515-516 for examples relating to the US establishment clause.

religion. There are, however, implications which can be drawn from his delineation of the themes in at least two respects. First, the open religious discourse in the public sphere envisaged by Witte's free public religion would seem to require at least some level of 'civility' in the equal voice liberalism sense. If equal voice liberalism requires principles of civility as Bader and Wolterstorff claim, and free public religion involves open religious discourse in the way equal voice liberalism advocates, it logically follows that free public religion would in turn require principles of civility. Consequently equal voice liberalism provides the aspect of civility necessary for Witte's version of free public religion to function as part of a healthy democracy.

Second, Witte mentions that freedom from public religion cannot prevent participation in public ceremonies or programs just because they are religious, and people should engage in a voluntary self-protection from public religion rather than rely on a state-enforced privatisation of religion. Anyone who participates in this kind of voluntary self-protection is in a sense putting into action the principles of civility. Rather than appealing to the state to censor religious perspectives they do not agree with, such persons are acknowledging the equal status and dignity of those with religious perspectives and recognising that they share a common identity as 'democratic citizen' which allows all perspectives to be publicly displayed and considered. Voluntary self-protection is not feasible without civic virtues such as honesty, forbearance and humility, and therefore the principles of civility support freedom from public religion as an aspect of free public religion.

Hence, the three criteria comprising equal voice liberalism provide an appropriate framework for facilitating Witte's conception of free public religion. However, it must be acknowledged that the preceding argument has made reference to 'freedom' and 'equality' without really defining or explaining them. Though both are crucial for the idea of democracy, the terms themselves require analysis for the argument to be meaningful, if not persuasive. In particular, 'acknowledgement of equality need not imply uniform treatment'.[86] Reasonable accommodation involving differential treatment can be made to maintain equality and preserve freedom. As such, the following part aims to give more analytical and evaluative precision to 'freedom' and 'equality' to bolster the argument that equal voice liberalism is an appropriate framework for facilitating free public religion.

---

[86] Roger Trigg, *Equality, Freedom and Religion* (Oxford, 2012) 3-4. Cf Ibid 139-140.

Preserving 'Freedom' and 'Equality'

To return to Senator Wong's statements at the beginning of this chapter, the basic arguments for discouraging free public religion stem from fundamental ideas of human dignity and equality, especially when public religion might discriminate against people of particular identities. As Trigg laments, 'when religion is pitted against [other] rights, religion is often sidelined'.[87] Of course, what is often forgotten is religion too is a fundamental human right; but when two rights such as 'religious freedom' and 'equality' are put in conflict this way, 'there seems little appetite from the standpoint of law for any reasonable accommodation. The views of the state have to be applied regardless of any conscientious dissent'.[88] If there is a clash of these fundamental rights, it appears 'the solution is for one to win, and not for any attempt to be made to satisfy both sides'.[89] But religious freedom is a basic right which cannot be simply discarded because it competes with other rights. The idea of religious freedom is to protect religious belief and practice from any prevailing orthodoxy (e.g. equality) which might oppose it. The idea is 'worthless' if it is allowed only when it fits in with that particular orthodoxy.[90]

This exigency makes finding some kind of reasonable balance between religious freedom and equality all the more pertinent. After all, freedom of religion 'arises in its most acute form when unpopular, or unfashionable, minority positions are in question. Freedom is safeguarded only when the majority allows beliefs to be manifested of which it disapproves'.[91] It is easy to talk about the freedom of those who think and act as we do. The problem is when there is fervent disagreement. Defending the right to disagree is 'important for the future of democracy', not least because one day we might be in the minority.[92] As Trigg powerfully observes, 'the essence of religious freedom is that people are allowed to follow their religion, even if it is a different one from that of the majority. The accommodation of minority beliefs is what distinguishes democracy from a totalitarian state'.[93] We must consider whether

---

[87]   Ibid 8.
[88]   Ibid.
[89]   Ibid.
[90]   Ibid 38-39.
[91]   Ibid 8.
[92]   Ibid 9.
[93]   Ibid 146, 151-152. Trigg alludes to the fact that secular thinking with its focus on 'equality' has now become the orthodox view in liberal societies, with the implication that religion is now a genuine minority (133).

we are willing to 'take account of conscientious objection' and 'find room for accommodation'.[94] Though it is always simpler to have a law which applies uniformly, important principles are at stake. Without exceptions unreasonable burdens can be placed on religious believers which are not operative on non-religious believers. Trigg provides the stock example of a law requiring cyclists to wear helmets. Such a law is eminently sensible and neutral, not targeting any particular group. But for Sikhs the law is unduly burdensome because of their requirement to wear a turban, and the law has granted an exception to them.[95] Therefore, 'if we really value religious freedom, including the right to deny all religion, we should be concerned if its claims are simply overridden'.[96] As Trigg explains, uniform treatment can make 'religious people feel like they are marginalised in their own society' because they alone are subject to an unequal burden through generally applicable legislation.[97] So religious people may resent their 'commitments being ignored and that they are being treated unfairly and unequally. A concern for equality can visibly diminish religious freedom'.[98]

It is becoming well known that social divisions, differences and fragmentation along religious and cultural lines can lead to conflict which undermines democratic freedom and equality. But this is only if the state fails to 'recognise and accommodate the various ethnicities, religions, languages and values in a particular country'.[99] Ten Napel proceeds to note that since 'religion is of profound importance to one's identity, from the point of view of cultural liberty, guaranteeing religious freedom in the best possible way is of foremost importance'.[100] Consequently Ten Napel contends that all civil society organisations, including religious ones, ought to enjoy a considerable degree of autonomy. Negotiation, reasonableness and accommodation is needed. This 'reasonable accommodation' is the way forward, including a 'proportionality principle' to 'weigh the seriousness of a particular infringement of a right against the importance of the conflicting private or public interest in precisely infringing upon this right', as opposed to an 'inadequately blunt' hierarchy

---

94 Ibid 9.
95 Ibid.
96 Ibid.
97 Ibid 31-32, 87-88, 114.
98 Ibid 32, 116, 119-120, 128-132.
99 Ten Napel, above n 31, 98.
100 Ibid 99.

of rights.[101] In this framework freedom is preserved by granting reasonable autonomy to religious organisations (and individuals). Equality is preserved by providing religious bodies with accommodations (as a function of autonomy) to remove unreasonable burdens, while ensuring any discrimination which occurs is a proportional and reasonable exercise of that autonomy in a liberal democracy.

It is also worth remembering that this accommodation can operate at multiple levels. For example, the term 'equality' can have different religious interpretations and conceptions as well. Views on equality may be understood differently by religious individuals and associations and therefore deeper views on plurality necessitate the accommodation of different views on equality as such.[102] However, any conception of equality must be reasonable in the context of a liberal democracy comprised of different, competing views. Hence we can finally characterise the principle of preserving freedom and equality as a proportionate, reasonable accommodation of difference in a liberal democracy.

Indeed, liberal democracy is a means of making it possible for a group to harmoniously exist despite deep difference. Equal voice liberalism in particular facilitates this by providing all citizens with an equal voice and ability to voice their perspectives in the public sphere according to the principles of civility with constitutional protections. The fact that citizens are allowed this kind of equal voice facilitates harmony in difference rather than coerced uniformity. In essence this is precisely the kind of free public religion envisaged by Witte, where a collection of religions are equally able to advocate for their distinct views without the state establishing or imposing them. Again, the idea is not to achieve a harmonious existence by eradicating difference or independent community (as in public reason liberalism, at least in the public sphere), but by tolerating these differences as much as possible through allowing them to be voiced within constitutional limits while exercising the principles of civility. All this entails 'both the existence of rules and the provision of accommodations' for religion.[103] Sadly, as Ten Napel incisively observes, 'what the fact that [the

---

[101]   Ibid 126.

[102]   See, for example, different religious and non-religious conceptions of equality in Tariq Modood, 'Muslim views on religious identity and racial equality' (2010) 19(3) *New Community* 513-519; Lucy Vickers, 'Promoting Equality or fostering resentment? The public sector equality duty and religion and belief' (2011) 31(1) *Legal Studies* 135-158; Wolterstorff, *Understanding Liberal Democracy*, above n 10, 177-226.

[103]   Ibid.

provision of religious accommodations] is becoming more controversial really demonstrates, therefore, is that the idea of liberal democracy as such is losing support'.[104]

This must not continue. Obviously there is no doubt equality legislation is an essential aspect of liberal democracy. But if administered in a coercive fashion without due attempts at accommodation and proportionality, it will burden some in society unnecessarily and inequitably.[105] It should be noted that associative and individual religious freedom is a special right in the context of liberal democracy, outweighing freedom of opinion and expression. 'Before one is able to express an opinion, one first needs to develop an idea, often in community with others. This idea, moreover, is likely to originate in a religious or non-religious worldview, which must thus be protected in order to make freedom of expression substantial'.[106] So religious associations in particular need legal protections to maintain their distinct identity such that they can continue to develop their ideas to inform opinions and expression in the public sphere. However, at the same time, this does not mean religious freedom should be pursued at the expense of other fundamental rights such as equality. Believers must recognise and respect opposing interests in a liberal democracy, especially if these are protected as fundamental rights.[107] That is why a proportionate, reasonable accommodation of difference is appropriate rather than unfettered religious freedom or pure mandated uniformity.[108]

John Inazu expresses this proportionate, reasonable accommodation of

---

[104] Ibid. See, eg, Paul Horwitz, 'Against Martyrdom: A Liberal Argument for Accommodation of Religion' (2016) 91 *Notre Dame Law Review* 1301. Cf Monica Mookherjee, *Democracy, Religious Pluralism and the Liberal Dilemma of Accommodation* (Springer, 2012) and Lori Beaman, *Reasonable Accommodation: Managing Religious Diversity* (UBC Press, 2012).

[105] Ten Napel, above n 31, 127. See also Thomas Berg, 'What Same-Sex Marriage Claims and Religious Liberty Claims Have in Common' (2010) 5(2) *Northwestern Journal of Law and Social Policy* 206.

[106] Ten Napel, above n 31, 127.

[107] Ibid.

[108] See also Trigg, above n 86, 91-96, 151-152 on the need to identify religious belief and practice as an area which needs to be specially safeguarded from state coercion to accepted majority views and practices. Democracy must tolerate the claims of conscience, because deeply felt moral and religious convictions provide the basis on which responsible decisions should be made. Morality has to constrain democratic discussion, so as to provide a vision for the kind of society to be achieved. Claims of conscience are the wellspring of democracy itself. (97)

difference as a 'confident pluralism' of 'mutual respect and coexistence'.[109] Such confident pluralism 'allows genuine difference to coexist without suppressing or minimising our firmly held convictions. We can embrace pluralism precisely because we are confident in our own beliefs, and in the groups and institutions that sustain them'.[110] To use a Dworkinism, confident pluralism takes both confidence and pluralism seriously.[111] 'Confidence without pluralism misses the reality of politics. It suppresses difference, sometimes violently. Pluralism without confidence misses the reality of people. It ignores or trivialises our stark differences for the sake of feigned agreement and false unity'.[112] Confident pluralism 'proposes the future of our democratic experiment requires finding a way to be steadfast in our personal convictions' while also allowing fundamental disagreement; we must have a 'principled commitment' to 'mutual respect' sufficient for at least coexistence and even flourishing.[113] This framework includes the premises of 'inclusion' (we seek for those within our boundaries to be part of the political community) and 'dissent' (we allow for people to dissent from the norms established by that community).[114]

Confident pluralism involves three constitutional commitments which essentially provide for the autonomy of religious associations and an ability for religious associations and individuals to freely develop and voice dissenting ideas in the public sphere – or, in short, enable a free public religion. These are considered in more detail when the chapter applies accommodationism to public religion. Confident pluralism also includes three 'civic practices': 'tolerance' (people are free to pursue their own beliefs and practices even if we find them morally objectionable), 'humility' (others will find our beliefs and practices morally objectionable and we can't always prove we are right and they are wrong), and 'patience' (restraint, persistence and endurance in our engagements across difference).[115]

Confident pluralism has affinities with equal voice liberalism in the sense that it consists of constitutional commitments (limits) which promote equal

---

109   John Inazu, *Confident Pluralism: Surviving and Thriving Through Deep Difference* (University of Chicago Press, 2016) 8 (*'Confident Pluralism'*).

110   Ibid 7.

111   See Ronald Dworkin, *Taking Rights Seriously* (Harvard, 1978).

112   Inazu, *Confident Pluralism*, above n 109, 6-7.

113   Ibid 8.

114   Ibid 9.

115   Ibid 10-11.

voice, and involves civic practices which are essentially the principles of civility. More significantly, these affinities suggest free public religion should be facilitated as part of a proportionate, reasonable accommodation of difference (accommodationism). In other words, accommodationism manifested as Inazu's 'civic practices' is a function of the civic virtues and moral engagement facilitated by equal voice liberalism. This implies an accommodationist approach to free public religion in the context of equal voice liberalism should include reasonable accommodations and exemptions for religious entities. These accommodations and exemptions provide the autonomy and freedom necessary for religious individuals and organisations to maintain distinct identities which form the basis for developing unique perspectives and modes of public expression, which is essential for free public religion.

Applying Accommodationism to Public Religion

The idea of religious exemptions to anti-discrimination law is contested. Some have advocated reducing or removing anti-discrimination exemptions for religious individuals and organisations because religion should not be a reason to discriminate in a secular state.[116] However, as the preceding analysis implies, broad anti-discrimination exemptions for religious individuals and organisations are necessary to preserve religious freedom and religious diversity in a liberal democracy.[117] Indeed, as Ten Napel observes on multiple occasions, there are strong affinities between Christianity, equal political voice liberal democracy, and the right to freedom of religion or belief.[118] What this means is as a general principle, free public religion and equal political voice (democracy) are mutually reinforcing symbiotic frameworks: preserving freedom of religion and association preserves the development of the structures, processes and content which are necessary for the preservation of democracy, which in turn just reinforces freedom

---

[116] Carolyn Evans and Leilani Ujvari, 'Non-Discrimination Laws and Religious Schools in Australia' (2009) 30 *Adelaide Law Review* 31; Douglas NeJaime, 'Marriage Inequality: Same-Sex Relationships, Religious Exemptions, and the Production of Sexual Orientation Discrimination' (2012) 100(5) *California Law Review* 1169.

[117] Charlotte Baines, 'A Delicate Balance: Religious Autonomy Rights and LGBTI Rights in Australia' (2015) 10(1) *Religion & Human Rights* 45; Patrick Parkinson, 'Accommodating Religious Beliefs in a Secular Age: The Issue of Conscientious Objection in the Workplace' (2011) 34(1) *University of New South Wales Law Journal* 281.

[118] Ten Napel, above n 31, 94-97, 106.

of religion and association.[119]

Associational Contexts

The remainder of the chapter will therefore focus on applying the principle of reasonable accommodation to religious freedom in associational contexts. It will first more specifically outline a rationale for recognising the religious freedom of associations as a function of equal voice liberalism facilitating free public religion, with concomitant allowance of reasonable accommodations or exemptions to equality legislation. It will then very briefly consider the specific example of religious educational institutions choosing not to employ those who do not, in word or deed, adhere to the doctrines of the religion. Other work has started doing this in individual contexts through, for example, developing proportionality tests which balance the need to preserve equality with the importance of individual religious freedom in a polity which desires to prioritise democracy. This kind of accommodationism takes into account both the harm suffered by those discriminated against and the harm suffered by those who are legally compelled against their conscience in trying to achieve some kind of reasonable balance or consideration of difference.[120] The principle also has utility in the associational context, where there is a tendency to characterise the religious freedom of associations as existing merely as a function of individual rights rather than as a right attaching to the group itself.[121]

However, as Nicholas Aroney cautions, 'much is at stake in the question whether freedom of religion is understood, in essence, to be an individual, associational or communal right'.[122] If it is purely an individual right such a conception 'has the tendency to suggest that the rights of religious groups

---

[119] Cf Ibid 106 where Ten Napel indicates Christianity in particular facilitates pluralistic liberal order and tolerant decision-making, and speculates that the decline of Christianity in the West is likely to detrimentally affect how democracy functions. John Milbank and Adrian Pabst go even further and argue Christianity is the source of democracy. See John Milbank and Adrian Pabst, *The Politics of Virtue: Post-Liberalism and the Human Future* (Rowman and Littlefield, 2016) 6-7; John Milbank, *Beyond Secular Order: The Representation of Being and the Representation of the People* (Blackwell, 2013) 10, 164.

[120] See Deagon, *Freedom and Discrimination*, above n 5, 276-286.

[121] See, eg, Jane Norton, *Freedom of Religious Organisations* (Oxford, 2016).

[122] Nicholas Aroney, 'Freedom of Religion as an Associational Right' (2014) 33(1) *University of Queensland Law Journal* 153, 154.

must always be subordinated to the rights, not only of their individual members, but the rights of individuals that do not belong to such groups but nonetheless make claims against them, such as through the universalising application of anti-discrimination and other regulatory laws'.[123] This assumption can result in 'massive and illegitimate' state intervention in the internal affairs of religious organisations, even in issues of core belief and practice.[124] Rather, Aroney claims that when this 'false and unarticulated' assumption is abandoned and the organisation or group itself is deemed as a bearer of rights, 'a more balanced assessment of the interaction between those rights and the rights of others can then be undertaken'.[125]

So religious freedom is not merely individual.[126] There is a general consensus among specialist scholars in the field that the right to hold and practice religion has personal, associational, communal, organisational and institutional dimensions.[127] As Carolyn Evans explains, at least at the level of international law:

> While human rights belong to individuals, the right to manifest religious freedom collectively means that it has an organisational dimension. When individuals choose to exercise their religion within an organised religious group, the state must respect the autonomy of this group with respect to decisions such as the freedom to choose their religious leaders, priests and teachers, the freedom to establish seminaries or religious schools and the freedom to prepare and distribute religious texts or publications.[128]

More broadly, as Cole Durham similarly observes:

> Protection of the right of religious communities to autonomy in structuring their religious affairs lies at the very core of protecting

---

[123] Ibid. See also Dwight Newman, *Community and Collective Rights: A Theoretical Framework for Rights Held by Groups* (Hart, 2011) 13-27.

[124] Bader, *Liberal-Democratic Constitutionalism*, above n 8, 23.

[125] Aroney, above n 121, 154-155. See also Mark E Chopko and Michael F Moses, 'Freedom to Be a Church: Confronting Challenges to the Right of Church Autonomy' (2005) 3 *Georgetown Journal of Law & Public Policy* 387.

[126] Julian Rivers, *The Law of Organized Religions: Between Establishment and Secularism* (Oxford, 2013) 317-318.

[127] Aroney, above n 122, 168, 181. See also, David Little, 'Religious Liberty' in John Witte and Frank S. Alexander (eds), *Christianity and Law: An Introduction* (Cambridge University Press, 2008) 249; Rex Ahdar and Ian Leigh, *Religious Freedom in the Liberal State* (Oxford University Press, 2nd ed, 2011) 375-377; Robert George, *Conscience and Its Enemies: Confronting the Dogmas of Liberal Secularism* (Intercollegiate Studies Institute, 2013) 76.

[128] Carolyn Evans, *Legal Protection of Religious Freedom in Australia* (Federation Press, 2012) 35.

religious freedom. We often think of religious freedom as an individual right rooted in individual conscience, but in fact, religion virtually always has a communal dimension, and religious freedom can be negated as effectively by coercing or interfering with a religious group as by coercing one of its individual members.[129]

Of course, all this does not mean religious freedom is absolute in this context. Interference by the state where necessary for public safety and the protection of other human rights (like equality) or legal rights (like property) in a liberal democracy would require significant justification but restrictions may be valid.[130]

Nevertheless, from the perspective of equal voice liberalism facilitating a free public religion which involves a proportionate, reasonable accommodation of difference, 'a resurrection of [this kind of] democracy … is not feasible without generous protection of the more associational and institutional dimensions of the right to freedom of religion or belief'.[131] Thinkers such as Wolterstorff who believe in the need to translate societal pluralism into true 'equal political voice liberalism' therefore give much weight to freedoms of association and assembly. They claim that 'in order for different voices to be heard, there is a need for places where people can find their voice', even if some of these ideas will not conform with majority opinion.[132] 'In such cases, it is furthermore required to be reluctant to interfere in the internal affairs of religious and other associations'.[133] Wolterstorff argues equal political voice liberalism is dependent on there being 'moral or religious communities in society that nourish the kind of convictions put forward by citizens and their political representatives'.[134] The implication is if these communities are not allowed to self-regulate, their ideas will dissipate and political voice will be impoverished as a result. Genuine equal political voice requires strong autonomy for religious groups to facilitate a free public religion. Consequently, all the state can do is facilitate the adaptation and development of the convictions of moral and

---

[129] W Cole Durham, 'The Right to Autonomy in Religious Affairs: A Comparative View' in Gerhard Robbers (ed), *Church Autonomy: A Comparative Survey* (Peter Lang, 2001) 1.

[130] Evans, above n 128, 35-36.

[131] Ten Napel, above n 31, 10.

[132] Ibid.

[133] Ibid.

[134] Ibid 92-93; Wolterstorff, *Understanding Liberal Democracy*, above n 10, 141.

religious communities by guaranteeing the freedoms of religion, expression, assembly and association.[135]

As discussed earlier, a way for the 'state to facilitate civil society associations in a democratic constitutional state' has been suggested by Inazu through three constitutional commitments and three civic practices. The civic practices have been outlined above. The constitutional commitments are: first, a 'voluntary groups' requirement which forbids state interference with the membership, leadership or internal practice of a voluntary group without a 'clearly articulated and precisely defined' compelling state interest; second, a 'public forum' requirement which holds that the public forum should allow dissenting voices absent a compelling state interest; and third a 'public funding' requirement which prevents government from restricting generally available public resources for facilitating a diversity of ideas on the basis of its own orthodoxy.[136] Inazu understands a 'compelling state interest' as requiring 'an extraordinary justification (for example, "we think your claim of human sacrifice as liturgy is actually murder")'.[137] So it is only instances where there are gross or substantive violations, harms or threats to others that associational freedom should be limited.

These constitutional commitments are also consistent with Bader's idea of associational governance of religious diversity, which formally recognises the plurality of religious groups and grants them strong associational freedoms and legal exemptions to ensure full representation of minority groups in the political process.[138] Thus equal voice liberalism facilitates free public religion by advocating for robust associational freedoms. These freedoms contribute to a healthy democracy by providing space for religious groups to develop and advocate their opinions in a public encounter of different perspectives.

Equal political voice liberalism consequently broadens the notion of politics beyond the political process to advancement of human development and the common good. Since religious groups in particular provide the associational structures (including visionary and didactic resources) for training in discourse concerning advancement of human development and the common good, it is essential for moral engagement and civic virtue (and

---

[135]   Ten Napel, above n 31, 93.

[136]   Inazu, *Confident Pluralism*, above n 109, 48, 64-65, 79. See also John Inazu, *Liberty's Refuge: The Forgotten Freedom of Assembly* (Yale University Press, 2012).

[137]   John Inazu, 'A Confident Pluralism' (2015) 88 *Southern California Law Review* 587, 605.

[138]   Bader, *Liberal-Democratic Constitutionalism*, above n 8, 18-19.

democracy itself) that these groups be protected by and from the state.[139] As Ten Napel argues, 'it is precisely within such faith and other communities that mature visions of the good life can develop, which simultaneously contribute to the notion of the common good'.[140] Thus religious groups should be free to run according to their own rules. The state must have a role in preserving the freedom of such groups because of the natural human tendency to form groups with common interests and 'a liberal society is itself sustained and protected by such groups'.[141] The point is well summarised by Galston:

> A liberal policy guided ... by a commitment to moral and political pluralism will be parsimonious in specifying binding public principles and cautious about employing such principles to intervene in the internal affairs of civil associations. It will rather pursue a policy of maximum feasible accommodation, limited only by the core requirements of individual security and civic unity. That there are costs to such a policy cannot reasonably be denied. It will permit internal associational practices (e.g. patriarchal gender relations) of which many disapprove. It will allow many associations to define their membership in ways that may be viewed as restraints on individual liberty ... Unless liberty individual and associational - is to be narrowed dramatically, however, we must accept these costs.[142]

Accepting these costs, then, the final question is what kind of specific exemptions and accommodations should exist for religious associations. Answering this question turns on what religious freedom means and the particular religious convictions involved. Religious freedom extends to worship, teaching, propagation, identifying conditions of membership and standards of conduct, and appointing officers, leaders and employees. Such practices are all protected, even if the organisations are formed for broader social or commercial purposes.[143] As for religious convictions, Aroney insightfully provides:

> ... some people who regard themselves as religious nonetheless tend to regard their religion as one aspect of their lives among many; others see their religion as definitive of their whole lives, so that even the most mundane activities are seen in religious terms. Such people frequently

---

[139] Ten Napel, above n 31, 94.

[140] Ibid 97.

[141] Ibid 123. See also Trigg, above n 86, 43-44.

[142] William Galston, 'Value Pluralism and Political Liberalism' (1996) 16(2) *Report from the Institute for Philosophy and Public Policy* 7, 7.

[143] Aroney, above n 122, 157-158.

gather together, not only for narrowly 'religious' activities such as prayer or scriptural study, but also for what might be described as social and cultural activities, such participation in games and sports, or the provision of educational, medical or charitable services. For many such people, such activities are deeply religious.[144]

These insights provide a persuasive basis for allowing, for example, religious educational institutions the autonomy to choose employees who share their doctrines as part of a proportionate, reasonable accommodation. A religious educational institution may want to preserve their distinctive identity as religious in order to be a community which approaches questions of education from that particular religious perspective. Indeed, they may see the practice of education itself as a religious injunction which is to be performed in accordance with their religious convictions. Maintaining this religious identity allows them to present a unique perspective in a democracy in accordance with equal voice liberalism and free public religion, and legally compelling them to accept employees with views or conduct inconsistent with that perspective undermines their religious identity and, consequently, their democratic position as equal and valued citizens.[145]

It is important to note the ability to 'discriminate' in this context is not only a function of religious freedom, but also preserves equality between religious and non-religious educational institutions. As Deagon argues:

> Generally applicable laws, such as anti-discrimination legislation, fall disproportionately or unequally on those whose religious practices conflict with them. Those who do not engage in religious belief or practice are not subject to the same practical restrictions resulting from the laws... the exemptions are necessary in order to preserve equality... specific exemptions are required to address this specific situation where there is an unequal or disproportionate application of law.[146]

In other words, such exemptions are a proportionate, reasonable accommodation of difference because they mitigate the effect of anti-discrimination laws that apply unequally to (in this case) religious educational institutions.[147] And as Trigg emphasises, 'the idea of reasonable

---

144   Ibid 161 at footnote 46. See also Wolterstorff, *Understanding Liberal Democracy*, above n 10, 298-299.

145   See Wolterstorff, *Understanding Liberal Democracy*, above n 10, 299; Trigg, above n 85, 51, 56-57.

146   Deagon, *Freedom and Discrimination*, above n 5, 276-278. Cf Evans and Ujvari, above n 115, 42.

147   See Trigg, above n 86, 3-4, 31-32, 87-88, 114.

accommodation highlights the need to adjust rules when they bear down unfairly on some categories, including religious believers'.[148] As such the need to accommodate religious practices can be traced to equality itself. The need to respect diversity and manage peaceful co-existence of difference requires respecting religion.[149] This proposition might well sit awkwardly with those who do not adhere to the doctrines of the particular religious institution. Nevertheless, if we desire a healthy democracy which genuinely and equally tolerates freedom to differ by giving equal voice to all perspectives within constitutional limits, we must allow associations the freedom to publicly conduct themselves in such a way as to maintain their unique identity on their terms.[150] Only this will facilitate a robust, collective political encounter of perspectives for consideration and critique by citizens so they are fully informed to pursue the public good.

A recent case illustrating this point has come out of the Supreme Court of Canada: *Trinity Western University v Law Society of Upper Canada*, 2018 SCC 33. In this case Trinity Western University ('TWU'), a private Christian college seeking accreditation of its law school, had a community Covenant prohibiting sexual activities outside heterosexual marriage in accordance with traditional Christian doctrine. The Law Society denied accreditation on the basis the covenant was discriminatory against LGBT persons and TWU eventually appealed to the Supreme Court. The Court held 7:2 that the denial was reasonable and proportionate. The scathing joint dissent identified the problem:

> The only proper purpose of a Law Society of Upper Canada ("LSUC") accreditation decision is to ensure that individual applicants who are graduates of the applicant institution are fit for licensing. As a consequence, the only defensible exercise of the LSUC's statutory discretion would have been to accredit TWU's proposed law school. The decision not to accredit TWU's proposed law school is, moreover, a *profound interference with the TWU community's freedom of religion*. Further, even were the "public interest" to be understood broadly as the LSUC and the majority contend, accreditation of TWU's law school would not be inconsistent with the LSUC's statutory mandate. *In a liberal and pluralist society, the public interest is served, and not undermined, by the accommodation of*

---

[148]   Ibid 124.

[149]   Ibid 124, 151-152.

[150]   Wolterstorff, *Understanding Liberal Democracy*, above n 10, 299, 304; Trigg, above n 86, 43-44.

difference. In our view, only a decision to accredit TWU's proposed law school would reflect a proportionate balancing of *Charter* rights and the statutory objectives which the LSUC sought to pursue.[151]

The dissent expressly concurs with the point this chapter is making, which is that associations are entitled to strong autonomy as part of an equal voice liberalism which facilitates free public religion. Trinity Western University is a private institution which is entitled to set a standard by which its community members will abide, as a function of religious freedom. The decision to not accredit them interferes with their religious freedom by effectively preventing them from running a law school in accordance with their religious convictions. No LGBT person, or any other person, is compelled to attend the institution and there are many other options; the accommodation of allowing accreditation of a private Christian law school with a 'discriminatory' Covenant is reasonable and proportionate. The presence of such a school and its ensuing graduates allow for the development and articulation of distinct views which will enrich the democratic process. As the dissenting justices so aptly put it, 'the unequal access resulting from the Covenant is a function not of condonation of discrimination, but of accommodating religious freedom, which freedom allows religious communities to flourish and thereby promotes diversity and pluralism in the public life of our communities'.[152] The fact the majority of the Supreme Court did not see this is concerning for the future of liberal democracy.

Conclusion

This chapter has argued that equal voice liberalism is an appropriate framework for facilitating free public religion, with the consequent implication that religious associations should have robust legal protections allowing them strong internal autonomy. The chapter began by clarifying the many manifestations of liberal democracy such as Bader's liberal-democratic constitutionalism, Wolterstorff's equal voice liberalism, and Billingham's argumentative democracy to construct a single framework of 'equal voice liberalism' which has three distinguishing features. The first is an anti-

---

[151] *Trinity Western University v Law Society of Upper Canada*, 2018 SCC 33 [57] Cote and Brown JJ (emphasis added).

[152] Ibid [81].

paternalist or equal voice approach to political discourse where there are no substantive limits on perspectives in policy discussion. Second, this free political discourse is guaranteed by constitutional protections of freedom of religion, speech, assembly and association. Finally, the discourse occurs according to the principles of civility to enhance a genuine engagement and solidarity between citizens.

The chapter further argued these features are important for facilitating a free public religion, which is a free, collective public encounter of religious perspectives without the state legally imposing any particular religious beliefs or practice. Finally, the chapter contended that for such an encounter to properly occur, religious associations need the space to independently form and develop unique perspectives which they can contribute to public discourse. As a function of a proportionate, reasonable accommodation of difference in a democracy, this space requires strong legal protection of associational freedoms and associational autonomy through, for example, exemptions in equality legislation. Though there is no doubt a cost to equality through allowing such exemptions, the cost to democracy is far greater by not allowing them. Reasonable accommodations of difference are part of a flourishing, pluralist community, and we must learn to live together harmoniously with our differences if the idea of liberal democracy is to retain currency today.

Bibliography

Ahdar Rex and Ian Leigh, *Religious Freedom in the Liberal State* (Oxford University Press, 2nd ed, 2011)

Aroney Nicholas, 'Freedom of Religion as an Associational Right' (2014) 33(1) *University of Queensland Law Journal*

Attorney-General (Vic); Ex rel Black v Commonwealth (1981) 146 CLR 559

Audi Robert, 'The Place of Religious Argument in a Free and Democratic Society' (1993) 30 *San Diego Law Review*

Audi Robert, *Democratic Authority and the Separation of Church and State* (Cambridge University Press, 2011)

Audi Robert, *Religious Commitment and Secular Reason* (Cambridge University Press, 2000)

Bader Veit, 'Included, Excluded or Foundational: Religion in Liberal-Democratic States' in Gavin D'Costa et al (eds), *Religion in a Liberal State* (Cambridge, 2013)

Bader Veit, 'Post-Secularism or Liberal-Democratic Constitutionalism?' (2012) 5(1) *Erasmus Law Review*

Bader Veit, 'Religious Pluralism: Secularism or Priority for Democracy' (1999) 27 *Political Theory*

Bader Veit, *Secularism or Democracy? Associational Governance of Religious Diversity* (Amsterdam University Press, 2007)

Baines Charlotte, 'A Delicate Balance: Religious Autonomy Rights and LGBTI Rights in Australia' (2015) 10(1) *Religion & Human Rights*

Beaman Lori, *Reasonable Accommodation: Managing Religious Diversity* (UBC Press, 2012)

Berg Thomas, 'What Same-Sex Marriage Claims and Religious Liberty Claims Have in Common' (2010) 5(2) *Northwestern Journal of Law and Social Policy*

Billingham Paul, 'Does Political Community Require Public Reason? On Lister's Defence of Political Liberalism' (2016) 15(1) *Politics, Philosophy and Economics*

Casanova Jose, *Public Religions in the Modern World* (University of Chicago Press, 2011)

Chopko E Mark and Michael F Moses, 'Freedom to Be a Church: Confronting Challenges to the Right of Church Autonomy' (2005) 3 *Georgetown Journal of Law & Public Policy*

Copan Paul, 'The Biblical Worldview Context for Religious Liberty' in A Menuge (ed), *Religious Liberty and the Law: Theistic and Non-Theistic Perspectives* (Routledge, 2018)

Curtis Kent Michael, 'A Unique Religious Exemption from Anti-Discrimination Laws in the Case of Gays? Putting the Call for Exemptions for Those Who Discriminate against Married or Marrying Gays in Context' cited in Michael Kent Curtis (ed), *The Rule of Law and the Rule of God* (Palgrave Macmillan, 2014)

Deagon Alex, 'Defining the Interface of Freedom and Discrimination: Exercising Religion, Democracy and Same-Sex Marriage' (2017) 20 *International Trade and Business Law Review*

Deagon Alex, 'Liberal Secularism and Religious Freedom in the Public Sphere: Reforming Political Discourse' (2018) 41(3) *Harvard Journal of Law and Public Policy*

Deagon Alex, 'On the Symbiosis of Law and Truth in Christian Theology: Reconciling Universal and Particular through the Pauline Law of Love' (2015) 23(4) *Griffith Law Review*

Deagon Alex, 'Secularism as a Religion: Questioning the Future of the

"Secular" State' (2017) 8 *The Western Australian Jurist*

Durham Cole W, 'The Right to Autonomy in Religious Affairs: A Comparative View' in Gerhard Robbers (ed), *Church Autonomy: A Comparative Survey* (Peter Lang, 2001)

Dworkin Ronald, *Taking Rights Seriously* (Harvard, 1978)

Eberle Christopher, *Religious Conviction in Liberal Politics* (Cambridge, 2002)

Evans Carolyn and Leilani Ujvari, 'Non-Discrimination Laws and Religious Schools in Australia' (2009) 30 *Adelaide Law Review*

Evans Carolyn, *Legal Protection of Religious Freedom in Australia* (Federation Press, 2012)

Galston William, 'Value Pluralism and Political Liberalism' (1996) 16(2) *Report from the Institute for Philosophy and Public Policy*

George Robert, *Conscience and Its Enemies: Confronting the Dogmas of Liberal Secularism* (Intercollegiate Studies Institute, 2013)

Gray Anthony, 'Reconciliation of Freedom of Religion With Anti-Discrimination Rights' (2016) 42(1) *Monash University Law Review*

Horwitz Paul, 'Against Martyrdom: A Liberal Argument for Accommodation of Religion' (2016) 91 *Notre Dame Law Review*

Inazu John, 'A Confident Pluralism' (2015) 88 *Southern California Law Review*

Inazu John, *Confident Pluralism: Surviving and Thriving Through Deep Difference* (University of Chicago Press, 2016)

Inazu John, *Liberty's Refuge: The Forgotten Freedom of Assembly* (Yale University Press, 2012)

Little David, 'Religious Liberty' in John Witte and Frank S. Alexander (eds), *Christianity and Law: An Introduction* (Cambridge University Press, 2008)

McConnell Michael, 'Why Protect Religious Freedom' (2013) 123 *Yale Law Journal*

McGraw Bryan, *Faith in Politics: Religion and Liberal Democracy* (Cambridge, 2010)

Menuge Angus, 'The Secular State's Interest in Religious Liberty' in A Menuge (ed), *Religious Liberty and the Law: Theistic and Non-Theistic Perspectives* (Routledge, 2018)

Milbank John and Adrian Pabst, *The Politics of Virtue: Post-Liberalism and the Human Future* (Rowman and Littlefield, 2016)

Milbank John, *Beyond Secular Order: The Representation of Being and the Representation of the People* (Blackwell, 2013)

Modood Tariq, 'Muslim views on religious identity and racial equality' (2010) 19(3) *New Community*

Mookherjee Monica, *Democracy, Religious Pluralism and the Liberal Dilemma of*

Accommodation (Springer, 2012)

NeJaime Douglas, 'Marriage Inequality: Same-Sex Relationships, Religious Exemptions, and the Production of Sexual Orientation Discrimination' (2012) 100(5) *California Law Review*

Newman Dwight, *Community and Collective Rights: A Theoretical Framework for Rights Held by Groups* (Hart, 2011)

Norton Jane, *Freedom of Religious Organisations* (Oxford, 2016)

Parkinson Patrick, 'Accommodating Religious Beliefs in a Secular Age: The Issue of Conscientious Objection in the Workplace' (2011) 34(1) *University of New South Wales Law Journal*

Rawls John, *Political Liberalism: Expanded Edition* (Columbia University Press, 2005)

Rivers Julian, *The Law of Organized Religions: Between Establishment and Secularism* (Oxford, 2013)

Ten Napel Hans-Martien, *Constitutionalism, Democracy and Religious Freedom* (Routledge, 2017)

Trigg Roger, *Equality, Freedom and Religion* (Oxford, 2012)

Trinity Western University v Law Society of Upper Canada, 2018 SCC 33

United States Constitution

Vickers Lucy, 'Promoting Equality or fostering resentment? The public sector equality duty and religion and belief' (2011) 31(1) *Legal Studies*

Waldron Jeremy, *Law and Disagreement* (Oxford, 1999)

Williams Rowan, *Faith in the Public Square* (Bloomsbury, 2012)

Witte Jr John, 'From Establishment to Freedom of Public Religion' (2004) 32 *Capital University Law Review*

Wolterstorff Nicholas, *Understanding Liberal Democracy: Essays in Political Philosophy* (Oxford University Press, 2012)

Wong Penny, 'The Separation of Church and State – The Liberal Argument for Equal Rights for Gay and Lesbian Australians' (Speech delivered at NSW Society of Labor Lawyers Frank Walker Memorial Lecture, 17 May 2017) <https://www.pennywong.com.au/speeches/the-separation-of-church-and-state-the-liberal-argument-for-equal-rights-for-gay-and-lesbian-australians-nsw-society-of-labor-lawyers-frank-walker-memorial-lecture-2017>

Woodhead Linda, 'Liberal Religion and Illiberal Secularism' in G D'Costa et al (eds), *Religion in a Liberal State* (Cambridge, 2013)

13

GETTING RELIGION AND BELIEF WRONG BY DEFINITION: A RESPONSE TO SULLIVAN AND HURD

IAIN T BENSON[1]

Abstract

This chapter rejects the definitional 'vagueness' argument against religious freedom of Winnifred Fallers Sullivan; the 'good religion/bad religion' paradigm and associated arguments of Elizabeth Shakman Hurd and their express or implied recourse to 'equality' as a supposed ground for liberty.[2] The first argument is, that religion is not as evasive of legal definition and utility as has been made out. Secondly, that all other terms argued as superior, such as 'equality' are even more difficult to define; they depend, in fact, on a context and a realisation that religion is an equality right itself – being universally listed as such within Constitutions and Bills of Rights in both domestic and international settings. No term is without ambiguity and language and thus

1   PhD (Wits), JD (Windsor), MA (Cambridge), BA (Hons.) (Queens); Professor of Law, School of Law, University of Notre Dame, Sydney, Australia; Extraordinary Professor of Law, Department of Public Law, University of the Free State, Bloemfontein, South Africa. The author thanks student Tara Veness for her assistance with this chapter.
2   WF Sullivan, *The Impossibility of Religious Freedom* (Princeton University Press, 2007); Elizabeth Shakman Hurd, *Beyond Religious Freedom: The New Global Politics of Religion* (Princeton University Press, 2015) ('*The New Global Politics of Religion*').

usually requires contextual interpretation.[3] Pluralism is about accommodating diversity and difference, and these are the grounds against which legal analysis of all terms must be placed. In addition, this chapter argues that terms such as 'belief', 'opinion', or 'conscience' in rights documents must be extended to include atheists and agnostics. The chapter argues that claims for 'state neutrality,' and 'international neutrality,' often import sub-textual atheistic or agnostic claims. More work is needed to expose the atheistic and agnostic biases that too often operate unobserved or uncommented upon in contemporary law and religion scholarship, policy work and judicial analysis. Finally, the sceptical approach taken by Hurd, which purports to express concern about categorising religions as 'good' or 'bad', harmful or unharmful is rejected as unworkable when viewed alongside that author's concerns about religion itself. Both theories are a sort of 're-warmed' secularism – concerns about religion in general are dressed up as a concern about International Relations and fail to respect religions themselves in their associational and lived dimensions. The threat to religious believers and their communities comes, not from sufficiently respectful governmental projects that encourage appropriate forms of inter-faith co-operation but, rather, in these instances, from scholars who overly 'problematise' religion in ways common to secularist anti-religious and sceptical sensibilities.

Keywords: *definition of religion, religious diversity, religion as an equality right, liberalism, atheism and agnosticism, secularism, legal definitions.*

Introduction

The public and associational importance of religion has been well recognised in the following passage from retired Justice Albi Sachs (himself an atheist) of South Africa as follows:

> [F]reedom of religion goes beyond protecting the inviolability of the individual conscience. For many believers, their relationship with God or creation is central to all their activities. It concerns their capacity to relate

---

3   I have written elsewhere about the necessity of contextual analysis that respects associational variation in relation to discrimination and equality. See, Iain T Benson, 'The Necessity for a Contextual Analysis for Equality and Non-discrimination' in Jane F Adolphe, Robert L Fastiggi and Michael A Vacca (eds), *Equality and Non-discrimination: Catholic Roots, Current Challenges* (Pickwick Publications, 2019) 63 – 75. ('*The Necessity for a Contextual Analysis*').

in an intensely meaningful fashion to their sense of themselves, their community and their universe. For millions in all walks of life, religion provides support and nurture and a framework for individual and social stability and growth. *Religious belief has the capacity to awake concepts of self-worth and human dignity which form the cornerstone of human rights. It affects the believer's view of society and founds the distinction between right and wrong. It expresses itself in the affirmation and continuity of powerful traditions that frequently have an ancient character transcending historical epochs and national boundaries.*[4] (emphasis added)

Justice Sachs recognises what some scholars do not; religions are critically important to and cannot be transmogrified into mere equality. Religions are not merely individual but strongly constitute associations worth taking into account for their contributions to human rights themselves. Religions, properly understood, and as understood within key international documents, support private and public dimensions as well as individual and group affiliations. As such, suggestions that religions 'privilege', 'marginalise', 'construct hierarchies of difference', 'sanctify a religious psychology that relies, even unwittingly, on a particular Christian or post-Christian notion of the autonomous subject', 'exclude other modes of living in the world', or 'disable others' all have a limited reach when viewed alongside how religious liberty is recognised in international documents and by international law.[5] Without religion, our very conceptions of 'human rights' (a fortiori 'dignity of the human person') and 'morals', both essential to any developed society, would be thin indeed.[6] Atheist and agnostic believers have no privileged moral viewpoint and what religion offers to culture as a category worthy of respect is not in any serious measure weakened by the law needing to define what it is any more

---

[4]   *Christian Education South Africa v Minister of Education* [2000] ZACC 11 [757].

[5]   All of these constructions are from Elizabeth Shakman Hurd, 'Politics of religious freedom in the Asia-Pacific: an introduction', (2018) 4 (1), *Journal of Religious and Political Practice*, 9-26. Commenting on Hurd's 'cynical' and 'state-centric analysis', one commentator, in an article which follows Hurd's introduction (just referred to), notes that Hurd 'caricatures religious actors, meanings and practices that challenge, transform as well as affirm political formations': Atalia Omer, 'When "good" religion is good', (2018) 4 (1), *Journal of Religious and Political Practice*, 122, 131. The very language of Article 18 of the *International Covenant on Civil and Political Rights*, contradicts Hurd's too easy understanding about the supposed "individual" nature of the rights of thought, belief, conscience and religion that are clearly personal and communal in that article.

[6]   In relation to principles of civil liberties and human rights requiring definitional line-drawing and the necessity of same as well as the importance of 'thought, conscience and religion' as 'fundamental rights' see Tom Bingham, *The Rule of Law* (Penguin 2011).

than any other rights category requires definition in relation to its exercise or protection. In Australia, the leading authority on the definition of religion, the *Scientology Case*,[7] gave no one definition of religion but in two judgements discussed the supposedly impossible term in this helpful manner: two justices including the Chief Justice (Mason ACJ and Brennan J) found that religion has a dual dimension, first, belief in a supernatural Being, Thing or Principle and, second, the acceptance of canons of conduct in order to give effect to that belief though canons of conduct which offend against the ordinary laws are outside the area of any immunity, privilege or right conferred on the grounds of religion.[8] Other justices (Wilson and Deane JJ) held that the important indicia of religion is 'belief in the supernatural' and that it deals with man's nature and place in the universe and his relation to things supernatural.[9] As with any definitions in law there are certainly going to be difficulties of application but that fact alone cannot possibly constitute, as Sullivan and Hurd suggest, any reasonable suggestion that religion is somehow more problematic of definition than many other terms with which law must deal.

Other significant blind spots occur in both Sullivan and Hurd's work. Both fail to engage the category of the fact or nature of atheism or agnosticism *as beliefs and belief systems*, and therefore miss an obvious area of difficulty for domestic or international law and policy making. Just as no regime should dominate culture with one religious perspective, so should no one regime dominate law or politics with atheistic or agnostic preconceptions. That this is missed entirely is a common error, but an error in any case. No doubt the category of religion has been distended, but one can readily deny that this leaves law without adequate frameworks to make important decisions about what counts as religion. Law must decide what counts as religion and how far aspects of religion might find support or rejection in open societies. The issue is not the need for definition but the assumptions about the context of religion and law that make all the difference to whether a religious claim is respected properly

---

7   *Church of the New Faith v. Commissioner of Pay-roll Tax* (1983) 154 CLR 120.

8   Ibid 134.

9   Ibid 174; see, for a discussion of this decision and others related to it, Peter Gerangelos et al, *Winterton's Australian Federal Constitutional Law* (Thomson Reuters, 2013) 950-951.

or not. Definition itself is not the problem – secularism is.[10] I take this point about the need for definition to be obvious and not at all nefarious as the authors suggest.

In common with many who are sceptical about 'tolerance', 'accommodation', 'religious hierarchies', and 'good' and 'bad' determinations, both scholars avoid the category of 'belief' as a human reality shared by religious *and non-religious* believers. This lacuna markedly tips the scale of analysis against religion and in favour of atheism and agnosticism. As such their analysis is a species of 'secularism' understood as an anti-religious movement.

I shall turn now to examine the three errors, firstly, exaggerating the problem of defining religion, secondly, suggesting 'equality' as a better or validly alternative ground for religious freedom and thirdly failing to engage 'non-religious beliefs' and their influence. A final point: despite the criticisms, I acknowledge both authors for providing a rich ground for disagreement and powerful stimulus to writing in an area that badly needs development and evaluation of many of its presuppositions.

It is a mystery why atheism and agnosticism have dominated law and politics for so long without being challenged as belief systems. What is needed now, in the 21st century is not so much the co-operation of church and state (for that has long been established in most open societies) but the separation of atheism and agnostic domination from the state.

---

[10]   Here one ought to be careful to define "secularism" as it should be but often is not. The proper approach to minimise confusion about the nature of secularism is to seek its meaning in the writings of the man who coined the term in 1851 – George Jacob Holyoake (Iain T Benson, 'Considering Secularism' in Douglas Farrow (ed), *Recognizing Religion in a Secular Society*, (McGill-Queen's University Press, 2004) 83-98) ('*Considering Secularism*'). Attempts to suggest there is such a thing as "open secularism" have confused the area. See a useful discussion in Ahdar and Leigh, below n 14. Though the authors do not deal with the original meaning of the term "secularism" or why the neologism of "open secularism" does anything but confuse an area in need of clarity. Secularisms proliferate and any attempt to define what secularism means with any precision is now extremely difficult since the term is used in such a bewildering number of ways none of which seem to have any idea of what Holyoake's original projected meaning entailed. Secularism as the ideology and secularist as the methodology is what is on display by Sullivan, Hurd and their ilk.

Religion as a 'Fundamental Definitional Ambiguity'[11]

It is not accurate to say that religion is any more difficult to define than, say, 'equality,' and the experience of courts and legislators show both that marginal or absurd claims can be ruled out. This, however, seems to trouble both Sullivan and Hurd. They claim that such 'ruling out' is offensive of some principle of inclusion. But there can no more be a blanket principle of 'inclusion' than there can be a blanket principle of 'equality'. Any legal regime is necessarily involved in line drawing and there is nothing inherently offensive about that. Scholars have shown that while some groups claiming to be religious may or may not be denied recognition (think here of Scientology), a sympathetic and wide latitude has been given (think of Buddhism). The fact is that any category of legislation and law requires specificity – or what a leading book on 'definition' refers to as 'stipulative' definitions in the circumstances of law.[12] Moreover, the same book points out that ambiguity is inevitable because 'all words are ambiguous and we are bound to make falsehoods if we start by insisting without investigation that some particular word has only one sense ... there is often a hidden identity and we should try hard to find it.'[13]

In similar fashion Sullivan and Hurd suggest that there is something inherently suspect in the exclusion of 'marginal' belief systems as if there is a pre-existing validity that law must recognise to all religious claims for any to be properly respected. This position is clearly untenable. If I wish to, for example, argue that Chief Boo Hoo is the leader of my religion and that the sacraments of my religion are LSD and marijuana then it might not be surprising that this 'religion' was found to be a mere front for drug usage and therefore illegitimate.[14] Most people, rightly, recognise that all definitions, by definition, require line drawing and will involve 'ins' and 'outs'.

There is something about the characterisation of the appropriate role not of religion, but of *law* in the work of both authors that is concerning.

---

11 Sullivan, above n 2, 29.
12 Richard Robinson, *Definition* (Oxford University Press, 1972) 59 ff.
13 Ibid 153.
14 For a detailed analysis of a wide variety of religious claims and the different approaches that may be used in relation to determining what is and is not counted as a 'religion' including the Chief Boo Hoo decision, see Rex Ahdar and Leigh Ian, *Religious Freedom in the Liberal State* (Oxford University Press, 2nd ed, 2015) 139-156 (142-143).

A clue may be found in the statement from Sullivan that 'at a very profound level religion competes with law - and also, perhaps more importantly, with science and a scientistic reading of law – for *comprehensive explanation and control.* Religion challenges the Rule of Law.'[15] Who claims that law has the role or competence to provide 'comprehensive explanation and control'? To ask this of law is to err in the direction of over-reach. Law simply does not, under the Rule of Law, have the competence to provide 'comprehensive explanations.'[16] That people (some of them judges) now may tend to speak in this way does not mean that they have the correct roles

---

[15]   Sullivan, above n 2, 155-156.

[16]   Note, for example, in his address at the opening of the 2018 law term, New South Wales Chief Justice, Tom Bathurst observed:

>The difficulty with the rule of law as a criterion for intervention is that it is far from being an objective and uncontested concept. Indeed, its authority is invoked in support of both sides of the ideological divide (citing George Brandis QC, "Address at the Opening of the International Bar Association annual Conference", 8 October 2017, Sydney). While conservatives tend to rely on thinner, procedural conceptions of the rule of law, progressives argue that procedural compliance alone is insufficient and that a conception of the Rule of Law unaccompanied by values of substantive equality is better labelled "rule of law": (citing Lord Goldsmith QC, "Government and the Rule of Law in the Modern Age", Speech delivered at the LSE Law Department and Clifford Chance Lecture Series on Rule of Law, London, 22 February 2006). Lord Goldsmith, for instance, posited that 'the rule of law comprehends some statement of values which are universal and ought to be respected as the basis of a free society'. In his famous book on the Rule of Law, former British judge Lord Bingham roundly rejects a thin definition on the basis that 'a state which savagely represses or persecutes sections of its people cannot…be regarded as observing the rule of law no matter how detailed, duly enacted or scrupulously observed are the laws which allow such persecution and repression' (Tom Bingham, *The Rule of Law*, (Penguin Books, 2011) 67).

of law or religion in mind.[17] Freedom from law is an important dimension of liberty. We rightly regard law 'all the way down' as the earmark of authoritarian regimes that give insufficient recognition to the private sphere or principles of ordering that leave, as much as possible, certain areas of life (friendship, the family, religious associations) as unregulated as possible.

Many terms such as 'equality', 'association', 'liberalism', and 'religion' itself all need to be examined on a case by case basis and, most importantly, in context. Thus, what might constitute an 'equality' issue in one setting (say, the refusal to hire someone due to a prohibited ground in an ordinary public setting) might not constitute a breach in another (say, the permitted requirement that a job only be open to co-religionists or a particular sex for a religious leadership appointment to take two commonly accepted examples). The point is that neither 'inclusion' nor 'equality' are sufficiently clear to give us an answer in a particular setting as to how the general terms apply. A diverse society is in the business of recognising and maintaining diverse settings as associational liberty (including religion) are key to the Rule of Law and the rights that operate within such systems. Context is essential in order to place respect properly the freedoms and rights that undergird abstractions such as "equality" or "inclusion".[18]

---

[17]   Some years ago an exchange of just this sort occurred between the then Chief Justice of the Supreme Court of Canada, Beverly McLachlin, and the late American political theorist, Jean Bethke Elshtain. Responding to the Chief Justice's claim that law carves out 'within itself' a place for religion, Elshtain rejected the Chief Justice's way of characterising the 'dialectic of normative commitments' and said:

> I will begin by querying this way of characterising the question before us as the framing of the question looks a bit different if one abstains from a strong version of comprehensive claims for law. Surely where the rule of law in the West is concerned, there is a great deal about which the law is simply silent: the "King's writ" does not extend to every nook and cranny. Indeed, a great deal of self-governing autonomy and authority is not only permitted but is necessary to a pluralistic, constitutional order characterized by limited government. In other words, the law need not be defined as total and comprehensive...

With respect, Sullivan and Hurd commit the same sort of error of legalistic over-reach viewing law as competent to make comprehensive claims. A better approach is to ask what are the limits of law, politics and religions or other associations in open societies mindful of the particular competencies of each sphere. See Jean Bethke Elshtain, 'Freedom of Religion and the Rule of Law' in Douglas Farrow (ed), *Recognizing Religion in a Secular Society* (McGill-Queens University Press) 69.

[18]   Benson, *The Necessity for a Contextual Analysis*, above n 3.

The Suggestion that Another Right Such as 'Equality' Is a Better Ground for Protection of the Individual: The Need for Contextual Evaluation Where Diversity is the Ground of Culture

As with the terms 'discrimination' and 'equality' it is essential to recognize that general terms must be understood against a prior background of diversity and difference within and between communities. Recognition of diverse contexts is the bedrock of contemporary open societies.[19] Failure to view 'equality' or 'discrimination' contextually produces an abstract conception that tends to gloss over the differential contexts of believers and belief communities themselves. This will likely be the result from any embrace of a de-contextualised notion of 'equality' or 'inclusion'. Case law and the language of international documents do not support Sullivan's assertion that equality is 'the higher principle': important, yes, 'higher', no.[20] Other terms, such as 'inclusive' or 'equality' cannot serve themselves as a better ground for protection owing to their dependence on matters that are prior to law itself – such as liberty, human groupings and human realities such as the family, friendship or associations which are compromised or completely eviscerated if subjected wholly to the law. Sullivan's claim, therefore, that 'equality' is a better ground for rights protection than religion fails to recognise the different ontological status of 'religions' and 'equality'.[21] Unless the importance of different contexts is understood to

---

[19]   Peter Westen, 'The Empty Idea of Equality' (1982) 95(3) *Harvard Law Review* 537-596.

[20]   Sullivan, above n 2, 157.

[21]   This quite apart from the fact that Bills of Rights invariably list religion as itself an equality right yet in the rhetorical and litigation battles (or in certain kinds of scholarship) this is somehow reimagined as 'equality *versus* religion' when it should be nothing of the sort, religion also being an equality right. This sort of twisting is inconsistent with the usual listing of 'religion' as both an equality right or, in some documents, a protected category under the heading 'discrimination.' See, for example, *The International Covenant on Civil and Political Rights* (1966) GA Res, 2200A, (XXI) Article 26; *The European Convention for the Protection of Human Rights and Fundamental Freedoms* (entered into force 3 September 1953) art 14; *Protocol No. 12 to the European Convention for the Protection of Human Rights and Fundamental Freedoms: prohibition of discrimination* (2000) European Treaty Series No. 187 (entered into force 1 July 2003), art 1; *Canadian Constitution Act* 1982 which at s 15 of the *Charter of Rights and Freedoms*, lists "religion" as one of the protected categories for non-discrimination and equality. Additionally, the *Constitution of the Republic of South Africa*, Act 108 of 1996, at s 9(3) lists 'religion, conscience and belief' amongst other 'equality rights'. In relation to 'discrimination' s 9(3) of the *South African Constitution* provides that the state may not 'unfairly discriminate' on the listed grounds suggesting, obviously, that 'fair discrimination' is not only permissible but expected.

be prior to the application of the general terms, the abstractions can become mere stalking horses for agendas of homogenisation rather than respectful disagreement and difference.

Litigation in the United States, Canada and increasingly in Europe has provided many cases in which the religious beliefs of individuals or groups have been subject to challenges as being 'discriminatory' or breaching some 'equality' or other. The implied legal viewpoint Sullivan and Hurd argue for is that religious believers or their communities ought to bend to generalised mandates (under the vague headings of 'equality' or 'discrimination') that elevate the challenger's viewpoint to that of the state - in short an implicitly statist viewpoint that raises a supposed good of homogeneity over diversity and the freedoms of associational autonomy, membership and exit.

Beliefs relating to the legitimacy of 'same-sex conduct' provide a good example though they are framed as identity recognition. Such cases are not discussed as 'moral disagreements' between citizens, though this is the most accurate way of characterising them. Such disputes tend not to be framed as a moral disagreement but, rather, as, in fact, a 'quest for equality' or 'equal treatment' – as seen in Australia's debate about 'marriage equality'.

Of course, use of a term such as 'marriage *equality*' begs the question as it fails to ask 'equal in relation to what'? For equality means treating likes alike and the whole point about same-sex marriage is that it is not entirely *like* heterosexual marriage but wishes to be treated the same – so this is treating 'unalikes alike' not treating likes alike. The choice to do so is one that cannot be reconciled between traditions that start off with fundamentally different ontological conceptions of the relevance (or irrelevance) of biology or moral traditions. With respect to the marriage debate, therefore, 'marriage equality' applied uniformly across a society will subordinate a 'difference' analysis about marriage (that men and women can be married but only to those of the opposite sex not those of the same sex) to a generalised homogenisation of what had been different moral and ethical viewpoints based on the natural fact of sexual differences. The point about the debate is that different communities differ *about what is relevant* with respect to marriage – for some marriage *just is*, about male and female and for others, marriage *just is* about love and not about male and female at all.[22] Neither the rhetoric of 'equality' nor 'inclusion' can sort out the difference between the two positions though they form the backdrop to powerful rhetorical claims and many current legal challenges. A better approach is to find out ways of formulating a modus vivendi that maximally respects different belief approaches instead of forcing opposing viewpoints into a 'winner takes all' litigation strategy.[23]

Respecting religious and non-religious belief differences is essential, and as I shall argue below, recognising atheism and agnosticism as 'belief systems' is a more useful, transparent and accurate way of framing diversity than embracing de-contextualised notions such as 'equality' or 'inclusion' in the abstract. The way to deal with 'religion' is precisely not in the abstract but as lived religion in relation to what it is and does. There is good in diversity since it provides a place for difference. Here there is an irony. To endorse inclusion or equality can, in fact, be good things as long as both are carefully delineated. We are 'included' in some ways in a common culture – we are, in some ways, similar as *persons* and as *citizens*. We operate under the same Rule of Law. We have, if our legal regime is a functioning one, the same sorts of rights and obligations before the law that should be clear and applied consistently. But note that being treated the same 'before the law' means in certain circumstances being treated differently on account of group memberships; that rule contains diversity it ought not to obliterate it.

Freedom in diverse treatment and the respect for difference applies irrespective of the numbers supporting one's particular position. This is what is wrong about focusing on 'minority/majority' analysis; everyone has a right to their moral beliefs (or religious beliefs) whether or not they form majority or minority positions. Here I agree with Hurd's call to be mindful of exclusion of the marginal groups. While law may take into account the potential that majority beliefs might make minority positions more difficult to argue for, it would be unfair to the free choices of citizens to subject majority viewpoints to disadvantage in terms of legal tests or to ignore the

---

[22]   See, for a useful discussion of the various ways of defining marriage and what the implications are: Sherif Girgis Robert George and Ryan T. Anderson, 'What is Marriage?' (2010) 34(1) *Harvard Journal of Law and Public Policy* 245-287.

[23]   For an argument along the lines of what I am sketching here but applied to sexual conduct disputes generally. See Shaun de Freitas, 'Religious Associational Rights and Sexual Conduct in South Africa: Towards a Furtherance of the Accommodation of a Diversity of Beliefs' (2013) 3 *Brigham Young University Law Review* 421-455.

importance of genuine rights of voice and exit from associations. Dissent, a category much mentioned by Sullivan and Hurd, is not a trump card against personal and associational life. That would be to provide a community solvent to the very fragmented liberal individualism that Sullivan and Hurd seem to rightly deprecate in other places in their writings.

Should legal tests fail to respect adequately the beliefs of religious individuals and their communities,[24] the appropriate response is not to declare religious liberty 'impossible' but to seek better and more fairly applied tests for courts that, for example, do not 'get inside' the doctrinal beliefs of religious associations but either accommodate them with broad definitions as the Australian High Court did in the *Scientology* case in 1983,[25] or in the manner of Canadian and South African courts, embark on only a cursory 'sincerity test' leaving the benefit of the doubt largely to religious belief and to the diverse forms of associational life.[26] Once again, genuine diversity is essential to ordered freedom. This will not satisfy scholars intent, as Hurd is, to insist as 'from on high' that religions be subjected to their own calculus of acceptability. What Hurd, and Sullivan, object to is, in actual fact, the normative differences of religions themselves. Note how Hurd characterises these in this quotation:

> One can study the ways in which religion is delimited and deployed in specific legal, institutional, historical and political contexts, by whom and for what purposes, as this book has done in the context of contemporary international relations. But religion is too unstable as a category to be treated otherwise. To the extent that scholars of religion and global politics fail to acknowledge this instability they risk reproducing the very

---

24   Sullivan, above n 2, 143.

25   *Church of the New Faith v. Commissioner of Pay-roll Tax* (1983) 154 CLR 120.

26   For respectful decisions by high courts that did not ask whether the religion in question mandated the religious practice at issue, imposing only a 'sincerity test' on the part of the believer, see from South Africa, *KwaZulu-Natal MEC for Education v. Pillay* (2008) (1) SA474 and from Canada, *Syndicat Northcrest v. Amselem* [2004] 2 SCR 551. If legal tests are insufficiently fair they should and can be adjusted. Similarly, on the possibility of an 'organic test' for religious employer exemptions rather than a 'job-parsing approach', see Iain T Benson, *An Associational Framework for the Reconciliation of Competing Rights Claims Involving the Freedom of Religion* (PhD dissertation, University of the Witwatersrand, 2013). The recent decision of the Gauteng High Court in Gaum et al. v Van Rensberg et al. Case No. 40819/17 (March 8, 2019) in which that Court held that the Dutch Reformed Church must change its doctrine on the nature of marriage and its rules of ordination is anomalous. The decision is not certain to be appealed but under existing South African case law is of dubious authority.

normative distinctions and discourses that are in need of interrogation and politicization.[27]

Religion is something here to be examined, 'problematised', 'interrogated', 'deployed' and 'politicised' since, we do not want its normative distinctions and discourses 'reproduced.' What seems to be behind all this 'problematising' is an attempt to blur the lines of orthodoxy of whatever religions there are that have settled frameworks, narrative traditions and belief systems however much there is internal dialogue within those traditions themselves. The view from 'on high' turns out to be an all conquering viewpoint – one that seeks to destabilise settled religion beyond the categories of 'good' and 'bad'. These approaches of Sullivan and Hurd are anything but neutral. They are loaded with normative beliefs that are, in every way, as dominant, hierarchical and hegemonic as the religious traditions or government initiatives they deride. What they lack and what governments and religions have, in fact, is accountability. Since they have no serious traditions of their own, and no clear normative commitments, there is nothing against which their own inferences can be measured.

Hurd's analysis throughout has a limited reach that is both extremely statist and cynical. It is also thoroughly philosophically incoherent since her whole approach to rejecting an ability to distinguish between 'good' and 'bad' religion relies upon our capacity to adjudge 'good' and 'bad' in relation to her own criticisms. If we are to agree with her, we must disagree with her model which suggests a general elision from judgment as to what constitutes 'good' and 'bad' religious practices. As Omer correctly observes, '[t]he main limitation of Hurd's work, therefore, is its power reductionism and lack of self-reflexivity as to her own positionality'.[28] If Sullivan errs with respect to 'problematising' the definition of religion on the microcosm, Hurd errs in her caricature of religions as individualistic, non-cooperative sources of manipulation by state actors in the macrocosm. Both offer what are, in effect, re-warmed secularist critiques of religion that seem to positively pine for the good old days of secularist domination when religions knew their place in the private sphere and kept out of sight and mind. Both their projects seem elaborate methodologies to manage religions back into their boxes, private, ineffectual and quiet. Both seem unaware that law does not 'construct' or

---

[27] Hurd, above n 2, 121.
[28] Omer, above n 5, 124.

'produce' religious groups but that it, rather, recognises them. What 'count' as religions are those that fit the general definitions and everything is defined at some point if it is to fit within law. Sullivan (who says definition is impossible) and Hurd (who sees definition as nefarious) object to the 'hierarchies of law' that, according to them, presuppose and *produce* religious groups with clearly defined orthodoxies and peaceable spokesmen. This, surely, gets the priority the wrong way around. Law may, in certain circumstances, regulate aspects of religious practice but it does not produce religion. There are, says Hurd, no such religions waiting in the wings with these characteristics because, in her world, 'that which falls under the heading of religion is a contested and shifting mash-up of families of beliefs, institutional forms, and fields of practice and experience. State-sponsored religious outreach forcibly distils that elusive and shifting field into something governable'.[29] Note here how she has, as Omer rightly points out, denied any valid agency to religions themselves. She and Sullivan could learn from the respectful stance of Justice Sachs and the International Documents which take associational life-worlds as they find them and "recognise" religion rather than assume that it is all created by power. That cynicism permeates the work of both scholars and those who employ their methodology and does little to advance important initiatives to bring peace between human communities in conflict whomever is behind the initiatives. One gets the sense that a deep anti-religious animus permeates the work rather than any genuine 'problem' – or, rather, that the cynicism itself is the problem not the definitional difficulties inherent in and between religious communities. Describing her project, Hurd states quite succinctly:[30]

> New interpretive possibilities emerge as a result of thinking differently about religion, of complicating and disaggregating the category. What if religion cannot be collapsed into a force for good or evil (or both)? What if it cannot simply stand in for whatever is considered to fall outside the secular? [this project] ... is intended, in part, as a thought experiment that provides a glimpse of what the world would look like after religion is dethroned as a stable, coherent legal and policy category.

Dethroned is the key term here. And who, we might ask, is to do the *de-throning*? Why, Hurd and her fellow traveller scholars, with their new 'problematising' of religion and religious communities of course; on the

---

29 Hurd, above n 2, 23.
30 Ibid 7.

other side are those who have respect for associations and their rights and freedoms and who rely upon the Rule of Law rather than the latest trends to protect them and their beliefs from hegemonic disassembly or dethroning.

Understanding that not all 'Beliefs' and 'Believers' are 'Religious' and the Difference that Makes

In his widely lauded Gifford Lectures for 1951-52, published some years later as *Personal Knowledge: Towards a Post-Critical Philosophy*, scientist and philosopher Michael Polanyi made the following observation:

> Our objectivism, which tolerates no open declaration of faith, has forced modern beliefs to take on implicit forms.... And no one will deny that those who have mastered the idioms in which these beliefs are entailed do also reason most ingeniously within these idioms, even while...they unhesitatingly ignore all that the idiom does not cover.[31]

As Polanyi notes, modern faiths have tended to take on implicit forms. Nowhere is this more evident than where people discuss 'belief' as if it is limited to 'religion' and analyse the difficulty of defining 'religion' as if it somehow gives a free pass to atheist and agnostic believers and the often unnoticed or uncommented upon dominance of these positions in law and public policy. It is a quirk of our post Enlightenment age that the category of 'believer' is more or less reserved for religious believers *and likely to be unevaluated as akin to religion*, for all others. Since everyone is a believer in something, the tendency to analyze only religion and religious belief as if problems of definition do not apply to atheist and agnostic believers causes a series of significant problems. First, problematising only religious belief as if it alone must make a case for itself, is inaccurate, unfair and likely to overlook important aspects about atheist and agnostic believers and, when present, their communities. It is not only religions that lead to human atrocities or unjustified restrictions on freedoms as the 20th century amply evidences.[32]

This is one of the primary errors in the approach of certain scholars

---

[31]   Michael Polanyi, *Personal Knowledge: Towards a Post-Critical Philosophy* (Routledge, 1958) 288.

[32]   A useful book in this area though it does not sufficiently note the category of 'non-religious believers' in the way I argue for it here is Martin D'Arcy, *The Nature of Belief* (Sheed and Ward, 2nd ed, 1945). On the deaths owing to deformed religiosity in the 20th century, see Michael Burleigh, *Sacred Causes: Religion and Politics from the European Dictators to Al Qaeda* (Harper, 2006).

including Sullivan and Hurd. Having identified, rightly, the difficulties in defining 'religion', they then erroneously and implicitly suggest that there is a belief framework outside of definitional uncertainty – that is, not surprisingly, the viewpoint they believe themselves to inhabit.

George Jacob Holyoake, who coined the term 'secularism' in 1851, well knew, as the subtitle to his work on the subject stated, that secularism was, in essence, 'A Confession of *Belief*.[33] Sullivan and Hurd are, therefore, believers and it would be honest and accurate and helpful of them to admit this so that their own method of analysis could be applied to their own orthodoxies. My own beliefs in the importance of diversity, associational independence and priority alongside rejection of 'civic totalism', statism, or moves towards legally enforced homogeneity I have set out in this chapter. I do not pre-emptively reject 'hierarchies' or 'dogma' or exclusivity of associational life as I view these as logically dictated by freedom under the Rule of Law. Sullivan and Hurd need to explain whether they accept diversity and the freedom to be different – as they express their theories thus far such a commitment on their part is far from clear. In handwringing over 'exclusions' there is precious little, if any, respect shown for religious associations themselves.

Unfortunately, neither Sullivan nor Hurd, identify their own community of beliefs, but only hint at 'tolerance' being problematic and 'hierarchies' and 'exclusions' being unacceptable. They suggest that only the religious have beliefs, then spend considerable time commenting how it is 'religious beliefs,' and not their own, that lead to marginalisation of others who do not share the beliefs of the particular religious believers.

Why, we might ask, is it *religious* beliefs and not, say, the atheo-agnostic beliefs (the beliefs of atheists and agnostics), that are singled out for analysis? The authors do not say and yet their focus on religion has a goal – the disengagement of governmental support for anything that could be said to further the 'good' or inhibit the 'bad' beliefs of religion. That some of what counts as government projects may be ill advised is undoubted; but where is there any analysis of the anti-religious aspects of contemporary governmental initiatives?

Every belief system, religious or atheo-agnostic, has its hierarchies, orthodoxies, heresies, marginalisations and inclusions. That religion alone

---

[33]   I have discussed Holyoake's work in some detail elsewhere. See Benson, *Considering Secularism*, above n 10, 83-94.

is identified in this way as subject to a definitional deficit is inaccurate and blind to the truly hegemonic dimensions of contemporary atheo-agnosticism itself. This kind of selectivity, bracketing religion out of its important and historical place of public importance is, frankly, little more than secularistic anti-religious bigotry masquerading as 'neutrality' or concern for excluded 'others'. In other words, the bewilderingly broad spectrum of political correctness is no less free of the definitional and practical issues that Sullivan and Hurd wish to lay at the door of religions. What is missing in their critique and in much of contemporary religion and law or political analysis, however, is seeing atheism and agnosticism as subject to the same weaknesses such scholars find in religion. For their theory to be fair, therefore, they would have to ask themselves where they sit in this new spectrum and why their perspective should be so privileged as to be free from analysis and judgment.

American political theorist William Galston respects associational diversity and has, on numerous occasions in his academic writing, pointed out the importance of the bulwark of co-existent belief systems against the liberal temptation towards homogenisation and the religious temptation to co-opt non-religious citizens. Galston[34] embraces John Gray's[35] conclusions with respect to *modus vivendi* liberalism or accommodational pluralism or what might be called 'deep diversity.' He stands for the affirmation of associational diversity within one sort of liberalism as against a convergence framework which, while calling itself liberal, may be anything but.

Other recent works such as *The Idea of Justice*,[36] by Amartya Sen and, more recently, Paul Horwitz's *The Agnostic Age*[37] are notable as two different calls for entirely new approaches to prevailing theories of justice. Both identify serious failures in the work of, amongst others, John Rawls,[38] and particularly in Sen's case, where Rawl's theory is criticised as hopelessly idealistic and unworkable, one imagines that Rawl's interesting theory will be useful in future only as a historical marker of a failed attempt to reach fairness 'without metaphysics' and in a way that is not ultimately useful for

---

[34]   William Galston, *The Practice of Liberal Pluralism* (Cambridge University Press, 2005).

[35]   John Gray, *Two Faces of Liberalism* (The New Press, 2000).

[36]   Amartya Sen, *The Idea of Justice* (The Belknap Press, 2009).

[37]   Paul Horwitz, *The Agnostic Age: Law Religion and the Constitution* (Oxford University Press, 2011).

[38]   John Rawls, *A Theory of Justice* (Harvard University Press, 1971).

law or politics. Ideas of justice must start from what is in the lived realities of differing communities in free societies rather than institutional idealism based on comprehensive schemes useful for law or politics.

Sen, after all, taught alongside Rawls for some years and his book is at some pains, not just to bury Rawls, but also to praise him. His work, though he ultimately shows why he considers Rawls' framework, 'unworkable,' is a consummate example of academic courtesy. Horwitz goes further and, in the *Agnostic Age*, calls for 'conventional liberals' and 'readers with strong religious views for or against the existence of God' to recognise that we can no longer reason together about the key questions related to Church and State 'while laying questions of religious truth aside'.[39] Horwitz argues that it is precisely a strategy of avoidance that characterises most judges and legal scholars' approach to religious truth and that this 'has led to the state of confusion and dissatisfaction that permeates the theory in practice of the religion clauses of the first amendment.'[40]

According to Horwitz, the theory of constitutional agnosticism that he propounds believes that these questions about religious truth must be confronted head-on rather than avoided and that such confrontation must be done with a measure of humility aware of the need to live amongst what he calls '…uncertainties, mysteries and doubts'.[41] Yet, 'questions of religious truth' are precisely what contemporary regimes believe they have bracketed out of the public sphere under the rubric of its 'neutrality.' What emerges therefore is an important fact: if, as I suggest, Justice Sachs is correct and essential notions undergirding human rights and conceptions of 'right and wrong' emerge paradigmatically from *within* religions, and if those religions therefore play an important role in relation to culture, then law must itself develop a greater, not lesser, respect for religious freedom. Far from such a quest being, 'impossible', as Sullivan alleges, it would seem both logically and theoretically essential. Key to the working of such a new jurisprudence, however, is a renewed sense of the role *and limits* of law and politics. So with respect to contesting the role of politics in relation to religion I agree in part with Hurd though I view co-operation with religions as not only permissible but essential whereas Hurd seems to imagine such co-operation

---

39   Joseph Koterski, 'Religion as the Root of Culture' in unknown (ed), *Christianity and Western Civilization* (Ignatius Press, 1993) xxiii, 26.

40   Horwitz, above n 37, xxiii.

41   Ibid.

in only negative ways. For Hurd, '...the deployment of religious rights is a technique of governance that authorizes particular forms of politics and regulates in which people live out their religion'.[42] If one returns to the quotation from Justice Albi Sachs near the beginning of this article, one sees a respectful view for the cultural role and nature of religions far removed from the statist, cynical and controlling stance adopted by scholars such as Hurd who view religion as something that can be understood from outside while at the same time claiming that it cannot be classified meaningfully as either 'good' or 'bad'.

Further, we should reject the idea of 'neutrality' and the metaphysical avoidance of questions of 'civic virtues' and therefore morals from just, necessary and limited government. Understanding atheism and agnosticism as 'faith commitments,' we should call for a richer engagement with moral traditions and politics instead of a quite unrealistic and stultifying avoidance of necessary metaphysical questions. Unlike Hurd, one need not believe that societies have the luxury of avoiding questions such as what makes for a just or good regime anymore than it can avoid thinking through the 'good' and 'bad' aspects of belief systems – religious and non-religious.

Horwitz, like that wise observer of authoritarianism, George Orwell, but unlike Sullivan, is suspicious of 'buzzwords' such as 'equality', 'neutrality' and 'equal liberty'.[43] Prevailing approaches to law or politics that depend upon such usually de-contextualised rhetorical terms play into a conception of law and religion that, while they purport to be neutral or to hold religious and non-religious beliefs alike in equal regard, in his words, 'routinely fail to do anything of the sort'.[44]

---

[42]   Hurd, above n 2, 17.

[43]   Sonia Orwell and Ian Angus (eds) 'Politics and the English Language' in *The Collected Essays, Journalism and Letters of George Orwell: Vol VI* (Penguin, 1945-1950) 161-162. In a similar way, George Orwell identifies "values", "equality" and "progressive" amongst the list of 'meaningless words' that he sees tending towards authoritarian politics. He also, somewhat cynically perhaps, lists "justice" though it could be argued that justice, as one of the cardinal virtues, only becomes "meaningless" when it is taken out of its historical entailments. On the non-entailed nature of the other terms Orwell mentions (but not of anything one could call a classical virtue, see Iain T Benson, 'Values Language: A Cuckoo's Egg or Useful Moral Framework?: An Unresolved Problem in Moral and Ethics Education and in Catholic Thought' in David Daintree (ed), *Creative Subversion: The Liberal Arts and Human Educational Fulfilment*, (Connor Court Publishing, 2018) 1-43.

[44]   Horwitz, above n 37, xxiv.

Horwitz rejects Rawlsian claims for 'public reason' as these bracket out claims for truth which, in many cases, are constitutive of our identity as persons and communities. Horwitz states, somewhat boldly, that:[45]

> ...we are now in the twilight of the liberal consensus as we have known it. It may survive, with important revisions. Or it may collapse all together, and new prophets will arise to predict what will come after it. *One thing, however, seems certain: the liberal consensus that emerged after the enlightenment, gelled in the nineteenth century, and reached a more or less stable form in the twentieth century, cannot last much longer as a basic, unquestioned assumption about the way we live.* From within and beyond its borders, the liberal consensus is under attack. On all sides we are hearing calls, sometimes measured and sometimes shrill, for a revision or an outright rejection of the terms of the liberal treaty. (emphasis added)

Sen endorses Gray's critique in *Two Faces* (favouring *modus vivendi* over convergence liberalism the latter being, in fact, illiberal) and, like Horwitz, calls for 'a substantial departure in the prevailing theories of justice'.[46]

Sen states that Rawls's, 'theory of justice, as formulated under the currently dominant transcendental institutionalism, reduces many of the most relevant issues of justice into empty – even if acknowledged to be – "well-meaning rhetoric"'.[47] He offers a succinct analysis of what he refers to as the 'seriously defective' main planks of the Rawlsian theory of justice.[48] This is a theory, it should be recalled, that claimed to be 'political rather than metaphysical,' as if such a bi-furcation was not only possible but advantageous when it is, in fact, neither.[49] Further discussion of these important themes cannot be developed here but it is critical to note that Sullivan and Hurd are writing at a time of transition within jurisprudence but using old forms of analysis on key points: they do not challenge seriously any of the main planks of widely discredited old liberal consensus.

This chapter, advocates for a richer engagement within and between

---

[45]   Ibid 22.

[46]   Sen, above n 36, 27.

[47]   Ibid 26.

[48]   Ibid 52-58; Ronald Beiner, *Civil Religion* (Cambridge University Press, 2011) 294-300; Charles Taylor, *Sources of the Self* (Harvard University Press, 1989) 89. Taylor and Beiner both refer to Rawls' theory as, on its deeper levels, 'incoherent' and Beiner mounts a strong set of arguments against Rawls' approach generally. Despite untold trenchant criticisms against Rawls' overall theory of justice it continues to exercise a powerful hold over certain sorts of liberal imaginations. See Rawls, above n 38.

[49]   Brian Bix, *Jurisprudence: Theory and Context* (Sweet & Maxwell, 4th ed, 2006) 110.

citizens, on the basis that all citizens are believers; the question is not *whether* they believe, but *what they believe in* and the law must be maximally respectful of differences of beliefs within and between communities. The law must be particularly careful not to dissolve diversity in the solvent of general and de-contextualized notions such as 'equality' and 'inclusion', elevating them over the inherently different and diverse commitments of religious believers and their communities. This condition of judicial and political over-reach is, unfortunately, what Sullivan and Hurd appear to call for by relocating the basis for religious liberty in undifferentiated de-contextualized notions of 'equality' or in characterising religions themselves as 'deployed' or 'privileged'. The better view however, is to understand that the existence of religious rights and the communities that are recognised but not created by such rights play crucial roles, as Justice Sachs understood, to the very understanding of 'right' and 'wrong', 'good' and 'bad' and 'human rights' themselves.

The Politics of Faith and the Politics of Scepticism

This heading is the title of Michael Oakeshott's posthumously published 1996 book.[50] He makes a distinction that is important for our consideration of some of the themes discussed by Sullivan and Hurd. He points out, ironically, 'the politics of faith' are held by those who would consider themselves to be 'unbelievers,' as the category is not typified by religious faith.[51] What marks out 'faith' in this account, he notes, is its correspondence with 'the modern disposition' that he called 'rationalism in politics,' which amounts to 'the ideological style of politics'.[52]

Opposed to this is the 'politics of scepticism' which 'finds human experience to be so varied and complex that no plan for ordering and reconstructing human affairs could ever succeed.'[53] In this latter category, according the Editor of Oakeshott's book:[54]

> The range of human experience, and the interminable altering of relations among individuals and groups, will always outstrip every effort to bring

---

[50]   Michael Oakeshott and Timothy Fuller, *The Politics of Faith and the Politics of Scepticism* (Yale University Press, 1996).

[51]   Ibid xii.

[52]   Ibid.

[53]   Ibid.

[54]   Ibid xi.

them under the control of a central design. To increase governmental power is to stimulate the mistaken aspiration to expand such control in order, collectively, to "pursue perfection as the crow flies."

In relation to Hurd and Sullivan, for example Oakeshott would characterise their appeal to some abstracted sense of 'equality' as representing 'the politics of faith.' It is a faith, obviously, without the identified community that typifies religions – as such it is even less capable of definition than the religions Sullivan and Hurd problematise and find evasive of definition.

Hurd longs for a situation in which 'established authorities' and 'hierarchies' are done away with, and 'dissenters, doubters, those who practice multiple traditions and those on the margins of the community' are placed in different positions once religions are 'destabilized and disaggregated';[55] but this would require massive interference with the associational liberties of religions. Such a viewpoint is highly statist and, frankly, disrespectful of diversity, open-government and due recognition of the limits of law and politics (domestic and international) itself as well as being an obliteration of subsidiarity in ignorance of the nature and importance of tradition. This is little more than wall-to-wall control 'of' religion under the guise that one is concerned about the control 'by' religion: the internal inconsistencies of Hurd's approach are startling. Hurd and Sullivan seem to endorse governmental involvement when it opposes the objectionable mores of settled religious communities (with their hierarchies and orthodoxies). This is, however, exactly what Oakeshott termed the 'politics of faith' and it is, frankly, statist in a way that exemplifies rather well the fears expressed by Gray and Galston and others about 'illiberalism' sailing under the flag of 'liberalism.' It is far better, for the sake of respecting the integrity of religious associations, to do what most Western courts have tried to do in various cases and stay out of the internal affairs of religions despite the temptations to meddle suggested by the vague languages of 'equality' and 'non-discrimination' especially when these are presented in an de-contextualised manner.[56]

Worse, Hurd makes some assertions that are simply not true in the way she states them. It is not accurate, for example, to suggest as she does, that the pressure to locate and fix individual and group religious identity and orthodoxy compels individuals who identify with several traditions to

---

55   Hurd, above n 2, 124-127.
56   Benson, *The Necessity for a Contextual Examination*, above n 3.

choose one over the other.[57] In any case, the integrity of traditions sometimes requires choices to be made and this cannot be rejected without sacrificing such traditions 'from outside' – an entirely hegemonic move. The freedom to choose something is necessarily the rejection of something else – this is basic philosophy in relation to the principle of non-contradiction and ought to form no part of the building of a stick with which to beat religions.

Conclusion

Inclusion, or equality, without the express safeguards of a religious commitment, even legal presumptions in favour of diversity, threaten religious accommodation and difference. This criticism of the work of these two contemporary American scholars argues that a commitment to accommodate religious differences is essential to a vision of society that is pluralistic, non-statist and that respects the forms of civil society within which diversity is at home. The new language of "inclusion" that suggests the "binding into" without a respect for the "difference from" poses a threat to the variety of differences that undergirds "deep diversity". Such an undifferentiated inclusion is the kind of thing that might favour "deep equality" rather than "deep diversity" and such a form of 'equality' while perhaps attractive to a certain form of statist, monist or 'civic totalist' is not consistent with respect for the communities that best nurture civic virtues in the various languages communities have developed over millennia.

---

[57]   See, in a South African context, for example, Peter Mtuzi, *The Essence of Xhosa Spirituality and the Nuisance of Cultural Imperialism* (Vivli, 2003). Here the author shows that Xhosa spiritual practices can co-exist quite comfortably with those of a variety of Christian traditions. This is not to deny Hurd's example of South Sudan in which the regime, apparently, demanded that certain religious adherents choose a distinct confessional identity and faith community. The argument here is not for the collapse of an appropriate jurisdictional line between 'church and state' remembering, of course, that 'co-operation' between religion and the state may be perfectly appropriate and 'strict separation' likely not so since it vests atheist and agnostic forms of belief that tend to go 'under the radar' for reasons discussed elsewhere in this chapter. South Africa, is in fact, at the cutting edge of our understanding of what counts as 'law'. Section 234 of the *Constitution of South Africa* recognizes expressly the possibility of 'additional charters' being created by civil society so as to 'deepen the culture of democracy.' The first use of this was the 2010 *South African Charter of Religious Rights and Freedoms* (of which the author was one of the drafters); how this is "law" or useful to standard law requires new approaches one that is well beyond the kind of analysis mounted by both Sullivan and Hurd.

A commitment to respect for different contexts and the various moral traditions that can co-exist in a respectful accommodational (but not a totalistic or 'vanguard') society is essential to the maintenance of freedoms for everyone. This will not give 'totalists' what they seek to achieve through the undifferentiated de-contextualised language of 'equality' or 'inclusion,' or by inappropriately problematising supposed definitional difficulties with the category of religion.

A recognition that law and politics *are themselves* inevitably powerful hierarchies of inclusion and exclusion ought to change our analysis of how both relate to other forms of authority within society. Purporting to respect 'religion' in any of its forms ('lived', 'expert' or 'governed') requires a deeper evaluation of the role and limits of law and politics themselves than we see in either Sullivan or Hurd. The very categorisation of 'faith' as coterminous with religion but not with non-religious beliefs is itself a power categorisation worthy of analysis.[58] The categories of 'thought', 'belief' and 'religion' as well as 'equality' can be respected in their proper relations *only* when they are placed alongside all 'beliefs,' not just religious ones.

Judges, for their part, need to begin to see through the claims to 'neutrality' that currently cloud the analysis of how different communities are to be given space under the Rule of Law. There is no 'trump card' for atheism and

---

[58] John Witte Jr, 'Facts and Fictions About the History of Separation of Church and State' (2006) 48(1) *Journal of Church and State* 15-45; R F A Hoérnle, Knowledge and Faith' in Daniel S. Robinson (ed) *Studies in Philosophy* (Harvard University Press, 1952) 55-61; Jon Butler, 'Disquieted History in a Secular Age' in Michael Warner, Jonathan Van Antwerpen and Craig Calhoune (eds), *Varieties of Secularism in a Secular Age* (Harvard University Press, 2010) 193-216. There is not scope in this chapter to develop the interesting and important philosophical and theological history of the term 'faith' and its correlate 'believer/non-believer' yet understanding both is important in order to unpack the manner in which the analysis at issue avoids seeing itself as implicated in the movements to control religion emanating from atheist and agnostic presuppositions. The power dimensions of 'atheism' and 'agnosticism' are deeply implicated in the contemporary analysis of the place of religion itself. The litigation against religious communities by those who further one side of the meaning of 'separation of church and state' for example, has a long history and deep philosophical and theological currents none of which are addressed in the work of Sullivan and Hurd. Though Hurd cites this article by Jon Butler, neither she, Butler nor Charles Taylor (whom Butler is criticising) appear to comprehend the realities and importance of 'atheist belief', 'agnostic belief' and the communities of believers that these movements exercise in relation to domestic and international policy despite their strong control of many courts and bureaucracies around the world today.

agnosticism operating within the 'implicit forms' of modern beliefs. Attempts, implicit or explicit, to stand 'outside' belief and control religions *as if one has the perspective to contain them with law and policy* are, precisely, the ultimate form of judging 'good' and 'bad' religion likely to be from a perspective devoid of accurate and honest moral evaluation as not all moral viewpoints are being considered. Judging 'good' and 'bad' in religion or anything else is both inevitable and necessary but the area within which such interferences with diversity may be allowable in an open society should be small. It is only over the sorts of matters that are covered by 'community exemptions' that law should exercise its jurisdiction and even then, with a great deal of judicious reticence.[59]

Bibliography

Ahdar, Rex and Leigh Ian, *Religious Freedom in the Liberal State* (Oxford University Press, 2nd ed, 2015)

Beaman, Lori, 'Defining Religion: The Promise and the Peril of Legal Interpretation' in Richard Moon (ed), *Law and Religious Pluralism in Canada* (UBC Press, 2008) 192

Beiner, Ronald, *Civil Religion* (Cambridge University Press, 2011)

Benson, Iain T, *An Associational Framework for the Reconciliation of Competing Rights Claims Involving the Freedom of Religion* (Phd dissertation, University of the Witwatersrand, 2013)

Benson, Iain T, 'Considering Secularism' in Douglas Farrow (ed), *Recognizing Religion in a Secular Society* (McGill-Queen's University Press, 2004) 83

Benson, Iain T, 'The Necessity for a Contextual Analysis for Equality and Non-discrimination' in Jane F Adolphe, Robert L Fastiggi and Michael A Vacca (eds), *Equality and Nondiscrimination: Catholic Roots, Current Challenges*

---

59   Though I do not agree with her focus on 'minority' and 'majority' religious viewpoints, Lori Beaman makes useful observations about some of the pitfalls of 'defining religions' and notes a point that I adopt as one of my conclusions to this chapter though she would likely not agree with my use of her comment in this context when she observes: 'one of the discursive strategies frequently employed by those seeking to minimize or reject a religious tradition is to use language that displaces or disrespects the practices of the religious group in question.' See Lori Beaman, 'Defining Religion: The Promise and the Peril of Legal Interpretation' in Richard Moon (ed), *Law and Religious Pluralism in Canada* (UBC Press, 2008) 192-216. In a more recent work, I have criticised extensively her argument in favour of 'deep equality' suggesting a notion of 'deep diversity preferable': see, Benson, *The Necessity for a Contextual Analysis*, above n 3.

(Pickwick Publications, 2019) 63

Benson, Iain T, 'Values Language: A Useful Moral Framework or a Cuckoo's Egg' in D. Daintree (ed), *Subverting Modernity: The Liberal Arts and Human Educational Fulfilment* (Connor Court, 2018) 1

Bingham, Tom, *The Rule of Law* (Penguin, 2011)

Bix, Brian, *Jurisprudence: Theory and Context* (Sweet & Maxwell, 4th ed, 2006)

Burleigh, Michael, *Sacred Causes: Religion and Politics from the European Dictators to Al Qaeda* (Harper, 2006)

Butler, Jon, 'Disquieted History in a Secular Age' in Michael Warner, Jonathan Van Antwerpen and Craig Calhoune (eds), *Varieties of Secularism in a Secular Age* (Harvard University Press, 2010) 193

Brandis, George, 'Address at the Opening of the International Bar Association Annual Conference' (8 October 2017, Sydney)

Canadian Constitution Act 1982

Church of the New Faith v Commissioner of Pay-roll Tax (1983) 154 CLR 120

Christian Education South Africa v Minister of Education [2000] ZACC 11 [757]

D'Arcy, Martin, *The Nature of Belief* (Sheed and Ward, 2nd ed, 1945)

de Freitas, Shaun, 'Religious Associational Rights and Sexual Conduct in South Africa: Towards a Furtherance of the Accommodation of a Diversity of Beliefs' (2013) 3 *Brigham Young University Law Review* 421

Elshtain, Jean Bethke, 'Freedom of Religion and the Rule of Law' in Douglas Farrow (ed), *Recognizing Religion in a Secular Society* (McGill-Queens University Press) 69

Galston, William, The Practice of Liberal Pluralism (Cambridge University Press, 2005)

Gerangelos, Peter, et al, *Winterton's Australian Federal Constitutional Law* (Thomson Reuters, 2013)

Girgis, Sherif, Robert George and Ryan T. Anderson, 'What is Marriage?' (2010) 34(1) *Harvard Journal of Law and Public Policy* 245

Gray, John, *Two Faces of Liberalism* (The New Press, 2000)

Hoérnle, R F A, 'Knowledge and Faith' in Daniel S. Robinson (ed) *Studies in Philosophy* (Harvard University Press, 1952) 55

Horwitz, Paul, *The Agnostic Age: Law Religion and the Constitution* (Oxford University Press, 2011)

Hurd, Elizabeth Shakman, *Beyond Religious Freedom: The New Global Politics of Religion* (Princeton University Press, 2015)

Hurd, Elizabeth Shakman, 'Politics of Religious Freedom in the Asia-Pacific: an introduction' in (2018) 4 (1), *Journal of Religious and Political Practice*, 9-26.

Koterski, Joseph, 'Religion as the Root of Culture' in unknown (ed), *Christianity and Western Civilization* (Ignatius Press, 1993)

KwaZulu-Natal MEC for Education v. Pillay (2008) (1) SA474

Mtuzi, Peter, *The Essence of Xhosa Spirituality and the Nuisance of Cultural Imperialism* (Vivli, 2003)

Oakeshott, Michael and Timothy Fuller, *The Politics of Faith and the Politics of Scepticism* (Yale University Press, 1996)

Omer, Atalia, 'When "good" religion is good', *Journal of Religious and Political Practice*, 121-131.

Orwell, Sonia and Ian Angus (eds) 'Politics and the English Language' in *The Collected Essays, Journalism and Letters of George Orwell: Vol VI* (Penguin, 1945-1950) 161

Polanyi, Michael, *Personal Knowledge: Towards a Post-Critical Philosophy* (Routledge, 1958)

Protocol No. 12 to the European Convention for the Protection of Human Rights and Fundamental Freedoms: prohibition of discrimination (2000) European Treaty Series No. 187 (entered into force 1 July 2003)

Rawls, John, *A Theory of Justice* (Harvard University Press, 1971)

Robinson, Richard, *Definition* (Oxford University Press, 1972)

Sen, Amartya, *The Idea of Justice* (The Belknap Press, 2009)

Sullivan, WF, *The Impossibility of Religious Freedom* (Princeton University Press, 2007)

Syndicat Northcrest v. Amselem [2004] 2 SCR 551

Taylor, Charles, *Sources of the Self* (Harvard University Press, 1989)

The European Convention for the Protection of Human Rights and Fundamental Freedoms (entered into force 3 September 1953)

The International Covenant on Civil and Political Rights (1966) GA Res, 2200A

Witte Jr, John, 'Facts and Fictions About the History of Separation of Church and State' (2006) 48(1) *Journal of Church and State* 15

Westen, Peter, 'The Empty Idea of Equality' (1982) 95(3) *Harvard Law Review* 537

INDEX

---

[1] *Convention on the Rights of Persons with Disabilities*, opened for signature 30 March 2007, 2515 UNTS 3 (entered into force 3 May 2008).

CPSIA information can be obtained
at www.ICGtesting.com
Printed in the USA
BVHW061551160919
558546BV00025B/2505/P

9 781925 826623